Record
Hits.

Record Hits.

The British Top 50 Charts
1954–1976

Compiled by Clive Solomon

Omnibus Press
London/New York/Sydney

Omnibus Press
(A division of Book Sales Limited)
Published in 1977.

Distributed by
Book Sales Limited,
78 Newman Street,
London W1P 3LA.

Book Sales Pty. Limited,
27 Clarendon Street,
Artarmon,
Sydney,
NSW 2064,
Australia.

Cover design by Paul May
Art Direction by Pearce Marchbank

Index Compiled By Martin Watson

1SBN 0.86001.314.6
OP 4019 D

Printed in England by
Lowe & Brydone Printers Limited, Thetford, Norfolk.

The Author wishes to thank Ivy Doran, Julian Hardstone,
his father, Charlie Gillett, Peter Wilsher, Avrom Sherr,
Steve and Sue, Roger Wilsher, Timmy Mallett and Adam
Cummings.

CONTENTS

HOW TO USE THIS BOOK

This book contains a log of every record to have made the British Top 50 Pop Charts between 1954 and 1976. The Preface explains how it is to be read.

Besides the log, there is an Index of song-titles compiled by Martin Watson. So when you want to trace a certain record in the log, but you are uncertain of the artist, you need only to refer to the Index.

Finally, there is an Appendix of "Chart-Toppers" for the period, and an Appendix of "Top Artists" based on various chart criteria.

Clive Solomon

This Log contains every Top 50 Pop Chart record since the
1st October 1954 (prior to this, 'New Musical Express' charts
referred to a Top 10 only) and covers the period through to the
5th June 1976. From the 1st January 1956, 'Record Mirror/'Record
Retailer' charts are used (and from the 12th March 1960), these
refer to a Top 50. From April 1969 'Record Retailer' (now called
'Music Week')/'Record Mirror' Top 50 Charts have been compiled
by the British Market Research Bureau (a company jointly financed
by 'Music Week', the B.B.C. and the record companies themselves
through the British Phonographic Industry) and are used by the
B.B.C.

Weeks of non-publication, such as the Christmas period and the
occasional printing strike (i.e. 1959 and 1971), have resulted in
other methods of chart compilation being employed, e.g. 'Record
Mirror' was not published from the 4th July to the 9th August 1959,
due to an industrial dispute, therefore, the charts of 'New Musical
Express' have been used for these weeks. Moreover, as noted by
Pete and Annie Fowler in the preface to 'Rock File', the charts of
'Record Mirror' at the beginning and end of each year, were
obviously inaccurate, as they tended to duplicate each other
(because of the Christmas period). Unfortunately, nothing could be
done about this.

Entries are arranged in this manner:
Artist (in alphabetical surname order); song-title; record label;
complete date of chart entry for those records which made the
Top 20 (but only the month and year of entry for those records
which made the Top 50 but did not make the Top 20, and for those
records which entered the charts prior to 1955. The reason for this
is that in the case of records which only made the lower reaches
of the charts, i.e. positions 20 - 50, the exact date of their chart
entry is frequently uncertain. This is particularly so for records
which entered the charts prior to 1955, when their obvious inaccuracy
is reflected in the fact that they tended to be repeated in successive
weeks); highest position reached; number of weeks in the Top 50 (if
the record made the charts prior to the 12th March 1960, this figure
obviously refers only to the number of weeks in the Top 20). There is
also a comprehensive list of relevant cross-references.

The following record labels have been abbreviated:

Blue Horizon	B. Horizon
Cameo-Parkway	Cameo P'way
Penny Farthing	P. Farthing
Private Stock	Pr. Stock
Pye International	Pye Int.
Regal Zonophone	R. Zonophone
Rolling Stones	R. Stones
Tamla Motown	T. Motown
United Artists	Un. Artists
Warner Brothers	Warner Bros.

Log.

	Label	Date of chart entry	Highest position reached	Number of weeks in charts
ABBA				
Waterloo	Epic	20 4 74	1	10
Ring Ring	Epic	- 7 74	32	5
I Do, I Do, I Do	Epic	- 7 75	38	6
S.O.S.	Epic	4 10 75	6	10
Mama Mia	Epic	10 1 76	1	14
ACE				
How Long	Anchor	7 12 74	20	10
ACT ONE				
Tom The Peeper	Mercury	- 5 74	40	5
CLIFF ADAMS ORCHESTRA				
The 'Lonely Man' Theme	Pye	- 4 60	39	2
ADAMS, MARIE				
see JOHNNY OTIS SHOW				
AKENS, JEWEL				
The Birds And The Bees	London	- 3 65	25	8
ALBERT, MORRIS				
Feelings	Decca	11 10 75	4	10
ALFIE AND HARRY				
The Trouble With Harry	London	23 3 56	15	3
ALICE COOPER				
School's Out	Warner Bros.	22 7 72	1	12
Elected	Warner Bros.	14 10 72	4	10
Hello Hurray	Warner Bros.	17 2 73	6	11
No More Mr. Nice Guy	Warner Bros.	5 5 73	10	10
Teenage Lament	Warner Bros.	2 2 74	12	7
ALLAN, RICHARD				
As Time Goes By	Parlophone	- 3 60	43	1
ALLISONS				
Are You Sure	Fontana	12 2 61	1	16
Words	Fontana	- 5 61	34	5
Lessons In Love	Fontana	- 2 62	30	6
ALL STAR HIT PARADE (E.Ps)(Various Artists)				
All Star Hit Parade (Vol. 1)	Decca	29 6 56	2	8
All Star Hit Parade (Vol. 2)	Decca	9 8 57	10	2
ALPERT, HERB (*AND THE TIJUANA BRASS)				
The Lonely Bull*	Stateside	- 1 63	22	9

Spanish Flea*	Pye	15 1 66	3	19
Tijuana Taxi*	Pye	- 3 66	37	4
Casino Royale*	A & M	- 4 67	27	14
This Guy's In Love With You	A & M	20 7 68	2	17
Without Her	A & M	- 6 69	36	4
Jerusalem*	A & M	- 12 70	42	3

AMEN CORNER

Gin House (Blues)	Deram	2 9 67	12	10
World Of Broken Hearts	Deram	- 10 67	24	6
Bend Me Shape Me	Deram	27 1 68	3	12
High In The Sky	Deram	17 8 68	6	13
(If Paradise Was) Half As Nice	Immediate	8 2 69	1	11
Hello Suzie	Immediate	5 7 69	4	11
(If Paradise Was) Half As· Nice (re-issue)	Immediate	- 2 76	34	5

AMERICA

Horse With No Name	Warner Bros.	15 1 72	3	12
Ventura Highway	Warner Bros.	- 11 72	43	4

AMERICAN BREED

Bend Me Shape Me	Stateside	- 2 68	24	6

AMES BROTHERS

Naughty Lady Of Shady Lane	HMV	4 4 55	6	6

ANDERSON, LYNN

Rose Garden	CBS	6 3 71	3	20

ANDERSON, MOIRA

Holy City	Decca	- 1 70	43	1

ANDREWS, CHRIS

Yesterday Man	Decca	21 10 65	3	15
To Whom It May Concern	Decca	18 12 65	13	10
Something On My Mind	Decca	- 4 66	41	3
What'cha Gonna Do Now	Decca	- 6 66	40	4
Stop That Girl	Decca	- 8 66	36	4

ANDREWS, EAMONN

The Shifting Whispering Sands	Parlophone	20 1 56	20	3

ANGELETTES

Don't Let Him Touch You	Decca	- 5 72	35	5

ANGELO, BOBBY

Baby Sittin'	HMV	- 8 61	30	6

ANGELS

My Boyfriend's Back	Mercury	- 10 63	50	1

ANIMALS

Baby Let Me Take You Home	Columbia	- 4 64	21	8
The House Of The Rising Sun	Columbia	4 7 64	1	11
I'm Crying	Columbia	26 9 64	8	10
Don't Let Me Be Misunderstood	Columbia	13 2 65	3	9
Bring It On Home To Me	Columbia	17 4 65	7	11
We've Got To Get Out Of This Place	Columbia	24 7 65	2	12

It's My Life	Columbia	6 11 65	7	11
Inside Looking Out	Decca	26 2 66	12	8
Don't Bring Me Down	Decca	4 6 66	6	8
House Of The Rising Sun	RAK Replay	- 10 72	25	6
(re-issue)				

(see also: ERIC BURDON AND THE ANIMALS)

ANKA, PAUL

Diana	Columbia	16 8 57	1	23
I Love You Baby	Columbia	8 11 57	3	13
You Are My Destiny	Columbia	31 1 58	6	10
All Of A Sudden My Heart				
Sings	Columbia	31 1 59	10	9
Lonely Boy	Columbia	9 8 59	3	12
Put Your Head On My Shoulder	Columbia	31 10 59	7	8
Puppy Love	Columbia	- 3 60	33	7
It's Time To Cry	Columbia	- 4 60	47	1
Hullo Young Lovers	Columbia	- 9 60	44	1
Love Me Warm And Tender	RCA	7 4 62	19	11
A Steel Guitar And A Glass				
Of Wine	RCA	- 7 62	41	4
(You're) Having My Baby	Un.Artists	12 10 74	6	10

ANTHONY, BILLIE

This Ole House	Columbia	- 10 54	4	14

ANTHONY, MIKI

If It Wasn't For The Reason				
That I Love You	Bell	- 2 73	27	7

ANTHONY, RICHARD

Walking Alone	Columbia	- 12 63	37	5
If I Loved You	Columbia	9 5 64	18	10

APHRODITES CHILD

Rain And Tears	Mercury	- 11 68	29	8

APPLEJACKS

Tell Me When	Decca	21 3 64	7	12
Like Dreamers Do	Decca	4 7 64	20	11
Three Little Words	Decca	- 10 64	23	5

APPLEWHITE, CHARLIE

Blue Star	Brunswick	23 9 55	20	1

ARCHIES

Sugar Sugar	RCA	18 10 69	1	26

ARGENT

Hold Your Head Up	Epic	1 4 72	5	12
Tragedy	Epic	- 6 72	34	7
God Gave Rock And Roll To				
You	Epic	21 4 73	18	8

ARMSTRONG, LOUIS

Theme From The Threepenny				
Opera	Philips	20 4 56	11	7
Hello Dolly	London	13 6 64	4	14
Wonderful World	HMV	16 3 68	1	29
Sunshine Of Your Love	Stateside	- 6 68	41	7

ARMY GAME (Cast From TV Show)

Army Game	HMV	6	6 58	5	6

ARNOLD, EDDY

Make The World Go Away	RCA	5	3 66	8	17
I Want To Go With You	RCA	-	5 66	46	3
If You Were Mine Mary	RCA	-	7 66	49	1

ARNOLD, P.P.

The First Cut Is The Deepest	Immediate	10	6 67	18	10
The Time Has Come	Immediate	-	8 67	47	2
Groovy	Immediate	-	1 68	41	4
Angel Of The Morning	Immediate	-	7 68	29	11

ARRIVAL

Friends	Decca	17	1 70	8	9
I Will Survive	Decca	20	6 70	16	10

ARROWS

A Touch Too Much	RAK	8	6 74	8	9
My Last Night With You	RAK	-	2 75	25	7

ARSENAL F.C.

Good Old Arsenal	Pye	22	5 71	16	7

ASHER, JOHN

Let's Twist Again	Creole	29	11 75	14	7

ASHTON, GARDNER AND DYKE

Resurrection Shuffle	Capitol	30	1 71	3	14

ASSOCIATION

Time For Living	Warner Bros.	-	5 68	23	8

ATKINS, CHET

Teensville	RCA	-	3 60	46	2

ATOMIC ROOSTER

Tomorrow Night	B & C	6	3 71	11	12
Devil's Answer	B & C	24	7 71	4	13

ATWELL, WINIFRED

Story Of Three Loves	Philips	-	10 54	19	1
Let's Have A Party	Philips	-	11 54	14	4
Let's Have Another Party	Philips	-	11 54	1	12
Let's Have A Ding Dong	Decca	4	11 55	3	10
Poor People Of Paris	Decca	16	3 56	1	15
Port-Au-Prince	Decca	18	5 56	20	6
Left Bank	Decca	20	7 56	14	4
Make It A Party	Decca	2	11 56	11	10
Let's Have A Ball	Decca	6	12 57	7	5
Piano Party	Decca	5	12 59	15	4

AUTUMN

My Little Girl	Pye	-	10 71	37	6

AVALON, FRANKIE

Why	HMV	16	1 60	15	3
Don't Throw Away All Those Teardrops	HMV	-	4 60	37	4

AVERAGE WHITE BAND

Pick Up The Pieces	Atlantic	8 3 75	6	9
Cut The Cake	Atlantic	- 4 75	31	4

AVONS

Seven Little Girls Sitting In The Back Seat	Columbia	21 11 59	4	9
We're Only Young Once	Columbia	- 6 60	45	2
Four Little Heels	Columbia	- 10 60	45	2
Rubber Ball	Columbia	- 1 61	30	4

AZNAVOUR, CHARLES

The Old Fashioned Way	Barclay	- 10 73	38	14
She	Barclay	22 6 74	1	13

AZZAM, BOB AND HIS ORCHESTRA

Mustapha	Decca	- 5 60	23	14

BABBITY BLUE

Don't Make Me Blue	Decca	- 2 65	48	2

BABS, ALICE

You've Gone	Fontana	- 8 63	43	1

BACHARACH, BURT

Trains And Boats And Planes	London	29 5 65	4	11

BACHELORS

Charmaine	Decca	2 3 63	6	19
Faraway Places	Decca	- 7 63	36	3
Whispering	Decca	21 9 63	18	10
Diane	Decce	8 2 64	1	19
I Believe	Decca	28 3 64	2	17
Ramona	Decca	13 6 64	4	13
I Wouldn't Trade You For The World	Decca	29 8 64	4	16
No Arms Could Ever Hold You	Decca	12 12 64	7	12
True Love For Evermore	Decca	- 4 65	35	6
Marie	Decca	29 5 65	9	12
In The Chapel In The Moonlight	Decca	- 10 65	27	9
Hello Dolly	Decca	- 1 66	38	4
Sound Of Silence	Decca	26 3 66	3	13
Can I Trust You	Decca	- 7 66	26	7
Walk With Faith In Your Heart	Decca	- 12 66	21	9
Oh How I Miss You	Decca	- 4 67	46	1
Marta	Decca	22 7 67	20	9

BACHMAN TURNER OVERDRIVE

You Ain't Seen Nothing Yet	Mercury	23 11 74	2	12
Roll On Down The Highway	Mercury	- 2 75	22	6

BAD COMPANY

Can't Get Enough	Island	29 6 74	15	8
Good Lovin' Gone Bad	Island	- 3 75	31	6
Feel Like Makin' Love	Island	11 10 75	20	9

BADFINGER

Come And Get It	Apple	17 1 70	4	12

Title	Label					
No Matter What	Apple	23	1	71	5	12
Day After Day	Apple	12	2	72	10	11

BAEZ, JOAN

Title	Label					
We Shall Overcome	Fontana	–	5	65	26	10
There But For Fortune	Fontana	17	7	65	8	12
It's All Over Now Baby Blue	Fontana	–	9	65	22	8
Farewell Angelina	Fontana	–	12	65	47	3
Pack Up Your Sorrows	Fontana	–	7	66	50	1
The Night They Drove Old Dixie Down	Vanguard	23	10	71	6	11

BAKER, ADRIAN

Title	Label					
Sherry	Magnet	9	8	75	10	8

BAKER: GEORGE BAKER SELECTION

Title	Label					
Una Paloma Blanca	Warner Bros.	4	10	75	10	10

BALDRY, LONG JOHN

Title	Label					
Let The Heartaches Begin	Pye	18	11	67	1	13
When The Sun Comes Shining Through	Pye	–	8	68	29	7
Mexico	Pye	9	11	68	15	8
It's Too Late Now	Pye	–	2	69	21	8

BAND

Title	Label					
The Weight	Capitol	–	9	68	21	9
Rag Mama Rag	Capitol	25	4	70	16	9

BAND OF THE BLACK WATCH

Title	Label					
Scotch On The Rocks	Spark	4	10	75	8	14
Dance Of The Cuckoos	Spark	–	12	75	37	8

BANDWAGON

see JOHNNY JOHNSON AND THE BANDWAGON

BARBER, CHRIS

Title	Label					
Petite Fleur	Pye Nixa	14	2	59	4	18
Revival	Columbia	–	1	62	43	4

BAR-KAYS

Title	Label					
Soul Finger	Stax	–	8	67	33	8

BARNES, RICHARD

Title	Label					
Take To The Mountains	Philips	–	5	70	35	6
Go North	Philips	–	10	70	38	4

BARRON KNIGHTS

Title	Label					
Call Up The Groups	Columbia	18	7	64	3	13
Come To The Dance	Columbia	–	10	64	42	2
Pop Go The Workers	Columbia	10	4	65	5	12
Merrie Gentle Pops	Columbia	25	12	65	9	7
Under New Management	Columbia	24	12	66	15	9
An Olympic Record	Columbia	–	11	68	35	4

BARRY, JOE

Title	Label					
I'm A Fool To Care	Mercury	–	8	61	49	1

BARRY, JOHN

Title	Label					
Hit And Miss	Columbia	27	2	60	12	8

Title	Label					
Beat For Beatniks	Columbia	–	4	60	40	3
Never Let Go	Columbia	–	7	60	49	1
Blueberry Hill	Columbia	–	8	60	34	3
Walk Don't Run	Columbia	18	9	60	11	14
Black Stockings	Columbia	14	1	61	13	9
Magnificent Seven	Columbia	–	2	61	45	6
Cutty Sark	Columbia	–	2	62	35	2
James Bond Theme	Columbia	24	11	62	13	11
From Russia With Love	Ember	–	11	63	39	3
The Persuaders (TV Theme)	CBS	15	1	72	13	15

BARRY, LEN

Title	Label					
1-2-3	Brunswick	13	11	65	3	14
Like A Baby	Brunswick	5	2	66	10	10

BASIE, COUNT

see FRANK SINATRA

BASS, FONTELLA

Title	Label					
Rescue Me	Chess	11	12	65	11	10
Recovery	Chess	–	1	66	32	5

BASSEY, SHIRLEY

Title	Label					
Banana Boat Song	Philips	8	3	57	7	6
Kiss Me Honey	Philips	3	1	59	4	13
As I Love You	Philips	17	1	59	2	15
With These Hands	Columbia	–	3	60	38	3
As Long As He Needs Me	Columbia	31	7	60	2	29
You'll Never Know	Columbia	7	5	61	6	17
Climb Every Mountain/Reach For The Stars	Columbia	29	7	61	1	18
I'll Get By	Columbia	18	11	61	10	9
Tonight	Columbia	–	2	62	21	8
Ave Maria	Columbia	–	4	62	31	4
Far Away	Columbia	–	5	62	24	13
What Now, My Love?	Columbia	22	9	62	5	18
What Kind Of Fool Am I	Columbia	–	2	63	47	2
I (Who Have Nothing)	Columbia	12	10	63	6	20
My Special Dream	Columbia	–	1	64	32	7
Gone	Columbia	–	4	64	36	5
Goldfinger	Columbia	–	10	64	21	9
No Regrets	Columbia	–	5	65	39	4
Big Spender	Un.Artists	–	10	67	21	15
Something	Un.Artists	4	7	70	4	22
Fool On The Hill	Un.Artists	–	1	71	48	1
(Where Do I Begin) Love Story	Un.Artists	–	3	71	34	10
For All We Know	Un.Artists	18	9	71	17	24
Diamonds Are Forever	Un.Artists	–	1	72	38	6
Never, Never, Never	Un.Artists	17	3	73	19	8

BAXTER, LES

Title	Label					
Unchained Melody	Capitol	13	5	55	10	9

BAY CITY ROLLERS

Title	Label					
Keep On Dancing	Bell	16	10	71	9	13
Remember (Sha La La)	Bell	23	2	74	6	12
Shang-A-Lang	Bell	4	5	74	2	10
Summerlove Sensation	Bell	3	8	74	3	10
All Of Me Loves All Of You	Bell	19	10	74	4	10
Bye Bye Baby	Bell	8	3	75	1	16
Give A Little Love	Bell	12	7	75	1	9
Money Honey	Bell	22	11	75	3	9
Love Me Like I Love You	Bell	10	4	76	4	6

B.B.C. ORCHESTRA

Music From Six Wives Of Henry VIII	B.B.C.	-	4 71	49	1

B. BUMBLE AND THE STINGERS

Nut Rocker	Top Rank	28	4 62	1	15
Nut Rocker (re-issue)	Stateside	7	7 72	19	11

BE-BOP DELUXE

Ships In The Night	Harvest	-	2 76	23	8

BEACH BOYS

Surfin' U.S.A.	Capitol	-	8 63	34	7
I Get Around	Capitol	25	7 64	7	13
When I Grow Up	Capitol	-	10 64	27	7
Dance Dance Dance	Capitol	-	1 65	24	6
Help Me Rhonda	Capitol	-	6 65	27	10
California Girls	Capitol	-	9 65	26	8
Barbara Anne	Capitol	26	2 66	3	10
Sloop John B	Capitol	30	4 66	2	15
God Only Knows/Wouldn't It Be Nice	Capitol	6	8 66	2	14
Good Vibrations	Capitol	5	11 66	1	13
Then I Kissed Her	Capitol	13	5 67	4	11
Heroes And Villains	Capitol	2	9 67	8	9
Wild Honey	Capitol	-	11 67	29	6
Darlin'	Capitol	3	2 68	11	13
Friends	Capitol	-	5 68	25	7
Do It Again	Capitol	10	8 68	1	14
Bluebirds Over The Mountain	Capitol	-	1 69	33	4
I Can Hear Music	Capitol	22	3 69	11	13
Breakaway	Capitol	28	6 69	6	11
Cottonfields	Capitol	30	5 70	5	17
California Saga	Reprise	-	3 73	37	5

BEATLES

Love Me Do	Parlophone	15	12 62	17	18
Please Please Me	Parlophone	3	2 63	2	18
From Me To You	Parlophone	27	4 63	1	21
My Bonnie (with TONY SHERIDAN)	Polydor	-	6 63	48	1
She Loves You	Parlophone	31	8 63	1	32
I Want To Hold Your Hand	Parlophone	7	12 63	1	21
Can't Buy Me Love	Parlophone	28	3 64	1	14
Ain't She Sweet	Polydor	-	6 64	29	6
A Hard Day's Night	Parlophone	18	7 64	1	13
I Feel Fine	Parlophone	5	12 64	1	13
Ticket To Ride	Parlophone	17	4 65	1	12
Help	Parlophone	31	7 65	1	14
Day Tripper/We Can Work It Out	Parlophone	11	12 65	1	12
Paperback Writer	Parlophone	18	6 66	1	11
Yellow Submarine/Eleanor Rigby	Parlophone	13	8 66	1	13
Penny Lane/Strawberry Fields Forever	Parlophone	25	2 67	2	14
All You Need Is Love	Parlophone	15	7 67	1	12
Hello Goodbye	Parlophone	2	12 67	1	12
Magical Mystery Tour E.P.	Parlophone	16	12 67	2	9
Lady Madonna	Parlophone	23	3 68	1	11
Hey Jude	Apple	14	9 68	1	16
Get Back	Apple	26	4 69	1	17
The Ballad Of John And Yoko	Apple	7	6 69	1	13
Something/Come Together	Apple	5	11 69	4	12

Let It Be	Apple	14	3 70	2	11
Yesterday	Apple	20	3 76	8	7
Hey Jude (re-issue)	Apple	10	4 76	12	7
Paperback Writer (re-issue)	Apple	-	3 76	23	5
Strawberry Fields Forever/ Penny Lane (re-issue)	Apple	-	4 76	32	4
Get Back (re-issue)	Apple	-	4 76	28	5
Help (re-issue)	Apple	-	4 76	37	5

BECAUD, GILBERT

A Little Love And Understanding	Decca	12	4 75	10	12

JEFF BECK GROUP

Hi Ho Silver Lining	Columbia	6	5 67	14	14
Tally Men	Columbia	-	8 67	30	3
Love Is Blue	Columbia	-	3 68	23	7
Hi Ho Silver Lining (re-issue)	RAK Replay	18	11 72	17	11
I've Been Drinking (re-issue) (with ROD STEWART)	RAK Replay	-	5 73	27	6

(see also: DONOVAN)

BEDROCKS

Ob-La-Di, Ob-La-Da	Columbia	4	1 69	20	7

BEE GEES

New York Mining Disaster, 1941	Polydor	13	5 67	12	10
To Love Somebody	Polydor	-	7 67	41	5
Massachusetts	Polydor	30	9 67	1	17
World	Polydor	2	12 67	9	16
Words	Polydor	10	2 68	8	10
Jumbo/Singer Sang His Song	Polydor	-	3 68	25	7
I Gotta Get A Message To You	Polydor	17	8 68	1	15
First Of May	Polydor	8	3 69	6	11
Tomorrow Tomorrow	Polydor	-	6 69	23	8
Don't Forget To Remember	Polydor	23	8 69	2	15
I.O.I.O.	Polydor	-	4 70	49	1
Lonely Days	Polydor	-	12 70	33	9
My World	Polydor	12	2 72	16	10
Run To Me	Polydor	12	8 72	9	10
Jive Talkin'	RSO	19	7 75	5	11

BEGINNING OF THE END

Funky Nassau (re-issue)	Atlantic	-	2 74	31	6

BELAFONTE, HARRY

Banana Boat Song (Day-O)	HMV	1	3 57	3	14
Island In The Sun/Coconut Woman	RCA	21	6 57	2	22
Scarlet Ribbons	HMV	20	9 57	18	2
Mary's Boy Child	RCA	15	11 57	1	9
Little Bernadette	RCA	22	8 58	18	4
Son Of Mary	RCA	19	12 58	17	2
Mary's Boy Child (re-issue)	RCA	5	12 58	10	5
Hole In The Bucket (with ODETTA)	RCA	-	9 61	32	8

BELL, ARCHIE AND THE DRELLS

Here I Go Again (re-issue)	Atlantic	11	11 72	11	10
There's Gonna Be A Showdown (re-issue)	Atlantic	-	1 73	36	5

BELL, FREDDIE AND THE BELL BOYS

Giddy Up A Ding Dong	Mercury	28 9 56	4	8

BELL, WILLIAM

Tribute To A King	Stax	– 6 68	31	7
Private Number	Stax	21 12 68	8	14
(with JUDY CLAY)				

BENNET, PETER E.

The Seagull's Name Was Nelson	RCA	– 11 70	45	1

BENNETT, BOYD

Seventeen	Parlophone	23 12 55	16	1

BENNETT, CLIFF AND THE REBEL ROUSERS

One Way Love	Parlophone	24 10 64	9	9
I'll Take You Home	Parlophone	– 2 65	42	3
Got To Get You Into My Life	Parlophone	10 9 66	6	11

BENNETT, TONY

Stranger In Paradise	Philips	15 4 55	1	16
Close Your Eyes	Philips	16 9 55	18	1
'Till/Seranata	Philips	– 12 61	35	2
The Good Life	CBS	– 7 63	27	13
If I Ruled The World	CBS	– 5 65	45	5
I Left My Heart In San Francisco	CBS	– 5 65	25	18
The Very Thought Of You	CBS	– 12 65	21	9

BENSON, GARY

Don't Throw It All Away	State	13 9 75	20	8

BENSON, GEORGE

Supership	CTI	– 10 75	30	6

BENTON, BROOK

Kiddio	Mercury	– 10 60	41	6
Fools Rush In	Mercury	– 2 61	50	1
The Boll Weevil Song	Mercury	– 7 61	30	9

BERNSTEIN, ELMER

Johnny Staccato Theme	Capitol	19 12 59	5	8

BERRY, CHUCK

School Days	London	29 6 57	20	1
Sweet Little Sixteen	London	19 4 58	11	6
Johnny B. Goode	London	7 6 58	17	1
Go Go Go	Pye	– 7 63	38	6
Memphis Tennessee/Let It Rock	Pye	26 10 63	6	10
Run Rudolph Run	Pye	– 12 63	36	6
Nadine	Pye	– 2 64	27	7
No Particular Place To Go	Pye	23 5 64	3	11
You Never Can Tell	Pye	– 8 64	25	8
Promised Land	Pye	– 1 65	26	6
My Ding-A-Ling	Chess	11 11 72	1	17
Reelin' And Rockin' (re-issue)	Chess	24 2 73	18	7

BERRY, DAVE (AND THE CRUISERS)

Memphis Tennessee	Decca	9 11 63	19	13

My Baby Left Me	Decca	– 1 64	37	9
Baby It's You	Decca	– 4 64	24	6
The Crying Game	Decca	22 8 64	5	13
One Heart Between Two	Decca	– 11 64	41	2
Little Things	Decca	10 4 65	6	12
This Strange Effect	Decca	– 7 65	37	6
Mama	Decca	23 7 66	5	16

BERRY, MIKE AND THE OUTLAWS

Tribute To Buddy Holly	HMV	4 11 61	18	6
Don't You Think It's Time	HMV	20 1 63	6	12
My Little Baby	HMV	– 4 63	34	7

BEVERLEY SISTERS

Little Drummer Boy	Decca	14 2 59	9	11
Little Donkey	Decca	28 11 59	16	2
Greenfields	Columbia	– 6 60	29	3

BIDDU ORCHESTRA

Summer Of '42	Epic	23 8 75	14	8
Rain Forest	Epic	– 4 76	39	4

BIG BEN BANJO BAND

Let's Get Together	HMV	9 12 55	15	4

BIG BOPPER

Chantilly Lace	Mercury	17 1 59	14	6

BIG THREE

Some Other Guy	Decca	– 4 63	34	7
By The Way	Decca	– 7 63	22	10

BILK, ACKER

Summer Set	Columbia	16 1 60	10	11
Goodnight Sweet Prince	Melodisc	– 6 60	50	1
White Cliffs Of Dover	Columbia	– 8 60	30	9
Buona Sera	Columbia	25 12 60	7	18
That's My Home	Columbia	22 7 61	7	17
Stars And Stripes/Creole Jazz	Columbia	11 11 61	17	11
Stranger On The Shore	Columbia	25 11 61	1	58
Frankie And Johnny	Columbia	10 3 62	20	6
Gotta See Baby Tonight	Columbia	– 7 62	24	9
Lonely	Columbia	13 10 62	14	11
A Taste Of Honey	Columbia	10 2 63	16	9

BILL BLACK COMBO

White Silver Sands	London	– 9 60	50	1
Don't Be Cruel	London	– 10 60	32	7

BIMBO JET

El Bimbo	EMI	16 8 75	12	10

BINDI, UMBERTO

Il Nostro Concerto	Oriole	– 11 60	47	1

BIRDS

Leaving Here	Decca	– 5 65	45	1

BIRKIN, JANE AND SERGE GAINSBOURG

Je T'Aime Moi Non Plus	Fontana	23 8 69	2	10

Je T'Aime Moi Non Plus	Major Minor	4 10 69	1	12
Je T'Aime Moi Non Plus (re-issue)	Antic	- 12 74	31	9

BLACK, BURUNDI STEIPHENSON

Burundi Black	Barclay	- 11 71	31	14

BLACK, CILLA

Love Of The Loved	Parlophone	- 10 63	35	6
Anyone Who Had A Heart	Parlophone	15 2 64	1	17
You're My World	Parlophone	16 5 64	1	17
It's For You	Parlophone	15 8 64	7	11
You've Lost That Lovin' Feeling	Parlophone	23 1 65	2	9
I've Been Wrong Before	Parlophone	15 5 65	17	7
Love's Just A Broken Heart	Parlophone	29 1 66	5	11
Alfie	Parlophone	9 4 66	9	12
Don't Answer Me	Parlophone	18 6 66	6	10
A Fool Am I	Parlophone	5 11 66	13	9
What Good Am I	Parlophone	- 6 67	24	7
I Only Live To Love You	Parlophone	- 12 67	26	11
Step Inside Love	Parlophone	30 3 68	8	9
Where Is Tomorrow	Parlophone	- 6 68	39	3
Surround Yourself With Sorrow	Parlophone	22 2 69	3	12
Conversations	Parlophone	26 7 69	7	12
If I Thought You'd Change Your Mind	Parlophone	10 1 70	20	9
Something Tells Me (Something's Gonna Happen Tonight)	Parlophone	4 12 71	3	14
Baby We Can't Go Wrong	EMI	- 2 74	36	6

BLACK, JEANNE

He'll Have To Stay	Capitol	- 6 60	41	6

BLACKBURN, TONY

So Much Love	MGM	- 1 68	31	4
It's Only Love	MGM	- 3 69	40	3

BLACKBYRDS

Walking In Rhythm	Fantasy	- 5 75	23	6

BLACKFOOT SUE

Standing In The Road	DJM	26 8 72	4	10
Sing Don't Speak	DJM	- 12 72	36	5

BLACK SABBATH

Paranoid	Vertigo	26 9 70	4	18

BLACKWELLS

Love Or Money	London	- 5 61	46	2

BLAND, BILLY

Let The Little Girl Dance	London	8 5 60	15	10

BLOE, MR

Groovin' With Mr. Bloe	DJM	30 5 70	2	18

BLOODSTONE

Natural High	Decca	- 8 73	40	4

BLOOD, SWEAT AND TEARS

You've Made Me So Very Happy	CBS	–	5 69	35	6

BLOOM, BOBBY

Montego Bay	Polydor	12	9 70	3	19
Heavy Makes You Happy	Polydor	–	1 71	31	5

BLUE, BARRY

Dancing On A Saturday Night	Bell	11	8 73	2	15
Do You Wanna Dance	Bell	10	11 73	7	12
School Love	Bell	16	3 74	11	9
Miss, Hit And Run	Bell	–	8 74	26	7
Hot Shot	Bell	–	10 74	23	5

BLUE HAZE

Smoke Gets In Your Eyes	A & M	–	3 72	32	6

BLUE MINK

Melting Pot	Philips	29	11 69	3	15
Good Morning Freedom	Philips	18	4 70	10	11
Our World	Philips	24	10 70	17	19
Banner Man	R.Zonophone	5	6 71	3	14
Stay With Me	R.Zonophone	2	12 72	11	14
By The Devil	EMI	–	3 73	26	8
Randy	EMI	14	7 73	9	10

BLUNSTONE, COLIN (FORMERLY NEIL MacARTHUR)

She's Not There	Deram	–	2 69	34	5
Say You Don't Mind	Epic	11	3 72	15	9
I Don't Believe In Miracles	Epic	–	11 72	31	6
How Could We Dare To Be Wrong	Epic	–	2 73	45	2

(see also: ZOMBIES)

BOB AND EARL

Harlem Shuffle (re-issue)	Island	19	4 69	7	13

BOB (ANDY) AND MARCIA (GRIFFITHS)

Young, Gifted And Black	Harry J	21	3 70	5	12
Pied Piper	Trojan	3	7 71	11	14

BOHANNON, HAMILTON

South African Man	Brunswick	–	2 75	22	8
Disco Stomp	Brunswick	14	6 75	6	12
Foot Stompin' Music	Brunswick	–	7 75	23	6
Happy Feeling	Brunswick	–	9 75	49	3

BOLAN, MARC

see T. REX

BONDS, GARY 'U.S.'

New Orleans	Top Rank	12	2 61	16	11
Quarter To Three	Top Rank	22	7 61	7	13

BONNEY, GRAHAM

Supergirl	Columbia	30	4 66	19	8

BONZO DOG DOO DAH BAND

I'm The Urban Spaceman	Liberty	30	11 68	5	14

BOOKER T AND THE MGs

Soul Limbo	Stax	–	12 68	30	9
Time Is Tight	Stax	31	5 69	4	17
Soul Clap	Stax	–	8 69	35	4

BOONE, DANIEL

Daddy Don't You Walk So Fast	P.Farthing	25	9 71	17	15
Beautiful Sunday	P.Farthing	–	4 72	21	10

BOONE, PAT

Ain't That A Shame	London	18	11 55	7	9
I'll Be Home	London	27	4 56	1	23
I Almost Lost My Mind	London	17	8 56	7	6
Long Tall Sally	London	24	8 56	19	2
Friendly Persuasion	London	21	12 56	3	17
Don't Forbid Me	London	8	2 57	2	14
Why Baby Why	London	10	5 57	17	1
Love Letters In The Sand	London	5	7 57	2	21
Remember You're Mine	London	4	10 57	5	13
April Love	London	20	12 57	8	18
It's Too Soon To Know/ A Wonderful Time Up There	London	4	4 58	2	14
Sugar Moon	London	27	6 58	5	10
If Dreams Come True	London	19	9 58	14	5
I'll Remember Tonight	London	31	1 59	17	3
For A Penny	London	18	7 59	19	1
'Twixt Twelve And Twenty	London	9	8 59	16	3
Walking The Floor Over You	London	–	6 60	39	5
Moody River	London	2	7 61	18	10
Johnny Will	London	2	12 61	4	14
I'll See You In My Dreams	London	10	3 62	19	9
Quando Quando Quando	London	–	5 62	41	4
Speedy Gonzales	London	21	7 62	2	19
The Main Attraction	London	1	12 62	12	11

BOOTHE, KEN

Everything I Own	Trojan	5	10 74	1	12
Crying Over You	Trojan	11	1 75	11	10

BOSWELL, EVE

Pickin' A Chicken	Parlophone	6	1 56	10	10

BOWIE, DAVID

Space Oddity	Philips	4	10 69	5	13
Starman	RCA	15	7 72	10	11
John I'm Only Dancing	RCA	7	10 72	12	10
The Jean Genie	RCA	23	12 72	2	13
Drive-In Saturday	RCA	14	4 73	3	10
Life On Mars	RCA	7	7 73	3	13
Laughing Gnome (re-issue)	Deram	29	9 73	6	12
Sorrow	RCA	20	10 73	3	15
Rebel Rebel	RCA	23	2 74	5	7
Rock And Roll Suicide	RCA	–	4 74	22	7
Diamond Dogs	RCA	–	6 74	21	6
Knock On Wood	RCA	28	9 74	10	6
Young Americans	RCA	8	3 75	18	7
Fame	RCA	23	8 75	17	8
Space Oddity (re-issue)	RCA	18	10 75	1	10
Golden Years	RCA	13	12 75	8	10

BOXTOPS

The Letter	Stateside	30	9 67	5	12
Cry Like A Baby	Bell	20	4 68	15	12
Soul Deep	Bell	–	8 69	22	9

BOYER, JACQUELINE

Tom Pillibi	Columbia	-	4 60	33	3

BRAMBLE, WILFRED AND HARRY H. CORBETT

At The Palace (Parts 1 and 2)	Pye	-	11 63	25	12

BRANDON, JOHNNY

Tomorrow	Polygon	11	3 55	8	6
Don't Worry	Polygon	1	7 55	18	4

BRASS CONSTRUCTION

Movin'	Un.Artists	-	4 76	23	6

BREAD

Make It With You	Elektra	22	8 70	5	14
Baby I'm-A-Want You	Elektra	29	1 72	14	10
Everything I Own	Elektra	-	4 72	32	6
Guitar Man	Elektra	28	10 72	16	9

BRECK, FREDDIE

So In Love With You	Decca	-	4 74	44	4

BRENNAN, ROSE

Tall Dark Stranger	Philips	-	12 62	31	10

BRENNAN, WALTER

Old Rivers	Liberty	-	6 62	32	3

BRENT, TONY

Cindy Oh Cindy	Columbia	14	12 56	16	3
Dark Moon	Columbia	19	7 57	17	5
The Clouds Will Soon Roll By	Columbia	5	9 58	16	5
Girl Of My Dreams	Columbia	27	9 58	14	3

BRESSLAW, BERNARD

Mad Passionate Love	HMV	12	9 58	5	9

BREWER, TERESA

Let Me Go Lover	Vogue-Coral	4	2 55	9	3
A Tear Fell	Vogue-Coral	13	4 56	2	15
Sweet Old Fashioned Girl	Vogue-Coral	13	7 56	3	13
How Do You Know It's Love	Coral	-	6 60	21	10

BRISTOL, JOHNNY

Hang On In There Baby	MGM	7	9 74	3	9

BROOK BROTHERS

Please Help Me, I'm Falling	Pye	14	8 60	16	7
Warpaint	Pye	5	3 61	5	14
Ain't Gonna Wash For A Week	Pye	19	8 61	13	10
Married	Pye	11	11 61	17	3
He's Old Enough To Know Better	Pye	-	1 62	37	1
Welcome Home Baby	Pye	-	8 62	33	6
Trouble Is My Middle Name	Pye	-	2 63	38	4

BROOK, NORMAN

Sky-Blue Shirt	London	-	11 54	17	1

BROTHERHOOD OF MAN

United We Stand	Deram	21 2 70	10	10
Where Are You Going To My Love	Deram	- 7 70	22	10

BROTHERS FOUR

Greenfields	Philips	- 6 60	40	3

EDGAR BROUGHTON BAND

Out Demons Out	Harvest	- 4 70	39	4
Apache Dropout	Harvest	- 1 71	31	6

CRAZY WORLD OF ARTHUR BROWN

Fire	Track	13 7 68	1	14

BROWN, JAMES (*AND THE FAMOUS FLAMES)

Papa's Got A Brand New Bag*	London	- 9 65	25	7
I Got You (I Feel Good)*	Pye	- 2 66	29	6
It's A Man's Man's Man's World*	Pye	9 7 66	13	9
Get Up I Feel Like Being A Sex Machine (Parts 1 and 2)	Polydor	- 10 72	32	7
Hey America	Mojo	- 11 72	47	3

BROWN, JOE (AND THE BRUVVERS)

Dark Town Strutters Ball	Decca	- 3 60	34	6
Shine	Pye	- 1 61	33	6
What A Crazy World We Live In	Pye	- 1 62	37	2
Picture Of You	Piccadilly	2 6 62	2	19
Your Tender Look	Piccadilly	- 9 62	31	6
It Only Took A Minute	Piccadilly	1 12 62	6	14
That's What Love Will Do	Piccadilly	24 2 63	3	14
Nature's Time For Love	Piccadilly	- 6 63	29	6
Sally Ann	Piccadilly	- 9 63	28	9
With A Little Help From My Friends	Pye	- 7 67	32	4
Hey Mama	Ammo	- 4 73	33	6

BROWN, POLLY

Up In A Puff Of Smoke	GTO	- 9 74	43	5

BROWNE, DUNCAN

Journey	RAK	- 8 72	23	6

BROWNS

Three Bells	RCA	12 9 59	5	11

BROWNSVILLE STATION

Smokin' In The Boys Room	Philips	- 3 74	27	6

BRUBECK, DAVE

Take Five	Fontana	21 10 61	6	16
It's A Raggy Waltz	Fontana	- 2 62	36	3
Unsquare Dance	CBS	9 6 62	14	12

BRUCE, TOMMY

Ain't Misbehavin'	Columbia	5 6 60	3	16
Broken Doll	Columbia	- 9 60	36	4
Babette	Columbia	- 2 62	50	1

BRUISERS

Blue Girl	Parlophone	- 8 63	31	6

BRYAN, DORA

All I Want For Christmas Is A Beatle	Fontana	- 12 63	22	6

BRYANT, ANITA

Paper Roses	London	- 5 60	24	4
My Little Corner Of The World	London	- 2 60	48	2

B.T. EXPRESS

Express	Pye	- 3 75	34	6

BUBBLEROCK

(I Can't Get No) Satisfaction	UK	- 1 74	29	5

BUCHANAN, ROY

Sweet Dreams	Polydor	- 3 73	40	3

BURDON, ERIC AND THE ANIMALS

Help Me Girl	Decca	12 11 66	14	9
When I Was Young	Decca	- 6 67	45	3
Good Times	MGM	7 10 67	20	1
San Franciscan Nights	MGM	4 11 67	7	10
Sky Pilot	MGM	- 2 68	40	3
Ring Of Fire	MGM	- 1 69	35	5
(see also: ANIMALS)				

BURNETTE, JOHNNY

Dreamin'	London	7 10 60	5	17
You're Sixteen	London	8 1 61	3	12
Little Boy Sad	London	9 4 61	12	12
Girls	London	- 8 61	37	5
Clown Shoes	Liberty	- 5 62	35	3

BURNS, RAY

Mobile	Columbia	11 2 55	2	13
That's How A Love Song Was Born	Columbia	26 8 55	14	6

BUSCH, LOU

Zambesi	Capitol	27 1 56	1	15

BUSTER, PRINCE

Al Capone	Bluebeat	1 4 67	18	13

BUTTERSCOTCH

Don't You Know	RCA	30 5 70	17	11

BYGRAVES, MAX

Gilly Gilly Ossenfeffer Katzenellen Bogen By The Sea	HMV	1 10 54	7	7
Mr. Sandman	HMV	21 1 55	16	1
Meet Me On The Corner	HMV	18 11 55	2	11
Davy Crockett	HMV	17 2 56	20	1
Out Of Town	HMV	15 6 56	18	2
Heart	Decca	5 4 57	14	7

You Need Hands/Tulips From Amsterdam	Decca	16 5 58	3	21
My Ukelele (I Love To Play)	Decca	10 1 59	16	2
Jingle Bell Rock	Decca	26 12 59	11	1
Fings Ain't What They Used To Be	Decca	13 3 60	6	8
Consider Yourself	Decca	- 7 60	50	1
Bells Of Avignon	Decca	- 5 61	36	5
You're My Everything	Pye	- 2 69	34	5
Deck Of Cards	Pye	27 10 73	13	15

BYRD, CHARLIE

see STAN GETZ

BYRDS

Mr. Tambourine Man	CBS	3 7 65	1	13
All I Really Want To Do	CBS	21 8 65	4	10
Turn Turn Turn	CBS	- 11 65	26	7
Eight Miles High	CBS	- 5 66	24	8
You Ain't Going Nowhere	CBS	- 6 68	45	3
Chestnut Mare	CBS	27 2 71	19	8

BYRNES, ED

see CONNIE STEVENS

BYSTANDERS

98.6	Piccadilly	- 2 67	45	1

C, ROY

Shotgun Wedding	Island	7 5 66	6	10
Shotgun Wedding (re-issue)	UK	9 12 72	8	13

CADETS

Jealous Heart	Pye	- 6 65	42	1

CADOGAN, SUSAN

Hurt So Good	Magnet	26 4 75	4	12
Love Me Baby	Magnet	- 7 75	22	7

CAIOLA, AL

The Magnificent Seven	HMV	- 6 61	34	6

CALVERT, EDDIE

Stranger In Paradise	Columbia	13 3 55	14	4
Cherry Pink	Columbia	8 4 55	1	21
John And Julie	Columbia	29 7 55	6	11
Zambesi	Columbia	9 3 56	13	5
Mandy	Columbia	21 2 58	13	11

CAMILLO, TONY

see TONY CAMILLO'S BAZUKA

CAMPBELL, ETHNA

The Old Rugged Cross	Philips	- 1 76	33	10

CAMPBELL, GLEN

Wichita Lineman	Ember	22 2 69	6	12
Galveston	Ember	24 5 69	14	10
All I Have To Do Is Dream (with BOBBIE GENTRY)	Capitol	13 12 69	3	14
Try A Little Kindness	Capitol	- 2 70	45	2

Honey Come Back	Capitol	23 5 70	4	18
Everything A Man Could Ever Need	Capitol	– 9 70	32	5
It's Only Make Believe	Capitol	28 11 70	4	14
Dream Baby	Capitol	– 3 71	39	4
Rhinestone Cowboy	Capitol	25 10 75	4	13

IAN CAMPBELL FOLK GROUP

Times They Are A Changin'	Transatlantic	– 3 65	42	4

CAMPBELL, JO ANNE

Motorcycle Michael	HMV	– 6 61	41	3

CAMPBELL, JUNIOR

Hallelujah Freedom	Deram	28 10 72	10	9
Sweet Illusion	Deram	16 6 73	15	9
(see also: MARMALADE)				

CAMPBELL, PAT

Deal	Major Minor	– 11 69	31	5

CANDLEWICK GREEN

Who Do You Think You Are	Decca	– 2 74	21	8

CANNED HEAT

On The Road Again	Liberty	24 8 68	8	15
Going Up Country	Liberty	15 2 69	19	10
Let's Work Together	Liberty	7 2 70	3	15
Sugar Bee	Liberty	– 7 70	49	1

CANNON, FREDDIE

Tallahassie Lassie	Top Rank	22 8 59	15	2
Way Down Yonder In New Orleans	Top Rank	3 1 60	4	10
California Here I Come	Top Rank	27 2 60	19	2
The Urge	Top Rank	22 5 60	18	10
Muskrat Ramble	Top Rank	– 4 61	32	5
Palisades Park	Stateside	14 7 62	20	9

CAPALDI, JIM

It's All Up To You	Island	– 7 74	27	5
Love Hurts	Island	8 11 75	4	11
(see also: TRAFFIC)				

CAPTAIN AND TENILLE

Love Will Keep Us Together	A & M	– 8 75	32	5
The Way I Want To Touch You	A & M	– 1 76	28	6

CARMEN, ERIC

All By Myself	Arista	24 4 76	12	7

CARAVELLES

You Don't Have To Be A Baby To Cry	Decca	17 8 63	6	13

CARPENTERS

Close To You	A & M	26 9 70	6	18
We've Only Just Begun	A & M	– 1 71	28	7
For All We Know/Superstar	A & M	6 11 71	18	13
Merry Christmas Darling	A & M	– 1 72	45	1
I Won't Last Another Day Without You	A & M	– 9 72	49	1
Goodbye To Love	A & M	21 10 72	9	15

Yesterday Once More	A & M	28 7 73	2	12
Top Of The World	A & M	27 10 73	5	18
Jambalaya	A & M	16 3 74	12	11
I Won't Last Another Day				
Without You (re-issue)	A & M	- 6 74	32	5
Please Mr. Postman	A & M	1 2 75	2	11
Only Yesterday	A & M	3 5 75	7	10
Solitaire	A & M	- 8 75	32	5
Santa Claus Is Coming To				
Town (re-issue)	A & M	- 12 75	37	4
There's A Kind Of Hush	A & M	- 3 76	22	6

CARR, JOE 'FINGERS'

The Portuguese Washer-Women	Capitol	6 7 56	20	1

CARR, LINDA AND THE LOVE-SQUAD

Highwire	Chelsea	2 8 75	15	8

CARR, PEARL AND TEDDY JOHNSON

Sing Little Birdie	Columbia	21 3 59	12	5
How Wonderful To Know	Columbia	- 4 61	23	11

CARR, VIKKI

It Must Be Him	Liberty	1 7 67	2	21
There I Go	Liberty	- 9 67	50	1
With Pen In Hand	Liberty	- 3 69	39	3

CARROL, RONNIE

Walk Hand In Hand	Philips	25 7 56	10	6
Wisdom Of A Fool	Philips	29 3 57	20	1
Footsteps	Philips	- 3 60	36	3
Ring A Ding Girl	Philips	- 2 62	46	3
Roses Are Red	Philips	18 8 62	3	16
If Only Tomorrow	Philips	- 11 62	33	4
Say Wonderful Things	Philips	23 3 63	6	14

CARROT, JASPER

Funky Moped/Magic Roundabout	DJM	30 8 75	5	15

CARTER, CLARENCE

Patches	Atlantic	17 10 70	2	13

CASCADES

Rhythm Of The Rain	Warner Bros.	16 3 63	5	16

CASH, JOHNNY

It Ain't Me Babe	CBS	- 6 65	28	8
A Boy Named Sue	CBS	20 9 69	4	18
What Is Truth	CBS	- 5 70	21	11
A Thing Called Love	CBS	29 4 72	4	14
(with the EVANGEL TEMPLE CHOIR)				

CASINOS

Then You Can Tell Me Goodbye	President	- 2 67	28	7

CASS, MAMA

Dream A Little Dream Of Me	RCA	31 8 68	11	12
It's Getting Better	Stateside	20 9 69	8	15
(see also: MAMAS AND PAPAS)				

CASSIDY, DAVID

Could It Be Forever	Bell	22 4 72	2	17
How Can I Be Sure?	Bell	16 9 72	1	11
Rock Me Baby	Bell	2 12 72	11	9
I'm A Clown/Some Kind Of				
A Summer	Bell	31 3 73	3	12
Daydreamer/Puppy Song	Bell	13 10 73	1	15
If I Didn't Care	Bell	25 5 74	9	8
Please Please Me	Bell	10 8 74	16	6
I Write The Songs/For Love	RCA	26 7 75	11	9
Darlin'	RCA	22 11 75	16	8
(see also: PARTRIDGE FAMILY)				

CASTLE, ROY

Little White Berry	Philips	- 12 60	40	3

CASUALS

Jesamine	Decca	14 9 68	3	18
Toy	Decca	- 12 68	30	8

CATS

Swan Lake	Baf	- 5 69	50	2

C.C.S.

Whole Lotta Love	RAK	14 11 70	13	13
Walking	RAK	27 3 71	7	17
Tap Turns On The Water	RAK	18 9 71	5	13
Brother	RAK	- 3 72	26	8
Band Played The Boogie	RAK	- 8 72	36	5

CHACKSFIELD, FRANK

In Old Lisbon	Decca	24 2 56	15	4

CHAD (STEWART) AND JEREMY (CLYDE)

Yesterday's Gone	Ember	- 11 63	37	7

CHAIRMEN OF THE BOARD

Give Me Just A Little More				
Time	Invictus	29 8 70	3	13
You've Got Me Dangling On				
A String	Invictus	21 11 70	5	13
Everything's Tuesday	Invictus	27 2 71	13	9
Pay To The Piper	Invictus	- 5 71	34	7
Chairman Of The Board	Invictus	- 9 71	48	2
Working On A Building Of				
Love	Invictus	19 8 72	20	8
Elmo James	Invictus	- 10 72	21	7
I'm On My Way To A Better				
Place	Invictus	- 12 72	30	8
Finders Keepers	Invictus	- 6 73	29	9

CHAMBERLAIN, RICHARD

Theme From 'Dr. Kildare'	MGM	23 6 62	12	10
Love Me Tender	MGM	24 11 62	15	12
Hi-Lili-Hi-Lo	MGM	9 3 63	20	9
True Love	MGM	- 7 63	30	6

CHAKACHAS

Jungle Fever	Polydor	- 5 72	29	7

LES CHAKACHAS

Twist Twist	RCA	- 1 62	48	1

CHAKARIS, GEORGE

Heart Of A Teenage Girl	Triumph	- 5 60	49	1

CHAMPS

Tequila	London	4	4 58	6	7
Too Much Tequila	London	–	3 60	49	1

CHANDLER, GENE

Nothing Can Stop Me Now (re-issue)	Soul City	–	6 68	41	4

CHANNEL, BRUCE

Hey Baby	Mercury	31	3 62	2	13
Keep On	Bell	3	8 68	11	16

CHANTAYS

Pipeline	London	25	5 63	16	14

CHAPIN, HARRY

W.O.L.D.	Elektra	–	5 74	35	5

CHAQUITO

Never On Sunday	Fontana	–	10 60	50	1

CHARLES, DON

Walk With Me My Angel	Decca	–	2 62	39	5

CHARLES, RAY

Georgia On My Mind	HMV	–	11 60	24	8
Hit The Road Jack	HMV	21	10 61	6	13
I Can't Stop Loving You	HMV	23	6 62	1	17
You Don't Know Me	HMV	29	9 62	9	13
Your Cheating Heart	HMV	29	12 62	13	8
Don't Set Me Free	HMV	–	3 63	37	3
Take These Chains From My Heart	HMV	1	6 63	5	19
No One	HMV	–	9 63	35	7
Busted	HMV	–	10 63	21	10
No One To Cry To	HMV	–	9 64	38	3
Makin' Whoopee	HMV	–	1 65	42	3
Cryin' Time	HMV	–	2 66	50	1
Together Again	HMV	–	4 66	48	1
Here We Go Again	HMV	–	7 67	38	3
Yesterday	Stateside	–	12 67	44	4
Eleanor Rigby	Stateside	–	8 68	36	8

CHARLES, TINA

I Love To Love (see also: 5,000 VOLTS)	CBS	21	2 76	1	11

DICK CHARLESWORTH ORCHESTRA

Billy Boy	Top Rank	–	4 61	43	1

CHECKER, CHUBBY

Pony Time	Columbia	8	4 61	19	6
Let's Twist Again	Columbia	–	8 61	37	3
Let's Twist Again (re-issue)	Columbia	20	1 62	2	30
The Twist (re-issue)	Columbia	13	1 62	12	10
Slow Twistin'	Columbia	–	4 62	23	8
Teach Me To Twist (with BOBBY RYDELL)	Columbia	–	4 62	45	1
Dancin' Party	Columbia	25	8 62	19	13
The Twist	Columbia	–	9 62	44	2
Limbo Rock	Cameo P'way	–	11 62	32	9

Jingle Bell Rock (with BOBBY RYDELL)	Cameo P'way	– 12 62	40	3
What Do You Say	Cameo P'way	– 10 63	37	4
Let's Twist Again/The Twist (re-issue)	London	6 12 75	5	10

CHECKMATES LTD. WITH SONNY CHARLES

Proud Mary	A & M	– 11 69	30	7

CHEETAHS

Mecca	Philips	– 10 64	36	3
Soldier Boy	Philips	– 1 65	39	3

CHELSEA F.C.

Blue Is The Colour	P.Farthing	26 2 72	5	13

CHEQUERS

Rock On Brother	Creole	– 10 75	21	5
Hey Miss Payne	Creole	– 2 76	32	5

CHER

All I Really Want To Do	Liberty	4 9 65	9	10
Bang Bang	Liberty	9 4 66	3	12
I Feel Something	Liberty	– 8 66	43	2
Sunny	Liberty	– 9 66	32	5
Gypsies, Tramps And Thieves	MCA	13 11 71	4	13
Dark Lady	MCA	– 2 74	36	4
(see also: SONNY AND CHER)				

CHEROKEES

Seven Daffodils	Columbia	– 9 64	33	5

CHERRY, DON

Band Of Gold	Philips	18 2 56	6	9

CHICAGO

I'm A Man	CBS	24 1 70	8	12
25 Or 6 To 4	CBS	15 8 70	7	13

CHICKEN SHACK

I'd Rather Go Blind	B.Horizon	7 6 69	14	13
Tears In The Wind	B.Horizon	– 9 69	29	5

CHICORY TIP

Son Of My Father	CBS	5 2 72	1	13
What's Your Name?	CBS	17 6 72	13	8
Good Grief Christina	CBS	5 5 73	17	13

CHIFFONS

He's So Fine	Stateside	4 5 63	16	12
One Fine Day	Stateside	– 7 63	29	6
Sweet Talking Guy	Stateside	– 5 66	31	8
Sweet Talking Guy (re-issue)	London	8 4 72	4	13

CHI-LITES

(For God's Sake) Give More Power To The People	MCA	– 8 71	32	6
Have You Seen Her	MCA	29 1 72	3	13
Oh Girl	MCA	24 6 72	14	9
Homely Girl	Brunswick	20 4 74	5	13
I Found Sunshine	Brunswick	– 7 74	34	5

Too Good To Be Forgotten	Brunswick	23 11 74	10	11
Have You Seen Her/Oh Girl (re-issue)	Brunswick	5 7 75	5	10
It's Time For Love	Brunswick	4 10 75	5	10

CHIPMUNKS (with DAVID SEVILLE)

Ragtime Cowboy Joe (see also: DAVID SEVILLE)	London	1 8 59	11	5

CHORDETTES

Mr. Sandman	Columbia	7 1 55	11	5
Born To Be With You	London	31 8 56	12	8
Lollipop	London	25 4 58	7	5

CHRISTIAN, NEIL

That's Nice	Strike	7 5 66	14	10

CHRISTIE

Yellow River	CBS	16 5 70	1	22
San Bernadino	CBS	7 11 70	7	14
Iron Horse	CBS	- 3 74	47	2

CHRISTIE, LOU

Lightnin' Strikes	MGM	5 3 66	11	8
Rhapsody In The Rain	MGM	- 4 66	37	2
I'm Gonna Make You Mine	Buddah	4 10 69	2	16
She Sold Magic	Buddah	- 1 70	25	7

CHRISTIE, TONY

Las Vegas	MCA	- 1 71	21	10
I Did What I Did For Maria	MCA	29 5 71	2	17
Is This The Way To Amarillo?	MCA	18 12 71	18	13
Avenues And Alleyways	MCA	- 2 73	37	4

CHUCKS

Loo-Be-Loo	Decca	- 1 63	23	7

CINQUETTI, GIGLIOLA

Non Ho L'Eta	Decca	30 5 64	17	17
Go	CBS	25 5 74	8	10

CLANTON, JIMMY

Another Sleepless Night	Top Rank	- 7 60	50	1

CLAPTON, ERIC

I Shot The Sheriff	RSO	10 8 74	9	9
Swing Low Sweet Chariot	RSO	7 6 75	19	9
Knockin' On Heaven's Door	RSO	- 8 75	38	4
(see also: CREAM, DELANEY AND BONNIE, DEREK AND THE DOMINOES)				

CLARK THE DAVE CLARK FIVE

Do You Love Me	Columbia	- 10 63	30	6
Glad All Over	Columbia	30 11 63	1	19
Bits And Pieces	Columbia	22 4 64	2	11
Can't You See That She's Mine	Columbia	13 6 64	10	9
Thinking Of You Baby	Columbia	- 8 64	26	4
Anyway You Want It	Columbia	- 10 64	25	5
Everybody Knows	Columbia	- 1 65	37	4
Reelin'n'Rockin'	Columbia	- 3 65	24	8

Come Home	Columbia	19	6 65	16	8
Catch Us If You Can	Columbia	31	7 65	5	11
Over And Over	Columbia	–	11 65	45	4
Look Before You Leap	Columbia	–	5 66	50	1
You Got What It Takes	Columbia	–	3 67	28	8
Everybody Knows	Columbia	18	11 67	2	14
No One Can Break A Heart Like You	Columbia	–	3 68	28	7
Red Balloon	Columbia	28	9 68	7	11
Live In The Sky	Columbia	–	11 68	38	2
Put A Little Love In Your Heart	Columbia	–	10 69	31	4
Good Old Rock 'n' Roll	Columbia	20	12 69	7	12
Everybody Get Together	Columbia	14	3 70	8	8
Here Comes Summer	Columbia	–	7 70	44	3
More Good Old Rock 'n' Roll	Columbia	–	11 70	34	6

CLARK, DEE

Just Keep It Up	London	12	9 59	19	1
Ride A Wild Horse	Chelsea	8	11 75	16	8

CLARK, PETULA

Majorca	Polygon	18	2 55	13	5
Suddenly There's A Valley	Nixa	25	11 55	8	10
With All My Heart	Nixa	2	8 57	6	16
Alone	Pye Nixa	22	11 57	9	9
Baby Lover	Pye Nixa	14	3 58	15	4
Sailor	Pye	15	1 61	1	15
Something Missing	Pye	–	4 61	44	1
Romeo	Pye	2	7 61	3	15
My Friend The Sea	Pye	18	11 61	7	14
I'm Counting On You	Pye	–	2 62	41	2
Ya Ya Twist	Pye	21	7 62	14	13
Casanova/Chariot	Pye	–	5 63	39	7
Downtown	Pye	21	11 64	2	15
I Know A Place	Pye	27	3 65	17	6
You Better Come Home	Pye	–	8 65	44	3
Round Every Corner	Pye	–	10 65	43	3
You're The One	Pye	–	11 65	23	8
My Love	Pye	19	2 66	4	9
A Sign Of The Times	Pye	–	4 66	49	1
I Couldn't Live Without Your Love	Pye	16	7 66	6	11
This Is My Song	Pye	11	2 67	1	14
Don't Sleep In The Subway	Pye	24	6 67	12	11
The Other Man's Grass	Pye	13	1 68	20	9
Kiss Me Goodbye	Pye	–	3 68	50	1
The Song Of My Life	Pye	–	1 71	32	13
I Don't Know How To Love Him	Pye	–	1 72	47	2

CLASSICS IV

Spooky	Liberty	–	2 68	46	1

CLAY, JUDY

see WILLIAM BELL

CLIFF, JIMMY

Wonderful World, Beautiful People	Trojan	1	11 69	6	12
Vietnam	Trojan	–	2 70	46	3
Wild World	Island	5	9 70	8	12

CLIFFORD, BUZZ

Baby Sittin' Boogie	Philips	19	2 61	17	13

CLINE, PATSY

She's Got You	Brunswick	– 4 62	43	1
Heartaches	Brunswick	– 11 62	31	5

CLOONEY, ROSEMARY

This Ole House	Philips	– 10 54	1	15
Mambo Italiano	Philips	– 12 54	1	13
Where Will The Dimple Be?	Philips	20 5 55	6	13
Hey There	Philips	30 9 55	4	11
Mangos	Philips	24 5 57	17	1

CLYDE VALLEY STOMPERS

Peter And The Wolf	Parlophone	– 8 62	25	8

COASTERS

Yakety Yak	London	15 8 58	10	7
Charlie Brown	London	28 3 59	5	10
Poison Ivy	London	21 11 59	15	2

COCHRAN, EDDIE

Summertime Blues	London	**28 11 58**	**18**	**2**
C'mon Everybody	London	**21 3 59**	**8**	**10**
Three Steps To Heaven	London	8 5 60	1	15
Lonely/Sweetie Pie	London	8 10 60	19	3
Weekend	London	11 6 61	15	17
Jeannie Jeannie Jeannie	London	– 11 61	31	4
My Way	Liberty	– 4 63	23	10
Summertime Blues (re-issue)	Liberty	– 4 68	34	8

COCKER, JOE

Marjorine	R.Zonophone	– 5 68	48	1
With A Little Help From My Friends	R.Zonophone	19 10 68	1	12
Delta Lady	R.Zonophone	25 10 69	10	11
The Letter	R.Zonophone	– 7 70	39	6

COCKEREL CHORUS

Nice One Cyril	Young Blood	10 3 73	14	12

(*STEVE HARLEY AND) COCKNEY REBEL

Judy Teen	EMI	1 6 74	5	11
Mr. Soft	EMI	24 8 74	8	9
Make Me Smile (Come Up And See Me)*	EMI	15 2 75	1	9
Mr. Raffles (Man It Was Mean)*	EMI	21 6 75	13	6

COGAN, ALMA

Little Things Mean A Lot	HMV	– 10 54	18	1
I Can't Tell A Waltz From A Tango	HMV	7 1 55	6	6
Dreamboat	HMV	27 5 55	1	16
Banjo's Back In Town	HMV	23 9 55	17	1
Go On By	HMV	14 10 55	16	4
Never Do A Tango With An Eskimo	HMV	23 12 55	6	5
Twenty Tiny Fingers	HMV	16 12 55	17	1
Willie Can	HMV	30 3 56	13	7
Why Do Fools Fall In **Love?**	HMV	11 8 56	19	2
Middle Of The House	HMV	23 11 56	20	2
You Me And Us	HMV	18 1 57	20	3
Sugartime	HMV	28 2 58	16	3
Train Of Love	HMV	– 8 60	23	5

Cowboy Jimmy Joe	Columbia	– 4	61	37	6

COGAN, SHAYE

Mean To Me	MGM	– 3	60	40	1

COLE, NAT 'KING'

Smile	Capitol	– 10	54	2	10
Make Her Mine	Capitol	– 10	54	11	8
A Blossom Fell	Capitol	25 2	55	3	10
My One Sin	Capitol	26 8	55	17	2
Dreams Can Tell A Lie	Capitol	27 1	56	12	9
Too Young To Go Steady	Capitol	18 5	56	12	10
Love Me As Though There Were No Tomorrow	Capitol	26 10	56	16	7
When I Fall In Love	Capitol	19 4	57	2	19
Time And The River	Capitol	– 3	60	47	1
That's You	Capitol	22 5	60	10	8
Just As Much As Ever	Capitol	– 11	60	21	10
The World In My Arms	Capitol	– 1	61	36	10
Let Your True Love Begin	Capitol	9 12	61	19	11
Brazilian Love Song	Capitol	– 3	62	34	4
The Right Thing To Say	Capitol	– 5	62	42	4
Let There Be Love (with GEORGE SHEARING)	Capitol	4 8	62	11	14
Ramblin' Rose	Capitol	6 10	62	5	14
Dear Lonely Hearts	Capitol	– 12	62	37	3

COLE, NATALIE

This Will Be	Capitol	– 10	75	32	5

COLLINS, DAVE AND ANSELL

Double Barrel	Technique	10 4	71	1	15
Monkey Spanner	Technique	3 7	71	7	12

COLLINS, JEFF

Only You	Polydor	– 11	72	40	6

COLLINS, JUDY

Both Sides Now	Elektra	21 2	70	14	12
Amazing Grace	Elektra	16 1	71	5	52
Amazing Grace (re-issue)	Elektra	– 4	72	21	23
Send In The Clowns	Elektra	24 5	75	6	9

COLLINS, ROGER

You Sexy Sugar Plumb	Fantasy	– 4	76	22	6

COMMODORES

Machine Gun	T.Motown	5 10	74	20	11
The Zoo	T.Motown	– 11	74	44	2

COMO, PERRY

Idle Gossip	HMV	– 10	54	14	4
Wanted	HMV	– 10	54	18	3
Papa Loves Mambo	HMV	– 12	54	16	3
Hot Diggity	HMV	25 5	56	4	12
More	HMV	5 10	56	11	8
Magic Moments	RCA	7 2	58	1	15
Catch A Falling Star	RCA	14 3	58	9	7
Kewpie Doll	RCA	16 5	58	11	5
I May Never Pass This Way Again	RCA	6 6	58	18	4
Moon Talk	RCA	3 10	58	19	4

Love Makes The World Go Round	RCA	7 11 58	5	8
Mandolins In The Moonlight	RCA	28 11 58	15	5
Tomboy	RCA	28 2 59	12	10
I Know	RCA	18 7 59	11	7
Delaware	RCA	20 2 60	3	14
Caterina	RCA	– 5 62	32	6
It's Impossible	RCA	13 2 71	4	23
I Think Of You	RCA	29 5 71	14	11
And I Love You So	RCA	5 3 73	3	35
For The Good Times	RCA	22 9 73	7	27
Walk Right Back	RCA	– 12 73	33	10
I Want To Give	RCA	– 5 74	31	6

CONGREGATION

Softly Whispering I Love You	Columbia	11 12 71	4	14

CONLEY, ARTHUR

Sweet Soul Music	Atlantic	20 5 67	7	14
Funky Street	Atlantic	– 4 68	46	1

CONNOLLY, BILLY

D.I.V.O.R.C.E.	Polydor	8 11 75	1	10

CONRAD, JESS

Cherry Pie	Decca	– 6 60	39	1
Mystery Girl	Decca	– 1 61	21	10
Pretty Jenny	Decca	– 10 62	50	2

CONSORTIUM

All The Love In The World	Pye	– 2 69	32	9

CONTOURS

Just A Little Misunderstanding	T.Motown	– 1 70	31	6

CONWAY, RUSS

More Party Pops	Columbia	26 12 58	10	3
Side Saddle	Columbia	28 2 59	1	17
Roulette	Columbia	23 5 59	1	11
China Tea	Columbia	22 8 59	4	10
Snow Coach	Columbia	14 11 59	6	8
More And More Party Pops	Columbia	28 11 59	9	6
Royal Event	Columbia	27 2 60	14	4
Fings Ain't What They Used To Be	Columbia	– 4 60	47	1
Lucky Five	Columbia	28 5 60	9	10
Passing Breeze	Columbia	– 9 60	22	10
Even More Party Pops	Columbia	– 11 60	27	9
Pepe	Columbia	31 12 60	14	9
Pablo	Columbia	– 5 61	45	2
Say It With Flowers (with DOROTHY SQUIRES)	Columbia	– 8 61	23	10
Toy Balloons	Columbia	9 12 61	7	12
Lesson No.1	Columbia	24 2 62	14	7
Always You And Me	Columbia	– 11 62	35	6

COOK, PETER AND DUDLEY MOORE

Goodbye	Decca	17 7 65	18	10
Ballad Of Spotty Muldoon (PETER COOK only)	Decca	– 7 65	34	5

COOKE, SAM

Only Sixteen	HMV	15 8 59	13	3

Wonderful World	HMV	– 7 60	27	8
Chain Gang	RCA	23 9 60	9	11
Cupid	RCA	5 8 61	7	14
Twisting The Night Away	RCA	17 3 62	6	14
Another Saturday Night	RCA	– 5 63	23	11
Frankie And Johnny	RCA	– 9 63	30	6

COOKIES

Chains	London	– 1 63	50	1

COOPER, TOMMY

Don't Jump Off The Roof Dad	Palette	– 6 61	40	3

CORDELL, FRANK

Black Bear	HMV	– 2 61	44	1

CORDET, LOUISE

I'm Just A Baby	Decca	11 8 62	13	13

CORNELL, DON

Hold My Hand	Vogue–Coral	– 10 54	5	15
Stranger In Paradise	Vogue–Coral	22 4 55	19	2

CORNELL, LYNN

Never On Sunday	Decca	22 10 60	18	8

CORONETS

Twenty Tiny Fingers	Columbia	25 11 55	20	1

COSTA, DON

Never On Sunday	London	– 10 60	27	9

COTTAGERS

Viva El Fulham	Sonet	– 5 75	46	1

COTTON, MIKE

Swing That Hammer	Columbia	– 6 63	36	4

COUGARS

Saturday Night At The Duckpond	Parlophone	– 2 63	33	8

COUNTRYMEN

I Know Where I'm Going	Piccadilly	– 5 62	45	2

COVAY, DON

It's Better To Have	Mercury	– 9 74	29	6

COX, MICHAEL

Angela Jones	Triumph	12 6 60	7	13
Along Came Caroline	HMV	8 10 60	20	4

CRAMER, FLOYD

On The Rebound	RCA	16 4 61	5	14
San Antonia Rose	RCA	– 7 61	36	8
Hot Pepper	RCA	– 8 62	46	2

CRANE, LES

Desiderata	Warner Bros.	18 3 72	7	14

CRAZY ELEPHANT

Gimme Gimme Gimme Good Lovin'	Major Minor	28 6 69	12	13

CREAM

Wrapping Paper	Reaction	– 10 66	34	6
I Feel Free	Reaction	21 1 67	11	12
Strange Brew	Reaction	1 7 67	17	9
Anyone For Tennis	Polydor	– 6 68	40	3
Sunshine Of Your Love	Polydor	– 10 68	25	7
White Room	Polydor	– 1 69	29	8
Badge	Polydor	26 4 69	18	9
Badge (re-issue)	Polydor	– 10 72	42	4

CREATION

Making Time	Planet	– 7 65	49	1
Painter Man	Planet	– 11 66	36	2

CREEDENCE CLEARWATER REVIVAL

Proud Mary	Liberty	21 6 69	8	12
Bad Moon Rising	Liberty	23 8 69	1	15
Green River	Liberty	27 12 69	19	11
Down On The Corner	Liberty	– 2 70	31	7
Travellin' Band	Liberty	18 4 70	8	12
Up Around The Bend	Liberty	27 6 70	3	12
As Long As I Can See The Light	Liberty	26 9 70	20	9
Have You Ever Seen The Rain	Liberty	– 2 71	36	10
Sweet Hitch Hiker	Un.Artists	– 7 71	36	8

CREW CUTS

Sh'Boom	Mercury	– 10 54	16	4
Earth Angel	Mercury	15 4 55	4	20

CRIBBINS, BERNARD

Hole In The Ground	Parlophone	24 2 62	9	13
'Right' Said Fred	Parlophone	21 7 62	10	10
Gossip Calypso	Parlophone	– 12 62	25	6

CRICKETS

That'll Be The Day	Vogue-Coral	27 9 57	1	12
Oh! Boy	Coral	10 1 58	3	12
Maybe Baby	Coral	21 3 58	4	8
Think It Over	Coral	1 8 58	13	5
It's So Easy	Coral	22 11 58	19	1
*Baby My Heart	Coral	– 5 60	33	4
Don't Ever Change	Liberty	7 7 62	5	13
My Little Girl	Liberty	10 2 63	17	10
Don't Try To Change Me	Liberty	– 6 63	37	4
(They Call Her) La Bamba (see also: BUDDY HOLLY)	Liberty	– 7 64	21	10

CRISPY AND COMPANY

Brazil	Creole	– 8 75	30	5
Get It Together	Creole	– 1 76	21	5

CRITTERS

Younger Girl	London	– 7 66	38	4

CROSBY, BING

Count Your Blessings	Brunswick	7 1 55	11	3

*All Records To Here, Feature BUDDY HOLLY

Stranger In Paradise	Brunswick	29	4 55	17	2
In A Little Spanish Town	Brunswick	14	4 56	20	1
True Love	Capitol	23	11 56	4	23
(with GRACE KELLY)					
Around The World	Brunswick	24	5 57	4	14
That's What Life Is All					
About	Un.Artists	–	8 75	41	4

CROSBY, STILLS AND NASH

Marrakesh Express	Atlantic	13	9 69	17	9

CRUSH, BOBBY

Borsalino	Philips	–	11 72	37	4

CRYIN' SHAMES

Please Stay	Decca	–	4 66	26	7

CRYSTALS

He's A Rebel	London	13	1 63	19	14
Da Doo Ron Ron	London	29	6 63	5	16
Then He Kissed Me	London	28	9 63	2	14
I Wonder	London	–	3 64	36	3
Da Doo Ron Ron/Then He Kissed Me (re-issue)	Warner-Spector	9	11 74	15	8

CUFFLINKS

Tracy	MCA	13	12 69	4	16
When Julie Comes Around	MCA	11	4 70	10	14

CUNNINGHAM, LARRY AND THE MIGHTY AVONS

Tribute To Jim Reeves	King	–	12 64	40	11

CUPID'S INSPIRATION

Yesterday Has Gone	NEMS	29	6 68	4	12
My World	NEMS	–	10 68	33	8

CURVED AIR

It Happened Today	Warner Bros.	–	2 71	47	2
Back Street Luv	Warner Bros.	4	9 71	4	12

CUTLER, ADGE AND THE WURZELS

Drink Up Thy Zider	Columbia	–	2 67	45	1

CYMBAL, JOHNNY

Mr. Bass Man	London	–	3 63	25	10

DAKOTAS

Cruel Sea	Parlophone	10	8 63	18	13
(see also: BILLY J. KRAMER)					

DALE AND GRACE

I'm Leaving It Up To You	London	–	1 64	42	2

DALE, JIM

Be My Girl	Parlophone	25	10 57	2	12
Sugar Time/Don't Let Go	Parlophone	8	3 58	17	1

DALE SISTERS

My Sunday Baby	Ember	–	11 61	36	6

DALTREY, ROGER

Giving It All Away	Track	28	4 73	5	11
I'm Free	Ode	25	8 73	13	10

(with THE LONDON SYMPHONY ORCHESTRA)
(see also: WHO)

DAMON, KENNY

While I Live	Mercury	-	5 66	45	2

DAMONE, VIC

On The Street Where You Live	Philips	16	5 58	1	15

DANA

All Kinds Of Everything	Rex	4	4 70	1	15
Who Put The Lights Out	Rex	13	3 71	16	11
Please Tell Him That I Said Hello	GTO	22	2 75	8	14
It's Gonna Be A Cold Cold Christmas	GTO	20	12 75	4	6
Never Gonna Fall In Love Again	GTO	-	3 76	31	4

DANKWORTH, JOHNNY

Experiments With Mice	Parlophone	29	4 56	5	8
African Waltz	Columbia	19	3 61	9	21

DANNY AND THE JUNIORS

At The Hop	HMV	17	1 58	4	13

DARIN, BOBBY

Splish Splash	London	29	8 58	15	1
Dream Lover	London	6	6 59	1	15
Mack The Knife	London	3	10 59	2	12
Beyond The Sea	London	30	1 60	8	6
Clementine	London	27	3 60	8	12
Bill Bailey	London	-	6 60	34	2
Lazy River	London	5	3 61	2	13
Nature Boy	London	-	7 61	24	7
You Must Have Been A Beautiful Baby	London	14	10 61	10	11
Multiplication	London	6	1 62	5	13
Things	London	4	8 62	2	17
If A Man Answers	Capitol	-	10 62	24	6
Baby Face	London	-	11 62	40	4
Eighteen Yellow Roses	Capitol	-	7 63	37	4
If I Were A Carpenter	Atlantic	29	10 66	9	12

BOBBY DARIN ORCHESTRA

Come September	London	-	10 61	50	1

DARRELL, GUY

I've Been Hurt	Santa Ponsa	15	9 73	12	13

DARREN, JAMES

Because They're Young	Pye	-	8 60	29	7
Goodbye Cruel World	Pye	6	1 62	15	10
Her Royal Majesty	Pye	-	3 62	36	4
Conscience	Pye	-	6 62	30	6

DAVID AND JONATHAN

Michelle	Columbia	29	1 66	11	6
Lovers Of The World Unite	Columbia	20	8 66	7	16

DAVID, ANN-MARIE

Wonderful Dream	Epic	12	5 73	13	9

DAVIDSON, PAUL

Midnight Rider	Tropical	24	1 76	10	9

DAVIES, DAVE

Death Of A Clown	Pye	29	7 67	3	10
Susannah's Still Alive	Pye	-	12 67	21	7
(see also: KINKS)					

DAVIES, WINDSOR AND DON ESTELLE

Whispering Grass	EMI	24	5 75	1	12
Paper Doll	EMI	-	10 75	41	3

DA VINCI, PAUL

Your Baby Ain't Your Baby Anymore	P.Farthing	17	8 74	20	8

DAVIS, BILLIE

Tell Him	Decca	9	3 63	10	12
He's The One	Decca	-	5 63	40	3
I Want You To Be My Baby	Decca	-	10 68	33	8

DAVIS, MAC

Baby Don't Get Hooked On Me	CBS	-	11 72	29	6

DAVIS, SKEETER

End Of The World	RCA	13	4 63	18	13

DAVIS JNR., SAMMY

Something's Gotta Give	Brunswick	29	7 55	11	7
Love Me Or Leave Me	Brunswick	9	9 55	8	8
That Old Black Magic	Brunswick	30	9 55	16	1
Hey There	Brunswick	7	10 55	19	1
Happy To Make Your Acquaintance	Brunswick	-	6 60	46	1
(with CARMEN McRAE)					
What Kind Of Fool Am I/ Gonna Build A Mountain	Reprise	-	3 62	26	8
Me And My Shadow	Reprise	29	12 62	20	9
(with FRANK SINATRA)					

SPENCER DAVIS GROUP

I Can't Stand It	Fontana	-	11 64	47	3
Every Little Bit Hurts	Fontana	-	2 65	41	3
Strong Love	Fontana	-	6 65	44	4
Keep On Runnin'	Fontana	25	12 65	1	14
Somebody Help Me	Fontana	2	4 66	1	10
When I Come Home	Fontana	17	9 66	12	9
Gimme Some Loving	Fontana	12	11 66	2	12
I'm A Man	Fontana	4	2 67	9	7
Time Seller	Fontana	-	8 67	30	5
Mr. Second Class	Un.Artists	-	1 68	35	4

DAWN (FEATURING TONY ORLANDO)

Candida	Bell	30	1 71	9	11
Knock Three Times	Bell	17	4 71	1	27
What Are You Doing Sunday?	Bell	14	8 71	3	12
Tie A Yellow Ribbon Round The Old Oak Tree	Bell	24	3 73	1	39
Say, Has Anybody Seen My Sweet Gypsy Rose?	Bell	1	9 73	12	15

Who's In The Strawberry Patch With Sally? (see also: TONY ORLANDO)	Bell	– 3 74	37	4

DAY, DORIS

Secret Love	Philips	– 10 54	8	8
Black Hills Of Dakota	Philips	– 10 54	9	7
If I Give My Heart To You	Philips	– 10 54	15	4
Ready Willing And Able	Philips	8 4 55	7	9
Love Me Or Leave Me	Philips	9 9 55	20	1
I'll Never Stop Loving You	Philips	21 10 55	17	3
Whatever Will Be Will Be (Que Sera Sera)	Philips	29 6 56	1	19
A Very Precious Love	Philips	4 7 58	20	5
Move Over Darling	CBS	11 4 64	8	16

DEAN, JIMMY

Big Bad John	Philips	21 10 61	2	14
Little Black Book	CBS	– 11 62	33	4

DE CASTRO SISTERS

Teach Me Tonight	London	11 2 55	20	1

DEE, DAVE, DOZY, BEAKY, MICK AND TITCH

You Make It Move	Fontana	– 1 66	26	7
Hold Tight	Fontana	26 3 66	4	17
Hideaway	Fontana	25 6 66	10	11
Bend It	Fontana	24 9 66	2	12
Save Me	Fontana	17 12 66	3	10
Touch Me Touch Me	Fontana	15 4 67	13	8
Okay	Fontana	10 6 67	4	11
Zabadak	Fontana	21 10 67	3	13
Legend Of Xanadu	Fontana	24 2 68	1	12
Last Night In Soho	Fontana	27 7 68	8	11
Wreck Of The Antoinette	Fontana·	12 10 68	14	9
Don Juan	Fontana	– 3 69	23	8
Snake In The Grass	Fontana	– 5 69	23	8
My Woman's Man (DAVE DEE only)	Fontana	– 3 70	42	4
Mr. President (DOZY, B. M. AND T.)	Fontana	– 8 70	23	8

DEE, JOEY AND THE STARLITERS

Peppermint Twist	Columbia	13 1 62	13	8

DEE, KIKI

Amoureuse	Rocket	8 12 73	13	13
I Got The Music In Me	Rocket	12 10 74	19	8
How Glad I Am	Rocket	– 4 75	33	4

DEENE, CAROLE

Sad Movies	HMV	– 10 61	44	3
Norman	HMV	– 1 62	24	8
Johnny Get Angry	HMV	– 7 62	32	4
Some People	HMV	– 8 62	25	10

DEEP FEELING

Do You Love Me	Page One	– 4 70	34	5

DEEP PURPLE

Black Night	Harvest	19 9 70	2	20

Strange Kind Of Woman	Harvest	20 3 71	8	12
Fireball	Harvest	11 12 71	15	13
Never Before	Purple	- 4 72	35	6

DEKKER, DESMOND AND THE ACES

007 (Shanty Town)	Pyramid	29 7 67	14	10
The Israelites	Pyramid	5 4 69	1	14
It Mek	Pyramid	12 7 69	7	11
Pickney Gal	Pyramid	- 1 70	45	3
You Can Get It If You Really Want It	Trojan	5 9 70	2	15
The Israelites (re-issue)	Cactus	24 5 75	10	9
Sing A Little Song	Cactus	27 9 75	16	7

DELANEY AND BONNIE AND FRIENDS

Comin' Home (with ERIC CLAPTON)	Atlantic	10 1 70	16	9

DELFONICS

Didn't I Blow Your Mind This Time (re-issue)	Bell	- 4 71	22	8
La-La Means I Love You	Bell	7 8 71	19	10
(re-issue)	Bell	7 8 71	19	10
Ready Or Not Here I Come	Bell	- 10 71	41	4

DELLS

Love Is Blue/I Can Sing A Rainbow	Chess	9 8 69	15	8

DE LOS RIOS, WALDO

Mozart Symphony No. 40	A & M	17 4 71	5	16

DENE, TERRY

White Sports Coat	Decca	21 6 57	16	2
Start Movin'	Decca	16 8 57	14	2
Stairway Of Love	Decca	23 5 58	12	2

DENNIS, JACKIE

La Dee Dah	Decca	28 3 58	6	7

DENNISONS

Be My Girl	Decca	- 8 63	46	4
Walkin' The Dog	Decca	- 5 64	36	7

DENVER, JOHN

Annie's Song	RCA	31 8 74	1	14

DENVER, KARL

Marcheta	Decca	18 6 61	8	19
Mexicali Rose	Decca	14 10 61	8	11
Wimoweh	Decca	3 2 62	4	17
Never Goodbye	Decca	7 4 62	9	18
A Little Love, A Little Kiss	Decca	16 6 62	19	10
Blue Weekend	Decca	- 9 62	33	5
Can You Forgive Me?	Decca	- 3 63	32	8
Indian Love Call	Decca	- 6 63	32	7
Still	Decca	7 9 63	13	10
My World Of Blue	Decca	- 3 64	29	6
Love Me With All Your Heart	Decca	- 6 64	37	6

DEODATO

Also Sprach Zarathustra-2001	Creed Taylor	12 5 73	7	9

DE PAUL, LYNSEY

Sugar Me	MAM	26 8 72	5	11
Getting A Drag	MAM	23 12 72	18	8
Won't Somebody Dance With Me	MAM	3 11 73	14	7
Ooh I Do	Warner Bros.	- 6 74	25	6
No Honestly	Jet	16 11 74	7	11
My Man And Me	Jet	- 3 75	40	4

DEREK AND THE DOMINOES

Layla (re-issue)	Polydor	19 8 72	7	11

DE SYKES, STEPHANIE

Born With A Smile On My Face	Bradleys	20 7 74	2	9
We'll Find Our Day	Bradleys	3 5 75	17	7

DETROIT EMERALDS

Feel The Need In Me	Janus	3 3 73	4	15
You Want It, You Got It	Westbound	2 6 73	12	9
I Think Of You	Westbound	- 8 73	27	9

DETROIT SPINNERS (FORMERLY MOTOWN SPINNERS)

Could It Be I'm Falling In Love	Atlantic	12 5 73	11	11
Ghetto Child	Atlantic	13 10 73	7	10

(see also: MOTOWN SPINNERS, DIONNE WARWICK)

DE VAUGHN, WILLIAM

Be Thankful For What You've Got	Chelsea	- 7 74	31	5

DIAMOND, NEIL

Cracklin' Rosie	UNI	21 11 70	3	16
Sweet Caroline (re-issue)	UNI	27 2 71	8	11
I Am ... I Said	UNI	22 5 71	4	12
Song Sung Blue	UNI	17 6 72	14	13

DIAMONDS

Little Darlin'	Mercury	7 6 57	4	15

DICK AND DEEDEE

The Mountains High	London	- 10 61	37	3

DICKENS, CHARLES

That's The Way	Pye	- 7 65	37	8

DICKIE, NEVILLE

Robin's Return	Major Minor	- 10 69	33	8

DICKSON, BARBARA

Answer Me	RSO	31 1 76	9	7

DIDDLEY, BO

Pretty Thing	Pye	- 10 63	34	6
Hey Good Lookin'	Chess	- 3 65	39	5

50

DI MUCCI, DION
see DION

DINNING, MARK

Teen Angel	MGM	– 3 60	40	3

DION

Lonely Teenager	Top Rank	– 1 61	47	1
Runaround Sue	Top Rank	4 11 61	11	10
The Wanderer	HMV	24 2 62	10	13

DISCO TEX AND THE SEX-O-LETTES

Get Dancing	Chelsea	7 12 74	8	12
I Wanna Dance Wit Choo (Do Dat Dance)	Chelsea	10 5 75	6	10

DISTEL, SACHA

Raindrops Keep Falling On My Head	Warner Bros.	28 2 70	14	24

DIVERSIONS

Fattie Bum Bum	Gull	– 9 75	34	3

DIXIE CUPS

Chapel Of Love	Pye	– 6 64	22	8
Iko Iko	Red Bird	– 5 65	23	7

DOBKINS, CARL

Lucky Devil	Brunswick	– 3 60	44	1

DODD, KEN

Love Is Like A Violin	Decca	17 7 60	8	18
Once In Every Lifetime	Decca	– 6 61	28	11
Pianissimo	Decca	– 2 62	21	15
Still	Columbia	– 8 63	37	5
Eight By Ten	Columbia	– 2 64	22	11
Happiness	Columbia	– 7 64	31	13
So Deep Is The Night	Columbia	– 11 64	31	7
Tears	Columbia	11 9 65	1	26
The River	Columbia	27 11 65	3	14
Promises	Columbia	21 5 66	6	14
More Than Love	Columbia	20 8 66	14	11
It's Love	Columbia	– 10 66	36	7
Let Me Cry On Your Shoulder	Columbia	4 2 67	11	10
Tears Won't Wash Away The Heartaches	Columbia	– 8 69	24	11
Broken Hearted	Columbia	19 12 70	15	10
When My Love Comes Round Again	Columbia	18 9 71	19	16
Just Out Of Reach	Columbia	– 11 72	29	11
(Think Of Me) Wherever You Are	EMI	– 11 75	21	8

DOLAN, JOE

Make Me An Island	Pye	19 7 69	3	18
Teresa	Pye	22 11 69	20	7
You're Such A Good Looking Woman	Pye	4 4 70	17	13

DOMINO, FATS

I'm In Love Again	London	24 8 56	9	5

Blueberry Hill	London	11	1 57	7	10
Ain't That A Shame	London	2	2 57	20	1
I'm Walking	London	19	4 57	15	1
The Big Beat	London	11	4 58	15	1
Margie	London	30	5 59	16	2
I Want To Walk You Home	London	7	11 59	19	2
Be My Guest	London	19	12 59	12	8
Country Boy	London	3	4 60	19	11
Walking To New Orleans	London	-	7 60	24	10
Three Nights A Week	London	-	11 60	45	2
My Girl Josephine	London	-	12 60	32	4
It Keeps Rainin'	London	-	7 61	49	1
What A Party	London	-	11 61	43	1
Jambalaya	London	-	3 62	41	1
Red Sails In The Sunset	HMV	-	10 63	34	6
Blueberry Hill (re-issue)	Un.Artists	-	4 76	41	5

DONEGAN, LONNIE

Rock Island Line	Decca	6	1 56	6	17
Lost John	Nixa	27	4 56	2	14
Skiffle Session EP	Nixa	6	7 56	20	1
Dead Or Alive	Pye Nixa	15	9 56	9	7
Bring A Little Water, Sylvie	Pye Nixa	14	9 56	8	8
Don't You Rock Me Daddy-O	Pye Nixa	18	1 57	4	15
Cumberland Gap	Pye Nixa	5	4 57	1	11
Puttin' On The Style/ Gambling Man	Pye Nixa	7	6 57	1	18
Dixie Darling	Pye Nixa	11	10 57	10	8
Jack O'Diamonds	Pye Nixa	20	12 57	16	6
Grand Coulee Dam/Nobody Loves Like An Irishman	Pye Nixa	25	4 58	5	9
Sally Don't You Grieve/ Betty Betty Betty	Pye Nixa	11	7 58	7	6
Tom Dooley	Pye Nixa	21	11 58	3	12
Skiffle Party EP	Pye Nixa	3	1 59	18	1
Does Your Chewing Gum Lose It's Flavour On The Bedpost Overnight	Pye Nixa	7	2 59	3	10
Fort Worth Jail	Pye Nixa	9	5 59	12	4
Battle Of New Orleans	Pye	20	6 59	2	14
Sal's Got A Sugar Lip	Pye	19	9 59	16	3
My Old Man's A Dustman	Pye	20	3 60	1	13
I Wanna Go Home	Pye	22	5 60	5	17
Lorelei	Pye	21	8 60	10	8
Lively	Pye	20	11 60	13	9
Virgin Mary	Pye	-	12 60	27	5
Have A Drink On Me	Pye	30	4 61	8	15
Michael Row The Boat Ashore/Lumbered	Pye	2	9 61	6	11
The Commancheros	Pye	27	1 62	14	10
The Party's Over	Pye	28	4 62	9	12
Pick A Bale Of Cotton	Pye	1	9 62	11	10

DONNER, RAL

You Don't Know What You've Got	Parlophone	4	11 61	16	11

DONOVAN

Catch The Wind	Pye	3	4 65	4	13
Colours	Pye	19	6 65	4	12
Turquoise	Pye	-	11 65	30	6
Sunshine Superman	Pye	17	12 66	2	11
Mellow Yellow	Pye	18	2 67	8	8
There Is A Mountain	Pye	4	11 67	8	11
Jennifer Juniper	Pye	2	3 68	5	11

Hurdy Gurdy Man	Pye	8 6 68	4	10
Atlantis	Pye	- 12 68	26	8
Goo Goo Babarabbajagal	Pye	26 7 69	12	9
(with the JEFF BECK GROUP)				

DOOBIE BROTHERS

Listen To The Music	Warner Bros.	- 3 74	29	7
(re-issue)				
Take Me In Your Arms	Warner Bros.	- 6 75	29	4

DOONICAN, VAL

Walk Tall	Decca	28 11 64	3	21
The Special Years	Decca	6 2 65	7	13
I'm Gonna Get There Somehow	Decca	- 4 65	23	5
Elusive Butterfly	Decca	26 3 66	5	12
What Would I Be?	Decca	19 11 66	2	17
Memories Are Made Of This	Decca	18 3 67	11	12
Two Streets	Decca	- 5 67	39	4
If The Whole World Stopped Loving	Pye	4 11 67	3	19
You're The Only One	Pye	- 2 68	37	4
Now	Pye	- 6 68	43	2
If I Knew Then What I Know Now	Pye	23 11 68	14	13
Ring Of Bright Water	Pye	- 4 69	48	1
Morning	Philips	18 12 71	12	12
Heaven Is My Woman	Philips	- 3 73	34	7

DOORS

Light My Fire	Elektra	- 8 67	49	1
Hello I Love You	Elektra	21 9 68	15	10
Riders On The Storm	Elektra	- 10 71	22	11
Riders On The Storm	Elektra	- 3 76	33	6
(re-issue)				

DORSEY, LEE

Get Out Of My Life Woman	Stateside	- 2 66	22	7
Confusion	Stateside	- 5 66	38	6
Workin' In The Coalmine	Stateside	3 9 66	8	11
Holy Cow	Stateside	12 11 66	6	12

TOMMY DORSEY ORCHESTRA

Tea For Two Cha Cha	Brunswick	7 11 58	4	13

DOUGLAS, CARL

Kung Fu Fighting	Pye	31 8 74	1	13
Dance The Kung Fu	Pye	- 11 74	35	5

DOUGLAS, CRAIG

A Teenager In Love	Top Rank	13 6 59	14	7
Only Sixteen	Top Rank	15 8 59	1	13
Pretty Blue Eyes	Top Rank	23 1 60	5	9
Heart Of A Teenage Girl	Top Rank	17 4 60	10	9
Oh What A Day	Top Rank	- 8 60	43	1
100 Pounds Of Clay	Top Rank	2 4 61	9	8
Time	Top Rank	25 6 61	9	14
When My Little Girl Is Smiling	Top Rank	7 4 62	9	13
Our Favourite Melodies	Columbia	14 7 62	9	10
Oh Lonesome Me	Decca	10 11 62	15	12
Town Crier	Decca	- 2 63	36	4

DOWLANDS

| All My Loving | Oriole | - 1 64 | 35 | 7 |

DOWNING, DON

| Lonely Days Lonely Nights | People | - 11 73 | 32 | 11 |

DRAKE, CHARLIE

Splish Splash/Hullo My Darlings	Parlophone	15 8 58	6	9
Mr. Custer	Parlophone	30 10 60	12	12
My Boomerang Won't Come Back	Parlophone	7 10 61	14	11
Puckwudgie	Columbia	- 1 72	47	1

DRAPER, RUSTY

| Mule Skinner Blues | Mercury | - 8 60 | 39 | 4 |

DREAMWEAVERS

| It's Almost Tomorrow | Brunswick | 10 2 56 | 1 | 16 |

DRENNON, EDDIE AND BBS UNLIMITED

| Let's Do The Latin Hustle | Pye | 13 3 76 | 20 | 6 |

DREW, ALAN

| Always The Lonely One | Columbia | - 9 63 | 48 | 2 |

DR. HOOK AND THE MEDICINE SHOW

| Sylvia's Mother | CBS | 8 7 72 | 2 | 13 |

DRIFTERS

Dance With Me	London	16 1 60	18	2
Save The Last Dance For Me	London	21 10 60	2	18
I Count The Tears	London	- 3 61	28	6
When My Little Girl Is Smiling	London	- 4 62	31	3
I'll Take You Home	London	- 10 63	37	5
Under The **Boardwalk**	Atlantic	- 10 64	45	4
At The Club	Atlantic	- 4 65	36	7
Come On Over To My Place	Atlantic	- 5 65	40	5
Baby What I Mean	Atlantic	- 2 67	49	1
At The Club/Saturday Night At The Movies (re-issue)	Atlantic	6 5 72	3	22
Come On Over To My Place (re-issue)	Atlantic	16 9 72	9	11
Like Sister And Brother	Bell	18 8 73	7	13
Kissing In The Back Row Of The Movies	Bell	22 6 74	2	13
Down On The Beach Tonight	Bell	26 10 74	7	9
Love Games	Bell	- 2 75	33	6
There Goes My First Love	Bell	20 9 75	3	12
Can I Take You Home Little Girl?	Bell	20 12 75	10	8
Hello Happiness	Bell	27 3 76	12	8

DRISCOLL, JULIE WITH THE BRIAN AUGER TRINITY

| This Wheel's On Fire | Marmalade | 25 5 68 | 5 | 16 |

D'RONE, FRANK

| Strawberry Blonde | Mercury | 18 12 60 | 13 | 2 |

DRUPI

Vado Via	A & M	12 1 74	17	12

DUBLINERS

Seven Drunken Nights	Major Minor	22 4 67	7	17
Black Velvet Band	Major Minor	23 9 67	15	15
Never Wed An Old Man	Major Minor	- 12 67	43	3

DUNCAN, JOHNNY

Last Train To San Fernando	Columbia	26 7 57	3	16

DUNN, CLIVE

Grandad	Columbia	12 12 70	1	30

DUPREE, SIMON (FORMERLY SIMON DUPREE AND THE BIG SOUND)

Kites	Parlophone	9 12 67	9	13
For Whom The Bell Tolls	Parlophone	- 4 68	43	4

DURHAM, JUDITH

see SEEKERS

DUSTY, SLIM

A Pub With No Beer	Columbia	14 2 59	3	11

DYLAN, BOB

Times They Are A-Changin'	CBS	3 4 65	7	11
Subterranean Homesick Blues	CBS	8 5 65	9	9
Maggie's Farm	CBS	- 6 65	22	8
Like A Rolling Stone	CBS	28 8 65	4	12
Positively 4th Street	CBS	6 11 65	8	12
Can You Please Crawl Out Your Window?	CBS	29 1 66	17	5
One Of Us Must Know	CBS	- 4 66	33	5
Rainy Day Women Nos. 12 and 35	CBS	21 5 66	7	7
I Want You	CBS	6 8 66	16	9
I Threw It All Away	CBS	- 5 69	30	6
Lay Lady Lay	CBS	27 9 69	5	12
Watching The River Flow	CBS	- 7 71	24	9
Knockin' On Heaven's Door	CBS	20 10 73	14	9
Hurricane	CBS	- 2 76	43	4

DYSON, RONNIE

When You Get Right Down To It	CBS	- 12 71	35	6

EAGLES

One Of These Nights	Asylum	- 8 75	23	7
Lyin' Eyes	Asylum	- 11 75	23	7
Take It To The Limit/Best Of My Love (re-issue)	Asylum	27 3 76	12	8

EARL, ROBERT

With Your Love	Philips	25 2 56	13	2
My September Love	Philips	17 3 56	14	2
I May Never Pass This Way Again	Philips	2 5 58	14	9

EAST OF EDEN

Jig-A-Jig	Deram	8 5 71	7	12

EASYBEATS

Friday On My Mind	Un.Artists	19 11 66	6	15
Hello, How Are You	Un.Artists	27 4 68	20	9

ECKSTINE, BILLY

No One But You	MGM	- 11 54	4	14
Gigi	Mercury	21 2 59	11	10
(see also: SARAH VAUGHAN)				

EDDY, DUANE

Rebel Rouser	London	12 9 58	13	5
Cannonball	London	3 1 59	14	4
The Lonely One	London	20 4 59	20	1
Peter Gunn/Yep	London	20 6 59	6	8
40 Miles Of Bad Road	London	5 9 59	6	8
Some Kinda Earthquake	London	12 12 59	7	6
Bonnie Came Back	London	13 2 60	9	4
Shazam	London	24 4 60	4	14
Because They're Young	London	17 7 60	2	18
Kommotion	London	6 11 60	13	10
Pepe	London	1 1 61	2	14
Theme From Dixie	London	9 4 61	7	10
Ring Of Fire	London	11 6 61	15	10
Drivin' Home	London	2 9 61	18	4
Caravan	London	- 10 61	42	3
Deep In The Heart Of Texas	RCA	23 6 62	19	8
Ballad Of Palladin	RCA	1 9 62	10	10
Dance With The Guitar Man	RCA	17 11 62	4	16
Boss Guitar	RCA	- 2 63	27	8
Lonely Boy, Lonely Guitar	RCA	- 5 63	35	4
Your Baby's Gone Surfin'	RCA	- 8 63	49	1
Play Me Like You Play Your Guitar	GTO	22 3 75	9	9
(with the REBELETTES)				

EDELMAN, RANDY

Concrete And Clay	20th Century	27 3 76	11	8

EDGAR BROUGHTON BAND

Out Demons Out	Harvest	- 4 70	39	4
Apache Dropout	Harvest	- 1 71	31	6

EDISON LIGHTHOUSE

Love Grows (Where My Rosemary Goes)	Bell	24 1 70	1	13
It's Up To You Petula	Bell	- 1 71	46	3

EDMUNDS, DAVE

I Hear You Knocking	MAM	21 11 70	1	14
Baby I Love You	Rockfield	17 2 73	8	13
Born To Be With You	Rockfield	30 6 73	5	12

EDWARDS, RUPIE

Ire Feelings (Skanga)	Cactus	30 11 74	9	10
Lego **Skanga**	Cactus	- 2 75	32	6

EDWARDS, TOMMY

It's All In The Game	MGM	10 10 58	1	15

ELBERT, DONNIE

Where Did Our Love Go?	London	22 1 72	8	10
I Can't Help Myself	Avco	11 3 72	11	10
A Little Piece Of Leather (re-issue)	London	- 4 72	27	9

ELECTRIC LIGHT ORCHESTRA

10538 Overture	Harvest	5	8 72	9	8
Roll Over Beethoven	Harvest	3	2 73	6	10
Showdown	Harvest	20	10 73	12	10
Ma-Ma-Ma Belle	Warner Bros.	-	3 74	22	8
Evil Woman	Jet	24	1 76	10	8

ELECTRIC PRUNES

I Had Too Much To Dream Last Night	Reprise	-	2 67	49	1
Get Me To The World On Time	Reprise	-	5 67	42	4

ELEGANTS

Little Star	HMV	11	10 58	20	1

ELGINS

Heaven Must Have Sent You (re-issue)	T.Motown	15	5 71	3	13
Put Yourself In My Place (re-issue)	T.Motown	-	10 71	28	7

ELIAS AND HIS ZIG ZAG JIVE FLUTES

Tom Hark	Columbia	2	5 58	2	12

ELLINGTON, RAY

The Madison	Ember	-	11 62	41	2

ELLIOTT, BERN AND THE FENMEN

Money (That's What I Want)	Decca	14	12 63	14	13
New Orleans	Decca	-	3 64	24	9

ELLIS, SHIRLEY

The Clapping Song	London	22	5 65	6	13

EMERSON, KEITH

Honky Tonk Train Blues	Manticore	-	4 76	21	5

EMERY, DICK

If You Love Her	Pye	-	3 69	32	4
You Are Awful	Pye	-	1 73	43	4

ENGLAND SISTERS

Heart Beat	HMV	-	3 60	33	1

ENGLAND WORLD CUP SQUAD

Back Home	Pye	2	5 70	1	15

ENGLISH, SCOTT

Brandy	Horse	30	10 71	12	10

EQUALS

I Get So Excited	President	-	2 68	44	4
Baby Come Back (re-issue)	President	25	6 68	1	18
Laurel And Hardy	President	-	8 68	35	5
Softly Softly	President	-	11 68	48	4
Michael And The Slipper Tree	President	-	4 69	24	7
Viva Bobby Joe	President	16	8 69	6	14
Rub A Dub Dub	President	-	1 70	34	6
Blackskin Blue-Eyed Boys	President	9	1 71	9	12

ESCORTS

The One To Cry	Fontana	- 7 64	49	2

ESSEX

Easier Said Than Done	Columbia	- 8 63	41	5

ESSEX, DAVID

Rock On	CBS	1 9 73	3	11
Lamplight	CBS	24 11 73	7	15
America	CBS	- 5 74	32	5
Gonna Make You A Star	CBS	19 10 74	1	17
Stardust	CBS	11 1 75	7	10
Rollin' Stone	CBS	12 7 75	5	7
Hold Me Close	CBS	20 9 75	1	10
If I Could	CBS	3 1 76	13	8
City Lights	CBS	- 3 76	24	4

ESTELLE, DON

see WINDSOR DAVIES AND DON ESTELLE

ETHIOPIANS

Train To Skaville	Rio	- 9 67	40	6

EVANS, MAUREEN

Love Kisses And Heartaches	Oriole	- 3 60	44	1
Paper Roses	Oriole	- 5 60	40	5
Like I Do	Oriole	22 12 62	3	18
I Love How You Love Me	Oriole	- 2 64	34	11

EVANS, PAUL AND THE CURLS

Seven Little Girls Sitting In The Back Seat	London	28 11 59	16	3
Midnight Special	London	- 3 60	41	1

EVERETT, BETTY

Getting Mighty Crowded	Fontana	- 1 65	29	7
It's In His Kiss (The Shoop Shoop Song) (re-issue)	President	- 11 68	34	7

EVERLY BROTHERS

Bye Bye Love	London	12 7 57	6	13
Wake Up Little Susie	London	15 11 57	2	12
All I Have To Do Is Dream/ Claudette	London	30 5 58	1	19
Bird Dog	London	12 9 58	2	16
Problems	London	24 1 59	5	8
Poor Jenny/Take A Message To Mary	London	30 5 59	11	7
('Til) I Kissed You	London	12 9 59	2	14
Let It Be Me	London	12 3 60	13	2
Cathy's Clown	Warner Bros.	10 4 60	1	18
When Will I Be Loved?	London	10 7 60	4	17
Lucille/So Sad	Warner Bros.	18 9 60	4	15
Like Strangers	London	25 12 60	11	10
Ebony Eyes/Walk Right Back	Warner Bros.	29 1 61	1	16
Temptation	Warner Bros.	4 6 61	1	15
Muskrat/Don't Blame Me	Warner Bros.	30 9 61	20	6
Cryin' In The Rain	Warner Bros.	27 1 62	6	16
How Can I Meet Her?	Warner Bros.	2 6 62	12	10
No One Can Make My Sunshine Smile	Warner Bros.	3 11 62	11	11
So It Will Always Be	Warner Bros.	- 3 63	23	10

It's Been Nice	Warner Bros.	- 6 63	26	5
The Girl Sang The Blues	Warner Bros.	- 10 63	25	9
Ferris Wheel	Warner Bros.	- 7 64	22	10
Gone Gone Gone	Warner Bros.	- 12 64	36	6
That'll Be The Day	Warner Bros.	- 4 65	30	5
The Price Of Love	Warner Bros.	29 5 65	2	14
I'll Never Get Over You	Warner Bros.	- 8 65	35	5
Love Is Strange	Warner Bros.	6 11 65	11	9
It's My Time	Warner Bros.	- 5 68	39	6

EXCITERS

Tell Him	Un.Artists	- 2 63	46	1
Reaching For The Best	20th Century	- 10 75	31	6

FABARES, SHELLEY

Johnny Angel	Pye	- 4 62	41	4

FACES

Stay With Me	Warner Bros.	15 1 72	6	13
Cindy Incidentally	Warner Bros.	17 2 73	2	9
Poolhall Richard/I Wish It Would Rain	Warner Bros.	22 10 73	8	11

FACES (with ROD STEWART)

You Can Make Me Dance, Sing Or Anything	Warner Bros.	21 12 74	12	9

FAIR, YVONNE

It Should Have Been Me	T.Motown	21 2 76	5	11

FAIRPORT CONVENTION

Si Tu Dois Partir	Island	- 7 69	21	8

FAIRWEATHER

Natural Sinner	RCA	8 8 70	6	12

FAIRWEATHER-LOW, ANDY

Reggae Tune	A & M	5 10 74	10	10
Wide Eyed And Legless	A & M	20 12 75	6	10

(see also: AMEN CORNER, FAIRWEATHER)

FAITH, ADAM

What Do You Want?	Parlophone	21 11 59	1	13
Poor Me	Parlophone	30 1 60	1	10
Someone Else's Baby	Parlophone	10 4 60	2	13
When Johnny Comes Marching Home/Made You	Parlophone	19 6 60	5	13
How About That	Parlophone	11 9 60	4	14
Lonely Pup	Parlophone	4 12 60	4	11
This Is It/Who Am I	Parlophone	29 1 61	5	14
Easy Going Me	Parlophone	23 4 61	12	10
Don't You Know It?	Parlophone	22 7 61	12	10
The Time Has Come	Parlophone	21 10 61	4	14
Lonesome	Parlophone	3 2 62	12	9
As You Like It	Parlophone	19 5 62	5	15
Don't That Beat All	Parlophone	8 9 62	8	11
Baby Take A Bow	Parlophone	- 12 62	22	6
What Now	Parlophone	- 1 63	31	5
Walkin' Tall	Parlophone	- 7 63	23	6
The First Time	Parlophone	5 10 63	5	13
We Are In Love	Parlophone	4 1 64	11	12
If He Tells You	Parlophone	- 3 64	25	9

I Love Being In Love With You	Parlophone	- 5 64	33	6
Message To Martha	Parlophone	12 12 64	12	11
Stop Feeling Sorry For Yourself	Parlophone	- 2 65	23	6
Someone's Taken Maria Away	Parlophone	- 6 65	34	5
Cheryl's Going Home	Parlophone	- 10 66	46	2

FAITH, HOPE AND CHARITY

Just One Look	RCA	- 1 76	38	4

FAITH, HORACE

Black Pearl	Trojan	3 10 70	13	10

PERCY FAITH ORCHESTRA

Theme From A Summer Place	Philips	27 2 60	4	12

FAITHFUL, MARIANNE

As Tears Go By	Decca	22 8 64	9	13
Come And Stay With Me	Decca	27 2 65	4	13
This Little Bird	Decca	15 5 65	6	11
Summer Nights	Decca	7 8 65	10	10
Is This What I Get For Loving You Baby	Decca	- 3 67	43	2

FAME, GEORGIE

Yeh Yeh	Columbia	26 12 64	1	12
In The Meantime	Columbia	- 3 65	22	7
Like We Used To Be	Columbia	- 7 65	33	7
Something	Columbia	- 10 65	23	6
Get Away	Columbia	2 7 66	1	11
Sunny	Columbia	8 10 66	13	8
Sittin' In The Park	Columbia	31 12 66	12	10
Because I Love You	CBS	15 4 67	15	8
Try My World	CBS	- 9 67	37	5
Ballad Of Bonnie And Clyde	CBS	30 12 67	1	13
Peaceful	CBS	9 8 69	16	9
Seventh Son	CBS	- 12 69	25	7

(see also: FAME AND PRICE)

FAME (GEORGIE) AND PRICE (ALAN)

Rosetta	CBS	24 4 71	11	10

FAMILY

No Mule's Fool	Reprise	- 11 69	29	7
Strange Band	Reprise	19 9 70	11	12
In My Own Time	Reprise	7 8 71	4	13
Burlesque	Reprise	21 10 72	13	12

FAMILY DOGG

Way Of Life	Bell	21 6 69	6	14

FANTASTICS

Something Old, Something New	Bell	24 4 71	9	16

FARDON, DON

Belfast Bay	Young Blood	- 4 70	32	5
Indian Reservation (re-issue)	Young Blood	31 10 70	3	18

FARLOWE, CHRIS

Think	Immediate	–	1 66	37	3
Out Of Time	Immediate	9	7 66	1	13
Ride On Baby	Immediate	–	10 66	31	7
My Way Of Giving	Immediate	–	2 67	49	1
Moanin'	Immediate	–	7 67	46	2
Handbags And Gladrags	Immediate	–	12 67	33	6
Out Of Time (re-issue)	Immediate	–	9 75	44	4

FATBACK BAND

Yum Yum (Gimme Some)	Polydor	–	9 75	40	6
Do The Bus Stop	Polydor	17	1 76	18	10
(Do The) Spanish Hustle	Polydor	6	3 76	10	7

FELICIANO, JOSÉ

Light My Fire	RCA	12	10 68	6	15
And The Sun Will Shine	RCA	–	10 69	25	7

FELIX, JULIE

El Condor Pasa (If I Could)	RAK	23	5 70	19	11
Heaven Is Here	RAK	–	10 70	22	8

FENDERMEN

Mule Skinner Blues	Top Rank	–	8 60	37	3

FENTON, PETER

Marble Breaks, Iron Bends	Fontana	–	11 66	46	3

FENTON, SHANE AND THE FENTONES

I'm A Moody Guy	Parlophone	–	10 61	22	8
Walk Away	Parlophone	–	2 62	38	5
It's All Over Now	Parlophone	–	4 62	45	1
The Mexican (FENTONES only)	Parlophone	–	4 62	41	3
Cindy's Birthday	Parlophone	4	8 62	19	8
The Breeze And I (FENTONES only)	Parlophone	–	9 62	48	1
(see also: ALVIN STARDUST)					

FERKO STRING BAND

Alabama Jubilee	London	12	8 55	20	1

FERRANTE AND TEICHER

Theme From 'The Apartment'	London	–	8 60	44	1
Theme From 'Exodus'	London	26	2 61	6	17

FERRY, BRYAN

A Hard Rain's A-Gonna Fall	Island	13	10 73	10	9
The 'In' Crowd	Island	1	6 74	12	6
Smoke Gets In Your Eyes	Island	28	9 74	17	8
You Go To My Head	Island	–	7 75	33	3
(see also: ROXY MUSIC)					

FIELDS, ERNIE

In The Mood	London	9	1 60	18	1

FIELDS, GRACIE

Around The World	Columbia	31	5 57	10	6

FIFTH DIMENSION

Aquarius/Let The Sun Shine In	Liberty	24	5 69	11	10

Wedding Bell Blues	Liberty	14 2 70	16	9

53rd AND A 3rd

Chick-A-Boom	UK	- 9 75	36	4

FIREBALLS
see JIMMY GILMER

FIRST CHOICE

Armed And Extremely Dangerous	Bell	9 6 73	16	10
Smarty Pants	Bell	18 8 73	9	11

FIRST CLASS

Beach Baby	UK	13 7 74	13	10

FISHER, EDDIE

I Need You Now	HMV	21 1 55	1	19
Wedding Bells	HMV	18 3 55	5	11
Cindy, Oh Cindy	HMV	23 11 56	6	13

FITZGERALD, ELLA

Swingin' Shepherd Blues	HMV	23 5 58	18	3
Mack The Knife	HMV	1 5 60	19	9
How High The Moon	HMV	- 10 60	46	1
Desafinado	Verve	- 11 62	38	6
Can't Buy Me Love	Verve	- 5 64	34	5

5,000 VOLTS

I'm On Fire	Philips	13 9 75	4	9

FLACK, ROBERTA

The First Time Ever I Saw Your Face	Atlantic	24 6 72	14	15
Where Is The Love (with DONNY HATHAWAY)	Atlantic	- 8 72	29	7
Killing Me Softly With His Song	Atlantic	3 3 73	6	14
Feel Like Makin' Love	Atlantic	- 8 74	34	7

FLAMINGOS

Boo Ga Loo Party (re-issue)	Philips	- 6 69	39	5

FLATT, LESTER AND EARL SCRUGGS

Foggy Mountain Breakdown	CBS	- 11 67	39	6

FLEE RAKKERS

Green Jeans	Triumph	- 5 60	23	13

FLEETWOOD MAC

Black Magic Woman	B. Horizon	- 4 68	37	7
I Need Your Love So Bad	B. Horizon	- 7 68	28	13
Albatross	B. Horizon	14 12 68	1	20
Man Of The World	B. Horizon	19 4 69	2	14
I Need Your Love So Bad (re-issue)	B. Horizon	- 7 69	32	9
Oh Well	Reprise	11 10 69	2	15
The Green Manalishi	Reprise	30 5 70	10	12
Albatross (re-issue)	CBS	2 6 73	2	15

FLEETWOODS

| Come Softly To Me | London | 25 4 59 | 6 | 8 |

FLOWERPOT MEN

| Let's Go To San Francisco | Deram | 9 9 67 | 4 | 12 |

FLOYD, EDDIE

Raise Your Hand	**Stax**	– 3 67	**45**	**3**
Knock On Wood	**Atlantic**	15 4 67	**19**	**19**
Things Get Better	**Stax**	– 8 67	**31**	**8**

FLOYD, KING

| Groove Me | Atlantic | – 2 71 | 41 | 2 |

FOCUS

| Sylvia | Polydor | 10 2 73 | 4 | 11 |
| Hocus Pocus | Polydor | 24 2 73 | 20 | 10 |

FONTANA, WAYNE (AND THE MINDBENDERS)

Hello Josephine	Fontana	– 7 63	46	2
Stop Look And Listen	Fontana	– 5 64	40	4
Um Um Um Um Um Um	Fontana	31 10 64	5	15
Game Of Love	Fontana	13 2 65	2	11
Just A Little Bit Too Late	Fontana	10 7 65	20	7
*She Needs Love	Fontana	– 9 65	32	6
It Was Easier To Hurt Her	Fontana	– 12 65	36	6
Come On Home	Fontana	4 6 66	16	12
Goodbye Bluebird	Fontana	– 8 66	49	1
Pamela Pamela	Fontana	7 1 67	11	12
(see also: MINDBENDERS)				

FORD, CLINTON

Too Many Beautiful Girls	Oriole	19 8 61	20	1
Fanlight Fanny	Oriole	– 3 62	22	10
Run To The Door	Piccadilly	– 1 67	25	13

FORD, EMILE AND THE CHECKMATES

What Do You Want To Make Those Eyes At Me For?	Pye	31 10 59	1	17
Slow Boat To China	Pye	30 1 60	4	10
You'll Never Know What You're Missing Till You Try	Pye	5 6 60	18	2
Them There Eyes	Pye	24 10 60	20	1
Counting Teardrops	Pye	25 12 60	6	6

FORD, TENNESSEE ERNIE

Give Me Your Word	Capitol	21 1 55	1	24
Sixteen Tons	Capitol	6 1 56	1	11
Ballad Of Davy Crockett	Capitol	13 1 56	4	7

FORMATIONS

| At The Top Of The Stairs (re-issue) | Mojo | – 7 71 | 28 | 10 |

FORMBY, GEORGE

| Happy Go Lucky Me/Banjo Boy | Pye | – 7 60 | 42 | 3 |

*All Records To Here, Feature MINDBENDERS

FORTUNE, LANCE

Be Mine	Pye	13 2 60	5	6
The Love I Have For You	Pye	- 4 60	26	5

FORTUNES

You've Got Your Troubles	Decca	17 7 65	2	14
Here It Comes Again	Decca	21 10 65	4	14
This Golden Ring	Decca	12 3 66	15	9
Freedom Come Freedom Go	Capitol	2 10 71	6	17
Storm In A Teacup	Capitol	12 2 72	7	11

FOUNDATIONS

Baby Now That I've Found You	Pye	21 10 67	1	16
Back On My Feet Again	Pye	17 2 68	18	10
Any Old Time (You're Lonely And Sad)	Pye	- 5 68	48	2
Build Me Up Buttercup	Pye	7 12 68	2	15
In The Bad Bad Old Days	Pye	22 3 69	8	10
Born To Live, Born To Die	Pye	- 9 69	46	3

FOUR ACES

Three Coins In The Fountain	Philips	- 10 54	8	6
Mr. Sandman	Brunswick	7 1 55	9	5
Stranger In Paradise	Brunswick	20 5 55	6	6
Love Is A Many Splendoured Thing	Brunswick	18 11 55	2	13
A Woman In Love	Brunswick	26 10 56	20	1

FOUR LADS

Standing On The Corner	Philips	- 4 60	34	4

FOUR PENNIES

Do You Want Me To?	Philips	- 1 64	47	2
Juliet	Philips	25 4 64	1	15
I Found Out The Hard Way	Philips	15 8 64	14	11
Black Girl	Philips	28 11 64	20	12
Until It's Time For You To Go	Philips	6 11 65	19	11
Trouble Is My Middle Name	Philips	- 2 66	32	5

FOUR PREPS

Big Man	Capitol	20 6 58	2	12
Got A Girl	Capitol	- 5 60	28	7
More Money For You And Me	Capitol	- 11 61	39	2

FOUR SEASONS (*FEATURING FRANKIE VALLI)

Sherry	Stateside	20 10 62	8	16
Big Girls Don't Cry	Stateside	27 1 63	13	10
Walk Like A Man	Stateside	13 4 63	12	12
Ain't That A Shame	Stateside	- 6 63	38	3
Rag Doll*	Philips	4 9 64	2	13
Let's Hang On*	Philips	4 12 65	4	16
Working My Way Back To You*	Philips	- 4 66	50	3
Opus 17 (Don't You Worry 'Bout Me)*	Philips	25 6 66	20	9
I've Got You Under My Skin*	Philips	15 10 66	12	11
Tell It To The Rain*	Philips	- 1 67	37	5
The Night (re-issue)	Mowest	3 5 75	7	9
Who Loves You	Warner Bros.	4 10 75	6	10
Oh What A Night-December '63	Warner Bros.	7 2 76	1	10

(see also: FRANKIE VALLI)

FOUR TOPS

I Can't Help Myself	T.Motown	- 7 65	23	9
It's The Same Old Song	T.Motown	- 9 65	34	8

Loving You Is Sweeter Than Ever	T.Motown	– 7 66	21	12
Reach Out, I'll Be There	T.Motown	15 10 66	1	16
Standing In The Shadows Of Love	T.Motown	14 1 67	6	9
Bernadette	T.Motown	15 4 67	8	10
Seven Rooms Of Gloom	T.Motown	1 7 67	12	9
You Keep Running Away	T.Motown	– 10 67	26	7
Walk Away Renee	T.Motown	23 12 67	3	11
If I Were A Carpenter	T.Motown	23 3 68	7	10
Yesterday's Dreams	T.Motown	7 9 68	20	15
I'm In A Different World	T.Motown	– 11 68	27	13
What Is A Man	T.Motown	28 6 69	16	10
Do What You've Gotta Do	T.Motown	11 10 69	11	11
I Can't Help Myself (re-issue)	T.Motown	11 4 70	10	11
It's All In The Game	T.Motown	20 6 70	5	17
Still Water (Love)	T.Motown	17 10 70	10	12
Just Seven Numbers	T.Motown	– 5 71	36	5
Simple Game	T.Motown	9 10 71	3	11
Bernadette (re-issue)	T.Motown	– 3 72	23	7
Walk With Me, Talk With Me Darling	T.Motown	– 8 72	32	6
Keeper Of The Castle	Probe	16 12 72	18	9
Sweet Understanding Love	Probe	– 11 73	29	10

(see also: SUPREMES)

FOURMOST

Hello Little Girl	Parlophone	5 10 63	9	16
I'm In Love	Parlophone	1 2 64	17	12
A Little Lovin'	Parlophone	2 5 64	6	13
How Can I Tell Her?	Parlophone	– 8 64	33	4
Baby I Need Your Lovin'	Parlophone	– 11 64	24	12
Girls Girls Girls	Parlophone	– 12 65	33	6

14 - 18

Good-Bye-Ee	Magnet	– 11 75	43	4

FOX

Only You Can	GTO	22 2 75	3	11
Imagine Me, Imagine You	GTO	7 6 75	15	8

FOXX, INEZ (AND CHARLIE)

Hurt By Love (INEZ FOXX only)	Sue	– 7 64	40	3
Mockingbird	Un.Artists	– 2 69	36	6

FRANCIS, CONNIE

Who's Sorry Now?	MGM	11 4 58	1	20
I'm Sorry I Made You Cry	MGM	4 7 58	12	8
Carolina Moon/Stupid Cupid	MGM	22 8 58	1	17
I'll Get By	MGM	21 11 58	19	1
Fallin'	MGM	28 11 58	20	1
You Always Hurt The One You Love	MGM	10 1 59	12	5
My Happiness	MGM	21 2 59	3	11
Lipstick On Your Collar	MGM	11 7 59	4	13
Plenty Good Lovin'	MGM	5 9 59	9	3
Among My Souvenirs	MGM	12 12 59	8	5
Valentino	MGM	– 3 60	27	8
Mama/Robot Man	MGM	15 5 60	2	17
Everybody's Somebody's Fool	MGM	14 8 60	5	13
My Heart Has A Mind Of It's Own	MGM	30 10 60	3	15
Many Tears Ago	MGM	15 1 61	12	9

Where The Boys Are/Baby Roo	MGM	19 3 61	5	14
Breakin' In A Brand New Broken Heart	MGM	25 6 61	12	11
Together	MGM	9 9 61	6	11
Baby's First Christmas	MGM	9 12 61	17	5
Don't Break The Heart That Loves You	MGM	- 4 62	39	3
Vacation	MGM	18 8 62	10	9
I'm Gonna Be Warm This Winter	MGM	- 12 62	48	1
My Child	MGM	- 6 65	26	6
Jealous Heart	MGM	- 1 66	44	2

FRANCOIS, CLAUDE

Tears On The Telephone	Bradleys	- 1 76	35	4

FRANKLIN, ARETHA

Respect	Atlantic	8 7 67	10	13
Baby I Love You	Atlantic	- 8 67	39	4
Chain Of Fools/Satisfaction	Atlantic	- 12 67	37	7
Since You've Been Gone	Atlantic	- 3 68	47	1
Think	Atlantic	- 5 68	26	9
I Say A Little Prayer	Atlantic	24 8 68	4	14
Don't Play That Song	Atlantic	12 9 70	13	11
Spanish Harlem	Atlantic	23 10 71	14	9
Angel	Atlantic	- 9 73	37	5
Until You Come Back To Me	Atlantic	- 2 74	26	8

FREBURG, STAN

Sh-Boom	Capitol	- 11 54	15	1
Yellow Rose Of Texas	Capitol	28 1 56	15	1

FRED, JOHN AND HIS PLAYBOY BAND

Judy In Disguise (With Glasses)	Pye	20 1 68	3	12

FREDDIE AND THE DREAMERS

If You Gotta Make A Fool Of Somebody	Columbia	1 6 63	3	14
I'm Telling You Now	Columbia	17 8 63	2	11
You Were Made For Me	Columbia	23 11 63	3	15
Over You	Columbia	29 2 64	13	11
I Love You Baby	Columbia	6 6 64	16	8
Just For You	Columbia	- 7 64	41	3
I Understand	Columbia	5 12 64	5	15
A Little You	Columbia	- 4 65	26	5
Thou Shalt Not Steal	Columbia	- 11 65	44	3

FREE

All Right Now	Island	20 6 70	2	16
My Brother Jake	Island	15 5 71	4	11
Little Bit Of Love	Island	17 6 72	13	10
Wishing Well	Island	20 1 73	7	9
All Right Now (re-issue)	Island	11 8 73	15	9

FRIJID PINK

House Of The Rising Sun	Deram	25 4 70	4	16

FROMAN, JANE

I Wonder	Capitol	17 6 55	14	4

BOBBY FULLER FOUR

I Fought The Law	London	-	4 66	33	4

FURY, BILLY

Maybe Tomorrow	Decca	11	4 59	17	4
Colette	Decca	6	3 60	18	2
That's Love	Decca	5	6 60	19	11
Wondrous Place	Decca	-	9 60	25	9
A Thousand Stars	Decca	-	1 61	21	10
Don't Worry	Decca	-	4 61	40	2
Halfway To Paradise	Decca	21	5 61	3	23
Jealousy	Decca	9	9 61	2	12
I'd Never Find Another You	Decca	9	12 61	5	16
Letter Full Of Tears	Decca	17	3 62	20	6
Last Night Was Made For Love	Decca	19	5 62	4	16
Once Upon A Dream	Decca	11	8 62	7	13
Because Of Love	Decca	10	11 62	18	14
Like I've Never Been Gone	Decca	2	3 63	3	14
When Will You Say I Love You	Decca	25	5 63	3	12
In Summer	Decca	3	8 63	5	11
Somebody Else's Girl	Decca	12	10 63	18	7
Do You Really Love Me Too (Fool's Errand)	Decca	11	1 64	13	10
I Will	Decca	9	5 64	14	11
It's Only Make Believe	Decca	1	8 64	10	10
I'm Lost Without You	Decca	6	2 65	16	10
In Thoughts Of You	Decca	7	8 65	9	11
Run To My Lovin' Arms	Decca	-	9 65	25	7
I'll Never Quite Get Over You	Decca	-	2 66	35	5
Give Me Your Word	Decca	-	8 66	27	7

GAINSBOURG, SERGE

see JANE BIRKIN

GALLAGHER AND LYLE

I Wanna Stay With You	A & M	13	3 76	6	9

GARFUNKEL, ART

I Only Have Eyes For You	CBS	27	9 75	1	11

(see also: SIMON AND GARFUNKEL)

GARLAND, JUDY

The Man That Got Away	Philips	10	6 55	18	2

GARRICK, DAVID

Lady Jane	Piccadilly	-	6 66	28	7
Dear Mrs. Applebee	Piccadilly	-	9 66	22	9

GAYE, MARVIN

Once Upon A Time (with MARY WELLS)	Stateside	-	7 64	50	1
How Sweet It Is (To Be Loved By You)	Stateside	-	12 64	49	1
Little Darling (I Need You)	T.Motown	-	10 66	50	1
It Takes Two (with KIM WESTON)	T.Motown	18	2 67	16	11
I Heard It Through The Grapevine	T.Motown	1	3 69	1	15
Too Busy Thinking About My Baby	T.Motown	16	8 69	5	16
Abraham, Martin And John	T.Motown	30	5 70	9	14
Save The Children	T.Motown	-	12 71	41	6
Let's Get It On	T.Motown	-	9 73	31	7

You Are Everything (with DIANA ROSS)	T.Motown	30 3 74	5	11
Stop, Look, Listen (with DIANA ROSS)	T.Motown	- 7 74	25	7

GAYE, MARVIN AND TAMMI TERRELL

If I Could Build My Whole World Around You	T.Motown	- 1 68	41	7
Ain't Nothing Like The Real Thing	T.Motown	- 6 68	34	7
You're All I Need To Get By	T.Motown	16 11 68	19	19
You Ain't Living Until You're Loving	T.Motown	- 1 69	21	8
Good Lovin' Ain't Easy To Come By	T.Motown	- 6 69	26	8
Onion Song	T.Motown	29 11 69	9	12

GAYNOR, GLORIA

Never Can Say Goodbye	MGM	11 1 75	2	13
Reach Out I'll Be There	MGM	29 3 75	14	8
All I Ever Need Is Your Sweet Lovin'	MGM	- 8 75	44	4
How High The Moon	MGM	- 1 76	33	4

G-CLEFS

I Understand	London	16 12 61	17	13

GENESIS

I Know What I Like	Charisma	- 4 74	21	7

GENEVIEVE

Once	CBS	- 5 66	43	1

GENTRY, BOBBIE

Ode To Billy Joe	Capitol	7 10 67	13	11
I'll Never Fall In Love Again	Capitol	13 9 69	1	17
All I Have To Do Is Dream (with GLEN CAMPBELL)	Capitol	13 12 69	3	14
Raindrops Keep Falling On My Head	Capitol	- 2 70	40	4

GEORDIE

Don't Do That	R.Zonophone	- 12 72	32	7
All Because Of You	EMI	14 4 73	6	13
Can You Do It	EMI	23 6 73	13	9
Electric Lady	EMI	- 8 73	32	6

GERRARD, DANYEL

Butterfly	CBS	2 10 71	11	12

GERRY AND THE PACEMAKERS

How Do You Do It?	Columbia	23 3 63	1	18
I Like It	Columbia	8 6 63	1	15
You'll Never Walk Alone	Columbia	19 10 63	1	19
I'm The One	Columbia	25 1 64	2	15
Don't Let The Sun Catch You Crying	Columbia	25 4 64	6	11
It's Gonna Be Alright	Columbia	- 9 64	24	7
Ferry Cross The Mersey	Columbia	9 1 65	8	13
I'll Be There	Columbia	3 4 65	12	9
Walk Hand In Hand	Columbia	- 11 65	29	6

GETZ, STAN AND CHARLIE BYRD

Desafinado	HMV	15 12 62	11	13
The Girl From Ipanema	Verve	- 7 64	29	10
(with ASTRUD GILBERTO)				

GIBB, ROBIN

Saved By The Bell	Polydor	19 7 69	2	17
August October	Polydor	- 2 70	45	3
(see also: BEE GEES)				

GIBBS, GEORGIA

Tweedle Dee	Mercury	22 4 55	20	1

GIBSON, DON

Sea Of Heartbreak	RCA	2 9 61	15	13
Lonesome No. 1	RCA	- 2 62	47	3

GIBSON, WAYNE

Kelly	Pye	- 9 64	48	2
Under My Thumb (re-issue)	Pye	11 1 75	17	11

GILBERTO, ASTRUD

see STAN GETZ

GILLIES, STUART

Amanda	Philips	7 4 73	13	10

GILMER, JIMMY AND THE FIREBALLS

Quite A Party (FIREBALLS only)	Pye	- 7 61	29	9
Sugar Shack	London	- 11 63	45	8

GILREATH, JAMES

Little Band Of Gold	Pye	- 5 73	29	10

GILSTRAP, JIM

Swing Your Daddy	Chelsea	29 3 75	4	11

GLITTER BAND

Angel Face	Bell	30 3 74	4	10
Just For You	Bell	17 8 74	10	8
Let's Get Together Again	Bell	26 10 74	8	8
Goodbye My Love	Bell	25 1 75	2	9
The Tears I Cried	Bell	19 4 75	8	8
Love In The Sun	Bell	30 8 75	15	8
People Like You, People Like Me	Bell	6 3 76	5	9
(see also: GARY GLITTER)				

GLITTER, GARY

Rock And Roll Parts 1 **And** 2	Bell	24 6 72	2	15
I Didn't Know I Loved You (Till I Saw You Rock **And** Roll)	Bell	30 9 72	4	11
Do You Wanna Touch Me (Oh Yeah)	Bell	27 1 73	2	11
Hello Hello I'm Back Again	Bell	7 4 73	2	14
I'm The Leader Of The Gang	Bell	21 7 73	1	10
I Love You Love Me Love	Bell	17 11 73	1	14
Remember Me This Way	Bell	30 3 74	3	8
Always Yours	Bell	15 6 74	1	9

Oh Yes, You're Beautiful (with GLITTER BAND)	Bell	23 11 74	2	10
Love Like You And Me	Bell	10 5 75	10	6
Doing Alright With The Boys	Bell	28 6 75	6	7
Papa Oom Mow Mow	Bell	- 11 75	38	5
You Belong To Me	Bell	- 3 76	40	5

GOLDEN EARRING

Radar Love	Track	12 1 74	7	13

GOLDIE AND THE GINGERBREADS

Can't You Hear My Heartbeat	Decca	- 2 65	25	5

GOLDSBORO, BOBBY

Honey	Un.Artists	4 5 68	2	15
Summer (The First Time)	Un.Artists	18 8 73	9	10
Hello Summertime	Un.Artists	17 8 74	14	10
Honey (re-issue)	Un.Artists	12 4 75	2	12

GOODIES

The Inbetweenies/Father Christmas Do Not Touch Me	Bradleys	21 12 74	7	9
The Funky Gibbon/Sick Man Blues	Bradleys	29 3 75	4	10
Black Pudding Bertha	Bradleys	19 6 75	19	7
Nappy Love/Wild Thing	Bradleys	- 9 75	21	6
Make A Daft Noise For Christmas	Bradleys	3 1 76	20	6

GOODWIN, RON

Blue Star	Parlophone	28 10 55	20	1

GOONS

Bluebottle Blues/The Goons I'm Walking Backwards For Christmas	Decca Decca	30 6 56 6 7 56	3 18	8 1
Ying Tong Song	Decca	14 9 56	4	8
Bloodnock's Rock And Roll	Decca	14 9 56	3	8
Ying Tong Song (re-issue)	Decca	4 8 73	9	9

GORE, LESLEY

It's My Party	Mercury	6 7 63	9	12
Maybe I Know	Mercury	24 10 64	20	1

GORME, EYDIE

Love Me Forever	HMV	8 2 58	20	1
Yes My Darling Daughter	CBS	30 6 62	10	9
Blame It On The Bossa Nova (see also: STEVE LAWRENCE)	CBS	- 1 63	32	6

GRACIE, CHARLIE

Butterfly	Parlophone	17 5 57	14	3
Fabulous	Parlophone	21 6 57	12	13
Wanderin' Eyes	London	30 8 57	4	11
I Love You So Much It Hurts	London	30 8 57	14	2

GRAHAM, EVE

see NEW SEEKERS

GRAND FUNK RAILROAD

Inside Looking Out	Capitol	- 2 71	40	4

GRANT, BOYSIE
see EZZ RECO

GRANT, GOGI

The Wayward Wind	London	29 6 56	8	9

GRANT, JULIE

Up On The Roof	Pye	- 1 63	33	3
Count On Me	Pye	- 3 63	24	9
Count To Me	Pye	- 9 64	31	5

GRAPEFRUIT

Dear Delilah	RCA	- 2 68	21	8
C'mon Marianne	RCA	- 8 68	25	10

GRAY, DOBIE

The 'In' Crowd	London	- 2 65	25	9
Out On The Floor	Black Magic	- 9 75	42	4

GRECO, BUDDY

Lady Is A Tramp	Fontana	- 7 60	26	8

GREEN, AL

Tired Of Being Alone	London	23 10 71	4	11
Let's Stay Together	London	22 1 72	7	13
Look What You Done For Me	London	- 5 72	45	4
I'm Still In Love With You	London	- 8 72	35	5
Sha La La (Makes Me Happy)	London	21 12 74	20	10
L.O.V.E.	London	- 3 75	24	8

GREEN, LORNE

Ringo	RCA	- 1 65	22	6

GREENBAUM, NORMAN

Spirit In The Sky	Reprise	11 4 70	1	20

GREGORY, IAN

Time Will Tell	Pye Int.	4 12 60	17	8
Can't You Hear The Beat Of A Broken Heart	Pye	- 1 62	39	2

GREY, DORIAN

I've Got You On My Mind	Parlophone	- 3 68	36	7

GREYHOUND

Black And White	Trojan	3 7 71	6	13
Moon River	Trojan	29 1 72	12	11
I Am What I Am	Trojan	29 3 72	20	9

GUESS WHO

His Girl	King	- 2 67	45	1
American Woman/No Sugar Tonight	RCA	4 7 70	19	7

GUNN

Race With The Devil	CBS	7 12 68	8	11

GUYS AND DOLLS

There's A Whole Lot Of Loving	Magnet	15 3 75	2	11

Here I Go Again	Magnet		– 5 75	36	5
You Don't Have To Say You Love Me	Magnet		6 3 76	5	8

HALEY, BILL AND THE COMETS

Shake, Rattle And Roll	Brunswick		– 12 54	4	11
Rock Around The Clock	Brunswick		7 1 55	17	2
Mambo Rock	Brunswick		15 4 55	14	2
Rock Around The Clock (re-issue)	Brunswick		14 10 55	1	17
Rock-A-Beatin' Boogie	Brunswick		6 1 56	3	8
See You Later Alligator	Brunswick		9 3 56	6	11
The Saints Rock 'n' Roll	Brunswick		1 6 56	3	22
Rockin' Through The Rye	Brunswick		17 8 56	3	19
Rock Around The Clock (re-issue)	Brunswick		21 9 56	7	11
Razzle Dazzle	Brunswick		28 9 56	16	4
See You Later Alligator (re-issue)	Brunswick		28 9 56	12	6
Rip It Up	Brunswick		16 11 56	2	14
Rudy's Rock	Brunswick		24 11 56	18	1
Rock The Joint	Brunswick		1 2 57	15	1
Don't Knock The Rock	Brunswick		8 3 57	10	7
Rock Around The Clock (re-issue)	MCA		6 4 68	20	11
Rock Around The Clock (re-issue)	MCA		6 4 74	12	10

HAMILTON IV, GEORGE

Why Don't They Understand	HMV		15 3 58	16	3

HAMILTON JOE FRANK AND REYNOLDS

Fallin' In Love	Pye		– 9 75	33	6

HAMILTON, RUSS

We Will Make Love/Rainbow	Oriole		7 6 57	3	16
Wedding Ring	Oriole		18 10 57	18	1

HAMLISCH, MARVIN

The Entertainer	MCA		– 3 74	25	12

HAMMOND, ALBERT

Free Electric Band	Mums		11 8 73	19	11

HANDLEY FAMILY

Wam Bam	GL		– 4 73	30	7

HAPPENINGS

I Got Rhythm	Stateside		– 5 67	28	9
My Mammy	Pye		– 8 67	34	5

HARDIN, TIM

Hang On To A Dream	Verve		– 1 67	50	1

HARDING, MIKE

Rochdale Cowboy	Rubber		– 8 75	22	8

HARDY, FRANÇOISE

Tous les Garçons Et Les Filles	Pye		– 6 64	36	7
Et Même	Pye		– 1 65	31	5

All Over The World	Pye	17 4 65	16	15

HARLEY QUINNE

New Orleans	Bell	18 10 72	19	8

HARLEY, STEVE

see COCKNEY REBEL

HARMONY GRASS

Move In A Little Closer	RCA	- 2 69	24	7

HARPER'S BIZARRE

59th Street Bridge Song (Feeling Groovy)	Warner Bros.	- 4 67	34	7
Anything Goes	Warner Bros.	- 10 67	33	6

HARPO

Movie Star	DJM	- 4 76	24	6

HARRIS, ANITA

Just Loving You	CBS	29 7 67	6	30
Playground	CBS	- 10 67	46	3
Anniversary Love	CBS	- 1 68	21	9
Dream A Little Dream Of Me	CBS	- 8 68	33	8

HARRIS, EMMYLOU

Here, There And Everywhere	Reprise	- 3 76	30	6

HARRIS, JET

Besame Mucho	Decca	- 5 62	22	7
Main Theme From 'The Man With The Golden Arm'	Decca	1 9 62	12	11
(see also: JET HARRIS AND TONY MEEHAN, SHADOWS)				

HARRIS, JET AND TONY MEEHAN

Diamonds	Decca	20 1 63	1	13
Scarlet O'Hara	Decca	4 5 63	2	12
Applejack	Decca	14 9 63	4	13

HARRIS, MAX

Gurney Slade	Philips	27 11 60	11	10

HARRIS, RICHARD

MacArthur Park	RCA	6 7 68	4	12
MacArthur Park (re-issue)	Probe	- 7 72	38	6

HARRIS, ROLF

Tie Me Kangaroo Down Sport	Columbia	24 7 60	9	14
Sun Arise	Columbia	10 11 62	3	16
Johnny Day	Columbia	- 2 63	44	2
Bluer Than Blue	Columbia	- 4 69	30	7
Two Little Boys	Columbia	29 11 69	1	25

HARRIS, RONNIE

Story Of Tina	Columbia	- 10 54	12	6

HARRISON, GEORGE

My Sweet Lord/Isn't It A Pity?	Apple	23 1 71	1	17

Bangla-Desh/Deep Blue	Apple	21 8 71	10	9
Give Me Love (Give Me Peace On Earth)	Apple	9 6 73	8	10
Ding Dong	Apple	- 12 74	38	5
You	Apple	- 10 75	38	5
(see also: BEATLES)				

HARRISON, NOEL

Windmills Of Your Mind	Reprise	15 3 69	8	14

HARRY J AND THE ALL STARS

The Liquidator	Trojan	15 11 69	9	20

HARVEY, ALEX

see SENSATIONAL ALEX HARVEY BAND

HATCH, TONY

Out Of This World	Pye	- 10 62	50	1

HATHAWAY, DONNY

see ROBERTA FLACK

THE EDWIN HAWKINS SINGERS

On Happy Day	Buddah	31 5 69	2	13

HAWKWIND

Silver Machine	Un.Artists	22 7 72	3	15
Urban Guerilla	Un.Artists	- 8 73	39	4

HAYES, BILL

The Ballad Of Davy Crockett	London	6 1 56	2	9

HAYES, ISAAC

Theme From 'Shaft'	Stax	4 12 71	4	12

HAYWARD, JUSTIN AND JOHN LODGE (BLUEJAYS)

Blue Guitar	Threshold	1 11 75	8	7
(see also: MOODY BLUES)				

HAZLEWOOD, LEE

see NANCY SINATRA

HEAD, MURRAY (WITH TRINIDAD SINGERS)/YVONNE ELLIMAN

Jesus Christ Superstar/I Don't Know How To Love Him	MCA	- 1 72	48	1

HEAD, ROY

Treat Her Right	Vocalion	- 11 65	30	5

TED HEATH BAND

The Faithful Hussar	Decca	3 8 56	15	3
Swingin' Shepherd Blues	Decca	28 3 58	4	10
Sucu Sucu	Decca	- 10 61	36	5

HEBB, BOBBY

Sunny	Philips	1 10 66	12	9
Love Love Love	Philips	- 8 72	32	6

HEDGEHOPPERS ANONYMOUS

It's Good News Week	Decca	21 10 65	5	12

HEINZ

Just Like Eddie	Decca	24 8 63	5	13
Country Boy	Decca	- 11 63	26	9
You Were There	Decca	- 2 64	26	8
Questions I Can't Answer	Columbia	- 10 64	39	2
Diggin' My Potatoes	Columbia	- 3 65	49	1

HELLO

Tell Him	Bell	30 11 74	6	12
New York Groove	Bell	8 11 75	9	9

HELMS, BOBBY

My Special Angel	Brunswick	7 12 57	16	3
Jacqueline	Brunswick	8 8 58	20	1

HELMS, JIMMY

Gonna Make You An Offer You Can't Refuse	Cube	3 3 73	8	9

HENDERSON, JOE 'MR. PIANO'

Sing It With Joe	Polygon	3 6 55	14	7
Trudie	Pye Nixa	8 8 58	14	6
Ooh La La	Pye	- 3 60	44	1

JIMI HENDRIX EXPERIENCE

Hey Joe	Polydor	21 1 67	6	11
Purple Haze	Track	15 4 67	3	13
And The Wind Cries Mary	Track	20 5 67	6	11
Burning Of The Midnight Lamp	Track	9 9 67	18	9
All Along The Watchtower	Track	2 11 68	5	11
Cross Town Traffic	Track	- 4 69	37	3
Voodoo Chile	Track	7 11 70	1	13
Gypsy Eyes/Remember	Track	- 10 71	35	5
Johnny B. Goode	Polydor	- 2 72	35	5

HENRY, CLARENCE 'FROGMAN'

But I Do	Pye Int.	7 5 61	3	19
You Always Hurt The One You Love	Pye Int.	15 7 61	6	12
Lonely Street/Why Can't You	Pye	- 9 61	42	2

HERD

From The Underworld	Fontana	7 10 67	6	13
Paradise Lost	Fontana	20 1 68	15	9
I Don't Want Our Loving To Die	Fontana	4 5 68	5	13

HERMAN'S HERMITS (FEATURING PETER NOONE)

I'm Into Something Good	Columbia	4 9 64	1	15
Show Me Girl	Columbia	5 12 64	19	9
Silhouettes	Columbia	27 2 65	3	12
Wonderful World	Columbia	1 5 65	7	10
Just A Little Bit Better	Columbia	18 9 65	15	9
A Must To Avoid	Columbia	8 1 66	6	11
You Won't Be Leavin'	Columbia	16 4 66	20	7
This Door Swings Both Ways	Columbia	9 7 66	18	7
East West	Columbia	- 12 66	33	7
No Milk Today	Columbia	15 10 66	7	10
There's A Kind Of Hush	Columbia	25 2 67	7	12

I Can Take Or Leave Your Loving	Columbia	27 1 68	11	9
Sleepy Joe	Columbia	11 5 68	12	9
Sunshine Girl	Columbia	3 8 68	8	13
Something's Happening	Columbia	4 1 69	6	15
My Sentimental Friend	Columbia	3 5 69	2	12
Here Comes The Star	Columbia	- 11 69	33	7
Years May Come, Years May Go	Columbia	21 2 70	7	12
Bet Yer Life I Do	RAK	- 5 70	23	10
(see also: PETER NOONE)				

HIGHLY LIKELY

Whatever Happened To You (Theme From 'The Likely Lads')	BBC	- 4 73	35	4

HIGHWAYMEN

Michael (Row The Boat Ashore)	HMV	9 9 61	1	14
Gypsy Rover	HMV	- 12 61	41	4

HILL, BENNY

Pepys' Diary/Gather In The Mushrooms	Pye	5 2 61	12	8
Transistor Radio	Pye	- 5 61	24	6
Harvest Of Love	Pye	1 6 63	20	8
Ernie (The Fastest Milkman In The West)	Columbia	20 11 71	1	18

HILL, CHRIS

Renta Santa	Philips	20 12 75	10	7

HILL, VINCE

The Rivers Run Dry	Piccadilly	- 6 62	41	2
Take Me To Your Heart Again	Columbia	22 1 66	13	11
Heartaches	Columbia	- 3 66	28	5
Merci Cherie	Columbia	- 6 66	36	6
Edelweiss	Columbia	18 2 67	2	17
Roses Of Picardy	Columbia	3 6 67	13	11
Love Letters In The Sand	Columbia	- 9 67	23	9
Importance Of Your Love	Columbia	- 6 68	38	12
Doesn't Anybody Know My Name	Columbia	- 2 69	50	1
Little Blue Bird	Columbia	- 10 69	42	1
Look Around	Columbia	30 10 71	12	16

HILLTOPPERS

Only You	London	27 1 56	4	21
Marianne	London	5 4 57	20	1

HILTON, RONNIE

I Still Believe	HMV	- 11 54	3	8
Veni Vidi Vici	HMV	- 12 54	12	4
A Blossom Fell	HMV	11 3 55	10	7
Stars Shine In Your Eyes	HMV	26 8 55	13	7
Yellow Rose Of Texas	HMV	11 11 55	15	2
Young And Foolish	HMV	10 2 56	12	3
No Other Love	HMV	20 4 56	1	13
Who Are We	HMV	13 7 56	12	8
A Woman In Love	HMV	6 10 56	20	1
Two Different Worlds	HMV	23 11 56	17	7
Around The World	HMV	24 5 57	5	15

Don't Let The Rain Come Down	HMV	–	5	64	21	9
A Windmill In Old Amsterdam	HMV	–	2	65	23	13

HOCKRIDGE, EDMOND

Young And Foolish	Nixa	17	2	56	11	7
Fountains Of Rome	Pye Nixa	7	9	56	17	4
No Other Love	Pye Nixa	12	5	56	16	4

HODGES, EDDIE

I'm Gonna Knock On Your Door	London	23	9	61	20	8

HOLLAND-DOZIER

Why Can't We Be Lovers	Invictus	–	10	72	29	5

HOLLIDAY, MICHAEL

Nothin' To Do	Columbia	30	3	56	16	1
Hot Diggity	Columbia	22	6	56	11	4
Gal With The Yaller Shoes	Columbia	15	6	56	17	3
The Story Of My Life	Columbia	17	1	58	1	14
Stairway Of Love	Columbia	23	5	58	6	11
Starry Eyed	Columbia	2	1	60	2	9
Skylark	Columbia	–	4	60	39	3
Little Boy Lost	Columbia	–	8	60	50	1

HOLLIES

Just Like Me	Parlophone	–	5	63	23	10
Searchin'	Parlophone	28	9	63	12	14
Stay	Parlophone	14	12	63	8	16
Just One Look	Parlophone	7	3	64	2	13
Here I Go Again	Parlophone	30	5	64	4	12
We're Through	Parlophone	3	10	64	7	11
Yes I Will	Parlophone	20	2	65	9	13
I'm Alive	Parlophone	12	6	65	1	14
Look Through Any Window	Parlophone	11	9	65	4	11
If I Needed Someone	Parlophone	15	1	66	20	9
I Can't Let Go	Parlophone	5	3	66	2	10
Bus Stop	Parlophone	25	6	66	5	9
Stop Stop Stop	Parlophone	22	10	66	2	12
On A Carousel	Parlophone	25	2	67	4	10
Carrie Anne	Parlophone	10	6	67	3	11
King Midas In Reverse	Parlophone	14	10	67	18	8
Jennifer Eccles	Parlophone	13	4	68	7	11
Listen To Me	Parlophone	19	10	68	11	11
Sorry Suzanne	Parlophone	15	3	69	3	12
He Ain't Heavy, He's My Brother	Parlophone	11	10	69	3	15
I Can't Tell The Bottom From The Top	Parlophone	2	5	70	7	10
Gasoline Alley Bred	Parlophone	17	10	70	14	7
Hey Willy	Parlophone	–	5	71	22	7
The Baby	Polydor	–	2	72	26	7
Long Cool Woman In A Black Dress	Polydor	–	9	72	32	8
The Day That Curly Billy Shot Crazy Sam McGee	Polydor	–	10	73	24	6
The Air That I Breathe	Polydor	23	2	74	2	13

HOLLY, BUDDY (AND THE CRICKETS)

Peggy Sue	Coral	3	1	58	4	12
Listen To Me	Coral	14	3	58	16	1
Rave On	Coral	27	6	58	4	12
Early In The Morning	Coral	29	8	58	15	2

It Doesn't Matter Anymore	Coral	7	3 59	1	19
Peggy Sue Got Married	Coral	12	9 59	14	8
Heartbeat	Coral	-	4 60	30	3
True Love Ways	Coral	-	5 60	25	7
Learning The Game	Coral	-	10 60	36	3
What To Do	Coral	-	1 61	35	6
Baby I Don't Care/Valley Of Tears	Coral	2	7 61	12	14
Listen To Me (re-issue)	Coral	-	3 62	48	1
Reminiscing	Coral	6	10 62	18	12
Brown-Eyed Handsome Man	Coral	16	3 63	3	17
Bo Diddley	Coral	15	6 63	4	12
Wishing	Coral	14	9 63	10	11
What To Do (re-issue)	Coral	-	12 63	27	8
You've Got Love	Coral	-	5 64	40	6
Love's Made A Fool Of You	Coral	-	9 64	39	6
Peggy Sue/Rave On (re-issue)	MCA	-	4 68	32	9
(see also: CRICKETS)					

HOLLYWOOD ARGYLES

Alley-Oop	London	-	7 60	24	10

HOLT, JOHN

Help Me Make It Through The Night	Trojan	11	1 75	6	14

HONEYBUS

I Can't Let Maggie Go	Deram	14	4 68	8	12

HONEYCOMBS

Have I The Right	Pye	8	8 64	1	15
Is It Because	Pye	-	10 64	38	6
Something Better Beginning	Pye	-	5 65	39	4
That's The Way	Pye	4	9 65	12	14

HOPKIN, MARY

Those Were The Days	Apple	14	9 68	1	20
Goodbye	Apple	19	4 69	2	14
Temma Harbour	Apple	7	2 70	6	11
Knock Knock Who's There	Apple	4	4 70	2	14
Think About Your Children	Apple	14	11 79	19	9
Let My Name Be Sorrow	Apple	-	7 71	46	1
If You Love Me	Good Earth	-	3 76	32	4

HORTON, JOHNNY

Battle Of New Orleans	Philips	18	7 59	16	1
North To Alaska	Philips	8	1 61	15	11

HOT BUTTER

Popcorn	Pye	29	7 72	5	17

HOT CHOCOLATE

Love Is Life	RAK	22	8 70	6	12
You Could've Been A Lady	RAK	-	2 71	22	10
I Believe (In Love)	RAK	11	9 71	8	11
You'll Always Be A Friend	RAK	-	10 72	23	8
Brother Louie	RAK	28	4 73	7	10
Rumours	RAK	-	8 73	44	3
Emma	RAK	23	3 74	3	10
Cheri Babe	RAK	-	11 74	31	9
Disco Queen	RAK	7	6 75	11	7
A Child's Prayer	RAK	30	8 75	7	10

You Sexy Thing	RAK	15 11 75	2	12
Don't Stop It Now	RAK	3 4 76	11	8

HOTLEGS

Neanderthal Man (see also: 10 C.C.)	Fontana	25 7 70	2	14

HOTSHOTS

Snoopy Versus The Red Baron	Mooncrest	16 6 73	4	15

HOWARD, BILLY

King Of The Cops	P.Farthing	10 1 76	6	12

HUDSON FORD

Pick Up The Pieces	A & M	1 9 73	8	9
Burn Baby Burn	A & M	2 3 74	15	9
Floating In The Wind (see also: STRAWBS)	A & M	- 6 74	35	2

HUES CORPORATION

Rock The Boat	RCA	3 8 74	6	10
Rock 'n' Soul	RCA	- 10 74	24	6

HUMBLE PIE

Natural Born Boogie	Immediate	30 8 69	4	10

HUMPERDINCK, ENGELBERT

Release Me	Decca	11 2 67	1	55
There Goes My Everything	Decca	3 6 67	2	29
The Last Waltz	Decca	26 8 67	1	27
Am I That Easy To Forget?	Decca	20 1 68	3	13
A Man Without Love	Decca	4 5 68	2	15
Les Bicyclettes De Belsize	Decca	12 10 68	5	15
The Way It Used To Be	Decca	15 2 69	3	14
I'm A Better Man	Decca	23 8 69	15	13
Winter World Of Love	Decca	22 11 69	7	13
My Marie	Decca	- 5 70	31	7
Sweetheart	Decca	- 9 70	22	7
Santa Lija	Decca	- 2 71	47	1
Another Time Another Place	Decca	2 10 71	13	12
Too Beautiful To Last	Decca	25 3 72	14	10
Love Is All	Decca	- 10 73	44	4

HUNT, MARSHA

Walk On Gilded Splinters	Track	- 5 69	46	2
Keep The Customer Satisfied	Track	- 5 70	41	1

HUNT, TOMMY

Crackin' Up	Spark	- 10 75	39	5

HUNTER, IAN

Once Bitten Twice Shy (see also: MOTT THE HOOPLE)	CBS	24 5 75	14	10

HUNTER, TAB

Young Love	London	8 2 57	1	17
Ninety Nine Ways	London	12 4 57	5	10

HYLAND, BRIAN

Itsy, Bitsy, Teenie, Weenie, Yellow Polka Dot Bikini	London	10 7 60	8	13
Four Little Heels	London	- 10 60	29	6

Ginny Come Lately	HMV	19 5 62	5	15
Sealed With A Kiss	HMV	18 8 62	3	15
Warmed Over Kisses	HMV	- 11 62	28	6
Gypsy Woman	UNI	- 3 71	42	6
Sealed With A Kiss (re-issue)	ABC	19 7 75	7	11

THE DICK HYMAN TRIO

Theme From 'A Threepenny Opera'	MGM	16 3 56	9	9

IDES OF MARCH

Vehicle	Warner Bros.	- 6 70	31	8

IFIELD, FRANK

Lucky Devil	Columbia	- 3 60	43	3
Gotta Get A Date	Columbia	- 9 60	49	1
I Remember You	Columbia	14 7 62	1	28
Lovesick Blues	Columbia	27 10 62	1	17
Wayward Wind	Columbia	3 2 63	1	13
Nobody's Darlin' But Mine	Columbia	20 4 63	4	16
I'm Confessin'	Columbia	6 7 63	1	16
Mule Train	Columbia	- 10 63	22	6
Don't Blame Me	Columbia	18 1 64	8	13
Angry At The Big Oak Tree	Columbia	- 4 64	25	8
I Should Care	Columbia	- 7 64	33	3
Summer Is Over	Columbia	- 10 64	25	6
Paradise	Columbia	- 8 65	26	11
No One Will Ever Know	Columbia	- 6 66	25	4
Call Her Your Sweetheart	Columbia	- 12 66	24	11

IMPRESSIONS

First Impressions	Curtom	20 12 75	16	10

IN CROWD

That's How Strong My Love Is	Parlophone	- 5 65	48	1

INKSPOTS

Melody Of Love	Parlophone	29 4 55	14	4

INMAN, JOHN

Are You Being Served Sir?	DJM	- 10 75	39	6

INTRUDERS

I'll Always Love My Mama	Philadelphia	- 4 74	32	7
She's A Winner	Philadelphia	20 7 74	14	9

IRVIN, BIG DEE

Swinging On A Star (with LITTLE EVA)	Colpix	21 12 63	7	17

ISLEY BROTHERS

Twist And Shout	Stateside	- 7 63	42	1
This Old Heart Of Mine	T.Motown	- 4 66	47	1
I Guess I'll Always Love You	T.Motown	- 9 66	45	2
This Old Heart Of Mine (re-issue)	T.Motown	2 11 68	3	15
I Guess I'll Always Love You (re-issue)	T.Motown	1 2 69	11	9
Behind The Painted Smile	T.Motown	3 5 69	5	12
It's Your Thing	Major Minor	- 6 69	30	5
Put Yourself In My Place	T.Motown	27 9 69	13	11

That Lady	Epic	20 10 73	14	9
Highways Of My Life	Epic	– 1 74	25	8
Summer Breeze	Epic	15 6 74	16	8

IVES, BURL

Little Bitty Tear	Brunswick	10 2 62	9	15
Funny Way Of Laughin'	Brunswick	– 5 62	29	10

IVY LEAGUE

Funny How Love Can Be	Piccadilly	13 2 65	8	9
That's Why I'm Crying	Piccadilly	– 4 65	22	10
Tossing And Turning	Piccadilly	10 7 65	3	13
Willow Tree	Piccadilly	– 7 66	50	1

JACKS, TERRY

Seasons In The Sun	Bell	23 3 74	1	12
If You Go Away	Bell	13 7 74	8	9
(see also: POPPY FAMILY)				

JACKSON FIVE

I Want You Back	T.Motown	14 2 70	2	13
ABC	T.Motown	23 5 70	8	11
The Love You Save/I Found That Girl	T.Motown	15 8 70	7	9
I'll Be There	T.Motown	5 12 70	4	17
Mama's Pearl	T.Motown	– 4 71	25	7
Never Can Say Goodbye	T.Motown	– 7 71	33	7
Lookin' Through The Windows	T.Motown	25 11 72	9	11
Santa Claus Is Coming To Town	T.Motown	– 12 72	43	2
Doctor My Eyes	T.Motown	24 2 73	9	10
Hallelujah Day	T.Motown	30 6 73	20	9
Sky Writer	T.Motown	– 9 73	25	8

JACKSON, MICHAEL

Got To Be There	T.Motown	26 2 72	5	11
Rockin' Robin	T.Motown	10 6 72	3	14
Ain't No Sunshine	T.Motown	2 9 72	8	11
Ben	T.Motown	2 12 72	7	14
(see also: JACKSON FIVE)				

JACKSON, MILLIE

My Man Is A Sweet Man (re-issue)	Mojo	– 11 72	50	1

JACKSON, TONY

Bye Bye Baby	Pye	– 10 64	38	3
(see also: SEARCHERS)				

JACKSON, WANDA

Let's Have A Party	Capitol	– 8 60	32	8
Mean Mean Mean	Capitol	– 1 61	40	3

JACKY

White Horses	Philips	27 4 68	10	14
(see also: JACKIE LEE)				

JAGGER, MICK

see ROLLING STONES

JAMES BOYS

Over And Over	P.Farthing	– 5 73	39	6

JAMES, DICK

Robin Hood	Parlophone	20	1 56	18	8
Garden Of Eden	Parlophone	25	1 57	18	2

JAMES, JIMMY AND THE VAGABONDS

Red Red Wine	Pye	–	9 68	36	8

JAMES, SONNY

Young Love	Capitol	8	2 57	9	7

JAMES, TOMMY AND THE SHONDELLS

Hanky Panky	Roulette	–	7 66	38	7
Mony Mony	Major Minor	6	7 68	1	18

JAN AND DEAN

Heart And Soul	London	–	8 61	24	8
Surf City	Liberty	–	8 63	26	10

JAN AND KJELD

Banjo Boy	Ember	–	7 60	36	4

JANKOWSKI, HORST

A Walk In The Black Forest	Mercury	7	8 65	3	18

JAVELLS (FEATURING NOSMO KING)

Goodbye, Nothing To Say	Pye	–	11 74	26	8

JAY, PETER AND THE JAYWALKERS

Can Can '62	Decca	–	11 62	31	11

JEFFERSON

Colour Of My Love	Pye	–	4 69	22	7

JETHRO TULL

Love Story	Island	–	1 69	29	8
Living In The Past	Island	14	6 69	3	14
Sweet Dream	Chrysalis	5	11 69	7	11
Witch's Promise/Teacher	Chrysalis	31	1 70	4	10
Life Is A Long Song/Up The Pool	Chrysalis	25	9 71	11	8

JIGSAW

Sky High	Splash	15	11 75	9	11

JOANS, JOHN PAUL

Man From Nazareth	RAK	–	12 70	25	7

JO JO GUNNE

Run Run Run	Asylum	15	4 72	6	12

JOHN, ELTON

Your Song	DJM	6	2 71	7	12
Rocket Man	DJM	6	5 72	2	13
Honky Cat	DJM	–	9 72	31	6
Crocodile Rock	DJM	11	11 72	5	14
Daniel	DJM	27	1 73	4	10
Saturday Night's Alright For Fighting	DJM	14	7 73	7	8
Goodbye Yellow Brick Road	DJM	6	10 73	6	14

Step Into Christmas	DJM	– 12 73	24	7
Candle In The Wind/Bennie And The Jets	DJM	9 3 74	11	9
Don't Let The Sun Go Down On Me	DJM	15 6 74	16	8
The Bitch Is Back	DJM	5 10 74	15	7
Lucy In The Sky With Diamonds	DJM	30 11 74	10	10
Philadelphia Freedom	DJM	22 3 75	12	9
Someone Saved My Life Tonight	DJM	– 6 75	22	5
Island Girl	DJM	25 10 75	14	8
Pinball Wizard	DJM	3 4 76	7	7

JOHN, ROBERT

If You Don't Want My Love	CBS	– 6 68	42	5

JOHNNY AND CHARLEY

La Yenka	Piccadilly	– 10 65	49	1

JOHNNY AND THE HURRICANES

Red River Rock	London	10 10 59	2	14
Reveille Rock	London	26 12 59	8	4
Beatnik Fly	London	13 3 60	8	19
Down Yonder	London	5 6 60	8	11
Rocking Goose	London	14 10 60	3	20
Ja Da	London	12 2 61	14	9
Old Smokey/High Voltage	London	2 7 61	12	8

JOHNSON, BRYAN

Looking High, High, High	Decca	3 4 60	17	1

JOHNSON, JOHNNY AND THE BANDWAGON

Breaking Down The Walls of Heartache (BANDWAGON only)	Direction	2 11 68	4	14
You	Direction	– 2 69	34	4
Let's Hang On	Direction	– 6 69	36	5
Sweet Inspiration	Bell	22 8 70	10	13
Blame It On The Pony Express	Bell	19 12 70	7	12

JOHNSON, KEVIN

Rock And Roll (I Gave You The Best Years Of My Life)	UK	– 1 75	23	6

JOHNSON, L.J.

Your Magic Put A Spell On Me	Philips	– 2 76	27	6

JOHNSON, LAURIE

Suku Suku	Pye	30 9 61	9	12

JOHNSON, LOU

Message To Martha	London	– 11 64	36	2

JOHNSON, MARV

You Got What It Takes	London	6 2 60	4	10
I Love The Way You Love	London	– 4 60	35	3
Ain't Gonna Be That Way	London	– 8 60	50	1
I'll Pick A Rose For My Rose	T.Motown	8 2 69	10	12
I Miss You Baby	T.Motown	– 10 69	25	8

JOHNSON, TEDDY

see PEARL CARR

JOHNSTON BROTHERS

Hernando's Hideaway	Decca	7 10 55	1	13

JONES, JANIE

Witch's Brew	HMV	- 1 66	46	3

JONES, JIMMY

Handy Man	MGM	13 3 60	3	22
Good Timin'	MGM	12 6 60	1	15
I Just Go For You	MGM	- 9 60	35	4
Ready For Love	MGM	- 11 60	46	1
I Told You So	MGM	- 3 61	33	3

JONES, JUGGY

Inside America	Contempo	- 2 76	39	4

JONES, PAUL

High Time	HMV	29 10 66	4	14
I've Been A Bad Bad Boy	HMV	28 1 67	5	9
Thinkin' Ain't For Me	HMV	- 8 67	32	8
Aquarius	Columbia	- 2 69	45	2
(see also: MANFRED MANN)				

JONES, TAMMY

Let Me Try Again	Epic	3 5 75	5	11

JONES, TOM

It's Not Unusual	Decca	20 2 65	1	14
Once Upon A Time	Decca	- 5 65	32	4
With These Hands	Decca	31 7 65	13	11
What's New Pussycat	Decca	28 8 65	11	10
Thunderball	Decca	- 1 66	35	4
Once There Was A Time/ Responsible	Decca	4 6 66	18	9
This And That	Decca	- 8 66	44	3
Green Green Grass Of Home	Decca	19 11 66	1	22
Detroit City	Decca	4 3 67	8	10
Funny Familiar Forgotten Feeling	Decca	29 4 67	7	15
I'll Never Fall In Love Again	Decca	5 8 67	2	25
I'm Coming Home	Decca	2 12 67	2	16
Delilah	Decca	9 3 68	2	17
Help Yourself	Decca	27 7 68	3	26
A Minute Of Your Time	Decca	14 12 68	15	15
Love Me Tonight	Decca	17 5 69	9	12
Without Love	Decca	20 12 69	10	11
Daughters Of Darkness	Decca	25 4 70	5	15
I (Who Have Nothing)	Decca	5 9 70	16	11
She's A Lady	Decca	30 1 71	13	11
Puppet Man	Decca	- 6 71	49	2
'Till	Decca	30 10 71	2	15
Young New Mexican Puppeteer	Decca	8 4 72	6	11
Letter To Lucille	Decca	- 4 73	31	7
Something 'Bout You Baby I Like	Decca	- 9 74	36	5

JORDAN, DICK

Hallelujah I Love Her So	Oriole	- 3 60	47	1
Little Christine	Oriole	- 6 60	39	3

JOYSTRINGS

It's An Open Secret	R.Zonophone	- 2 64	32	7
A Starry Night	R.Zonophone	- 12 64	34	4

JUDGE DREAD

Big Six	Big Shot	23 9 72	11	18
Big Seven	Big Shot	23 12 72	8	18
Big Eight	Big Shot	28 4 73	10	14
Je T'Aime	Cactus	12 7 75	9	9
Big Ten	Cactus	4 10 75	14	8
Christmas In Dreadland/ Come Outside	Cactus	20 12 75	14	7

JUICY LUCY

Who Do You Love	Vertigo	18 4 70	14	12
Pretty Woman	Vertigo	- 10 70	44	5

JUNE, ROSEMARY

I'll Be With You In Apple Blossom Time	Pye	7 2 59	12	4

JUSTICE, JIMMY

When My Little Girl Is Smiling	Pye	21 4 62	9	13
Ain't That Funny	Pye	23 6 62	8	11
Spanish Harlem	Pye	15 9 62	20	11

JUSTIS, BILL

Raunchy	London	14 2 58	11	4

KAEMPFERT, BERT

Bye Bye Blues	Polydor	- 12 65	24	10

KALIN TWINS

When	Brunswick	25 7 58	1	16

KALLEN, KITTY

Little Things Mean A Lot	Brunswick	- 10 54	6	10

GUNTHER KALLMAN CHOIR

Elizabethan Seranade	Polydor	- 12 64	39	3

KANE, EDEN

Well I Ask You	Decca	28 5 61	1	21
Get Lost	Decca	16 9 61	11	11
Forget Me Not	Decca	27 1 62	3	14
I Don't Know Why	Decca	26 5 62	7	13
Boys Cry	Decca	22 2 64	8	14

KASENATZ KATZ SINGING ORCHESTRAL CIRCUS

Quick Joey Small (Run Joey Run)	Buddah	1 2 69	19	15

KAYE SISTERS

Paper Roses	Philips	31 7 60	7	18

(see also: THREE KAYES, FRANKIE VAUGHAN)

K.C. AND THE SUNSHINE BAND

Queen Of Clubs	Jay Boy	7 9 74	7	12
Sound Your Funky Horn (re-issue)	Jay Boy	21 12 74	17	9
Get Down Tonight	Jay Boy	- 3 75	21	10
That's The Way (I Like It)	Jay Boy	23 8 75	4	10
I'm So Crazy	Jay Boy	- 11 75	34	3

K-DOE, ERNIE

Mother-In-Law	London	- 5 61	29	7

KEATING, JOHNNY

The Theme From 'Z Cars'	Piccadilly	10 3 62	8	14

KEENE, NELSON

Image Of A Girl	HMV	- 8 60	37	5

KEITH

98.6	Mercury	- 1 67	24	7
Tell It To My Face	Mercury	- 3 67	50	1

KELLER, JERRY

Here Comes Summer	London	29 8 59	2	12

KELLY, GRACE

see BING CROSBY

KELLY, KEITH

Tease Me	Parlophone	- 4 60	27	4
Ooh! La, La	Parlophone	17 4 60	13	6
Listen Little Girl/Uh Huh	Parlophone	31 7 60	15	5

KENDRICKS, EDDIE

Keep On Truckin'	T.Motown	15 12 73	18	14
Boogie Down	T.Motown	- 3 74	39	4
(see also: TEMPTATIONS)				

KENDRIK, LINDA

I Will See You There	Philips	- 4 69	41	1

KENNY

Heart Of Stone	RAK	10 3 73	11	10
Give It To Me Now	RAK	- 6 73	38	3
The Bump	RAK	11 1 75	3	15
Fancy Pants	RAK	15 3 75	4	9
Baby I Love You, OK	RAK	21 6 75	12	7
Julie-Ann	RAK	30 8 75	10	8

KIDD, JOHNNY AND THE PIRATES

Shakin' All Over	HMV	26 6 60	3	19
Restless	HMV	7 10 60	18	7
Linda Lu	HMV	- 4 61	47	1
Shot Of Rhythm And Blues	HMV	- 1 63	48	1
I'll Never Get Over You	HMV	10 8 63	4	16
Hungry For Love	HMV	7 12 63	20	10
Always And Ever	HMV	- 4 64	46	1

KIM, ANDY

Rock Me Gently	Capitol	7 9 74	2	12

KING, BEN E.

First Taste Of Love	London	15 1 61	16	11
Stand By Me	London	- 1 61	27	6
Amor	London	- 10 61	38	4

(see also: DRIFTERS)

KING BROTHERS

A White Sports Coat	Parlophone	7 6 57	8	11
In The Middle Of An Island	Parlophone	20 9 57	20	3
Wake Up Little Suzie	Parlophone	21 12 57	19	1
Standing On The Corner	Parlophone	17 4 60	4	11
Mais Qui	Parlophone	- 7 60	21	10
Doll House	Parlophone	- 1 61	21	8
76 Trombones	Parlophone	- 2 61	25	10

KING, CAROLE

It Might As Well Rain Until September	London	6 10 62	3	13
It's Too Late/I Feel The Earth Move	A & M	28 8 71	6	12
It Might As Well Rain Until September (re-issue)	London	- 10 72	43	4

KING, DAVE

Memories Are Made Of This	Decca	17 2 56	5	13
You Can't Be True To Two	Decca	20 4 56	10	7
Story Of My Life	Decca	24 1 58	20	1

KING, JONATHAN

Everyone's Gone To The Moon	Decca	7 8 65	4	11
Let It All Hang Out	Decca	- 1 70	26	7
Lazybones	Decca	- 5 71	23	8
Hooked On A Feeling	Decca	- 11 71	23	10
Flirt	Decca	- 2 72	22	9
Una Paloma Blanca	UK	20 9 75	5	11

(see also: BUBBLEROCK, 53rd AND A 3rd,
    HEDGEHOPPERS ANONYMOUS, PIGLETS,
    ST. CECILIA, SAKHARIN, SHAG, WEATHERMEN)

KING, NOSMO

see JAVELLS

KING, SOLOMON

She Wears My Ring	Columbia	20 1 68	3	18
When We Were Young	Columbia	- 5 68	21	10

KINGSMEN

Louie Louie	Pye	- 1 64	26	7

KINGSTON TRIO

Tom Dooley	Capitol	21 11 58	4	12

KINKS

You Really Got Me	Pye	22 8 64	1	12
All Day And All Of The Night	Pye	7 11 64	2	14
Tired Of Waiting For You	Pye	30 1 65	1	10
Everybody's Gonna Be Happy	Pye	10 4 65	11	8
Set Me Free	Pye	12 6 65	9	11
See My Friend	Pye	21 8 65	10	9

Till The End Of The Day	Pye	25 12 65	8	12
Dedicated Follower Of Fashion	Pye	12 3 66	4	11
Sunny Afternoon	Pye	18 6 66	1	13
Dead End Street	Pye	3 12 66	5	11
Waterloo Sunset	Pye	20 5 67	2	11
Autumn Almanac	Pye	28 10 67	3	11
Wonderboy	Pye	– 4 68	37	6
Days	Pye	3 8 68	12	10
Plastic Men	Pye	– 4 69	31	4
Victoria	Pye	– 1 70	33	4
Lola	Pye	11 7 70	2	14
Apeman	Pye	2 1 71	5	15
Supersonic Rocketship	RCA	17 6 72	16	8
(see also: DAVE DAVIES)				

KIRBY, KATHY

Dance On	Decca	31 8 63	11	13
Secret Love	Decca	16 11 63	4	17
Let Me Go Lover	Decca	7 3 64	10	11
You're The One	Decca	30 5 64	17	9
I Belong	Decca	– 3 65	36	3

KISSOON, MAC AND KATIE

Chirpy Chirpy Cheep Cheep	Young Blood	– 6 71	41	1
Sugar Candy Kisses	Polydor	1 2 75	3	10
Don't Do It Baby	State	17 5 75	9	8
Like A Butterfly	State	27 9 75	18	9

KITT, EARTHA

Under The Bridges Of Paris	HMV	4 4 55	7	9

KNIGHT, FREDERICK

I've Been Lonely For So Long	Stax	– 6 72	22	10

KNIGHT, GLADYS AND THE PIPS

Take Me In Your Arms And Love Me	T.Motown	22 7 67	13	15
I Heard It Through The Grapevine	T.Motown	– 12 67	47	1
Just Walk In My Shoes (re-issue)	T.Motown	– 6 72	35	8
Help Me Make It Through The Night	T.Motown	9 12 72	11	16
Look Of Love	T.Motown	– 3 73	21	9
Neither One Of Us (Can Be The First To Say Goodbye)	T.Motown	– 5 73	31	7
The Way We Were/Try To Remember	Buddah	17 5 75	4	15
The Best Thing That Ever Happened To Me	Buddah	16 8 75	7	11
Part Time Love	Buddah	– 11 75	30	5

KNIGHT, ROBERT

Everlasting Love	Monument	– 6 68	40	2
Love On A Mountain Top (re-issue)	Monument	15 12 73	10	16
Everlasting Love (re-issue)	Monument	30 3 74	19	8

KNOX, BUDDY

Party Doll	Columbia	25 5 57	17	1
She's Gone	Liberty	– 8 62	45	2

MOE KOFFMAN QUARTETTE

Swingin' Shepherd Blues	London	22 3 58	20	1

KOKOMO
| Asia Minor | London | – 4 61 | 35 | 7 |

KONGOS, JOHN
| He's Gonna Step On You Again | Fly | 12 6 71 | 4 | 14 |
| Tokoloshe Man | Fly | 27 11 71 | 4 | 11 |

KRAFTWERK
| Autobahn | Vertigo | 24 5 75 | 11 | 9 |

KRAMER, BILLY J. AND THE DAKOTAS
Do You Want To Know A Secret	Parlophone	11 5 63	2	15
Bad To Me	Parlophone	10 8 63	1	14
I'll Keep You Satisfied	Parlophone	16 11 63	4	13
Little Children	Parlophone	7 3 64	1	13
From A Window	Parlophone	8 8 64	10	7
Trains And Boats And Planes	Parlophone	29 5 65	12	8
(see also: DAKATOS)

KREWCUTS
| Trambone | HMV | – 3 61 | 33 | 9 |

KUNZ, CHARLIE
| New Piano Medley | Decca | – 12 54 | 16 | 1 |

LA ROSA, JULIUS
| Torero | RCA | 1 8 58 | 15 | 3 |

LA RUE, DANNY
| On Mother Kelly's Doorstep | Page One | – 12 68 | 33 | 9 |

LABELLE
| Lady Marmalade | Epic | 12 4 75 | 17 | 9 |

LAINE, CLEO
| Let's Slip Away | Fontana | – 12 60 | 42 | 1 |
| You'll Answer To Me | Fontana | 16 9 61 | 5 | 13 |

LAINE, FRANKIE
My Friend	Philips	– 10 54	4	10
There Must Be A Reason	Philips	– 10 54	9	8
Rain Rain Rain	Philips	– 10 54	8	13
In The Beginning	Philips	11 3 55	20	1
Cool Water	Philips	24 6 55	2	22
Strange Lady In Town	Philips	15 7 55	6	13
Humming Bird	Philips	11 11 55	16	1
Hawkeye	Philips	25 11 55	7	8
Sixteen Tons	Philips	20 1 56	15	3
A Woman In Love	Philips	14 9 56	1	19
Moonlight Gambler	Philips	28 12 56	9	9
Love Is A Golden Ring	Philips	10 5 57	16	2
Rawhide	Philips	14 11 59	11	11
Gunslinger	Philips	– 5 61	50	1

LAKE, GREG
| I Believe In Father Christmas | Manticore | 13 12 75 | 2 | 7 |

LANCASTRIANS

We'll Sing In The Sunshine	Pye	- 12 64	47	2

LANCE, MAJOR

Um Um Um Um Um Um	Columbia	- 2 64	40	2

LANE, RONNIE

How Come	GM	26 1 74	11	8
The Poacher	GM	- 6 74	36	4
(see also: FACES, SMALL FACES)				

LANG, DON

Cloudburst	HMV	4 11 55	11	4
Witchdoctor	HMV	23 5 58	4	10

LANZA, MARIO

Drinking Song	HMV	4 2 55	13	1
I'll Walk With God	HMV	18 2 55	18	1
Serenade	HMV	22 4 55	15	3
I'll Walk With God (re-issue)	HMV	6 5 55	20	1

LAUREL AND HARDY

The Trail Of The Lonesome Pine (re-issue)	Un.Artists	6 12 75	2	10

LAWRENCE, LEE

Suddenly There's A Valley	Columbia	2 12 55	14	3

LAWRENCE, STEVE

Footsteps	HMV	10 4 60	9	13
Girls Girls Girls	London	- 8 60	49	1
I Want To Stay Here	CBS	31 8 63	3	13
(with EYDIE GORME)				

LEANDROS, VICKY

Come What May	Philips	22 4 72	2	16
The Love In Your Eyes	Philips	- 12 72	46	3
When Bouzoukis Played	Philips	- 7 73	43	5

LEE, BRENDA

Sweet Nothin's	Brunswick	3 4 60	5	19
I'm Sorry/That's All You Gotta Do	Brunswick	3 7 60	10	16
I Want To Be Wanted	Brunswick	- 10 60	31	6
Let's Jump The Broomstick	Brunswick	12 2 61	15	15
Emotions	Brunswick	- 4 61	45	1
Dum Dum	Brunswick	- 7 61	22	8
Fool No. 1	Brunswick	18 11 61	18	5
Break It To Me Gently	Brunswick	- 2 62	46	2
Speak To Me Pretty	Brunswick	21 4 62	3	12
Here Comes That Feeling	Brunswick	7 7 62	5	12
It Started All Over Again	Brunswick	6 10 62	15	11
Rockin' Around The Christmas Tree	Brunswick	8 12 62	6	7
All Alone Am I	Brunswick	27 1 63	7	17
Losing You	Brunswick	20 4 63	10	17
I Wonder	Brunswick	27 7 63	14	9
Sweet Impossible You	Brunswick	- 11 63	28	5
As Usual	Brunswick	18 1 64	5	15
Think	Brunswick	- 4 64	26	8
Is It True?	Brunswick	26 9 64	17	8

Christmas Will Be Just Another Lonely Day	Brunswick	– 12 64	25	5
Thanks A Lot	Brunswick	– 2 65	41	2
Too Many Rivers	Brunswick	– 7 65	22	12

LEE, BYRON AND THE DRAGONAIRES

Elizabethan Reggae	Duke	– 1 70	22	13

LEE, CURTIS

Pretty Little Angel Eyes	London	– 8 61	47	2

LEE, JACKIE

Rupert	Pye	13 2 71	14	17
(see also: JACKY)				

LEE, LEAPY

Little Arrows	MCA	7 9 68	2	22
Good Morning	MCA	– 12 69	22	11

LEE, PEGGY

Mr. Wonderful	Brunswick	24 5 57	8	13
Fever	Capitol	22 8 58	6	8
'Til There Was You	Capitol	– 3 61	30	4

LEEDS UNITED FOOTBALL CLUB

Leeds United	Chapter One	13 5 72	10	9

RAYMOND LEFEVRE ORCHESTRA

Soul Coaxing	Major Minor	– 5 68	46	2

LEMON PIPERS

Green Tambourine	Kama Sutra	24 2 68	7	11
Rice Is Nice	Pye	– 6 68	41	5

LENNON, JOHN (*AND THE PLASTIC ONO BAND) (*YOKO ONO)

Instant Karma (JOHN ONO LENNON)	Apple	21 2 70	5	8
Power To The People*	Apple	20 3 71	7	9
Happy Christmas (War Is Over)* (with the HARLEM COMMUNITY CHOIR)	Apple	16 12 72	4	8
Mind Games	Apple	– 11 73	26	9
Whatever Gets You Through The Night	Apple	– 10 74	36	4
Happy Christmas (War Is Over) (re-issue)*	Apple	– 1 75	48	1
No. 9 Dream	Apple	– 2 75	23	8
Stand By Me	Apple	– 5 75	30	7
Imagine	Apple	15 11 75	6	11
(see also: PLASTIC ONO BAND, BEATLES)				

LESTER, KETTY

Love Letters	London	5 5 62	4	12
But Not For Me	London	– 7 62	45	4

LETTERMEN

Way You Look Tonight	Capitol	– 11 61	36	3

LEVINE, HANK

Image	HMV	– 12 61	45	4

LEWIS, GARY AND THE PLAYBOYS

My Heart's Symphony (re-issue)	Un.Artists	– 2 75	36	7

LEWIS, JERRY

Rock-a-Bye Your Baby	Brunswick	8 2 57	14	5

LEWIS, JERRY LEE

Whole Lotta Shakin' Goin' On	London	4 10 57	8	7
Great Balls Of Fire	London	20 12 57	1	11
Breathless	London	18 4 58	8	5
High School Confidential	London	24 1 59	10	5
Lovin' Up A Storm	London	2 5 59	20	1
Baby Bye Bye	London	– 6 60	47	1
What'd I Say	London	30 4 61	8	13
Sweet Little Sixteen	London	– 9 62	38	5
Good Golly Miss Molly	London	– 6 63	31	6
Chantilly Lace (re-issue)	Mercury	– 5 72	33	5

LEWIS, LINDA

Rock-A-Doodle Doo	Raft	7 7 73	15	12
It's In His Kiss	Arista	26 7 75	6	8
Baby I'm Yours	Arista	– 4 76	33	6

RAMSEY LEWIS TRIO

Wade In The Water (re-issue)	Chess	– 4 72	31	8

LEYTON, JOHN

Johnny Remember Me	Top Rank	29 7 61	1	15
Wild Wind	Top Rank	30 9 61	2	11
Son, This Is She	HMV	9 12 61	15	10
Lone Rider	HMV	– 3 62	40	5
Lonely City	HMV	26 5 62	14	11
Down The River Nile	HMV	– 8 62	42	3
Cupboard Love	HMV	– 2 63	22	12
I'll Cut Your Tail Off	HMV	– 7 63	36	3
Make Love To Me	HMV	– 2 64	49	1

LIBERACE

Unchained Melody	Philips	17 6 55	20	1

LIEUTENANT PIGEON

Mouldy Old Dough	Decca	23 9 72	1	19
Desperate Dan	Decca	13 1 73	17	10

LIGHTFOOT, GORDON

If You Could Read My Mind	Reprise	– 6 71	30	9
Sundown	Reprise	– 8 74	33	7

LIGHTFOOT, TERRY

True Love	Columbia	– 9 61	33	4
King Kong	Columbia	– 11 61	29	13
Tavern In The Town	Columbia	– 5 62	49	1

LIMMIE AND THE FAMILY COOKING

You Can Do Magic	Avco	4 8 73	3	13
Dreamboat	Avco	– 10 73	31	5
A Walkin' Miracle	Avco	13 4 73	6	10

LIND, BOB

Elusive Butterfly	Fontana	26 3 66	5	8

Remember The Rain	Fontana	- 5 66	46	1

LINDISFARNE

Meet Me On The Corner	Charisma	18 3 72	5	11
Lady Eleanor (re-issue)	Charisma	20 5 72	3	11
All Fall Down	Charisma	- 9 72	34	5

LITTLE EVA

The Locomotion	London	22 9 62	2	16
Keep Your Hands Off My Baby	London	- 1 63	30	5
Let's Turkey Trot	London	30 3 63	13	12
The Locomotion (re-issue)	London	19 8 72	11	5

(see also: BIG DEE IRWIN)

LITTLE RICHARD

Long Tall Sally	London	15 2 57	3	14
The Girl Can't Help It	London	15 3 57	4	11
She's Got It	London	22 3 57	8	8
Tutti Frutti	London	6 4 57	18	1
Lucille	London	5 7 57	7	7
Jenny Jenny	London	13 9 57	11	5
Keep A Knocking (But You Can't Come In)	London	7 12 57	15	2
Good Golly Miss Molly	London	7 3 58	8	7
Baby Face	London	10 1 59	2	11
By The Light Of The Silvery Moon	London	4 4 59	15	3
He Got What He Wanted	London	- 10 62	38	4
Bamalama Loo	London	27 6 64	20	7

LITTLE TONY

Too Good	Decca	2 1 60	13	4

LIVINGSTONE, DANDY

Suzanne Beware Of The Devil	Horse	23 9 72	14	11
Big City/Think About That	Horse	- 1 73	26	8

LOBO

Me And You And A Dog Named Boo	Philips	3 7 71	4	14
I'd Love You To Want Me (re-issue)	UK	22 6 74	5	11

LOCKLIN, HANK

Please Help Me I'm Falling	RCA	4 9 60	10	19
From Here, To There, To You	RCA	- 2 62	44	3
We're Gonna Go Fishin'	RCA	29 12 62	18	11
I Feel A Cry Coming On	RCA	- 5 66	29	8

LOCOMOTIVE

Rudy's In Love	Parlophone	- 10 68	25	11

LODGE, JOHN

see JUSTIN HAYWARD AND JOHN
   LODGE (BLUEJAYS)

LONDON, LAURIE

He's Got The Whole World In His Hands	Parlophone	29 11 57	12	8

LONDON STRING CHORALE

Galloping Home (Theme From 'Black Beauty')	Polydor	- 12 73	31	14

LONG AND THE SHORT

| The Letter | Decca | − 9 64 | 35 | 5 |
| Choc Ice | Decca | − 12 64 | 40 | 3 |

LONG, SHORTY

| Here Comes The Judge | T.Motown | − 7 68 | 30 | 7 |

LOPEZ, TRINI

If I Had A Hammer	Reprise	21 9 63	4	18
Kansas City	Reprise	− 12 63	35	5
I'm Comin' Home Cindy	Reprise	− 5 66	28	5
Gonna Get Along Without You Now	Reprise	− 4 67	41	5

LORDAN, JERRY

| Who Could Be Bluer? | Parlophone | 20 2 60 | 14 | 6 |
| Sing Like An Angel | Parlophone | − 5 60 | 36 | 2 |

LOREN, SOPHIA

see PETER SELLERS

LOS BRAVOS

| Black Is Black | Decca | 16 7 66 | 2 | 13 |
| I Don't Care | Decca | 8 10 66 | 16 | 11 |

LOS INDIOS TABAJARAS

| Maria Elena | RCA | 16 11 63 | 5 | 16 |

LOS MACHUCAMBOS

| Pepito | Decca | 26 8 61 | 19 | 9 |

JOE LOSS ORCHESTRA

Wheels Cha Cha	HMV	− 6 61	21	21
Sucu Sucu	HMV	− 10 61	48	1
The Maigret Theme	HMV	21 4 62	20	10
Must Be Madison	HMV	17 11 62	20	13
March Of The Mods	HMV	− 11 64	31	7

LOUDERMILK, JOHN D.

| The Language Of Love | RCA | 20 1 62 | 13 | 10 |

LOVE AFFAIR

Everlasting Love	CBS	13 1 68	1	12
Rainbow Valley	CBS	11 5 68	5	12
A Day Without Love	CBS	5 10 68	6	12
One Road	CBS	15 3 69	16	10
Bringing On Back The Good Times	CBS	2 8 69	9	10

LOVE SCULPTURE

| Sabre Dance | Parlophone | 14 12 68 | 6 | 14 |

LOVE UNLIMITED

| Walkin' In The Rain With The One I Love | UNI | 8 7 72 | 14 | 10 |
| It May Be Winter Outside | 20th Century | 15 2 75 | 11 | 9 |

LOVE UNLIMITED ORCHESTRA

| Love Theme | Pye | 9 2 74 | 10 | 10 |

LOVIN' SPOONFUL

Daydream	Pye	23	4 66	2	13
Summer In The City	Kama Sutra	30	7 66	8	11
Nashville Cats	Kama Sutra	–	1 67	26	7
Darling Be Home Soon	Kama Sutra	–	3 67	44	2

LOWE, JIM

The Green Door	London	8	11 56	10	5

LULU (AND THE LUVVERS)

Shout	Decca	6	6 64	7	14
Here Comes The Night	Decca	–	11 64	50	1
*Satisfied	Decca	–	4 65	50	1
Leave A Little Love	Decca	3	7 65	8	10
Try To Understand	Decca	–	9 65	25	8
The Boat That I Row	Columbia	29	4 67	6	11
Let's Pretend	Columbia	29	7 67	11	8
Love, Loves To Love, Love	Columbia	–	11 67	32	6
Me, The Peaceful Heart	Columbia	9	3 68	9	9
Boys	Columbia	29	6 68	15	7
I'm A Tiger	Columbia	23	11 68	9	11
Boom Bang-A-Bang	Columbia	29	3 69	4	13
Oh Me Oh My (I'm A Fool For You Baby)	Atco	–	11 69	47	2
The Man Who Sold The World	Polydor	2	2 74	3	9
Take Your Mama For A Ride	Chelsea	–	4 75	37	4

LUMAN, BOB

Let's Think About Living	Warner Bros.	23	9 60	7	18
Why Why Bye Bye	Warner Bros.	–	12 60	46	1
Great Snowman	Warner Bros.	–	4 61	49	2

LUVVERS

see LULU

LYMON, FRANKIE

see TEENAGERS

LYNCH, KENNY

Mountain Of Love	HMV	–	6 60	33	3
Puff	HMV	–	9 62	33	6
Up On The Roof	HMV	6	1 63	10	12
You Can Never Stop Me Loving You	HMV	13	7 63	10	13
Stand By Me	HMV	–	4 64	39	7
What Am I To You	HMV	–	8 64	37	6
I'll Stay By You	HMV	–	6 65	29	7

LYNN, PATTI

Johnny Angel	Fontana	–	5 62	37	5

LYNN, TAMMI

I'm Gonna Run Away From You (re-issue)	Mojo	5	6 71	4	14
I'm Gonna Run Away From You (re-issue)	Contempo	–	5 75	36	6

LYNN, VERA

My Son, My Son	Decca	–	10 54	1	12
A House With Love In It	Decca	30	11 56	17	6
Travellin' Home	Decca	5	7 57	20	1

*All Records To Here, Feature The LUVVERS

LYON, BARBARA

| Stowaway | Columbia | 24 6 55 | 12 | 8 |

LYTTLETON, HUMPHREY

| Bad Penny Blues | Parlophone | 13 7 56 | 17 | 3 |

McBETH, DAVID

| Mr. Blue | Pye | 31 10 59 | 14 | 2 |

McBRIDE, FRANKIE

| Five Little Fingers | Emerald | 14 10 67 | 19 | 15 |

McCAFFERTY, DAN

| Out Of Time | Mountain | - 9 75 | 41 | 3 |

(see also: NAZARETH)

McCALL, C.W.

| Convoy | MGM | 21 2 76 | 2 | 10 |

McCALLUM, DAVID

| Communication | Capitol | - 4 66 | 32 | 4 |

McCARTNEY, PAUL

Another Day	Apple	6 3 71	2	12
Back Seat Of My Car	Apple	- 8 71	39	5
Junior's Farm/Sally G	Apple	14 12 74	16	10
Listen To What The Man Said	EMI	7 6 75	6	8
Letting Go	EMI	- 10 75	41	3

(see also: BEATLES, McCARTNEY'S
    WINGS, WINGS)

McCARTNEY'S WINGS

My Love	Apple	21 4 73	9	11
Live And Let Die	Apple	16 6 73	9	13
Helen Wheels	Apple	24 11 73	12	12
Jet	Apple	2 3 74	7	9
Band On The Run	Apple	13 7 74	3	11

(see also: PAUL McCARTNEY, WINGS)

McCOY, VAN

| The Hustle | Avco | 14 6 75 | 3 | 12 |
| Change With The Times | Avco | - 11 75 | 36 | 4 |

McCOYS

| Hang On Sloopy | Immediate | 18 9 65 | 5 | 14 |
| Fever | Immediate | - 12 65 | 44 | 4 |

McCRAE, GEORGE

Rock Your Baby	Jay Boy	6 7 74	1	14
I Can't Leave You Alone	Jay Boy	19 10 74	9	9
You Can Have It All	Jay Boy	- 12 74	23	9
Sing A Happy Song	Jay Boy	- 3 75	38	4
It's Been So Long	Jay Boy	9 8 75	4	11
I Ain't Lying	Jay Boy	1 11 75	12	7
Honey I	Jay Boy	- 1 76	33	5

McDANIELS, GENE

| Tower Of Strength | London | - 11 61 | 49 | 2 |

CHAS McDEVITT SKIFFLE GROUP (WITH NANCY WHISKEY)

Freight Train	Oriole	13 4 57	5	15

McGEAR, MIKE
see SCAFFOLD

McGUINNESS FLINT

When I'm Dead And Gone	Capitol	5 12 70	2	15
Malt And Barley Blues	Capitol	15 5 71	5	12

McGUIRE, BARRY

Eve Of Destruction	RCA	18 9 65	3	13

McGUIRE SISTERS

No More	Vogue-Coral	4 4 55	20	1
Sincerely	Vogue-Coral	15 7 55	14	4
Sugar Time	Vogue-Coral	21 2 58	20	1

McKELLAR, KENNETH

A Man Without Love	Decca	- 3 66	30	4

McLAIN, TOMMY

Sweet Dreams	London	- 9 66	49	1

McLEAN, PAUL

Small Sad Sam	Top Rank	- 1 62	34	4

McTELL, RALPH

Streets Of London	Warner Bros.	14 12 74	2	12
Dreams Of You	Warner Bros.	- 12 75	36	6

MAAZEL AND THE NEW PHILHARMONIC ORCHESTRA

Thus Spake Zarathustra	Columbia	- 8 69	33	6

MACKENZIE, SCOTT

San Francisco (Flowers In Your Hair)	CBS	15 7 67	1	17
Like An Old Time Movie	CBS	- 11 67	50	1

MACKINTOSH, KEN

Raunchy	HMV	14 2 58	19	2

MACLEAN, DON

American Pie	Un.Artists	5 2 72	2	16
Vincent	Un.Artists	27 5 72	1	15
Everyday	Un.Artists	- 4 73	38	5

MACRAE, JOSH

Talkin' Army Blues	Rank	19 6 60	12	13
Wild Side Of Life	Rank	20 11 60	13	9
Messing About On The River	Rank	22 1 61	15	6

MAGIC LANTERNS

Excuse Me Baby	CBS	- 7 66	44	2

MAIN INGREDIENT

Just Don't Want To Be Lonely	RCA	- 6 74	27	7

MAKADOPOLOUS

Never On Sunday	Palette	- 10 60	36	14

MALCOLM, CARL

Fattie Bum Bum	UK	20 9 75	8	8

MAMAS AND PAPAS

California Dreamin'	RCA	- 4 66	23	9
Monday Monday	RCA	21 5 66	3	13
I Saw Her Again	RCA	13 8 66	11	11
Words Of Love	RCA	- 2 67	47	3
Dedicated To The One I Love	RCA	22 4 67	2	17
Creeque Alley	RCA	5 8 67	9	11

MANCHESTER UNITED F.C.

Manchester United	Decca	- 5 76	50	1

HENRY MANCINI ORCHESTRA

Moon River	RCA	- 12 61	41	4
How Soon	RCA	17 10 64	10	12
Theme From 'Cade's Country'	RCA	- 3 72	42	2

MANDEL, STEVE

see ERIC WEISSBERG

M AND O BAND

Let's Do The Hustle	Creole	27 3 76	16	6

MANFRED MANN

5-4-3-2-1	HMV	1 2 64	5	13
Hubble Bubble Toil And Trouble	HMV	25 4 64	11	8
Doo Wah Diddy Diddy	HMV	25 7 64	1	14
Sha La La	HMV	24 10 64	3	12
Come Tomorrow	HMV	23 1 65	4	9
Oh No Not My Baby	HMV	1 5 65	11	9
If You Gotta Go, Go Now	HMV	23 9 65	2	12
Pretty Flamingo	HMV	30 4 66	1	12
You Gave Me Somebody To Love	HMV	- 7 66	36	4
Just Like A Woman	Fontana	20 8 66	10	10
Semi-Detached Suburban Mr. Jones	Fontana	5 11 66	2	12
Ha! Ha! Said The Clown	Fontana	8 4 67	4	11
Sweet Pea	Fontana	- 5 67	36	4
The Mighty Quinn	Fontana	3 2 68	1	11
My Name Is Jack	Fontana	29 6 68	8	11
Fox On The Run	Fontana	18 1 69	5	12
Ragamuffin Man	Fontana	17 5 69	8	11
(see also: MANFRED MANN'S EARTHBAND)				

MANFRED MANN'S EARTHBAND

Joybringer	Vertigo	22 9 73	9	10
(see also: MANFRED MANN)				

MANHATTAN TRANSFER

Tuxedo Junction/Operator	RCA	- 2 76	24	6

MANILOW, BARRY

Mandy	Arista	15 3 75	11	9

JOHNNY MANN SINGERS

Up Up And Away	Liberty	29 7 67	6	13

MANTOVANI

Lonely Ballerina	Decca	11	2 55	16	4
Around The World	Decca	7	6 57	20	1
Exodus	Decca	26	3 61	20	7

MANUEL AND HIS MUSIC OF THE MOUNTAINS

Never On Sunday	Columbia	-	10 60	29	9
Somewhere My Love	Columbia	-	10 66	42	2
Roderigo's Guitar Concerto D'Aranjuez	EMI	14	2 76	3	9

MARAUDERS

That's What I Want	Decca	-	8 63	43	4

MARBLES

Only One Woman	Polydor	19	10 68	5	12
The Walls Fell Down	Polydor	-	3 69	29	6

MARCELS

Blue Moon	Pye Int.	26	3 61	1	13
Summertime	Pye	-	6 61	46	4

MARDI GRAS

Too Busy Thinkin' 'Bout My Baby	Bell	16	9 72	19	9

MARINI, MARINO

Volare	Durium	10	10 58	13	5
Come Prima	Durium	10	10 58	2	17

MARKHAM, PIGMEAT

Here Comes The Judge	Chess	3	8 68	19	8

MARLEY, BOB AND THE WAILERS

No Woman, No Cry	Island	-	9 75	22	8

MARMALADE

Lovin' Things	CBS	15	6 68	6	13
Wait For Me Marianne	CBS	-	10 68	30	5
Ob-La-Di, Ob-La-Da	CBS	21	12 68	1	20
Baby Make It Soon	CBS	5	7 69	9	13
Reflections Of My Life	Deram	10	1 70	3	12
Rainbow	Decca	1	8 70	3	14
My Little One	Decca	1	5 71	15	11
Cousin Norman	Decca	11	9 71	6	11
Back On The Road	Decca	-	11 71	35	8
Radancer	Decca	22	4 72	6	11
Falling Apart At The Seams	Target	13	3 76	9	11

MARSHALL, JOY

The More I See You	Decca	-	6 66	34	2

MARTHA (REEVES) AND THE VANDELLAS

Dancing In The Street	Stateside	-	10 64	28	8
Nowhere To Run	T.Motown	-	4 65	21	8
I'm Ready For Love	T.Motown	-	12 66	22	8
Jimmy Mack	T.Motown	-	4 67	21	9
*Honey Chile	T.Motown	-	1 68	30	9
Dancing In The Street (re-issue)	T.Motown	1	2 69	4	11
Nowhere To Run (re-issue)	T.Motown	-	4 69	42	3
Jimmy Mack (re-issue)	T.Motown	-	8 70	21	12

*Shown as: MARTHA REEVES AND THE VANDELLAS, from here

Forget Me Not (re-issue)	T.Motown	27	2 71	11	9
Bless You	T.Motown	-	1 72	33	5

MARTIN, DEAN

Sway	Capitol	-	10 54	10	7
How Do You Speak To An Angel	Capitol	-	10 54	15	4
Naughty Lady Of Shady Lane	Capitol	28	1 55	5	10
Mambo Italiano	Capitol	4	2 55	14	2
Let Me Go Lover	Capitol	25	2 55	3	9
Under The Bridges Of Paris	Capitol	4	4 55	6	8
Memories Are Made Of This	Capitol	10	2 56	1	14
Young And Foolish	Capitol	2	3 56	20	1
Return To Me	Capitol	27	6 58	2	16
Volare	Capitol	29	8 58	2	12
Everybody Loves Somebody	Capitol	18	9 64	11	13
The Door Is Still Open	Capitol	-	11 64	43	4
Gentle On My Mind	Reprise	1	3 69	2	23

MARTIN, TONY

Stranger In Paradise	HMV	22	4 55	7	13
Walk Hand In Hand	HMV	13	7 56	4	14

MARTINAS AND HIS ORCHESTRA

Cha Cha Momma Brown	Columbia	19	12 58	18	1

MARTINDALE, WINK

Deck Of Cards	London	19	12 59	19	1
Deck Of Cards (re-issue)	London	18	5 63	5	20
Deck Of Cards (re-issue)	Dot	-	10 73	22	11

MARTINO, AL

Story Of Tina	Capitol	-	10 54	11	7
Wanted	Capitol	-	10 54	17	3
Man From Laramie	Capitol	23	9 55	19	3
Summer Time	Top Rank	-	3 60	49	1
I Love You Because	Capitol	-	8 63	48	1
Spanish Eyes (re-issue)	Capitol	28	7 73	5	22

MARVELLETTES

When You're Young And In Love	T.Motown	15	7 67	13	10

MARVIN, LEE AND CLINT EASTWOOD

Wanderin' Star/I Talked To The Trees	Paramount	14	2 70	1	20

MARVIN, HANK

see CLIFF RICHARD

MASSIEL

La La La	Philips	-	4 68	35	4

MASTERS, SAMMY

Rocking Red Wing	Warner Bros.	-	6 60	36	5

MASTERSINGERS

Highway Code	Parlophone	-	4 66	25	6
Weather Forecast	Parlophone	-	11 66	45	2

MATHEWS, AL

Fool	CBS	13	9 75	16	8

MATHIS, JOHNNY

A Certain Smile	Fontana	3 10 58	4	14
Winter Wonderland	Fontana	26 12 58	17	1
Someone	Fontana	1 8 59	8	12
The Best Of Everything	Fontana	28 11 59	18	1
Misty	Fontana	30 1 60	13	4
You Are Beautiful	Fontana	– 3 60	39	7
Starbright	Fontana	– 7 60	47	2
My Love For You	Fontana	30 9 60	14	17
What Will Mary Say	CBS	– 4 63	49	1
I'm Stone In Love With You	CBS	22 2 75	10	12

MATTHEWS SOUTHERN COMFORT

Woodstock	UNI	17 10 70	1	17

MATTHIEU, MIRIELLE

La Dernière Valse	Columbia	– 12 67	26	7

MAUGHAN, SUSAN

Bobby's Girl	Philips	3 11 62	3	19
Hand A Hankerchief To Helen	Philips	– 2 63	41	3
She's New To You	Philips	– 5 63	45	3

MAURIAT, PAUL AND HIS ORCHESTRA

Love Is Blue	Philips	23 3 68	12	13

MAY, BILLY

Main Title	Capitol	4 5 56	7	9

MAY, MARY

Anyone Who Had A Heart	Fontana	– 2 64	49	1

MAYFIELD, CURTIS

Move On Up	Buddah	28 8 71	12	10

MAYTALS

Monkey Man	Trojan	– 4 70	47	4

MEDICINE HEAD

(And The) Pictures In The Sky	Dandelion	– 6 71	22	8
One And One Is One	Polydor	19 5 73	3	13
Rising Sun	Polydor	18 8 73	11	9
Slip And Slide	Polydor	– 2 74	22	7

MEEHAN, TONY

Song Of Mexico	Decca	– 1 64	39	4

(see also: JET HARRIS AND TONY
   MEEHAN, SHADOWS)

MELACHRINO, GEORGE

Autumn Concerto	HMV	19 10 56	18	4

MELANIE

Ruby Tuesday	Buddah	24 10 70	9	17
Brand New Key	Buddah	15 1 72	4	12
Will You Still Love Me Tomorrow	Neighborhood	– 2 74	37	5

MELODIANS

Sweet Sensation	Trojan	– 1 70	41	2

MELVIN, HAROLD AND THE BLUENOTES

If You Don't Know Me By Now	CBS	27 1 73	9	9
The Love I Lost	Philadelphia	- 1 74	21	8
Satisfaction Guaranteed	Philadelphia	- 4 74	32	6
Get Out	Philadelphia	- 5 75	35	5

MENZIES, IAN

Fish Man	Nixa	18 9 60	15	8

MERSEYBEATS

It's Love That Really Counts	Fontana	- 9 63	24	12
I Think Of You	Fontana	1 2 64	5	17
Don't Turn Around	Fontana	2 5 64	13	11
Wishin' And Hopin'	Fontana	18 7 64	13	10
Last Night	Fontana	- 11 64	40	3
I Love You Yes I Do	Fontana	- 10 65	25	8
I Stand Accused	Fontana	- 1 66	38	3
(see also: MERSEYS)				

MERSEYS (FORMERLY MERSEYBEATS)

Sorrow	Fontana	14 5 66	4	12

M.F.S.B. (MOTHER, FATHER, SISTER, BROTHER)

T.S.O.P. (The Sound Of Philadelphia)	Philadelphia	- 4 74	22	8
Sexy	Philadelphia	- 7 75	37	6

MICHELL, KEITH

I'll Give You The Earth	Spark	- 3 71	30	11

MICROBE (IAN DOODY)

Groovy Baby	CBS	- 5 69	29	7

MIDDLE OF THE ROAD

Chirpy Chirpy Cheep Cheep	RCA	12 6 71	1	33
Tweedle Dee Tweedle Dum	RCA	18 9 71	2	17
Soley Soley	RCA	18 12 71	5	12
Sacremento	RCA	- 3 72	23	8
Samson And Delilah	RCA	- 7 72	26	6

MIGHTY AVENGERS

So Much In Love	Decca	- 11 64	46	2

MIGIL FIVE

Mockingbird Hill	Pye	18 4 64	10	14
Near You	Pye	- 7 64	31	7

MIKI AND GRIFF

Hold Back Tomorrow	Pye	3 10 59	20	1
Rockin' Alone	Pye	- 10 60	44	3
Little Bitty Tear	Pye	24 3 62	19	13
I Wanna Stay Here	Pye	- 8 63	23	7

MILES, JOHN

Highfly	Decca	1 11 75	17	6
Music	Decca	27 3 76	3	9

MILLER, GARY

Yellow Rose Of Texas	Nixa	21 10 55	13	5
Robin Hood	Nixa	13 1 56	11	6
The Ballad Of Davy Crockett	Pye Nixa	21 1 56	18	1
Garden Of Eden	Pye Nixa	11 1 57	12	4

The Story Of My Life	Pye Nixa	17	1 58	10	5
The Night Is Young/There Goes That Song Again	Pye	-	12 61	29	9

GLENN MILLER ORCHESTRA

Moonlight Serenade/Little Brown Jug (re-issue)	RCA	7	2 76	13	8

MILLER, JODY

Home Of The Brave	Capitol	-	10 65	49	1

MILLER, MITCH

Yellow Rose Of Texas	Philips	7	10 55	2	13

MILLER, NED

From A Jack To A King	London	16	3 63	2	20
Do What You Do Do, Well	London	-	2 65	48	1

MILLER, ROGER

King Of The Road	Philips	17	4 65	1	15
Engine Engine No. 9	Philips	-	6 65	33	5
Kansas City Star	Philips	-	10 65	48	1
England Swings	Philips	22	1 66	13	8
Little Green Apples	Philips	11	5 68	19	10
Little Green Apples (re-issue)	Mercury	-	4 69	40	3

MILLER, SUZI

Happy Days, Lonely Nights	Decca	21	1 55	14	2

MILLICAN AND NESBITT

Vaya Con Dios	Pye	5	1 74	20	11
For Old Time's Sake	Pye	-	5 74	38	3

MILLIE (SMALL)

My Boy Lollipop	Fontana	11	4 64	2	18
Sweet William	Fontana	-	6 64	30	9
Bloodshot Eyes	Fontana	-	11 65	48	1

MILLS, GARY

Look For A Star	Top Rank	3	7 60	5	17
Top Teen Baby	Top Rank	21	10 60	20	8
I'll Step Down	Decca	-	7 61	39	5

MILLS, HAYLEY

Let's Get Together	Decca	14	10 61	11	11

MRS. MILLS

Mrs. Mills Medley	Parlophone	-	12 61	21	6

MINDBENDERS

A Groovy Kind Of Love	Fontana	29	1 66	2	14
Can't Live With You, Can't Live Without You	Fontana	-	5 66	28	7
Ashes To Ashes	Fontana	17	9 66	14	9
The Letter	Fontana	-	9 67	42	4

(see also: WAYNE FONTANA)

MINEO, SAL

Start Movin'	Philips	26	7 57	11	6

MINGRABI, MARCELLO

Zorba's Dance	Durium	14 8 65	6	16

MIRACLES

Love Machine (see also: SMOKEY ROBINSON)	T.Motown	17 1 76	3	9

MISS X

Christine	Ember	- 8 63	37	6

MITCHELL, GUY

Singing The Blues	Philips	7 12 56	1	20
Knee Deep In The Blues	Philips	22 2 57	3	11
Rock-a-Billy	Philips	26 4 57	1	11
Call Rosie On The Phone	Philips	18 10 57	17	3
Heartaches By The Number	Philips	28 11 59	5	8

MITCHELL, JONI

Big Yellow Taxi	Reprise	25 7 70	11	15

MITCHELL, WILLIE

Soul Seranade	London	- 4 68	43	1

MIXTURES

Pushbike Song	Polydor	23 1 71	2	20

MODUGNO, DOMENICO

Volare	Oriole	5 9 58	13	8

MOJOS

Everything's All Right	Decca	11 4 64	9	10
Why Not Tonight	Decca	- 6 64	25	10
Seven Daffodils	Decca	- 9 64	30	5

MOMENTS (*AND WHATNAUTS)

Girls*	All Platinum	15 3 75	3	10
Dolly My Love	All Platinum	9 8 75	10	9
Look At Me (I'm In Love)	All Platinum	- 10 75	42	3

MONEY, ZOOT AND THE BIG ROLL BAND

Big Time Operator	Columbia	- 8 66	25	8

MONKEES

I'm A Believer	RCA	14 1 67	1	17
Last Train To Clarksville	RCA	- 1 67	23	7
A Little Bit Me, A Little Bit You	RCA	8 4 67	3	12
Alternate Title	RCA	1 7 67	2	12
Pleasant Valley Sunday	RCA	26 8 67	11	8
Daydream Believer	RCA	2 12 67	5	17
Valleri	RCA	6 4 68	12	9
D.W. Washburn	RCA	6 7 68	17	6
Teardrop City	RCA	- 3 69	44	1
Someday Man	RCA	- 6 69	47	1

MONRO, MATT

Portrait Of My Love	Parlophone	18 12 60	5	16
My Kind Of Girl	Parlophone	26 2 61	5	12
Why Not Now/Can This Be Love	Parlophone	- 5 61	24	8

Gonna Build A Mountain	Parlophone	- 9 61	44	3
Softly As I Leave You	Parlophone	3 3 62	10	18
When Love Comes Along	Parlophone	- 6 62	46	3
My Love And Devotion	Parlophone	- 11 62	29	5
From Russia With Love	Parlophone	30 11 63	20	13
Walk Away	Parlophone	10 10 64	4	20
For Mama	Parlophone	- 12 64	23	4
Without You	Parlophone	- 3 65	33	5
Yesterday	Parlophone	30 10 65	8	12
And You Smiled	EMI	- 11 73	28	8

MONROE, GERRY

Sally	Chapter One	13 6 70	4	20
Cry	Chapter One	- 9 70	38	5
My Prayer	Chapter One	5 12 70	9	13
It's A Sin To Tell A Lie	Chapter One	8 5 71	13	12
Little Drops Of Silver	Chapter One	- 8 71	37	6
Girl Of My Dreams	Chapter One	- 2 72	43	2

MONTENEGRO, HUGO AND HIS ORCHESTRA

The Good, The Bad And The Ugly	RCA	19 10 68	1	26
Hang 'Em High	RCA	- 1 69	50	1

MONTEZ, CHRIS

Let's Dance	London	20 10 62	2	18
Some Kinda Fun	London	27 1 63	10	9
The More I See You	Pye	16 7 66	3	13
There Will Never Be Another You	Pye	- 9 66	37	4
Let's Dance (re-issue)	London	4 11 72	9	14

MOODY BLUES

Go Now	Decca	2 1 65	1	14
I Don't Want To Go On Without You	Decca	- 3 65	33	8
From the Bottom Of My Heart	Decca	- 6 65	22	9
Everyday	Decca	- 12 65	44	2
Nights In White Satin	Deram	17 2 68	19	11
Voices In The Sky	Deram	- 8 68	23	10
Ride My See Saw	Deram	- 12 68	42	1
Question	Threshold	9 5 70	2	12
Isn't Life Strange?	Threshold	27 5 72	13	10
Nights In White Satin (re-issue)	Deram	16 12 72	9	11
I'm Just A Singer (In A Rock And Roll Band)	Threshold	- 2 73	36	4

MOONTREKKERS

Night Of The Vampire	Parlophone	- 11 61	50	1

MOORE, DUDLEY

see PETER COOK

MORGAN, DERRICK

Moon Hop	Crab	- 1 70	49	1

MORGAN, JANE

The Day The Rains Came Down	London	12 12 58	4	11
Romantica	London	- 7 60	39	5

MORGAN, RAY

The Long And Winding Road	B & C	-	7 70	32	6

MOST, MICKIE

Mr. Porter	Decca	-	7 63	45	1

MOTOWN SPINNERS

It's A Shame	T.Motown	19	12 70	20	11
(see also: DETROIT SPINNERS)					

MOTT THE HOOPLE

All The Young Dudes	CBS	19	8 72	3	11
Honaloochie Boogie	CBS	7	7 73	12	9
All The Way From Memphis	CBS	22	9 73	10	8
Roll Away The Stone	CBS	1	12 73	8	12
Golden Age Of Rock And Roll	CBS	13	4 74	16	7
Foxy Foxy	CBS	-	6 74	33	5
Saturday Gig	CBS	-	11 74	41	3

MOUTH AND MACNEAL

I See A Star	Decca	25	5 74	8	10

MOVE

Night Of Fear	Deram	14	1 67	2	10
I Can Hear The Grass Grow	Deram	22	4 67	5	10
Flowers In The Rain	R.Zonophone	16	9 67	2	13
Fire Brigade	R.Zonophone	17	2 68	3	12
Blackberry Way	R.Zonophone	18	1 69	1	11
Curly	R.Zonophone	9	8 69	12	12
Brontosaurus	R.Zonophone	9	5 70	7	10
Tonight	Harvest	17	7 71	11	10
China Town	Harvest	-	10 71	23	8
California Man	Harvest	27	5 72	7	14

MUD

Crazy	RAK	7	4 73	12	12
Hypnosis	RAK	4	8 73	16	13
Dyna-Mite	RAK	3	11 73	4	12
Tiger Feet	RAK	19	1 74	1	11
The Cat Crept In	RAK	13	4 74	2	9
Rocket	RAK	3	8 74	6	9
Lonely This Christmas	RAK	7	12 74	1	9
The Secrets That You Keep	RAK	22	2 75	3	9
Oh Boy	RAK	26	4 75	1	9
Moonshine Sally	RAK	28	6 75	10	9
One Night	RAK	-	8 75	32	5
L - L - Lucy	Pr.Stock	11	10 75	10	7
Show Me You're A Woman	Pr.Stock	6	12 75	8	8

MUDLARKS

Lollipop	Columbia	2	5 58	5	9
Book Of Love	Columbia	13	6 58	6	7

MULDAUR, MARIA

Midnight At The Oasis	Reprise	-	6 74	21	8

MUNGO JERRY

In The Summertime	Dawn	6	6 70	1	20
Baby Jump	Dawn	20	2 71	1	13
Lady Rose	Dawn	5	6 71	5	12

You Don't Have To Be In The Army (To Fight In The War)	Dawn	9 10 71	13	8
Open Up	Dawn	- 4 72	21	8
Alright, Alright, Alright	Dawn	21 7 73	3	11
Wild Love	Dawn	- 11 73	32	5
Long Legged Woman Dressed In Black	Dawn	27 4 74	13	10

MURRAY, ANNE

Snowbird	Capitol	- 10 70	23	17
Destiny	Capitol	- 10 72	41	4

MURRAY, RUBY

Heartbeat	Columbia	- 12 54	3	11
Softly Softly	Columbia	28 1 55	1	23
Happy Days And Lonely Nights	Columbia	4 2 55	6	8
If Anyone Finds This I Love You	Columbia	11 3 55	4	11
Let Me Go Lover	Columbia	4 3 55	5	7
Evermore	Columbia	1 7 55	3	17
I'll Come When You Call	Columbia	14 10 55	6	7
You Are My First Love	Columbia	31 8 56	19	1
Real Love	Columbia	12 12 58	18	3
Goodbye Jimmy Goodbye	Columbia	20 6 59	10	7

NAPOLEON XIV

They're Coming To Take Me Away Ha_Ha	Warner Bros.	20 8 66	4	10

NASH, JOHNNY

Hold Me Tight	R.Zonophone	24 8 68	5	16
You Got Soul	Major Minor	25 1 69	6	12
Cupid	Major Minor	19 4 69	6	13
Stir It Up	CBS	22 4 71	13	11
I Can See Clearly Now	CBS	8 7 72	5	15
There Are More Questions Than Answers	CBS	14 10 72	9	9
Tears On My Pillow	CBS	21 6 75	1	11
Let's Be Friends	CBS	- 10 75	42	3

NASHVILLE TEENS

Tobacco Road	Decca	25 7 64	6	13
Google Eye	Decca	7 11 64	10	10
Find My Way Back Home	Decca	- 3 65	34	5
This Little Bird	Decca	- 5 65	38	4
The Hard Way	Decca	- 2 66	45	3

NATURALS

I Should Have Known Better	Parlophone	- 8 64	24	9

NAZARETH

Broken Down Angel	Mooncrest	19 5 73	9	11
Bad Bad Boy	Mooncrest	28 7 73	10	9
This Flight Tonight	Mooncrest	27 10 73	11	11
Shanghai'd In Shanghai	Mooncrest	- 3 74	41	4
My White Bicycle	Mooncrest	28 6 75	14	8
Holy Roller	Mountain	- 11 75	36	4

NELSON, RICKY (*RICK)

Stood Up	London	22 2 58	18	1
Poor Little Fool	London	22 8 58	5	13
Someday	London	21 11 58	9	9

It's Late/There'll Never Be Anyone Else But You	London	18	4 59	3	18
Just A Little Too Much/ Sweeter Than You	London	5	9 59	9	8
Young Emotions	London	–	7 60	40	1
Hello Mary Lou/Travellin' Man	London	14	5 61	3	18
*Everlovin'	London	2	12 61	20	6
*Young World	London	5	5 62	19	13
*Teenage Idol	London	–	8 62	39	4
*It's Up To You	London	–	1 63	22	9
*Fools Rush In	Brunswick	2	11 63	12	9
*For You	Brunswick	15	2 64	14	10
*Garden Party	MCA	–	10 72	41	4

NELSON, SANDY

Teen Beat	Top Rank	31	10 59	7	11
Let There Be Drums	London	9	12 61	2	17
Drums Are My Beat	London	–	3 62	30	6
Drummin' Up A Storm	London	–	6 62	39	8

NERO AND THE GLADIATORS

Entry Of The Gladiators	Decca	–	3 61	37	5
In The Hall Of The Mountain King	Decca	–	7 61	48	1

NEW GENERATION

Smokey Blues Away	Spark	–	6 68	38	4

NEW SEEKERS

What Have They Done To My Song, Ma	Philips	–	10 70	44	2
Never-Ending Song Of Love	Philips	24	7 71	2	19
I'd Like To Teach The World To Sing	Polydor	25	12 71	1	21
Beg, Steal, Or Borrow	Polydor	11	3 72	2	14
Circles	Polydor	1	7 72	4	13
Come Softly To Me	Polydor	20	1 73	20	11
Pinball Wizard/See Me, Feel Me	Polydor	10	3 73	16	8
Nevertheless (I'm In Love With You)	Polydor	–	4 73	34	5
(featuring EVE GRAHAM) Goodbye Is Just Another Word	Polydor	–	6 73	36	5
You Won't Find Another Fool Like Me	Polydor	1	12 73	1	16
I Get A Little Sentimental Over You	Polydor	16	3 74	5	9

NEW VAUDEVILLE BAND

Winchester Cathedral	Fontana	24	9 66	4	19
Peek A Boo	Fontana	11	2 67	7	11
Finchley Central	Fontana	27	5 67	11	8
Green Street Green	Fontana	–	8 67	37	4

NEW WORLD

Rose Garden	RAK	13	3 71	15	12
Tom Tom Turnaround	RAK	10	7 71	6	15
Kara Kara	RAK	8	1 72	17	13
Sister Jane	RAK	27	5 72	9	13
Roof Top Singing	RAK	–	5 73	50	1

NEW YORK CITY

| I'm Doing Fine Now | RCA | 25 | 8 | 73 | 20 | 11 |

NEWBEATS

| Bread And Butter | Hickory | 3 | 10 | 64 | 15 | 9 |
| Run Baby Run (re-issue) | London | 13 | 11 | 71 | 10 | 13 |

NEWLEY, ANTHONY

Idle On Parade EP	Decca	2	5	59	13	2
I've Waited So Long	Decca	2	5	59	4	13
Personality	Decca	20	6	59	6	10
Why	Decca	9	1	60	1	12
Do You Mind?	Decca	20	3	60	2	15
If She Could Come To You	Decca	17	7	60	7	15
Strawberry Fair	Decca	20	11	60	3	11
And The Heavens Cried	Decca	5	3	61	8	12
Pop Goes The Weasel/Bee-Bum	Decca	4	6	61	9	9
What Kind Of Fool Am I	Decca	-	7	61	36	8
D-Darling	Decca	-	1	62	25	6
That Noise	Decca	-	7	62	34	5

NEWMAN, BRAD

| Somebody To Love | Fontana | - | 2 | 62 | 47 | 2 |

NEWMAN, THUNDERCLAP

| Something In The Air | Track | 21 | 6 | 69 | 1 | 12 |
| Accidents | Track | - | 6 | 70 | 46 | 1 |

NEWTON-JOHN, OLIVIA

If Not For You	Pye	3	4	71	7	12
Banks Of The Ohio	Pye	13	11	71	6	17
What Is Life	Pye	8	4	72	16	8
Take Me Home Country Roads	Pye	10	2	73	15	13
Long Live Love	Pye	30	3	74	11	9
I Honestly Love You	Pye	-	10	74	22	6

NICE

| America | Immediate | - | 7 | 68 | 21 | 15 |

NICHOLLS, SUE

| Where Will You Be | Pye | 20 | 7 | 68 | 17 | 8 |

NIGHTINGALE, MAXINE

| Right Back Where We Started From | Un.Artists | 15 | 11 | 75 | 8 | 9 |

NILSSON

Everybody's Talkin'	RCA	-	9	69	23	14
Without You	RCA	19	2	72	1	19
Coconut	RCA	-	6	72	42	5

NINA AND FREDERICK

Listen To The Ocean	Columbia	-	4	60	46	1
Little Donkey	Columbia	20	11	60	5	10
Longtime Boy	Columbia	-	9	61	43	3
Sucu Sucu	Columbia	7	10	61	17	13

1910 FRUITGUM CO.

| Simon Says | Pye | 6 | 4 | 68 | 2 | 16 |

NIRVANA

Rainbow Chaser	Island	–	5 68	34	6

NOONE, PETER

Lady Barbara	RAK	12	12 70	13	13
(with HERMAN'S HERMITS)					
Oh You Pretty Thing	RAK	29	5 71	12	9
(see also: HERMAN'S HERMITS)					

NOTES, FREDDIE AND THE RUDIES

Montego Bay	Trojan	–	10 70	45	2

O'BRIEN, DERMOT

Merry Ploughboy	Envoy	–	10 66	46	2

OCEAN, BILLY

Love Really Hurts Without You	GTO	28	2 76	2	10

O'CONNOR, DES

Careless Hands	Columbia	25	11 67	6	17
I Pretend	Columbia	15	6 68	1	36
1, 2, 3, O'Leary	Columbia	30	11 68	4	11
Dick-A-Dum-Dum	Columbia	31	5 69	14	10
Loneliness	Columbia	20	12 69	18	11
I'll Go On Hoping	Columbia	–	3 70	30	7
Tips Of My Fingers	Columbia	17	10 70	15	15

ODETTA

see HARRY BELAFONTE

OHIO EXPRESS

Yummy Yummy Yummy	Pye	29	6 68	5	15

O'JAYS

Back Stabbers	CBS	14	10 72	14	9
Love Train	CBS	24	3 73	9	13
I Love Music	Philadelphia	21	2 76	13	9

OLDFIELD, MIKE

Mike Oldfield's Single	Virgin	–	7 74	31	6
(Theme From 'Tubular Bells')					
In Dulce Jubilo/On Horseback	Virgin	17	1 76	4	10

OLIVER

Good Morning Starshine	CBS	30	8 69	6	16

OLYMPICS

Western Movies	HMV	10	10 58	12	7
I Wish I Could Shimmy Like My Sister Kate	Vogue	–	1 61	40	1

ONO, YOKO

see JOHN LENNON

OFARIM, ESTHER AND ABI

Cinderella Rockafella	Fontana	24	2 68	1	13
One More Dance	Philips	6	7 68	13	9

ORBISON, ROY

Only The Lonely	London	14 8 60	1	24
Blue Angel/Today's Teardrops	London	30 10 60	11	15
Runnin' Scared	London	21 5 61	9	15
Cryin'	London	- 7 61	25	9
Dream Baby	London	17 3 62	2	14
The Crowd	London	- 6 62	40	4
Workin' For The Man	London	- 11 62	50	1
In Dreams	London	30 3 63	6	22
Falling	London	8 6 63	9	11
Blue Bayou/Mean Woman Blues	London	28 9 63	3	19
Borne On The Wind	London	7 3 64	15	10
It's Over	London	9 5 64	1	16
Oh Pretty Woman	London	18 9 64	1	17
Pretty Paper	London	28 11 64	6	11
Goodnight	London	20 2 65	14	9
(Say) You're My Girl	London	- 7 65	23	8
Ride Away	London	- 9 65	34	6
Crawlin' Back	London	4 12 65	19	8
Breakin' Up Is Breakin' My Heart	London	- 1 66	23	6
Twinkle Toes	London	- 4 66	29	5
Lana	London	2 7 66	15	9
Too Soon To Know	London	27 8 66	3	17
There Won't Be Many Coming Home	London	17 12 66	12	9
So Good	London	- 2 67	32	6
Walk On	London	- 7 68	38	10
Heartache	London	- 9 68	44	4
My Friend	London	- 5 69	35	5
Penny Arcade	London	- 9 69	27	12

ORLANDO, TONY

Bless You	Fontana	30 9 61	7	11

(see also: DAWN)

ORLONS

Don't Hang On	Cameo P'way	- 12 62	39	3

OSBOURNE, TONY

Man From Madrid	HMV	- 2 61	50	1
The Shepherd's Song	Philips	- 2 73	46	2

OSIBISA

Sunshine Day	Bronze	31 1 76	17	6

OSMOND, DONNY

Puppy Love	MGM	24 6 72	1	18
Too Young	MGM	23 9 72	5	13
Why	MGM	18 11 72	3	21
12th Of Never	MGM	10 7 73	1	14
Young Love	MGM	18 8 73	1	10
When I Fall In Love	MGM	17 11 73	4	13
Where Did All The Good Times Go?	MGM	14 12 74	18	10

(see also: DONNY AND MARIE OSMOND)

OSMOND, DONNY AND MARIE

I'm Leaving It All Up To You	MGM	17 8 74	2	12
Morning Side Of The Mountain	MGM	18 1 75	5	11
Make The World Go Away	MGM	5 7 75	18	6
Deep Purple	MGM	- 1 76	25	7

OSMOND, LITTLE JIMMY

Long-Haired Lover From Liverpool	MGM	9 12 72	1	27
Tweedle Dee	MGM	7 4 73	4	12
I'm Gonna Knock On Your Door	MGM	13 4 74	11	10

OSMOND, MARIE

Paper Roses	MGM	24 11 73	2	15

(see also: DONNY AND MARIE OSMOND)

OSMONDS

One Bad Apple	MGM	- 3 71	43	1
Down By The Lazy River	MGM	- 3 72	40	5
Crazy Horses	MGM	18 11 72	2	18
Going Home	MGM	14 7 73	4	10
Let Me In	MGM	3 11 73	2	14
I Can't Stop (re-issue)	MGM	11 5 74	12	10
Love Me For A Reason	MGM	24 8 74	1	9
Having A Party	MGM	- 3 75	28	8
The Proud One	MGM	31 5 75	5	8
I'm Still Gonna Need You	MGM	- 11 75	32	4

O'SULLIVAN, GILBERT

Nothing Rhymed	MAM	12 12 70	8	12
Underneath The Blanket Go	MAM	- 4 71	40	4
We Will	MAM	28 8 71	16	11
No Matter How I Try	MAM	4 12 71	5	13
Alone Again (Naturally)	MAM	18 3 72	3	12
Ooh-Wakka-Doo-Wakka-Day	MAM	24 6 72	8	12
Clair	MAM	21 10 72	1	14
Get Down	MAM	24 3 73	1	13
Ooh Baby	MAM	29 9 73	18	7
Why Oh Why Oh Why	MAM	17 11 73	6	14
Happiness Is Me And You	MAM	2 3 74	19	7
A Woman's Place	MAM	- 8 74	42	3
Christmas Song	MAM	- 12 74	44	1
I Don't Love You But I Think I Like You	MAM	28 6 75	14	6

JOHNNY OTIS SHOW (*WITH MARIE ADAMS AND THE THREE TONS OF JOY)

Ma (He's Making Eyes At Me)*	Capitol	22 11 57	2	15
Bye Bye Baby	Capitol	7 2 58	17	3

OUTLAWS

Swingin' Low	HMV	- 4 61	46	2
Ambush	HMV	- 6 61	43	2

OVERLANDERS

Michelle	Pye	22 1 66	1	10

OWEN, REG

Manhattan Spiritual	Pye Int.	7 3 59	18	3
Obsession	Palette	- 10 60	43	3

PACKABEATS

As Long As He Needs Me	Columbia	- 2 61	49	1

PAGE, HAL AND THE WHALERS

Going Back To My Home Town	Melodisc	- 8 60	50	1

PAGLIARO
Loving You Ain't Easy	Pye	–	2 72	31	7

PAPER DOLLS
Something Here In My Heart	Pye	20	4 68	11	13

PAPER LACE
Billy Don't Be A Hero	Bus Stop	2	3 74	1	14
The Night Chicago Died	Bus Stop	11	5 74	3	11
Black Eyed Boys	Bus Stop	14	9 74	11	9

PARAMOUNTS
Poison Ivy	Parlophone	–	1 64	35	7

NORRIE PARAMOUR ORCHESTRA
Theme From 'A Summer Place'	Columbia	–	3 60	36	2
Theme From 'Z Cars'	Columbia	–	3 62	33	6

PARCHMENT
Light Up The Fire	Pye	–	9 72	31	5

SIMON PARK ORCHESTRA
Eye Level	Columbia	–	11 72	41	2
Eye Level (re-issue)	Columbia	22	9 73	1	22

PARKER, ROBERT
Barefootin'	Island	3	9 66	19	9

PARKINSON, JIMMY
The Great Pretender	**Columbia**	2	3 56	10	10
Walk Hand In Hand	Columbia	4	8 56	18	2
Middle Of The House	Columbia	7	12 56	20	1

PARRISH, DEAN
I'm On My Way (re-issue)	UK	–	2 75	38	4

PARTRIDGE, DON
Rosie	Columbia	24	2 68	4	10
Blue Eyes	Columbia	8	6 68	3	13
Breakfast On Pluto	Columbia	–	2 69	26	7

PARTRIDGE FAMILY (FEATURING DAVID CASSIDY)
I Think I Love You	Bell	27	2 71	18	10
It's One Of Those Nights (Yes Love)	Bell	18	3 72	11	11
Breaking Up Is Hard To Do	Bell	15	7 72	3	13
Looking Through The Eyes Of Love	Bell	17	2 73	9	9
Walking In The Rain	Bell	2	6 73	10	11
(see also: DAVID CASSIDY)					

PAUL AND PAULA
Hey Paula	Philips	2	3 63	8	17
Young Lovers	Philips	11	5 63	9	12

PAUL, BILLY
Me And Mrs. Jones	Epic	27	1 73	12	9
Thanks For Saving My Life	Philadelphia	–	1 74	33	6

PAUL, LYN

It Ought To Sell A Million (see also: NEW SEEKERS)	Polydor	-	6 75	37	6

PAVONE, RITA

Heart	RCA	-	12 66	27	12
You Only You	RCA	-	1 67	21	7

PAYNE, FREDA

Band Of Gold	Invictus	12	9 70	1	19
Deeper And Deeper	Invictus	-	11 70	33	9
Cherish What Is Dear To You	Invictus	-	3 71	46	2

PEARLS

Third Finger Left Hand	Bell	-	4 72	37	6
You Came, You Saw, You Conquered	Bell	-	9 72	32	5
You Are Everything	Bell	-	3 73	41	3
Guilty	Bell	22	6 74	10	10

JOHNNY PEARSON ORCHESTRA

Sleepy Shores ('Owen M.D. Theme)	P.Farthing	25	12 71	8	12

PEDDLERS

Let The Sunshine In	Philips	-	1 65	50	1
Birth	CBS	20	9 69	17	9
Girlie	CBS	-	1 70	34	4

PEEBLES, ANNE

I Can't Stand The Rain	London	-	4 74	41	3

PEERS, DONALD

Games That Lovers Play	Parlophone	-	12 66	46	1
Please Don't Go	Columbia	1	2 69	3	20
Give Me One More Chance	Decca	-	6 72	36	6

PENTANGLE

Once I Had A Sweetheart	Big T	-	5 69	46	1
Light Flight	Big T	-	2 70	45	3

PEOPLE'S CHOICE

Do It Anyway You Wanna	Philadelphia	-	9 75	36	5

PEPPERMINT, DANNY AND THE JUMPING JACKS

Peppermint Twist	London	-	1 62	26	8

PEPPERS

Pepper Box	Spark	9	11 74	6	12

PERCIVAL, LANCE

Shame And Scandal In The Family	Parlophone	-	10 65	37	3

PERICOLI, EMILIO

Al Di Da	Warner Bros.	-	6 62	30	14

PERKINS, CARL

Blue Suede Shoes	London	18	5 56	13	7

PERRY, STEVE

Step By Step	HMV	– 7 60	41	1

PETER AND GORDON

World Without Love	Columbia	28 3 64	1	13
Nobody I Know	Columbia	20 6 64	10	11
True Love Ways	Columbia	24 4 65	2	15
To Know You Is To Love You	Columbia	3 7 65	5	10
Baby I'm Yours	Columbia	13 11 65	19	9
Woman	Columbia	– 2 66	28	7
Lady Godiva	Columbia	15 10 66	16	11

PETER, PAUL AND MARY

Blowing In The Wind	Warner Bros.	9 11 63	13	16
Go Tell It On The Mountain	Warner Bros.	– 4 64	33	4
The Times They Are A-Changin'	Warner Bros.	– 10 64	44	2
Leaving On A Jet Plane	Warner Bros.	24 1 70	2	14

PETERS AND LEE

Welcome Home	Philips	9 6 73	1	24
By Your Side	Philips	– 11 73	39	4
Don't Stay Away Too Long	Philips	27 4 74	3	15
Rainbow	Philips	7 9 74	17	7
Hey Mr. Music Man	Philips	3 4 76	16	7

PETERSON, RAY

Answer Me	RCA	– 3 60	47	1
Corinne Corrina	London	– 1 61	41	7

PHILIPS, ESTHER

What A Difference A Day Makes	Kudu	18 10 75	6	8

PIAF, EDITH

Milord	Columbia	– 5 60	41	4
Milord (re-issue)	Columbia	13 11 60	17	13

PICKETT, BOBBY 'BORIS' AND THE CRYPT-KICKERS

Monster Mash (re-issue)	London	22 9 73	3	13

PICKETT, WILSON

In The Midnight Hour	Atlantic	14 10 65	12	11
Don't Fight It	Atlantic	– 11 65	29	8
634 - 5789	Atlantic	– 3 66	36	4
Land Of 1000 Dances	Atlantic	– 9 66	22	9
Mustang Sally	Atlantic	– 12 66	28	7
Funky Broadway	Atlantic	– 9 67	42	3
I'm A Midnight Mover	Atlantic	– 9 68	38	6
Hey Jude	Atlantic	15 2 69	16	8

PICKETTYWITCH

That Same Old Feeling	Pye	7 3 70	5	14
(It's Like A) Sad Old Kinda Movie	Pye	18 7 70	16	10

PIGLETS

Johnny Reggae	Bell	6 11 71	3	12

PILOT

Magic	EMI	16 11 74	11	12

January	EMI	25 1 75	1	10
Call Me 'Round	EMI	– 4 75	34	4
Just A Smile (re-issue)	EMI	– 9 75	31	4

PILTDOWN MEN

McDonald's Cave	Capitol	7 10 60	12	18
Piltdown Rides Again	Capitol	1 1 61	13	10
Goodnight Mrs. Flintstone	Capitol	5 3 61	18	8

PING PING AND AL VERLAINE

Sucu Sucu	Oriole	– 9 61	41	4

PINK FLOYD

Arnold Layne	Columbia	22 4 67	20	8
See Emily Play	Columbia	8 7 67	6	12

PINKERTON'S ASSORTED COLOURS

Mirror Mirror	Decca	12 2 66	9	8
Don't Stop Lovin' Me Baby	Decca	– 4 66	50	1

PIONEERS

Long Shot, Kick The Bucket	Trojan	– 10 69	21	12
Let Your Yeah Be Yeah	Trojan	21 8 71	5	12
Give And Take	Trojan	– 1 72	35	5

PIPKINS

Gimme Dat Ding	Columbia	11 4 70	6	10

PITNEY, GENE

I Wanna Love My Life Away	London	– 3 61	26	11
Town Without Pity	HMV	– 3 62	32	6
24 Hours From Tulsa	Un.Artists	14 12 63	5	19
That Girl Belongs To Yesterday	Un.Artists	14 3 64	8	12
It Hurts To Be In Love	Un.Artists	– 10 64	36	4
I'm Gonna Be Strong	Stateside	21 11 64	2	14
I Must Be Seeing Things	Stateside	27 2 65	6	10
Looking Thru' The Eyes Of Love	Stateside	19 6 65	3	12
Princess In Rags	Stateside	20 11 65	9	12
Backstage	Stateside	26 2 66	4	10
Nobody Needs Your Love	Stateside	18 6 66	2	13
Just One Smile	Stateside	26 11 66	8	11
Cold Light Of Day	Stateside	– 2 67	38	6
Something's Gotten Hold Of My Heart	Stateside	25 11 67	5	13
Somewhere In The Country	Stateside	4 5 68	19	9
Yours Until Tomorrow	Stateside	– 11 68	34	7
Maria Elena	Stateside	– 3 69	25	6
Street Called Hope	Stateside	– 3 70	37	5
Shady Lady	Stateside	– 10 70	29	8
24 Sycamore	Pye	– 4 73	34	7
Blue Angel	Bronze	– 11 74	39	4

PLASTIC ONO BAND

Give Peace A Chance	Apple	19 7 69	2	13
Cold Turkey	Apple	5 11 69	14	9
(see also: JOHN LENNON AND PLASTIC ONO BAND)				

PLASTIC PENNY

Everything I Am	Page One	27 1 68	6	10

PLATTERS

The Great Pretender/Only You	Mercury	7 9 56	5	11
My Prayer	Mercury	2 11 56	4	10
I'm Sorry	Mercury	31 5 57	18	2
Twilight Time	Mercury	6 6 58	3	12
Smoke Gets In Your Eyes	Mercury	17 1 59	1	19
Harbour Lights	Mercury	30 1 60	12	5

PLUTO (SHERVINGTON)

Dat	Opal	21 2 76	6	8
Ram Goat Liver	Trojan	- 4 76	43	4

POETS

Now We're Through	Decca	- 10 64	31	5

PONI-TAILS

Born Too Late	HMV	19 9 58	6	10

POOLE, BRIAN AND THE TREMELOES

Twist And Shout	Decca	13 7 63	4	14
Do You Love Me?	Decca	21 9 63	1	14
I Can Dance	Decca	- 11 63	31	8
Candy Man	Decca	15 2 64	6	13
Someone, Someone	Decca	30 5 64	2	17
Twelve Steps To Love	Decca	- 8 64	32	7
Three Bells	Decca	30 1 65	17	10
I Want Candy	Decca	- 7 65	25	8
(see also: TREMELOES)				

POOLE, GLYN

Milly Molly Mandy	York	- 10 73	35	8

POPPY FAMILY

Which Way You Goin', Billy?	Decca	12 9 70	7	14

POSEY, SANDY

Born A Woman	MGM	- 9 66	24	11
Single Girl	MGM	28 1 67	15	13
What A Woman In Love Won't Do	MGM	- 4 67	48	3
Single Girl (re-issue)	MGM	- 9 75	35	5

MIKE POST COALITION

Afternoon Of The Rhino	Warner Bros.	- 8 75	47	3

POTTERS

We'll Be With You	Pye	- 4 72	34	2

POWELL, COZY

Dance With The Devil	RAK	22 12 73	3	15
The Man In Black	RAK	15 6 74	18	8
Na Na Na	RAK	24 8 74	10	10

PRADO, PEREZ

Cherry Pink	HMV	25 3 55	1	17
Patricia	RCA	8 8 58	9	11

PRELUDE

After The Goldrush	Dawn	- 1 74	21	9

PRESLEY, ELVIS

Heartbreak Hotel	HMV	11 5 56	3	19

Title	Label	Date		
Blue Suede Shoes	HMV	25 5 56	9	8
I Want You, I Need You, I Love You	HMV	17 8 56	14	6
Hound Dog	HMV	21 9 56	2	22
Don't Be Cruel	HMV	10 11 56	17	3
Blue Moon	**HMV**	16 11 56	8	8
Love Me Tender	HMV	7 12 56	11	9
Rip It Up	HMV	– 2 57	24	1
Too Much	HMV	10 5 57	7	8
All Shook Up	HMV	28 6 57	1	18
Teddy Bear	RCA	12 7 57	2	18
Paralysed	HMV	30 8 57	9	8
Let's Have A Party/	RCA	4 10 57	2	14
Got A Lot Of Living To Do	RCA	18 10 57	17	3
Tryin' To Get You/	HMV	1 11 57	16	3
Lawdy Miss Clawdy	HMV	8 11 57	15	3
Santa Bring My Baby Back To Me	RCA	15 11 57	7	7
I'm Left, You're Right, She's Gone	RCA	18 1 58	17	3
Jailhouse Rock	RCA	24 1 58	1	13
Jailhouse Rock EP	RCA	31 1 58	18	3
Don't/I Beg Of You	RCA	28 2 58	2	10
Wear My Ring Around Your Neck	RCA	2 5 58	2	7
Hard Headed Woman	RCA	25 7 58	2	8
King Creole	RCA	3 10 58	2	10
I Got Stung/One Night	RCA	24 1 59	1	12
A Fool Such As I/I Need Your Love Tonight	RCA	25 4 59	1	14
Big Hunk Of Love/My Wish Came True	RCA	25 7 59	4	8
Stuck On You/Fame And Fortune	RCA	3 4 60	2	15
The Girl Of My Best Friend/ Mess Of Blues	RCA	24 7 60	2	19
It's Now Or Never	RCA	30 10 60	1	19
Are You Lonesome Tonight/ I Gotta Know	RCA	8 1 61	1	15
Wooden Heart	RCA	26 2 61	1	27
Surrender	RCA	14 5 61	1	15
Wild In The Country/I Feel So Bad	RCA	2 9 61	2	12
(Marie's The Name) His Latest Flame/Little Sister	RCA	28 10 61	1	14
Rock-A-Hula Baby/Can't Help Falling In Love With You	RCA	3 2 62	1	20
Good Luck Charm	RCA	12 5 62	1	17
She's Not You	RCA	8 9 62	1	14
Return To Sender	RCA	8 12 62	1	14
One Broken Heart For Sale	RCA	16 3 63	12	9
(You're The) Devil In Disguise	RCA	13 7 63	1	12
Bossa Nova Baby	RCA	2 11 63	13	8
Kiss Me Quick	RCA	28 12 63	14	10
Viva Las Vegas	RCA	28 3 64	17	11
Kissin' Cousins	RCA	4 7 64	10	11
Such A Night	RCA	29 8 64	13	10
Ain't That Loving You Baby	RCA	7 11 64	15	8
Blue Christmas	RCA	19 12 64	11	7
Do The Clam	RCA	20 3 65	19	7
Crying In The Chapel	RCA	5 6 65	1	15
Tell Me Why	RCA	27 11 65	15	10
Blue River	RCA	– 2 66	22	7
Frankie And Johnny	RCA	– 4 66	21	9
Love Letters	RCA	16 7 66	6	10
All That I Am	RCA	5 11 66	18	8

If Everyday Was Like Christmas	RCA	10 12 66	9	9
Indescribably Blue	RCA	- 2 67	21	5
You've Gotta Stop/The Love Machine	RCA	- 5 67	38	5
Long Legged Girl	RCA	- 8 67	49	2
Guitar Man	RCA	23 3 68	19	9
U.S. Male	RCA	25 5 68	15	8
Your Time Hasn't Come Yet Baby	RCA	- 7 68	22	11
You'll Never Walk Alone	RCA	- 10 68	44	3
If I Can Dream	RCA	8 3 69	11	10
In The Ghetto	RCA	21 6 69	2	16
Clean Up Your Own Backyard	RCA	- 9 69	21	6
Suspicious Minds	RCA	6 12 69	2	14
Don't Cry Daddy	RCA	7 3 70	8	11
Kentucky Rain	RCA	- 5 70	21	12
The Wonder Of You/Mama Liked The Roses	RCA	11 7 70	1	21
I've Lost You	RCA	28 11 70	9	12
You Don't Have To Say You Love Me	RCA	16 1 71	9	11
There Goes My Everything	RCA	27 3 71	6	11
Rags To Riches	RCA	29 5 71	9	11
Heartbreak Hotel/Hound Dog (re-issue)	RCA	7 8 71	10	12
I'm Leaving	RCA	- 10 71	23	9
I Just Can't Help Believing	RCA	25 12 71	6	16
Jailhouse Rock (re-issue)	RCA	- 12 71	42	5
Until It's Time For You To Go	RCA	15 4 72	5	10
American Trilogy	RCA	1 7 72	8	11
Burning Love	RCA	7 10 72	7	9
Always On My Mind	RCA	6 1 73	9	13
Polk Salad Annie	RCA	- 5 73	23	7
Fool	RCA	1 9 73	15	10
Raised On Rock	RCA	- 11 73	36	5
I've Got A Thing About You Baby	RCA	- 3 74	33	5
If You Talk In Your Sleep	RCA	- 7 74	40	3
My Boy	RCA	30 11 74	5	13
Promised Land	RCA	25 1 75	9	8
Trouble	RCA	- 5 75	31	4
Green Green Grass Of Home	RCA	- 11 75	29	7

PRESTON, BILLY
_____

That's The Way God Planned It	Apple	12 7 69	11	9
Outa Space	A & M	- 9 72	44	3

PRESTON, JOHNNY
_____

Running Bear	Mercury	6 2 60	1	11
Cradle Of Love	Mercury	1 5 60	2	16
I'm Starting To Go Steady	Mercury	- 7 60	49	1
Feel So Fine (re-issue)	Mercury	- 8 60	21	10
Charming Billy	Mercury	- 12 60	34	3

PRESTON, MIKE
_____

Mr. Blue	Decca	24 10 59	9	7
I'd Do Anything	Decca	- 8 60	23	10
Togetherness	Decca	- 12 60	41	5
Marry Me	Decca	12 3 61	13	10

PRETTY THINGS
_____

Rosalyn	Fontana	- 6 64	41	5

Don't Bring Me Down	Fontana	14 11 64	10	11
Honey I Need	Fontana	13 3 65	13	9
Cry To Me	Fontana	- 7 65	28	7
Midnight To Six Man	Fontana	- 1 66	46	1
Come See Me	Fontana	- 5 66	43	5
A House In The Country	Fontana	- 7 66	50	2

ALAN PRICE (SET)

I Put A Spell On You	Decca	16 4 66	9	10
Hi-Lili-Hi-Lo	Decca	6 8 66	11	12
Simon Smith And His Amazing Dancing Bear/Tickle Me	Decca	18 3 67	4	9
The House That Jack Built	Decca	12 8 67	4	10
Shame	Decca	- 11 67	45	2
Don't Stop The Carnival	Decca	10 2 68	13	8
Rosetta	CBS	24 4 71	11	10
(with GEORGIE FAME)				
The Jarrow Song (ALAN PRICE)	**Warner Bros.**	8 6 **74**	6	9
(see also: ANIMALS, FAME AND PRICE)				

PRICE, LLOYD

Stagger Lee	HMV	14 2 59	6	13
Where Were You On Our Wedding Day?	HMV	9 5 59	15	5
Personality	HMV	6 6 59	9	9
I'm Gonna Get Married	HMV	19 9 59	20	2
Lady Luck	HMV	- 4 60	45	1

PROBY, P.J.

Hold Me	Decca	27 6 64	3	15
Together	Decca	18 9 64	8	11
Somewhere	Liberty	19 12 64	6	12
I Apologise	Liberty	6 3 65	11	8
Let The Water Run Down	Liberty	31 7 65	19	8
That Means A Lot	Liberty	- 9 65	30	6
Maria	Liberty	4 12 65	8	9
You've Come Back	Liberty	- 2 66	25	7
To Make A Big Man Cry	Liberty	- 5 66	34	3
I Can't Make It Alone	Liberty	- 10 66	37	5
It's Your Day Today	Liberty	- 3 68	32	4

PROCOL HARUM

A Whiter Shade Of Pale	Deram	3 6 67	1	15
Homburg	R.Zonophone	14 10 67	6	10
Quite Rightly So	R.Zonophone	- 4 68	50	1
A Salty Dog	R.Zonophone	- 6 69	44	3
A Whiter Shade Of Pale (re-issue)	Magni Fly	27 5 72	13	13
Conquistador	Chrysalis	- 8 72	24	7
Pandora's Box	Chrysalis	13 9 75	16	7

PROTHEROE, BRIAN

Pinball	Chrysalis	- 9 74	22	6

PROVINE, DOROTHY

Don't Bring Lulu	Warner Bros.	6 1 62	14	13
Crazy Words, Crazy Tune	Warner Bros.	- 6 62	45	3

PUCKETT, GARY AND THE UNION GAP (*Shown as THE UNION GAP FEATURING GARY PUCKETT)

Young Girl*	CBS	4 5 68	1	17
Lady Willpower	CBS	7 9 68	5	16
Woman Woman (re-issue)*	CBS	- 8 68	47	2
Young Girl (re-issue)	**CBS**	6 7 74	6	13

PYRAMIDS
Train Tour To Rainbow City	President	− 11 67	35	4

PYTHON LEE JACKSON
In A Broken Dream	Young Blood	7 10 72	3	12

QUATRO, SUZI
Can The Can	RAK	26 5 73	1	14
48 Crash	RAK	4 8 73	3	9
Daytona Demon	RAK	17 11 73	14	13
Devil Gate Drive	RAK	9 2 74	1	11
Too Big	RAK	13 7 74	14	6
The Wild One	RAK	16 11 74	7	10
Your Mama Won't Like Me	RAK	− 2 75	31	15

QUEEN
Seven Seas Of Rhye	EMI	23 3 74	10	10
Killer Queen	EMI	2 11 74	2	12
Now I'm Here	EMI	1 2 75	11	7
Bohemian Rhapsody	EMI	15 11 75	1	17

? (QUESTION MARK) AND THE MYSTERIANS
96 Tears	Cameo P'way	− 11 66	37	4

QUICKLY, TOMMY
Wild Side Of Life	Pye	− 10 64	33	8

QUIET FIVE
When The Morning Sun Dries The Dew	Parlophone	− 5 65	45	2
Homeward Bound	Parlophone	− 4 66	46	2

RACE, STEVE
Pied Piper	Parlophone	− 2 63	29	9

RADHA KRISHNA TEMPLE
Hare Krishna Mantra	Apple	20 9 69	12	9
Govinda	Apple	− 4 70	23	8

RAGTIMERS
The Sting	Pye	− 3 74	31	8

RAINBOW COTTAGE
Seagull	P.Farthing	− 3 76	33	4

RAINWATER, MARVIN
Whole Lotta Woman	MGM	14 3 58	1	14
I Dig You Baby	MGM	20 6 58	14	3

RAMRODS
Riders In The Sky	London	5 2 61	7	12

RARE BIRD
Sympathy	Charisma	− 2 70	27	8

RATTLES
The Witch	Decca	31 10 70	8	15

RAY, JOHNNY

If You Believe	Philips	8	4 55	7	11
Paths Of Paradise	Philips	20	5 55	20	1
Hernando's Hideaway	Philips	7	10 55	11	5
Hey There	Philips	14	10 55	5	9
Song Of The Dreamer	Philips	28	10 55	10	5
Who's Sorry Now	Philips	17	2 56	17	2
Ain't Misbehavin'	Philips	20	4 56	18	4
Just Walkin' In The Rain	Philips	12	10 56	1	18
You Don't Owe Me A Thing/	Philips	25	1 57	14	10
Look Homeward, Angel	Philips	22	3 57	7	10
Yes, Tonight Josephine	Philips	10	5 57	1	15
Build Your Love	Philips	13	9 57	17	3

RECO, EZZ AND THE LAUNCHERS WITH BOYSIE GRANT

King Of Kings	Columbia	-	3 64	44	4

REDBONE

Witch Queen Of New Orleans	Epic	9	10 71	2	12

REDDING, OTIS

My Girl	Atlantic	8	1 66	11	16
(I Can't Get No) Satisfaction	Atlantic	-	4 66	33	4
My Lover's Prayer	Atlantic	-	7 66	37	6
I Can't Turn You Loose	Atlantic	-	8 66	29	8
Fa-Fa-Fa-Fa-Fa (Sad Song)	Atlantic	-	11 66	23	9
Try A Little Tenderness	Atlantic	-	1 67	46	4
Day Tripper	Stax	-	3 67	43	6
Let Me Come On Home	Stax	-	5 67	48	1
Shake	Stax	-	6 67	28	10
Tramp	Stax	19	8 67	18	11
(with CARLA THOMAS)					
Knock On Wood	Stax	-	10 67	35	5
(with CARLA THOMAS)					
Dock Of The Bay	Stax	9	3 68	3	12
My Girl (re-issue)	Atlantic	-	2 68	36	8
Happy Song	Stax	-	6 68	24	5
Hard To Handle	Atlantic	31	8 68	15	11
Love Man	Atco	-	7 69	34	3

REDDY, HELEN

Angie Baby	Capitol	1	2 75	5	10

REED, JIMMY

Shame, Shame, Shame	Stateside	-	9 64	45	2

REED, LOU

Walk On The Wild Side	RCA	26	5 73	10	9

REEVES, JIM

He'll Have To Go	RCA	10	4 60	11	31
Whispering Hope	RCA	-	3 61	50	1
You're The Only Good Thing					
That's Happened To Me	RCA	2	12 61	12	20
Adios Amigo	RCA	-	6 62	23	21
I'm Gonna Change Everything	RCA	-	11 62	42	2
Welcome To My World	RCA	29	6 63	6	15
Guilty	RCA	-	10 63	29	7
I Love You Because	RCA	14	3 64	5	38
I Won't Forget You	RCA	4	7 64	3	27
There's A Heartache Following					
Me	RCA	14	11 64	6	13
It Hurts So Much	RCA	13	2 65	8	11

Not Until The Next Time	RCA	15	5 65	13	11
How Long Has It Been	RCA	–	5 65	45	5
This World Is Not My Home	RCA	–	7 65	22	9
Is It Really Over?	RCA	4	12 65	17	9
Distant Drums	RCA	3	9 66	1	25
I Won't Come In While He's There	RCA	11	2 67	12	11
Trying To Forget	RCA	–	7 67	33	5
I Heard A Heart Break Last Night	RCA	–	11 67	38	6
That's When I See The Blue	RCA	–	3 68	33	5
When Two Worlds Collide	RCA	2	8 69	17	16
But You Love Me, Daddy	RCA	27	12 69	15	17
Nobody's Fool	RCA	–	3 70	32	5
Angels Don't Lie	RCA	–	9 70	32	3
I Love You Because (re-issue)	RCA	–	6 71	34	8
You're Free To Go	RCA	–	2 72	48	2

REEVES, MARTHA

see MARTHA AND THE VANDELLAS

REGAN, JOAN

If I Give My Heart To You	Decca	–	10 54	20	1
Wait For Me Darling	Decca	–	11 54	18	2
Prize Of Gold	Decca	25	3 55	6	9
Groci Di Oro	Decca	14	1 56	18	1
May You Always	HMV	6	6 59	12	8
Happy Anniversary	HMV	13	2 60	20	1
Papa Loves Mama	Pye	–	7 60	29	8

REID, MIKE

The Ugly Duckling	Pye	5	4 75	10	8

REID, NEIL

Mother Of Mine	Decca	25	12 71	2	21
That's What I Want To Be	Decca	–	4 72	45	5

REPARATA (*AND THE DELRONS)

Captain Of Your Ship*	Bell	6	4 68	13	10
Shoes	Dart	–	10 75	42	2

REUNION

Life Is A Rock (But The Radio Rolled Me)	RCA	–	9 74	33	4

REYNOLDS, DEBBIE

Tammy	Vogue-Coral	6	9 57	3	15

RICH, CHARLIE

The Most Beautiful Girl	CBS	23	2 74	2	14
Behind Closed Doors (re-issue)	Epic	18	5 74	16	10
We Love Each Other	Epic	–	2 75	37	5

RICHARD, CLIFF (AND THE SHADOWS THROUGH TO 1967)

Move It	Columbia	26	9 58	3	11
High Class Baby	Columbia	28	11 58	6	9
Never Mind/Mean Streak	Columbia	25	4 59	8	10
Livin' Doll	Columbia	11	7 59	1	18
Travellin' Light	Columbia	10	10 59	1	14
A Voice In The Wilderness	Columbia	16	1 60	2	10
Expresso Bongo EP	Columbia	16	1 60	8	4

Title	Label					
Fall In Love With You/ Willie And The Hand Jive	Columbia	20	3	60	2	16
Please Don't Tease	Columbia	26	6	60	1	18
Nine Times Out Of Ten	Columbia	18	9	60	2	12
I Love You	Columbia	27	11	60	2	16
Theme For A Dream	Columbia	19	2	61	4	14
Gee Whizz, It's You	Columbia	26	3	61	8	14
A Girl Like You	Columbia	11	6	61	3	14
When The Girl In Your Arms Is The Girl In Your Heart	Columbia	14	10	61	2	17
The Young Ones	Columbia	13	1	62	1	21
Do You Want To Dance/I'm Looking Out The Window	Columbia	12	5	62	2	17
It'll Be Me	Columbia	8	9	62	2	12
The Next Time/Bachelor Boy	Columbia	8	12	62	1	18
Summer Holiday	Columbia	2	3	63	1	17
Lucky Lips	Columbia	18	5	63	4	14
It's All In The Game	Columbia	31	8	63	2	13
Don't Talk To Him	Columbia	16	11	63	2	14
I'm The Lonely One	Columbia	15	2	64	8	10
Constantly	Columbia	9	5	64	4	13
On The Beach	Columbia	11	7	64	7	13
Twelfth Of Never	Columbia	17	10	64	8	11
I Could Easily Fall	Columbia	12	12	64	6	11
The Minute You're Gone	Columbia	27	3	65	1	14
On My Word	Columbia	26	6	65	12	10
The Time In Between	Columbia	–	8	65	22	8
Wind Me Up	Columbia	20	11	65	2	15
Blue Turns To Grey	Columbia	2	4	66	15	9
Visions	Columbia	30	7	66	7	12
Time Drags By	Columbia	29	10	66	10	11
In The Country	Columbia	31	12	66	6	10
It's All Over	Columbia	1	4	67	9	10
I'll Come Running	Columbia	–	6	67	26	8
The Day I Met Marie	Columbia	9	9	67	10	14
All My Love	Columbia	25	11	67	6	12
Congratulations	Columbia	30	3	68	1	13
I'll Love You Forever Today	Columbia	–	6	68	27	6
Marianne	Columbia	–	9	68	22	8
Don't Forget To Catch Me	Columbia	–	11	68	21	10
Good Times (Better Times)	Columbia	8	3	69	12	11
Big Ship	Columbia	14	6	69	8	9
Throw Down A Line (with HANK MARVIN)	Columbia	20	9	69	7	9
With The Eyes Of A Child	Columbia	20	12	69	20	12
Joy Of Living (with HANK MARVIN)	Columbia	–	2	70	25	9
Goodbye Sam, Hello Samantha	Columbia	13	6	70	6	12
I Ain't Got Time Anymore	Columbia	–	9	70	21	7
Sunny Honey Girl	Columbia	20	2	71	19	8
Silvery Rain	Columbia	–	4	71	27	6
Flying Machine	Columbia	–	7	71	37	7
Sing A Song Of Freedom	Columbia	27	11	71	13	12
Jesus	Columbia	–	3	72	37	4
Living In Harmony	Columbia	16	9	72	12	10
Power To All Our Friends	EMI	17	3	73	4	11
Help It Along/Tomorrow Rising	EMI	–	5	73	29	6
Take Me High	EMI	–	12	73	27	12
(You Keep Me) Hanging On	EMI	1	6	74	13	8
Miss You Nights	EMI	6	3	76	15	10

RIGHTEOUS BROTHERS

Title	Label					
You've Lost That Lovin' Feeling	London	23	1	65	1	10
Unchained Melody	London	11	9	65	14	12

Ebb Tide	London	– 1 66	48	2
(You're My) Soul And Inspiration	Verve	7 5 66	15	10
White Cliffs Of Dover	London	– 11 66	21	9
Island In The Sun	Verve	– 12 66	24	5
You're Lost That Lovin Feeling (re-issue)	London	1 3 69	10	11

RILEY, JEANNIE C.

Harper Valley P.T.A.	Polydor	30 11 68	12	15

RIMSHOTS

7-6-5-4-3-2-1 (Blow Your Whistle)	All Platinum	– 7 75	26	5

RIOS, MIGUEL

Song Of Joy	A & M	8 8 70	16	12

RIPPERTON, MINNIE

Loving You	Epic	26 4 75	2	10

RITCHIE FAMILY

Brazil	Polydor	– 8 75	41	4

RITTER, TEX

The Wayward Wind	Capitol	29 6 56	8	11

RIVERS, DANNY

Can't You Hear My Heart	Decca	– 1 61	36	3

ROBERTS, AUSTIN

Rocky	Pr.Stock	– 10 75	22	7

ROBERTS, MALCOLM

Time Alone Will Tell	RCA	– 5 67	45	2
May I Have The Next Dream With You	Major Minor	23 11 68	8	14
Love Is All	Major Minor	29 11 69	12	12

ROBERTSON, DON

The Happy Whistler	Capitol	18 5 56	8	7

ROBBINS, MARTY

El Paso	Fontana	23 1 60	17	2
Big Iron	Fontana	– 5 60	48	1
Devil Woman	CBS	27 10 62	5	16
Ruby Ann	CBS	– 1 63	24	6

ROBINSON, FLOYD

Makin' Love	RCA	17 10 59	8	7

ROBINSON, SMOKEY AND THE MIRACLES

Going To A Go-Go	T.Motown	– 2 66	44	5
(Come 'Round Here) I'm The One You Need	T.Motown	– 12 66	37	2
I Second That Emotion	T.Motown	– 12 67	27	11
If You Can Want	T.Motown	– 4 68	50	1
Tracks Of My Tears (re-issue)	T.Motown	31 5 69	9	13
Tears Of A Clown	T.Motown	15 8 70	1	14

(Come 'Round Here) I'm The One You Need (re-issue)	T.Motown	20 2 71	13	9
I Don't Blame You At All	T.Motown	26 6 71	11	10
Just My Soul Responding	T.Motown	– 2 74	35	6

(SMOKEY ROBINSON only)
(see also: MIRACLES)

ROCK CANDY

Remember	MCA	– 9 71	31	6

ROCKIN' BERRIES

I Didn't Mean To Hurt You	Piccadilly	– 10 64	43	1
He's In Town	Piccadilly	31 10 64	3	13
What In The World's Come Over You	Piccadilly	– 1 65	23	7
Poor Man's Son	Piccadilly	22 5 65	5	11
You're My Girl	Piccadilly	– 8 65	40	7
The Water Is Over My Head	Piccadilly	– 1 66	43	2

LORD ROCKINGHAM'S XI

Hoots Mon	Decca	24 10 58	1	16
Wee Tom	Decca	7 2 59	11	3

RODGERS, CLODAGH

Come Back And Shake Me	RCA	19 4 69	3	14
Goodnight Midnight	RCA	26 7 69	4	12
Biljo	RCA	– 11 69	22	8
Everybody Go Home	RCA	– 4 70	47	2
Jack In The Box	RCA	27 3 71	4	10
Lady Love Bug	RCA	– 10 71	28	11

RODGERS, JIMMY

Honeycomb	Columbia	2 11 57	20	1
Kisses Sweeter Than Wine	Columbia	20 12 57	6	10
Oh! Oh! I'm Falling In Love Again	Columbia	4 4 58	15	5
English Country Garden	Columbia	30 6 62	5	13

RODGERS, JULIE

The Wedding	Mercury	4 9 64	3	23
Like A Child	Mercury	2 1 65	20	9
Hawaiian Wedding Song	Mercury	– 3 65	28	6

ROE, TOMMY

Sheila	HMV	22 9 62	3	14
Susie Darlin'	HMV	– 12 62	37	5
The Folk Singer	HMV	30 3 63	4	13
Everybody	HMV	12 10 63	9	14
Dizzy	Stateside	10 5 69	1	19
Heather Honey	Stateside	– 7 69	27	8

ROGERS, KENNY AND THE FIRST EDITION

Ruby (Don't Take Your Love To Town)	Reprise	15 11 69	2	23
Something's Burning	Reprise	7 3 70	8	14

ROLLING STONES

Come On	Decca	– 7 63	21	14
I Wanna Be Your Man	Decca	7 12 63	12	16
Not Fade Away	Decca	7 3 64	3	15
It's All Over Now	Decca	11 7 64	1	15
Little Red Rooster	Decca	28 11 64	1	12
The Last Time	Decca	13 3 65	1	13

(I Can't Get No) Satisfaction	Decca	28 8 65	1	12
Get Off My Cloud	Decca	30 10 65	1	11
19th Nervous Breakdown	Decca	12 2 66	2	8
Paint It Black	Decca	21 5 66	1	10
Have You Seen Your Mother Baby? (Standing In The Shadows)	Decca	1 10 66	5	9
Let's Spend The Night Together/Ruby Tuesday	Decca	28 1 67	3	10
We Love You/Dandelion	Decca	26 8 67	8	8
Jumping Jack Flash	Decca	1 6 68	1	11
Honky Tonk Women	Decca	12 7 69	1	17
Memo From Turner (MICK JAGGER)	Decca	- 11 70	32	5
Brown Sugar/Bitch/Let It Rock	R.Stones	1 5 71	2	14
Street Fighting Man (re-issue)	Decca	- 7 71	21	8
Tumbling Dice	R.Stones	29 4 72	5	8
Angie	R.Stones	8 9 73	5	10
It's Only Rock And Roll	R.Stones	10 8 74	10	7
Out Of Time	Decca	- 9 75	45	2

ROMEO, MAX

Wet Dream	Unity	2 8 69	10	24

RONETTES

Be My Baby	London	26 10 63	4	13
Baby I Love You	London	1 2 64	11	14
The Best Part Of Breaking Up	London	- 8 64	43	3
Do I Love You	London	- 10 64	35	4

RONSTADT, LINDA

Tracks Of My Tears	Asylum	- 5 76	42	3

ROOFTOP SINGERS

Walk Right In	Fontana	17 2 63	10	12

ROSS, DIANA

Reach Out And Touch (Somebody's Hand)	T.Motown	- 7 70	33	5
Ain't No Mountain High Enough	T.Motown	26 9 70	6	12
Remember Me	T.Motown	17 4 71	7	12
I'm Still Waiting	T.Motown	31 7 71	1	14
Surrender	T.Motown	20 11 71	10	11
Doobedood'ndoobe, etc.	T.Motown	3 6 72	12	9
Touch Me In The Morning	T.Motown	28 7 73	9	13
All Of My Life	T.Motown	19 1 74	9	13
You Are Everything (with MARVIN GAYE)	T.Motown	30 3 74	5	11
Last Time I Saw Him	T.Motown	- 5 74	35	4
Stop, Look, Listen (with MARVIN GAYE)	T.Motown	- 7 74	25	7
Love Me	T.Motown	- 10 74	38	5
Sorry Doesn't Always Make It Right	T.Motown	- 3 75	23	9
Do You Know Where You're Going To (Theme From 'Mahogany')	T.Motown	10 4 76	5	8

ROSS, DIANA AND THE SUPREMES

Reflections	T.Motown	16 9 67	5	14

In And Out Of Love	T.Motown	9 12 67	13	13
Forever Came Today	T.Motown	– 4 68	28	8
Some Things You Never Get Used To	T.Motown	– 7 68	34	6
Love Child	T.Motown	7 12 68	15	14
I'm Gonna Make You Love Me (with TEMPTATIONS)	T.Motown	8 2 69	3	11
Living In Shame	T.Motown	10 5 69	14	9
No Matter What Sign You Are	T.Motown	– 7 69	38	7
I Second That Emotion (with TEMPTATIONS)	T.Motown	4 10 69	18	8
Someday We'll Be Together (see also: SUPREMES)	T.Motown	17 1 70	13	13

ROSSO, NINI

Il Silenzio	Durium	18 9 65	8	14

ROUSSOS, DEMIS

Happy To Be On An Island In The Sun	Philips	6 12 75	5	10
Can't Say How Much I Love You (see also: APHRODITES CHILD)	Philips	– 2 76	35	5

ROUTERS

Let's Go	Warner Bros.	– 12 62	32	7

ROWLES, JOHN

If I Only Had Time	MCA	30 3 68	3	18
Hush, Not A Word To Mary	MCA	29 6 68	12	10

ROXY MUSIC

Virginia Plain	Island	2 9 72	4	12
Pyjamarama	Island	31 3 73	10	12
Street Life	Island	1 12 73	9	12
All I Want Is You	Island	19 10 74	12	8
Love Is The Drug	Island	25 10 75	2	10
Both Ends Burning	Island	– 1 76	25	6

R.A.F. BAND

Dambusters March	HMV	21 10 55	18	1

ROYAL, BILLY JOE

Down In The Boondocks	CBS	– 10 65	38	4

ROYAL GUARDSMEN

Snoopy Vs. The Red Baron	Stateside	4 2 67	8	13
Return Of The Red Baron	Stateside	– 4 67	37	4

ROYAL SCOTS DRAGOON GUARDS BAND

Amazing Grace	RCA	15 4 72	1	25
Heykens Serenade/The Day Is Over	RCA	– 8 72	30	7
Little Drummer Boy	RCA	16 12 72	13	9

ROZA, LITA

Hey There	Decca	7 10 55	17	2
Jimmy Unknown	Decca	23 3 56	13	5

RUBETTES

Sugar Baby Love	Polydor	11 5 74	1	11

Tonight	Polydor	27 7 74	12	8
Juke Box Jive	Polydor	23 11 74	3	12
I Can Do It	State	15 3 75	7	9
Foe-Dee-O-Dee	State	5 7 75	15	6
Little Darling	State	– 11 75	30	6
You're The Reason Why	State	– 5 76	28	4

RUBY AND THE ROMANTICS

Our Day Will Come	London	– 3 63	38	6

RUFFIN, BRUCE

Rain	Trojan	22 5 71	19	11
Mad About You	Rhino	22 7 72	9	12

RUFFIN, DAVID

Walk Away From Love	T.Motown	31 1 76	10	8

(see also: TEMPTATIONS)

RUFFIN, JIMMY

What Becomes Of The Broken-Hearted	T.Motown	3 12 66	8	15
I've Passed This Way Before	T.Motown	– 2 67	29	7
Gonna Give Her All The Love I Got	T.Motown	– 4 67	29	6
I've Passed This Way Before (re-issue)	T.Motown	– 8 69	45	5
Farewell Is A Lonely Sound (re-issue)	T.Motown	4 4 70	8	16
I'll Say Forever My Love (re-issue)	T.Motown	18 7 70	7	12
It's Wonderful To Be Loved By You (re-issue)	T.Motown	31 10 70	6	14
What Becomes Of The Broken-Hearted (re-issue)	T.Motown	10 8 74	4	12
Farewell Is A Lonely Sound (re-issue)	T.Motown	– 11 74	30	5
Tell Me What You Want	Polydor	– 11 74	39	4

RUNDGREN, TODD

I Saw The Light (re-issue)	Bearsville	– 6 73	36	6

RYAN, BARRY

Eloise	MGM	2 11 68	2	12
Love Is Love	MGM	– 2 69	25	4
Hunt	Polydor	– 10 69	34	5

RYAN, MARION

Love Me Forever	Pye Nixa	24 1 58	7	10
It's You That I Love	Pye	18 12 60	20	8

RYAN, PAUL AND BARRY

Don't Bring Me Your Heartaches	Decca	27 11 65	13	9
Have Pity On The Boy	Decca	12 2 66	18	6
I Love Her	Decca	28 5 66	17	7
I Love How You Love Me	Decca	– 7 66	21	7
Have You Ever Loved Somebody	Decca	– 10 66	49	1
Missy Missy	Decca	– 12 66	43	4
Keep It Out Of Sight	Decca	– 3 67	30	6
Clare	Decca	– 7 67	47	2

RYDELL, BOBBY

Wild One	Columbia	13 3 60	12	7
Swingin' School	Columbia	- 6 60	44	1
Volare	Columbia	- 8 60	22	7
Sway	Columbia	1 1 61	14	12
Good Time Baby	Columbia	- 3 61	41	7
Teach Me To Twist	Columbia	- 4 62	45	1
(with CHUBBY CHECKER)				
Jingle Bell Rock	Cameo P'way	- 12 62	40	3
(with CHUBBY CHECKER)				
Forget Him	Cameo P'way	15 6 63	13	14

RYDER, MITCH AND THE DETROIT WHEELS

| Jenny Takes A Ride | Stateside | - 2 66 | 33 | 5 |

SADLER, STAFF SGT. BARRY

| Ballad Of The Green Berets | RCA | - 3 66 | 24 | 8 |

SAGAR, MIKE

| Deep Feeling | HMV | - 12 60 | 44 | 5 |

SAILOR

| Glass Of Champagne | Epic | 20 12 75 | 2 | 12 |
| Girls, Girls, Girls | Epic | 10 4 76 | 7 | 8 |

ST. ANDREW'S CHORALE

| Cloud 99 | Decca | - 2 76 | 31 | 5 |

ST. CECILIA

| Leap Up And Down (Wave Your Knickers In The Air) | Polydor | 17 7 71 | 12 | 17 |

ST. JOHN, BARRY

| Come Away Melinda | Columbia | - 12 65 | 47 | 1 |

ST. LOUIS UNION

| Girl | Decca | 5 2 66 | 11 | 10 |

ST. PETERS, CRISPIAN

You Were On My Mind	Decca	29 1 66	2	14
Pied Piper	Decca	16 4 66	5	13
Changes	Decca	- 9 66	47	4

SAINTE-MARIE, BUFFY

| Soldier Blue | RCA | 14 8 71 | 7 | 18 |
| I'm Gonna Be A Country Girl Again | Vanguard | - 3 72 | 34 | 5 |

SAKAMOTO, KYU

| Sukiyaki | HMV | 20 7 63 | 6 | 13 |

SAKHARIN

| Sugar Sugar | RCA | 8 5 71 | 12 | 14 |

SAM AND DAVE

Soothe Me	Stax	- 3 67	35	7
Soul Man	Stax	- 11 67	24	14
I Thank You	Stax	- 3 68	34	9
Soul Sister, Brown Sugar	Atlantic	8 2 69	15	8

SAM THE SHAM AND THE PHAROAHS

Woolly Bully	MGM	17 7 65	11	15
Lil' Red Riding Hood	MGM	- 8 66	46	3

MIKE SAMMES SINGERS

Somewhere My Love	HMV	22 7 67	14	38

SAMPSON, DAVE

Sweet Dreams	Columbia	- 5 60	29	6

SAN REMO STRINGS

Festival Time	T.Motown	- 12 71	39	8

SANDFORD, CHRIS

Not Too Little, Not Too Much	Decca	21 12 63	17	9

SANDPIPERS

Guantanamera	Pye	1 10 66	7	17
Quando Ln'Innamoro	A & M	- 1 67	33	6
Kum Baya	A & M	- 3 69	38	1

SANDS, JODIE

Someday	HMV	17 10 58	16	8

SANDS, TOMMY

Old Oaken Bucket	Capitol	- 7 60	25	7

SANTO AND JOHNNY

Sleep Walk	Pye	10 10 59	14	2
Teardrops	Parlophone	- 3 60	50	1

SANTANA

Samba Pa Ti	CBS	- 9 74	27	8

SARNE, MIKE

Come Outside	Parlophone	26 5 62	1	19
Will I What	Parlophone	15 9 62	18	10
Just For Kicks	Parlophone	- 1 63	22	7
Code Of Love	Parlophone	- 3 63	29	7

SARSTEDT, PETER

Where Do You Go To My Lovely?	Un.Artists	8 2 69	1	16
Frozen Orange Juice	Un.Artists	28 6 69	10	9

SAVAGE, EDNA

Arriverderci Darling	Parlophone	13 1 56	19	1

SAVALAS, TELLY

If	MCA	1 3 75	1	9
You've Lost That Lovin' Feeling	MCA	- 5 75	47	3

SAXON, AL

Only Sixteen	Fontana	29 8 59	17	1
Blue Eyed Boy	Fontana	- 12 60	39	2
There I've Said It Again	Piccadilly	- 9 61	48	1

SAYER, LEO

The Show Must Go On	Chrysalis	22 12 73	2	13
One Man Band	Chrysalis	22 6 74	6	9
Long Tall Glasses	Chrysalis	28 9 74	4	9
Moonlighting	Chrysalis	6 9 75	2	8

SCAFFOLD

Thank U Very Much	Columbia	9 12 67	4	12
Do You Remember	Columbia	- 3 68	34	5
Lily The Pink	Columbia	23 11 68	1	24
Gin Gan Goolie	Parlophone	- 11 69	38	12
Liverpool Lou	Warner Bros.	15 6 74	7	9
Leave It (MIKE McGEAR only)	Warner Bros.	- 10 74	36	5

SCOTLAND WORLD CUP SQUAD

Easy Easy	Polydor	29 6 74	20	4

SCOTT, JACK

My True Love	London	17 10 58	10	7
What In The World's Come Over You	Top Rank	27 2 60	6	8
Burning Bridges	Top Rank	- 5 60	32	2

SCOTT, LINDA

I've Told Every Little Star	Columbia	28 5 61	9	13
Don't Bet Money Honey	Columbia	- 9 61	50	1

SCOTT, SIMON

Move It Baby	Parlophone	- 8 64	37	8

SEARCHERS

Sweets For My Sweet	Pye	13 7 63	1	16
Sugar And Spice	Pye	2 11 63	2	13
Sweet Nothin's	Philips	- 10 63	48	2
Needles And Pins	Pye	25 1 64	1	15
Don't Throw Your Love Away	Pye	18 4 64	1	10
Someday We're Gonna Love Again	Pye	25 7 64	11	9
When You Walk In The Room	Pye	3 10 64	3	12
What Have They Done To The Rain	Pye	19 12 64	13	11
Goodbye My Love	Pye	13 3 65	4	11
He's Got No Love	Pye	24 7 65	12	10
When I Get Home	Pye	- 10 65	35	3
Take Me For What I'm Worth	Pye	22 1 66	20	8
Take It Or Leave It	Pye	- 4 66	31	6
Have You Ever Loved Somebody	Pye	- 10 66	48	2

SEASHELLS

Maybe I Know	CBS	- 9 72	32	5

SECOMBE, HARRY

On With The Motley	Philips	9 12 55	16	3
If I Ruled The World	Philips	21 12 63	18	16
This Is My Song	Philips	11 3 67	2	15
(see also: GOONS)				

SECOND CITY SOUND

Tchaikovsky One	Decca	- 1 66	22	7
Dream Of Oliver	Major Minor	- 4 69	43	2

SEDAKA, NEIL

I Go Ape	RCA	2	5 59	9	10
Oh! Carol	RCA	14	11 59	3	13
Stairway To Heaven	RCA	8	5 60	13	15
You Mean Everything To Me	RCA	–	8 60	45	3
Calender Girl	RCA	22	1 61	10	15
Little Devil	RCA	14	5 61	12	12
Happy Birthday Sweet 16	RCA	16	12 61	4	18
King Of Clowns	RCA	–	4 62	23	11
Breaking Up Is Hard To Do	RCA	11	8 62	7	16
Next Door To An Angel	RCA	–	11 62	29	4
Let's Go Steady Again	RCA	–	5 63	43	3
Oh Carol/Breaking Up Is Hard To Do/Little Devil (re-issue)	RCA	2	12 72	19	13
Beautiful You	RCA	–	11 72	43	3
That's When The Music Takes Me	RCA	24	3 73	18	9
Standing On The Inside	MGM	–	6 73	26	9
Our Last Song Together	MGM	–	8 73	31	8
A Little Lovin'	Polydor	–	2 74	34	6
Laughter In The Rain	Polydor	20	7 74	15	9
Queen Of 1964	Polydor	–	3 75	35	5

SEEKERS

I'll Never Find Another You	Columbia	30	1 65	1	23
World Of Our Own	Columbia	1	5 65	3	17
The Carnival Is Over	Columbia	6	11 65	1	17
Someday One Day	Columbia	9	4 66	11	11
Walk With Me	Columbia	24	9 66	10	12
Morningtown Ride	Columbia	3	12 66	2	15
Georgy Girl	Columbia	4	3 67	3	11
Olive Tree (JUDITH DURHAM only)	Columbia	–	6 67	33	5
When Will The Good Apples Fall	Columbia	7	10 67	11	12
Emerald City	Columbia	–	12 67	50	1

SELLERS, PETER

Any Old Iron	Parlophone	20	9 57	17	2
Goodness Gracious Me (with SOPHIA LOREN)	Parlophone	13	11 60	5	14
Bangers And Mash (with SOPHIA LOREN)	Parlophone	–	1 61	22	5
A Hard Day's Night (see also: GOONS)	Parlophone	8	1 66	14	7

SEMPRINI

Theme From 'Exodus'	HMV	–	3 61	25	8

SENSATIONAL ALEX HARVEY BAND

Delilah	Vertigo	2	8 75	7	7
Gambling Bar Room Blues	Vertigo	–	11 75	38	8

SETTLERS

The Lightning Tree	York	–	10 71	36	5

SEVERINE

Un Banc, Une Arbre, Une Rue	Philips	15	5 71	9	11

SEVILLE, DAVID

Witch Doctor (see also: CHIPMUNKS)	London	23	5 58	15	5

SEYTON, DENNY

The Way You Look Tonight	Mercury	– 9 64	48	1

SHADOWS

Apache	Columbia	17 7 60	1	20
Man Of Mystery/The Stranger	Columbia	6 11 60	2	16
F.B.I.	Columbia	29 1 61	4	18
Frightened City	Columbia	30 4 61	3	20
Kon-Tiki	Columbia	2 9 61	1	15
The Savage	Columbia	11 11 61	9	9
Wonderful Land	Columbia	3 3 62	1	19
Guitar Tango	Columbia	11 8 62	4	15
Dance On	Columbia	22 12 62	1	14
Foot Tapper	Columbia	16 3 63	1	16
Atlantis	Columbia	15 6 63	2	17
Shindig	Columbia	28 9 63	6	12
Geronimo	Columbia	14 12 63	11	12
Theme For Young Lovers	Columbia	21 3 64	12	10
The Rise And Fall Of Flingel Bunt	Columbia	23 5 64	5	13
Rhythm And Greens	Columbia	– 9 64	22	7
Genie With The Light Brown Lamp	Columbia	9 1 65	17	10
(Next Time I See) Mary Anne	Columbia	27 2 65	17	10
Stingray	Columbia	26 6 65	19	7
Don't Make My Baby Blue	Columbia	14 8 65	10	10
War Lord	Columbia	25 12 65	18	10
I Met A Girl	Columbia	– 3 66	22	5
A Place In The Sun	Columbia	– 7 66	24	6
The Dreams I Dream	Columbia	– 11 66	42	6
Maroc 7	Columbia	– 4 67	24	8
Let Me Be The One	EMI	5 4 75	12	9
(see also: CLIFF RICHARD AND THE SHADOWS)				

SHAG

Loop-Di-Love	UK	28 10 72	4	12

SHAND, JIMMY

Bluebell Polka	Parlophone	23 12 55	18	2
Sing With Shand	Parlophone	1 12 56	19	1

SHANGRI-LAS

Remember (Walking In The Sand)	Red Bird	14 11 64	14	13
Leader Of The Pack	Red Bird	30 1 65	11	9
Leader Of The Pack (re-issue)	Kama Sutra	4 11 72	3	12

SHANNON, DEL

Runaway	London	23 4 61	1	22
Hats Off To Larry	London	2 9 61	9	12
So Long Baby	London	9 12 61	10	12
Hey Little Girl	London	31 3 62	2	15
Cry Myself To Sleep	London	– 9 62	29	6
Swiss Maid	London	20 10 62	2	17
Little Town Flirt	London	27 1 63	4	13
Two Kinds Of Teardrops	London	4 5 63	5	13
Two Silhouettes	London	– 8 63	23	8
Sue's Gonna Be Mine	London	– 10 63	21	8
Mary Jane	Stateside	– 3 64	35	4
Handy Man	Stateside	– 7 64	36	4
Keep Searchin'	Stateside	23 1 65	3	11
Stranger In Town	Stateside	– 3 65	40	2

SHAPIRO, HELEN

Don't Treat Me Like A Child	Columbia	16 4 61	4	20
You Don't Know	Columbia	2 7 61	1	23
Walkin' Back To Happiness	Columbia	23 9 61	1	20
Tell Me What He Said	Columbia	24 2 62	2	15
Let's Talk About Love	Columbia	- 5 62	23	7
Little Miss Lonely	Columbia	28 7 62	8	11
Keep Away From Other Girls	Columbia	- 10 62	40	6
Queen For Tonight	Columbia	- 2 63	33	5
Woe Is Me	Columbia	- 4 63	35	5
Look Who It Is	Columbia	- 10 63	47	3
Fever	Columbia	- 1 64	38	4

SHARONETTES

Papa Oom Mow Mow	Black Magic	- 4 75	26	5
Going To A Go-Go	Black Magic	- 7 75	46	3

SHAW, SANDIE

(There's) Always Something There To Remind Me	Pye	17 10 64	1	11
Girl Don't Come	Pye	19 12 64	3	12
I'll Stop At Nothing	Pye	27 2 65	4	11
Long Live Love	Pye	22 5 65	1	14
Message Understood	Pye	7 10 65	6	10
How Can You Tell	Pye	- 11 65	21	9
Tomorrow	Pye	12 2 66	9	9
Nothing Comes Easy	Pye	4 6 66	14	9
Run	Pye	- 9 66	32	5
Think Sometimes About Me	Pye	- 11 66	32	5
I Don't Need Anything	Pye	- 1 67	50	1
Puppet On A String	Pye	25 3 67	1	18
Tonight In Tokyo	Pye	- 7 67	21	6
You've Not Changed	Pye	21 10 67	18	12
Today	Pye	- 2 68	27	7
Monsieur Dupont	Pye	1 3 69	6	15
Think It All Over	Pye	- 5 69	42	4
Rose Garden	Pye	- 3 71	41	3

SHEARING, GEORGE

Let There Be Love (with NAT KING COLE)	Capitol	4 8 62	11	14
Baubles, Bangles And Beads	Capitol	- 10 62	49	1

SHEARSTON, GARY

I Get A Kick Out Of You	Charisma	12 10 74	9	10

SHEER ELEGANCE

Milky Way	Pye	24 1 76	18	10

SHELDON, DOUG

Runaround Sue	Decca	- 11 61	36	3
Your Ma Said You Cried In Your Sleep Last Night	Decca	- 1 62	29	6
I Saw Linda Yesterday	Decca	- 2 63	36	6

SHELLEY, PETER

Gee Baby	Magnet	28 9 74	4	10
Love Me Love My Dog	Magnet	5 4 75	3	11

SHELTON, ANNE

Arriverderci Darling	HMV	16 12 55	17	4

Seven Days	Philips	20	4 56	18	3
Lay Down Your Arms	Philips	31	8 56	1	13
Sailor	Philips	15	1 61	7	8

SHEPHERD SISTERS

Alone	HMV	22 11 57	14	3

SHERIDAN, TONY
see BEATLES

SHERMAN, ALLAN

Hello Muddah, Hello Faddah	Warner Bros.	5 10 63	14	10

SHERMAN, BOBBY

Julie Do Ya Love Me	CBS	- 10 70	28	4

SHERVINGTON, PLUTO
see PLUTO

SHERWOOD, HOLLY

Day By Day	Bell	- 2 72	29	7

SHEVETON, TONY

Million Drums	Oriole	- 2 64	49	1

SHIRELLES

Will You Still Love Me Tomorrow?	Top Rank	29 1 61	3	14
Soldier Boy	HMV	- 5 62	23	9
Foolish Little Girl	Stateside	- 5 63	38	5

SHIRLEY AND COMPANY

Shame, Shame, Shame	All Platinum	15 2 75	6	13

SHOCKING BLUE

Venus	P.Farthing	14 2 70	8	12
Mighty Joe	P.Farthing	- 4 70	43	3

SHONDELL, TROY

This Time	London	25 11 61	14	12

SHOWADDYWADDY

Hey Rock'n'Roll	Bell	1 6 74	2	14
Rock'n'Roll Lady	Bell	31 8 74	15	9
Hey Mister Christmas	Bell	4 1 75	13	8

SHOWSTOPPERS

Ain't Nothing But A House-Party	Beacon	30 3 68	11	15
Eeny Meeny	MGM	- 12 68	33	7

SIFFRE, LABI

It Must Be Love	Pye	11 12 71	14	12
Crying, Laughing, Loving, Lying	Pye	15 4 72	11	9
Watch Me	Pye	- 7 72	29	6

SILKIE

You've Got To Hide Your Love Away	Fontana	- 9 65	28	6

SILVER CONVENTION

Save Me	Magnet	-	4 75	30	7
Fly Robin Fly	Magnet	-	11 75	28	7

SILVERSPOON, DOOLEY

Let Me Be The No. 1	Sevile	-	1 76	44	3

SIMON AND GARFUNKEL

Homeward Bound	CBS	16	4 66	9	12
I Am A Rock	CBS	2	7 66	17	10
Mrs'. Robinson	CBS	20	7 68	4	11
Mrs. Robinson EP	CBS	8	2 69	9	7
The Boxer	CBS	10	5 69	6	14
Bridge Over Troubled Water	CBS	28	2 70	1	19
America (re-issue)	CBS	-	10 72	25	7

SIMON, CARLY

You're So Vain	Elektra	2	1 73	3	15
The Right Thing To Do	Elektra	12	5 73	17	10
Mockingbird	Elektra	-	3 74	34	5
(with JAMES TAYLOR)					

SIMON, JOE

Step By Step (re-issue)	Mojo	14	7 73	14	10

SIMON, PAUL

Mother And Child Reunion	CBS	26	2 72	5	12
Me And Julio Down By The Schoolyard	CBS	27	5 72	15	9
Take Me To The Mardi Gras	CBS	30	6 73	7	11
Loves Me Like A Rock	CBS	-	5 74	39	5
50 Ways To Leave Your Lover	CBS	-	1 76	23	6
(see also: SIMON AND GARFUNKEL)					

SIMON, TITO

This Monday Morning Feeling	Horse	-	2 75	45	4

SIMONE, NINA

I Put A Spell On You	Philips	-	8 65	49	1
Ain't Got No-I Got Life	RCA	16	11 68	2	18
I Put A Spell On You (re-issue)	Philips	-	1 69	28	4
To Love Somebody	RCA	1	2 69	5	9

SINATRA, FRANK

Three Coins In The Fountain	Capitol	-	10 54	1	10
You My Love	Capitol	10	6 55	13	6
Learnin' The Blues	Capitol	5	8 55	2	15
Not As A Stranger	Capitol	2	9 55	18	1
Love And Marriage	Capitol	13	1 56	3	8
Love Is The Tender Trap	Capitol	20	1 56	2	9
Songs For Swingin' Lovers	Capitol	22	6 56	12	5
All The Way/Chicago	Capitol	13	12 57	5	16
Witchcraft	Capitol	14	2 58	17	6
Mr. Success	Capitol	19	12 58	18	2
High Hopes	Capitol	19	9 59	9	10
It's Nice To Be Travellin'	Capitol	-	4 60	48	2
River, Stay 'Way From My Door	Capitol	12	6 60	16	9
Nice'n'Easy	Capitol	11	9 60	20	12
Ole McDonald	Capitol	20	11 60	14	8

My Blue Heaven	Capitol	– 4 61	33		7
Granada	Reprise	23 9 61	13		8
Coffee Song	Reprise	– 11 61	39		3
Everybody's Twisting	Reprise	– 4 62	22		12
Me And My Shadow (with SAMMY DAVIS JNR.)	Reprise	29 12 62	20		9
My Kind Of Girl (with COUNT BASIE)	Reprise	– 3 63	35		6
Hello Dolly (with COUNT BASIE)	Reprise	– 9 64	47		1
Strangers In The Night	Reprise	21 5 66	1		20
Summer Wind	Reprise	– 10 66	36		5
That's Life	Reprise	– 12 66	45		5
Somethin' Stupid (with NANCY SINATRA)	Reprise	1 4 67	1		18
The World We Knew	Reprise	– 8 67	33		9
My Way	Reprise	10 5 69	5		125
Love's Been Good To Me	Reprise	25 10 69	8		18
I Will Drink The Wine	Reprise	20 3 71	16		13
*My Way (re-entry)	Reprise	2 1 71	18		125
I Believe I'm Gonna Love You	Reprise	– 12 75	34		7

SINATRA, NANCY

These Boots Are Made For Walking	Reprise	5 2 66	1		15
How Does That Grab You, Darlin'	Reprise	14 5 66	19		8
Sugar Town	Reprise	4 2 67	8		10
You Only Live Twice	Reprise	15 7 67	11		18
Ladybird (with LEE HAZLEWOOD)	Reprise	– 11 67	47		1
Highway Song	Reprise	– 11 69	21		10
Did You Ever (with LEE HAZLEWOOD)	Reprise	4 9 71	2		,13

(see also: FRANK SINATRA)

SINGING DOGS

The Singing Dogs	Nixa	25 11 55	13		4

SINGING NUNS

Dominique	Philips	14 12 63	7		14

SIR DOUGLAS QUINTET

She's About A Mover	London	10 7 65	15		10

SISTER SLEDGE

Mama Never Told Me	Atlantic	19 7 75	20		6

SKATALITES

Guns Of Navarone	Island	– 4 67	36		6

SKELLERN, PETER

You're A Lady	Decca	30 9 72	3		11
Hold On To Love	Decca	26 4 75	14		8

SLADE

Get Down And Get With It	Polydor	7 8 71	16		14
Coz I Luv You	Polydor	6 11 71	1		15
Look Wot You Dun	Polydor	12 2 72	4		10
Take Me Bak 'Ome	Polydor	10 6 72	1		13
Mama Weer All Crazee Now	Polydor	2 9 72	1		10

*'My Way' spent a total of 125 weeks in the Top 50, re-entering the Top 20 on the 2nd January 1971

Gudbuy T'Jane	Polydor	25 11 72	2	13
Cum On Feel The Noize	Polydor	3 3 73	1	12
Skweeze Me Pleeze Me	Polydor	30 6 73	1	10
My Friend Stan	Polydor	6 10 73	2	8
Merry Christmas Everybody	Polydor	8 12 73	1	9
Everyday	Polydor	6 4 74	3	7
Bangin' Man	Polydor	6 7 74	3	7
Far Far Away	Polydor	19 10 74	2	6
How Does It Feel	Polydor	8 3 75	15	7
Thanks For The Memory	Polydor	17 5 75	7	7
In For A Penny	Polydor	29 11 75	11	8
Let's Call It Quits	Polydor	21 2 76	11	7

SLEDGE, PERCY

When A Man Loves A Woman	Atlantic	28 5 66	4	17
Warm And Tender Love	Atlantic	- 8 66	34	7

SLIK

Forever And Ever	Bell	24 1 76	1	9

SLOANE, P.F.

Sins Of A Family	RCA	- 11 65	38	3

SLY AND THE FAMILY STONE

Dance To The Music (re-issue)	CBS	3 8 68	7	15
M'Lady	Direction	- 10 68	32	7
Everyday People	Direction	- 3 69	36	4
Family Affair	Epic	5 2 72	15	8
Runnin' Away	Epic	6 5 72	17	8

SMALL, MILLIE

see MILLIE

SMALL FACES

Whatcha Gonna Do About It	Decca	30 9 65	14	10
Sha La La La Lee	Decca	19 2 66	3	11
Hey Girl	Decca	21 5 66	10	9
All Or Nothing	Decca	20 8 66	1	12
My Mind's Eye	Decca	26 11 66	4	11
I Can't Make It	Decca	- 3 67	26	7
Here Comes The Nice	Immediate	24 6 67	12	10
Itchycoo Park	Immediate	19 8 67	3	15
Tin Soldier	Immediate	23 12 67	9	12
Lazy Sunday	Immediate	27 4 68	2	11
Universal	Immediate	27 7 68	16	11
Afterglow	Immediate	- 3 69	36	1
Itchycoo Park (re-issue)	Immediate	17 1 76	9	11
Lazy Sunday (re-issue)	Immediate	- 3 76	39	5
(see also: FACES, HUMBLE PIE)				

SMITH BROTHERS

I'm In Favour Of Friendship	Decca	22 7 55	20	1

SMITH, HURRICANE

Don't Let It Die	Columbia	19 6 71	2	12
Oh Babe, What Would You Say	Columbia	13 5 72	4	16
Who Was It	Columbia	- 9 72	23	7

SMITH, JIMMY

Got My Mojo Working	Verve	- 4 66	48	3

SMITH, KEELEY

You're Breaking My Heart	Reprise	3 4 65	14	10

SMITH, O.C.

Son Of Hickory Holler's Tramp	CBS	15 6 68	2	15

SMITH, WHISTLING JACK

I Was Kaiser Bill's Batman	Deram	18 3 67	5	11

SMOKE

My Friend Jack	Columbia	– 3 67	45	3

SMOKEY

If You Think You Know How To Love Me	RAK	26 7 75	3	9
Don't Play Your Rock And Roll To Me	RAK	18 10 75	8	7
Something's Been Making Me Blue	RAK	28 2 76	17	8

SONNY

Laugh At Me	Atlantic	4 9 65	9	11
(see also: SONNY AND CHER)				

SONNY AND CHER

I Got You Babe	Atlantic	21 8 65	1	12
Baby Don't Go (re-issue)	Reprise	30 9 65	11	9
But You're Mine	Atlantic	6 11 65	17	8
What Now, My Love	Atlantic	12 3 66	13	11
Have I Stayed Too Long	Atlantic	– 7 66	42	3
Little Man	Atlantic	17 9 66	4	10
Living For You	Atlantic	– 11 66	44	4
Beat Goes On	Atlantic	– 2 67	29	8
All I Ever Need Is You	MCA	29 1 72	8	13
(see also: CHER, SONNY)				

SORROWS

Take A Heart	Piccadilly	– 9 65	21	8

SOUL BROTHERS

I Keep Ringing My Baby	Decca	– 4 65	43	3

SOUL, JIMMY

If You Wanna Be Happy	Stateside	– 7 63	39	2

SOUND 9418

In The Mood	UK	– 2 76	46	3

SOUNDS INCORPORATED

The Spartans	Columbia	– 4 64	30	6
Spanish Harlem	Columbia	– 7 64	35	6

SOUNDS NICE

Love At First Sight	Parlophone	4 10 69	18	10

SOUNDS ORCHESTRAL

Cast Your Fate To The Wind	Piccadilly	2 1 65	5	16
Moonglow	Piccadilly	– 7 65	43	2

SOUTH, JOE

Games People Play	Capitol	15 3 69	6	11

SOUTHLANDERS

Alone	Decca	29 11 57	17	6
Put A Light In The Window	Decca	15 2 58	20	1

SOVEREIGN COLLECTION

Mozart 40	Capitol	– 4 71	27	6

SOXX, BOB B. AND THE BLUE JEANS

Zip-A-Dee-Doo-Dah	London	– 1 63	45	2

SPARKS

This Town Ain't Big Enough For The Both Of Us	Island	18 5 74	2	10
Amateur Hour	Island	27 7 74	7	9
Never Turn Your Back On Mother Earth	Island	2 11 74	13	7
Something For The Girl With Everything	Island	8 2 75	17	7
Get In The Swing	Island	– 7 75	27	7
Look, Looks, Looks	Island	– 10 75	26	5

SPEARS, BILLIE JO

Blanket On The Ground	Un.Artists	9 8 75	6	13

SPEDDING, CHRIS

Motor Biking	RAK	13 9 75	14	8

JOHNNY SPENCE ORCHESTRA

Theme From 'Dr. Kildare'	Parlophone	31 3 62	15	15

SPENCER, DON

Fireball XL5	HMV	– 3 63	32	12

SPINNERS

see DETROIT SPINNERS, MOTOWN SPINNERS

SPLINTER

Costafine Town	Dark Horse	30 11 74	17	10

SPOTNIKS

Orange Blossom Special	Oriole	– 6 62	29	10
The Rocket Man	Oriole	– 9 62	38	9
Hava Nagila	Oriole	17 2 63	13	12
Just Listen To My Heart	Oriole	– 4 63	36	6

SPRINGFIELD, DUSTY

I Only Want To Be With You	Philips	7 12 63	4	18
Stay Awhile	Philips	29 2 64	13	10
I Just Don't Know What To Do With Myself	Philips	11 7 64	3	12
Losing You	Philips	21 11 64	9	13
Your Hurtin' Kind Of Love	Philips	– 1 65	37	4
In The Middle Of Nowhere	Philips	10 7 65	8	10
Some Of Your Lovin'	Philips	7 10 65	8	12
Little By Little	Philips	19 2 66	17	9
You Don't Have To Say You Love Me	Philips	9 4 66	1	13

Goin' Back	Philips	16 7 66	10	10
All I See Is You	Philips	24 9 66	9	12
I'll Try Anything	Philips	14 3 67	13	9
Give Me Time	Philips	8 7 67	19	7
I Close My Eyes (And Count To Ten)	Philips	27 7 68	4	12
Son Of A Preacher Man	Philips	21 12 68	9	9
Am I The Same Girl	Philips	– 9 69	43	4
How Can I Be Sure	Philips	– 9 70	36	4
(see also: SPRINGFIELDS)				

SPRINGFIELDS

Breakaway	Philips	– 8 61	31	8
Bambino	Philips	6 1 62	15	12
Island Of Dreams	Philips	20 1 63	5	26
Say I Won't Be There	Philips	13 4 63	5	15
Come On Home	Philips	– 7 63	31	6

SPRINGWATER

I Will Return	Polydor	6 11 71	5	12

SQUIRES, DOROTHY

Say It With Flowers	Columbia	– 8 61	23	10
(with RUSS CONWAY)				
For Once In My Life	President	– 9 69	24	11
'Till	President	– 2 70	25	11
My Way	President	– 8 70	25	24

STAFFORD, JIM

Spiders And Snakes	MGM	11 5 74	14	9
My Girl Bill	MGM	27 7 74	20	8

STAFFORD, JO

Suddenly There's A Valley	Philips	9 12 55	12	6

STAFFORD, TERRY

Suspicion	London	– 5 64	31	9

STAIFFI AND HIS MUSTAPHAS

Mustapha	Pye	– 7 60	43	1

STAMFORD BRIDGE

Chelsea	P.Farthing	– 1 71	48	1

STANG, ARNOLD

Ivy Will Cling	Fontana	5 12 59	18	1

STAPLE SINGERS

I'll Take You There	Stax	– 6 72	30	8
If You're Ready (Come Go With Me)	Stax	– 6 74	34	6

STAPLETON, CYRIL

Elephant Tango	Decca	27 5 55	19	4
Blue Star	Decca	23 9 55	2	12
The Italian Theme	Decca	6 4 56	18	1

STARDUST, ALVIN

My Coo-Ca-Choo	Magnet	24 11 73	2	21

Jealous Mind	Magnet	23 2 74	1	11
Red Dress	Magnet	11 5 74	7	8
You You You	Magnet	7 9 74	6	10
Tell Me Why	Magnet	14 12 74	16	8
Good Love Can Never Die	Magnet	15 2 75	11	9
Sweet Cheatin' Rita	Magnet	– 7 75	37	4
(see also: SHANE FENTON AND THE FENTONES)				

STARGAZERS

Somebody	Decca	11 3 55	20	1
Crazy Otto Rag	Decca	3 6 55	18	3
Close The Door	Decca	9 9 55	6	9
Twenty Tiny Fingers	Decca	11 11 55	4	11
Hot Diggity	Decca	9 6 56	17	1

STARR, EDWIN

Stop Her On Sight	Polydor	– 5 66	35	7
Headline News	Polydor	– 8 66	39	3
SOS/Headline News (re-issue)	Polydor	18 1 69	11	11
25 Miles (re-issue)	T.Motown	– 9 69	36	6
War	T.Motown	24 10 70	3	12
Stop The War Now	T.Motown	– 2 71	33	4

STARR, FREDDIE

It's You	Tiffany	2 3 74	9	10
White Christmas	Thunderbird	– 12 75	41	4

STARR, KAY

Am I A Toy Or A Treasure	Capitol	– 10 54	17	3
Rock And Roll Waltz	HMV	17 2 56	1	18

STARR, RINGO

It Don't Come Easy	Apple	24 4 71	4	11
Back Off Boogaloo	Apple	8 4 72	2	10
Photograph	Apple	10 11 73	8	13
You're Sixteen	Apple	23 2 74	4	10
Only You	Apple	– 11 74	28	11
(see also: BEATLES)				

STATLER BROTHERS

Flowers On The Wall	CBS	– 2 66	38	4

STATUS QUO

Pictures Of Matchstick Men	Pye Int.	10 2 68	7	11
Ice In The Sun	Pye Int.	21 9 68	8	12
Are You Growing Tired Of My Love	Pye	– 6 69	46	2
Down The Dustpipe	Pye	20 6 70	12	17
In My Chair	Pye	– 11 70	21	14
Paper Plane	Vertigo	27 1 73	8	11
Mean Girl	Pye	26 5 73	20	10
Caroline	Vertigo	29 9 73	5	13
Break The Rules	Vertigo	18 5 74	8	8
Down Down	Vertigo	14 12 74	1	11
Roll Over Lay Down EP	Vertigo	24 5 75	9	8
Rain	Vertigo	21 2 76	7	7

STEALERS WHEEL

Stuck In The Middle With You	A & M	2 6 73	8	10
Everything Will Turn Out Fine	A & M	– 9 73	33	6
Star	A & M	– 1 74	25	6

STEAM

Na Na, Hey Hey, Kiss Him Goodbye	Fontana	7 3 70	9	14

STEELE, ANTHONY AND THE RADIO REVELLERS

West Of Zanzibar	Polygon	- 10 54	13	6

STEELE, TOMMY

Rock With The Cave Man	Decca	2 11 56	11	3
Singing The Blues	Decca	21 12 56	1	10
Knee Deep In The Blues	Decca	22 2 57	16	4
Butterfingers	Decca	17 5 57	9	15
Shiralee	Decca	23 8 57	14	3
Water Water/Handful Of Songs	Decca	30 8 57	5	13
Nairobi	Decca	7 3 58	3	10
Happy Guitar/Princess	Decca	25 4 58	14	4
The Only Man On The Island	Decca	18 7 58	15	7
Come On, Let's Go	Decca	21 11 58	9	11
Give Give Give/Tallahassie Lassie	Decca	15 8 59	17	3
Little White Bull	Decca	28 11 59	6	10
What A Mouth	Decca	26 6 60	5	11
Must Be Santa	Decca	- 12 60	40	1
The Writing On The Wall	Decca	12 8 61	18	6

STEELEYE SPAN

Gaudete (re-issue)	Chrysalis	22 12 73	14	9
All Around My Hat	Chrysalis	22 11 75	5	10

STEELY DAN

Do It Again (re-issue)	ABC	- 8 75	39	4

STEPPENWOLF

Born To Be Wild (re-issue)	Stateside	- 6 69	30	9

STEVENS, CAT

I Love My Dog	Deram	- 10 66	28	7
Matthew And Son	Deram	14 1 67	2	10
I'm Gonna Get Me A Gun	Deram	22 4 67	6	10
A Bad Night	Deram	26 8 67	20	8
Kitty	Deram	- 12 67	47	1
Lady D'Arbanville	Island	11 7 70	8	13
Moon Shadow	Island	- 8 71	22	11
Morning Has Broken	Island	15 1 72	9	14
Can't Keep It In	Island	20 1 73	13	12
Another Saturday Night	Island	28 9 74	19	8

STEVENS, CONNIE

Kookie, Kookie Lend Me Your Comb	Warner Bros.	1 5 60	20	9
(with EDDIE BYRNES)				
Sixteen Reasons	Warner Bros.	15 5 60	12	11

STEVENS, RAY

Everything Is Beautiful	CBS	23 5 70	6	16
Bridget The Midget	CBS	20 3 71	2	15
Turn Your Radio On	CBS	- 3 72	33	4
The Streak	Janus	1 6 74	1	12
Misty	Janus	28 6 75	2	10
Indian Love Call	Janus	- 9 75	34	4

STEVENS, RICKY

I Cried For You	Columbia	- 12 62	34	8

STEVENSON'S ROCKET

Alright Baby	Magnet	- 11 75	37	5

STEWART, ANDY

Donald Where's Your Trousers	Top Rank	- 12 60	37	1
A Scottish Soldier	Top Rank	- 1 61	23	30
The Battle's O'er	Top Rank	- 5 61	28	13
Doctor Finlay	HMV	- 8 65	44	5

STEWART, BILLY

Summertime	Chess	- 9 66	39	2

STEWART, ROD

Maggie May/Reason To Believe	Mercury	11 9 71	1	22
You Wear It Well	Mercury	19 8 72	1	12
Angel/What Made Milwaukee Famous	Mercury	25 11 72	4	11
Oh No, Not My Baby	Mercury	15 9 73	6	8
Farewell/Bring It On Home To Me/You Send Me	Mercury	12 10 74	7	7
Sailing	Warner Bros.	23 8 75	1	11
This Old Heart Of Mine	Warner Bros.	22 11 75	4	9

(see also: JEFF BECK GROUP, FACES, PYTHON LEE JACKSON)

STILLS, STEPHEN

Love The One You're With	Atlantic	- 2 71	37	8

(see also: CROSBY, STILLS AND NASH)

STOLLER, RHET

Chariot	Decca	8 1 61	19	9

STOLOFF, MORRIS

Moonglow/Theme From 'Picnic'	Brunswick	1 6 56	9	8

STONE, R. AND J.

We Do It	RCA	17 1 76	5	9

STORM, DANNY

Honest I Do	Piccadilly	- 4 62	42	4

STORM, GALE

I Hear You Knocking	London	17 3 56	17	1

STRAKER, PETER WITH DR. TELENY

Spirit Is Willing	RAK	- 2 72	40	4

STRAWBS

Lay Down	A & M	25 11 72	12	13
Part Of The Union	A & M	27 1 73	2	11
Shine On Silver Sun	A & M	- 10 73	34	3

STREISAND, BARBRA

Second Hand Rose	CBS	19 2 66	14	13
Stoney End	CBS	- 1 71	27	11
The Way We Were	CBS	- 3 74	32	6

STRETCH

Why Did You Do It?	Anchor	22 11 75	16	9

STRING-A-LONGS

Wheels	London	12 2 61	12	16

STYLISTICS

Betcha By Golly Wow	Avco	22 7 72	13	12
I'm Stone In Love With You	Avco	11 11 72	9	10
Break Up To Make Up	Avco	– 3 73	34	5
Peek-A-Boo	Avco	– 6 73	36	6
Rockin'Roll Baby	Avco	26 1 74	6	9
You Make Me Feel Brand New	Avco	27 7 74	2	14
Let's Put It All Together	Avco	2 11 74	9	9
Star On A T.V. Show	Avco	8 2 75	12	8
Sing Baby Sing	Avco	17 5 75	3	10
I Can't Give You Anything (But My Love)	Avco	2 8 75	1	11
Na Na Is The Saddest Word	Avco	29 11 75	5	10
Funky Weekend	Avco	28 2 76	10	7

SUNDRAGON

Green Tambourine	MGM	– 2 68	50	1

SUNNY

Doctor's Orders	CBS	13 4 74	7	10

SUPERTRAMP

Dreamer	A & M	8 3 75	13	10

SUPREMES

Where Did Our Love Go?	Stateside	11 9 64	3	13
Baby Love	Stateside	31 10 64	1	15
Come See About Me	Stateside	– 1 65	27	6
Stop In The Name Of Love	T.Motown	10 4 65	6	12
Back In My Arms Again	T.Motown	– 6 65	40	5
I Hear A Symphony	T.Motown	– 12 65	39	5
You Can't Hurry Love	T.Motown	17 9 66	3	12
You Keep Me Hangin' On	T.Motown	10 12 66	8	10
Love Is Here And Now You're Gone	T.Motown	25 3 67	17	10
The Happening	T.Motown	27 5 67	6	12
Why (Must We Fall In Love) (with TEMPTATIONS)	T.Motown	– 3 70	34	7
Up On The Ladder To The Roof	T.Motown	30 5 70	6	15
Stoned Love	T.Motown	30 1 71	3	13
River Deep Mountain High (with FOUR TOPS)	T.Motown	10 7 71	11	11
Nathan Jones	T.Motown	4 9 71	5	11
You Gotta Have Love In Your Heart (with FOUR TOPS)	T.Motown	– 11 71	25	10
Floy Joy	T.Motown	18 3 72	9	10
Automatically Sunshine	T.Motown	29 7 72	10	9
Bad Weather	T.Motown	– 4 73	37	4
Baby Love (re-issue)	T.Motown	14 9 74	12	10

(see also: DIANA ROSS AND THE SUPREMES, DIANA ROSS)

SUPRISE SISTERS

La Booga Rooga	Good Earth	– 3 76	38	3

SURFARIS
Wipe Out	London	3 8 63	5	14

SUZUKI, PAT
I Enjoy Being A Girl	RCA	- 4 60	49	1

SWAN, BILLY
I Can Help	Monument	21 12 74	6	9
Don't Be Cruel	Monument	- 5 75	42	4

SWEET
Funny Funny	RCA	10 4 71	13	15
Co-Co	RCA	19 6 71	2	15
Alexander Graham Bell	RCA	- 10 71	33	5
Poppa Joe	RCA	26 2 72	11	12
Little Willy	RCA	24 6 72	4	14
Wig-Wam Bam	RCA	23 9 72	4	13
Blockbuster	RCA	13 1 73	1	15
Hell Raiser	RCA	5 5 73	2	11
Ballroom Blitz	RCA	22 9 73	2	9
Teenage Rampage	RCA	19 1 74	2	8
The Six Teens	RCA	13 7 74	9	7
Turn It Down	RCA	- 11 74	41	2
Fox On The Run	RCA	29 3 75	2	10
Action	RCA	26 7 75	15	6
Lies In Your Eyes	RCA	- 1 76	35	5

SWEET DREAMS
Honey Honey	Bradleys	17 8 74	10	12

SWEET SENSATION
Sad Sweet Dreamer	Pye	28 9 74	1	10
Purely By Coincidence	Pye	25 1 75	11	7

SWINGING BLUE JEANS
It's Too Late Now	HMV	- 6 63	30	9
Hippy Hippy Shake	HMV	4 1 64	2	17
Good Golly Miss Molly	HMV	4 4 64	11	10
You're No Good	HMV	20 6 64	3	13
Don't Make Me Over	HMV	- 1 66	31	8

SYLVIA (AMERICAN)
Pillow Talk	London	21 7 73	14	11

SYLVIA (SWEDISH)
Y Viva Espana	Sonet	24 8 74	4	16
Hasta La Vista	Sonet	- 4 75	38	5

SYMBOLS
Bye Bye Baby	President	- 8 67	44	3
Best Part Of Breaking Up	President	- 1 68	25	11

SYREETA
Spinnin' And Spinnin'	T.Motown	- 9 74	49	3
Your Kiss Is Sweet	T.Motown	15 2 75	12	8
Harmour Love	T.Motown	- 7 75	32	4

T. REX (FORMERLY TYRANNOSAURUS REX)
Deborah	R.Zonophone	- 5 68	34	7
One Inch Rock	R.Zonophone	- 9 68	28	7

King Of The Rumbling Spires	R.Zonophone	- 8 69	44	1
Ride A White Swan	Fly	21 11 70	2	21
Hot Love	Fly	6 3 71	1	17
Get It On	Fly	17 7 71	1	12
Jeepster	Fly	20 11 71	2	15
Telegram Sam	T.Rex	29 1 72	1	12
Metal Guru	T.Rex	13 5 72	1	14
Deborah/One Inch Rock (re-issue)	Magni Fly	15 4 72	7	10
Children Of The Revolution	T.Rex	16 9 72	2	10
Solid Gold Easy Action	EMI - MARC	9 12 72	2	11
20th Century Boy	EMI - MARC	10 3 73	3	9
Groover	EMI - MARC	16 6 73	4	9
Truck On (Tyke)	EMI - MARC	1 12 73	12	11
Teenage Dream (MARC BOLAN)	EMI - MARC	9 2 74	13	5
Light Of Love	EMI - MARC	- 7 74	22	5
Zip Gun Boogie	EMI - MARC	- 11 74	41	3
New York City	EMI	26 7 75	15	8
Dreamy Lady	EMI	- 10 75	30	5
London Boys	EMI	- 3 76	40	3

TAMS

Be Young Be Foolish Be Happy	Stateside	- 2 70	37	5
Hey Girl Don't Bother Me (re-issue)	Probe	21 8 71	1	17

TANEGA, NORMA

Walking My Cat Named Dog	Stateside	- 4 66	22	8

TARRIERS

Banana Boat Song	Columbia	8 3 57	11	6

TAYLOR, FELICE

I Feel Love Coming On	President	18 11 67	11	12

TAYLOR, JAMES

Fire And Rain	Warner Bros.	- 11 70	42	3
You've Got A Friend	Warner Bros.	11 9 71	4	15
Mockingbird (with CARLY SIMON)	Elektra	- 3 74	34	5

TAYLOR, R. DEAN

Gotta See Jane	T.Motown	20 7 68	17	11
Indiana Wants Me	T.Motown	1 5 71	2	15
There's A Ghost In My House	T.Motown	25 5 74	3	12
Window Shopping	Polydor	- 8 74	36	5
Gotta See Jane (re-issue)	T.Motown	- 9 74	41	4

TAYLOR, VINCE

I'll Be Your Hero/Jet Black Machine	Palette	18 9 60	15	9

TEACH-IN

Ding-A-Dong	Polydor	19 4 75	13	7

TEDDY BEARS

To Know Him Is To Love Him	London	10 1 59	2	10

TEENAGERS, FRANKIE LYMON AND THE

Why Do Fools Fall In Love	Columbia	6 7 56	1	14
I'm Not A Juvenile Delinquent	Columbia	12 4 57	7	6

Baby Baby	Columbia	12 4 57	2	9

TEMPERANCE SEVEN

You're Driving Me Crazy	Parlophone	26 3 61	1	16
Pasadena	Parlophone	4 6 61	4	17
Hard Hearted Hannah/Chilli Bom-Bom	Parlophone	30 9 61	19	6
The Charleston	Parlophone	2 12 61	14	9

TEMPO, NINO AND APRIL STEVENS

Deep Purple	London	7 12 63	17	11
Whispering	London	8 2 64	20	8

TEMPTATIONS

My Girl	Stateside	– 3 65	43	1
It's Growing	T.Motown	– 4 65	45	2
Ain't Too Proud To Beg	T.Motown	– 7 66	21	11
Beauty Is Only Skin Deep	T.Motown	12 11 66	18	10
(I Know) I'm Losing You	T.Motown	14 1 67	19	9
You're My Everything	T.Motown	– 9 67	26	15
I Wish It Would Rain	T.Motown	– 3 68	45	1
I Could Never Love Another	T.Motown	– 6 68	47	1
I'm Gonna Make You Love Me	T.Motown	8 2 69	3	11
(with DIANA ROSS AND THE SUPREMES)				
Get Ready (re-issue)	T.Motown	22 3 69	10	9
Cloud Nine	T.Motown	13 9 69	15	10
I Second That Emotion	T.Motown	4 10 69	18	8
(with DIANA ROSS AND THE SUPREMES)				
I Can't Get Next To You	T.Motown	31 1 70	13	9
Why (Must We Fall In Love)	T.Motown	– 3 70	34	7
(with DIANA ROSS AND THE SUPREMES)				
Psychedelic Shack	T.Motown	– 6 70	33	7
Ball Of Confusion	T.Motown	10 10 70	7	15
Just My Imagination	T.Motown	19 6 71	8	16
Superstar (Remember How You Got Where You Are)	T.Motown	– 2 72	32	6
Take A Look Around	T.Motown	6 5 72	13	10
Papa Was A Rolling Stone	T.Motown	20 1 73	14	8
Law Of The Land	T.Motown	– 9 73	41	4

10 C.C.

Donna	UK	7 10 72	2	13
Rubber Bullets	UK	2 6 73	1	15
The Dean And I	UK	8 9 73	10	8
Wall Street Shuffle	UK	29 6 74	10	10
Silly Love	UK	– 9 74	24	7
Life Is A Minestrone	Mercury	19 4 75	7	8
I'm Not In Love	Mercury	7 6 75	1	11
Art For Art's Sake	Mercury	20 12 75	5	10
I'm Mandy Fly Me	Mercury	27 3 76	6	8

TEN YEARS AFTER

Love Like A Man	Deram	18 7 70	10	18

TERRELL, TAMMI

see MARVIN GAYE

TERRY DACTYL AND THE DINOSAURS

Seaside Shuffle (re-issue)	UK	22 7 72	2	12
On A Saturday Night	UK	– 1 73	45	4

THEM

Baby Please Don't Go/Gloria	Decca	16 1 65	10	9

Here Comes The Night	Decca	3	4 65	2	12

THIN LIZZY

Whisky In The Jar	Decca	10	2 73	6	12

THOMAS, B.J.

Raindrops Keep Falling On My Head	Wand	-	2 70	42	4

THOMAS, EVELYN

Weak Spot	20th Century	-	1 76	26	7
Doomsday	20th Century	-	4 76	41	4

THOMAS, JAMO

I Spy For The F.B.I. (re-issue)	Polydor	-	5 69	44	2

THOMAS, NICKY

Love Of The Common People	Trojan	4	7 70	9	14

THOMAS, RUFUS

Do The Funky Chicken	Stax	23	5 70	18	12

THOMAS, TIMMY

Why Can't We Live Together	Mojo	24	3 73	12	11

THOMPSON, SUE

Sad Movies (Make Me Cry)	Polydor	-	11 61	46	2
Paper Tiger	Hickory	-	1 65	30	7

THORNE, DAVID

Alley Cat Song	Stateside	-	1 63	28	8

KEN THORNE ORCHESTRA

Theme Form 'The Legion's Last Patrol'	HMV	3	8 63	4	13

THREE DEGREES

The Year Of Decision	Philadelphia	4	5 74	13	10
When Will I See You Again?	Philadelphia	20	7 74	1	16
Get Your Love Back	Philadelphia	-	11 74	34	4
Take Good Care Of Yourself	Philadelphia	26	4 75	9	9
Long Lost Lover	Philadelphia	-	7 75	40	4
Toast Of Love	Philadelphia	-	5 76	36	4

THREE DOG NIGHT

Mama Told Me Not To Come	Stateside	22	8 70	3	14
Joy To The World	Probe	-	5 71	24	10

THREE GOOD REASONS

Nowhere Man	Mercury	-	3 66	47	3

THREE KAYES

Ivory Tower (see also: KAYE SISTERS)	HMV	8	6 56	20	1

THUNDERTHIGHS

Central Park Arrest	Philips	-	6 74	30	5

TILLOTSON, JOHNNY

Poetry In Motion	London	20 11 60	1	15
Jimmy's Girl	London	- 1 61	43	2
It Keeps Right On A-Hurtin'	London	- 7 62	31	11
Send Me The Pillow You Dream On	London	- 10 62	21	9
I Can't Help It	London	- 12 62	41	7
Out Of My Mind	London	- 5 63	34	5

TIMEBOX

Beggin'	Deram	- 7 68	38	4

TINY TIM

Great Balls Of Fire	Reprise	- 2 69	45	1

TITANIC

Sultana	CBS	9 10 71	5	12

TODD, NICK

At The Hop	London	22 2 58	14	2

TOKENS

The Lion Sleeps Tonight	London	13 1 62	16	12

TONY CAMILLO'S BAZUKA

Dynomite	A & M	- 5 75	28	5

TOPOL

If I Were A Rich Man	CBS	17 6 67	9	20

TORME, MEL

Mountain Greenery	Vogue-Coral	18 5 56	4	17
Comin' Home Baby	London	20 1 63	13	8

TORNADOES

Telstar	Decca	15 9 62	1	25
Globe Trotter	Decca	20 1 63	5	11
Robot	Decca	13 4 63	17	12
The Ice Cream Man	Decca	29 6 63	18	9
Dragonfly	Decca	- 10 63	41	2

TOROK, MITCHELL

When Mexico Gave Up The Rhumba	Brunswick	5 10 56	7	15

TOYS

A Lover's Concerto	Stateside	20 11 65	5	13
Attack	Stateside	- 1 66	36	4

TRAFFIC

Paper Sun	Island	17 6 67	5	10
A Hole In My Shoe	Island	23 9 67	2	14
Here We Go Round The Mulberry Bush	Island	9 12 67	8	12
No Face, No Name, No Number	Island	- 3 68	40	4

TRAMMPS

Zing Went The Strings Of My Heart	Buddah	- 11 74	29	11

Sixty Minute Man	Buddah	- 2 75	40	4
Hold Back The Night	Buddah	25 10 75	5	8
Where The Happy People Go	Buddah	- 3 76	35	8

TRASH

Golden Slumbers/Carry That Weight	Apple	- 10 69	35	3

TREMELOES

Here Comes My Baby	CBS	18 2 67	4	11
Silence Is Golden	CBS	6 5 67	1	15
Even The Bad Times Are Good	CBS	12 8 67	4	13
Be Mine	CBS	- 11 67	39	2
Suddenly You Love Me	CBS	27 1 68	6	11
Helule Helule	CBS	25 5 68	14	10
My Little Lady	CBS	5 10 68	6	12
I Shall Be Released	CBS	- 12 68	29	5
Hello World	CBS	19 4 69	14	8
(Call Me) Number One	CBS	1 11 69	2	14
By The Way	CBS	- 3 70	35	6
Me And My Life	CBS	26 9 70	4	18
Right Wheel Left Hammer Sham	CBS	- 2 71	46	4
Hello Buddy	CBS	- 7 71	32	7

(see also: BRIAN POOLE)

TRENT, JACKIE

Where Are You Now My Love	Pye	8 5 65	1	10
When The Summertime Is Over	Pye	- 7 65	39	2
I'll Be There	Pye	- 4 69	41	4

TRIBE, TONY

Red Red Wine	Downtown	- 7 69	46	2

TROGGS

Wild Thing	Fontana	14 5 66	2	12
With A Girl Like You	Fontana	23 7 66	1	12
I Can't Control Myself	Page One	8 10 66	2	13
Anyway That You Want Me	Page One	31 12 66	8	10
Give It To Me	Page One	11 3 67	12	10
Night Of The Long Grass	Page One	17 6 67	17	6
Hi Hi Hazel	Page One	- 7 67	42	3
Love Is All Around	Page One	4 11 67	5	14
Little Girl	Page One	- 3 68	37	4

TROUBADOURS DU ROI BAUDOIN

Sanctus	Philips	- 3 69	31	11

TROY, DORIS

What'cha Gonna Do About It	Atlantic	- 11 64	37	12

TRUTH

Girl	Pye	- 2 66	27	6

TUCKER, TOMMY

Hi Heel Sneakers	Pye	- 3 64	23	10

TURNER, IKE AND TINA

River Deep Mountain High	London	18 6 66	3	13
Tell Her I'm Not At Home	Warner Bros.	- 8 66	48	1
A Love Like Yours (Don't Come Knocking Everyday)	London	26 11 66	16	10

River Deep Mountain High (re-issue)	London	– 2 69	33	7
Nutbush City Limits	Un.Artists	22 9 73	4	13

TURNER, SAMMY

Always	London	14 11 59	20	1

TURTLES

Happy Together	London	15 4 67	12	12
She'd Rather Be With Me	London	24 6 67	4	15
Eleanore	London	16 11 68	7	15

TWICE AS MUCH

Sittin' On A Fence	Immediate	– 6 66	25	9

TWINKLE

Terry	Decca	19 12 64	4	15
Golden Lights	Decca	– 2 65	21	5

TWITTY, CONWAY

It's Only Make Believe	MGM	14 11 58	1	14
Hey Little Lucy	MGM	16 5 59	20	1
Mona Lisa	MGM	15 8 59	6	13
Is A Blue Bird Blue	MGM	– 7 60	43	3
C'Est Si Bon	MGM	– 2 61	40	3

TYMES

So Much In Love	Cameo P'way	– 7 63	21	8
People	Direction	8 2 69	16	10
You Little Trustmaker	RCA	19 10 74	18	9
Ms. Grace	RCA	11 1 75	1	11
God's Gonna Punish You	RCA	– 1 76	41	3

TYPICALLY TROPICAL

Barbados	Gull	12 7 75	1	11

TYRANNOSAURUS REX

see T. REX

UNDERTAKERS

Just A Little Bit	Pye	– 4 64	49	1

UNION GAP

see GARY PUCKETT

UNIT 4 + 2

Green Fields	Decca	– 2 64	48	2
Concrete And Clay	Decca	20 3 65	1	15
You've Never Been In Love Like This Before	Decca	5 6 65	14	11
Baby Never Say Goodbye	Decca	– 3 66	49	1

PHIL UPCHURCH COMBO

You Can't Sit Down	Sue	– 5 66	39	2

UPSETTERS

Return Of Django	Upsetter	18 10 69	5	14

VALANCE, RICKY

Tell Laura I Love Her	Columbia	21 8 60	1	16

VALENS, RITCHIE

Donna	London	28 3 59	20	2

VALENTE, CATERINA

The Breeze And I	Polydor	19 8 55	5	14

VALENTINE, DICKIE

Endless	Decca	- 11 54	19	1
Finger Of Suspicion	Decca	7 1 55	1	12
Mr. Sandman	Decca	7 1 55	5	9
A Blossom Fell	Decca	18 2 55	9	10
I Wonder	Decca	3 6 55	4	15
Christmas Alphabet	Decca	25 11 55	1	7
Old Pianna Rag	Decca	16 12 55	20	3
Christmas Island	Decca	14 12 56	20	1
One More Sunrise	Pye	24 10 59	14	4

VALINO, JOE

Garden Of Eden	HMV	19 1 57	17	2

VALLI, FRANKIE

You're Ready Now (re-issue)	Philips	16 1 71	11	13
My Eyes Adored You	Pr.Stock	22 2 75	5	11
Swearin' To God	Pr.Stock	- 6 75	31	5
(see also: FOUR SEASONS)				

VAN DYKE, LEROY

Walk On By	Mercury	13 1 62	5	17
Big Man In A Big House	Mercury	- 4 62	34	3

VANILLA FUDGE

You Keep Me Hangin' On	Atlantic	16 9 67	18	11

VANITY FARE

I Live For The Sun	Page One	28 9 68	20	9
Early In The Morning	Page One	9 8 69	8	12
Hitchin' A Ride	Page One	7 2 70	16	13

VAUGHAN, FRANKIE

Happy Days And Lonely Nights	HMV	28 1 55	12	3
Tweedle Dee	Philips	22 4 55	17	1
Seventeen	Philips	2 12 55	18	3
My Boy Flat Top	Philips	3 2 56	20	2
The Green Door	Philips	9 11 56	2	15
Garden Of Eden	Philips	11 1 57	1	12
Man On Fire/Wanderin' Eyes	Philips	4 10 57	6	11
You Gotta Have Somethin' In The Bank, Frank (with KAYE SISTERS)	Philips	1 11 57	7	8
Kisses Sweeter Than Wine	Philips	27 12 57	11	8
Can't Get Along Without You/We Are Not Alone	Philips	7 3 58	10	4
Kewpie Doll	Philips	16 5 58	8	9
Come Softly To Me	Philips	25 4 59	9	8
Heart Of A Man	Philips	25 7 59	6	12
Kookie Little Paradise	Philips	- 9 60	31	5
Milord	Philips	- 10 60	34	6
Tower Of Strength	Philips	11 11 61	1	14
Don't Stop, Twist	Philips	10 2 62	14	12
Hercules	Philips	- 9 62	42	4
Loop De Loop	Philips	10 2 63	5	12
Hey Mama	Philips	- 6 63	21	9

Hello Dolly	Philips	27 6 64	18	11
Someone Must Have Hurt You A Lot	Philips	- 3 65	46	1
There Must Be A Way	Columbia	16 9 67	7	21
So Tired	Columbia	- 11 67	21	8
Nevertheless	Columbia	- 3 68	29	5

VAUGHAN, MALCOLM

Every Day Of My Life	HMV	1 7 55	5	16
With Your Love	HMV	27 1 56	17	2
St. Theresa Of The Roses	HMV	16 11 56	3	18
Chapel Of The Roses	HMV	10 5 57	16	6
My Special Angel	HMV	29 11 57	3	14
To Be Loved	HMV	4 4 58	14	8
More Than Ever	HMV	17 10 58	6	13
Wait For Me	HMV	28 2 59	15	6

VAUGHAN, NORMAN

Swingin' In The Rain	Pye	- 5 62	34	5

VAUGHAN, SARAH

Broken-Hearted Melody	Mercury	26 9 59	9	10
Lets/Seranata	Columbia	- 12 61	37	4
Passing Strangers (with BILLY ECKSTINE)	Mercury	26 4 69	17	13

VAUGHN, BILLY

The Shifting Whispering Sands	London	27 1 56	9	6
Theme From 'The Threepenny Opera'	London	23 3 56	12	5

VEE, BOBBY

Rubber Ball	London	8 1 61	3	11
More Than I Can Say/Staying In	London	23 4 61	3	16
How Many Tears	London	12 8 61	13	14
Take Good Care Of My Baby	London	28 10 61	1	17
Run To Him	London	6 1 62	10	15
Please Don't Ask About Barbara	Liberty	- 3 62	29	9
Sharing You	Liberty	16 6 62	10	13
A Forever Kind Of Love	Liberty	15 12 62	13	19
The Night Has A Thousand Eyes	Liberty	17 2 63	3	12
Bobby Tomorrow	Liberty	- 6 63	21	10

VELVELETTES

These Things Will Keep Me Loving You (re-issue)	T.Motown	- 7 71	34	7

VELVETS

Lucky Old Sun	London	- 5 61	46	1
Tonight	London	- 8 61	50	1

VENTURES

Walk Don't Run	London	11 9 60	8	14
Perfidia	London	4 12 60	5	13
Ram-Bunk-Shush	London	- 3 61	45	1
Lullaby Of The Leaves	London	- 5 61	43	4

VERNON GIRLS FEATURING MAUREEN

Lover Please	Decca	16 6 62	16	16

Loco Motion	Decca	– 9 62	47	1
You Know What I Mean	Decca	– 10 62	37	4
Funny All Over	Decca	– 1 63	31	8
Do The Bird	Decca	– 4 63	44	2

VIENNA PHILHARMONIC ORCHESTRA

Theme From 'The Onedin Line'	Decca	15 1 72	15	14

VINCENT, GENE

Be-Bop-A-Lula	Capitol	24 8 56	17	2
Blue Jean Bop	Capitol	9 11 56	12	2
Wild Cat	Capitol	– 3 60	48	1
My Heart	Capitol	12 3 60	16	16
Pistol Packing Mama	Capitol	12 6 60	11	9
She She Little Sheila	Capitol	– 5 61	22	11
I'm Going Home	Capitol	– 8 61	36	4

VINTON, BOBBY

Roses Are Red	Columbia	18 8 62	15	8
There I've Said It Again	Columbia	– 12 63	34	10

VIPERS

Don't You Rock Me Daddy-O	Parlophone	1 2 57	8	6
Cumberland Gap	Parlophone	29 3 57	9	4
Maggie May	Parlophone	20 4 57	20	1

VIRTUES

Guitar Boogie Shuffle	HMV	16 5 59	19	3

VISCOUNTS

Shortnin' Bread	Pye	14 10 60	13	8
Who Put The Bomp	Pye	7 10 61	15	10

WADE, ADAM

Take Good Care Of Her	HMV	– 6 61	38	6

WAIKIKIS

Hawaii Tattoo	Pye	– 3 65	41	2

WAKELIN, JOHNNY AND THE KINSHASA BAND

Black Superman (Muhammed Ali)	Pye	8 2 75	7	10

WALKER BROTHERS

Love Her	Philips	19 6 65	20	13
Make It Easy On Yourself	Philips	28 8 65	1	14
My Ship Is Coming In	Philips	11 12 65	3	12
The Sun Ain't Gonna Shine Anymore	Philips	12 3 66	1	11
(Baby) You Don't Have To Tell Me	Philips	30 7 66	13	8
Another Tear Falls	Philips	8 10 66	12	8
Deadlier Than The Male	Philips	– 12 66	32	6
Stay With Me Baby	Philips	– 2 67	26	6
Walking In The Rain	Philips	– 5 67	26	6
No Regrets	GTO	31 1 76	7	9
(see also: GARY WALKER, JOHN WALKER, SCOTT WALKER)				

WALKER, GARY

You Don't Love Me	CBS	– 2 66	26	6
Twinkie Lee	CBS	– 5 66	26	5
(see also: WALKER BROTHERS)				

WALKER, JOHN

Annabella	Philips	–	7	67	24	6

(see also: WALKER BROTHERS)

WALKER, JUNIOR AND THE ALL STARS

How Sweet It is (To Be Loved By You)	T.Motown	–	8	66	22	10
(I'm A) Roadrunner/Shotgun (re-issue)	T.Motown	26	4	69	12	11
What Does It Take (To Win Your Love)	T.Motown	5	11	69	13	12
Walk In The Night	T.Motown	23	9	72	16	11
Take Me Girl, I'm Ready	T.Motown	17	2	73	16	9
Way Back Home	T.Motown	–	6	73	35	5

WALKER, SCOTT

Jackie	Philips	6	1	68	20	9
Joanna	Philips	18	5	68	7	11
Lights Of Cincinatti	Philips	28	6	69	13	10

(see also: WALKER BROTHERS)

WALLACE, JERRY

You're Singing Our Love Song To Somebody Else	London	–	6	60	46	1

WALLIS, BOB

I'm Shy Mary Ellen, I'm Shy	Pye	–	7	61	44	2
Come Along Please	Pye	–	1	62	33	5

WAR

Low Rider	Island	7	2	76	12	7

WARD, BILLY

Stardust	London	13	9	57	17	3

WARD, CLIFFORD T.

Gaye	Charisma	21	7	73	8	11
Scullery	Charisma	–	1	74	37	5

WARD, MICHAEL

Let There Be Peace On Earth (Let It Begin With Me)	Philips	27	10	73	15	11

WARM SOUNDS

Birds And Bees	Deram	–	5	67	27	6

WARWICK, DIONNE

Anyone Who Had A Heart	Pye	–	2	64	42	3
Walk On By	Pye	2	5	64	9	14
You'll Never Get To Heaven	Pye	15	8	64	20	8
Reach Out For Me	Pye	–	10	64	23	7
You Can Have Him	Pye	–	4	65	34	5
Valley Of The Dolls	Pye	–	3	68	28	8
Do You Know The Way To San José?	Pye	25	5	68	8	10
Then Came You	Atlantic	–	10	74	29	6

(with DETROIT SPINNERS)

WASHINGTON, DINAH

September In The Rain	Mercury	2	12	61	17	6

WASHINGTON, GENO AND THE RAM JAM BAND

Water	Piccadilly	–	5 66	39	8
Hi Hi Hazel	Piccadilly	–	7 66	45	3
Que Sera Sera	Piccadilly	–	10 66	43	3
Michael	Piccadilly	–	1 67	39	5

WEATHERMEN

It's The Same Old Song	B & C	13	2 71	19	10

WEBER, JOAN

Let Me Go Lover	Philips	18	2 55	16	1

WEEDON, BERT

Guitar Boogie Shuffle	Top Rank	9	5 59	6	8
Big Beat Boogie	Top Rank	–	3 60	50	1
Twelfth Street Rag	Top Rank	–	6 60	47	2
Apache	Top Rank	–	7 60	24	4
Sorry Robbie	Top Rank	13	11 60	18	11
Ginchy	Top Rank	–	1 61	31	5
Mr. Guitar	Top Rank	–	4 61	47	1

WEIR, FRANK

Caribbean Honeymoon	Oriole	28	8 60	18	8

WEISSBERG, ERIC AND STEVE MANDEL

Duelling Banjos ('Deliverance' Soundtrack)	Warner Bros.	21	4 73	17	7

WELK, LAWRENCE

Calcutta	RCA	5	2 61	19	7

WELLS, HOUSTON

Only The Heartaches	Parlophone	–	8 63	22	10

WELLS, MARY

My Guy	Stateside	6	6 64	5	14
Once Upon A Time (with MARVIN GAYE)	Stateside	–	7 64	50	1
My Guy (re-issue)	T.Motown	29	7 72	14	10

WELSH, ALEX

Tansy	Columbia	–	8 61	45	4

WEST, DODIE

Goin' Out Of My Head	Decca	–	1 65	39	4

WEST HAM UNITED

I'm Forever Blowing Bubbles	Pye	–	5 75	31	2

WEST, KEITH

Excerpt From A Teenage Opera	Parlophone	26	8 67	2	16
Sam	Parlophone	–	11 67	38	3

WESTON, KIM

see MARVIN GAYE

WHISKEY, NANCY

see CHAS McDEVITT

WHITE, BARRY

I'm Gonna Love You Just A Little Bit More, Baby	Pye	- 6 73	23	7
Never Never Gonna Give Ya Up	Pye	23 2 74	14	11
Can't Get Enough Of Your Love Baby	Pye	7 9 74	8	12
You're The First, The Last My Everything	20th Century	9 11 74	1	14
What Am I Gonna Do With You?	20th Century	15 3 75	5	8
I'll Do For You Anything You Want Me To	20th Century	14 6 75	20	6
Let The Music Play	20th Century	17 1 76	9	7
You See The Trouble With Me	20th Century	13 3 76	2	10

(see also: LOVE UNLIMITED ORCHESTRA)

WHITE, CHRIS

Spanish Wine	Charisma	- 3 76	37	4

WHITE PLAINS

My Baby Loves Lovin'	Deram	21 2 70	9	11
I've Got You On My Mind	Deram	16 5 70	17	11
Julie Do Ya Love Me?	Deram	14 11 70	8	14
When You Are A King	Deram	3 7 71	13	11
Step Into A Dream	Deram	- 2 73	23	9

WHITE, TAM

What In The World's Come Over You?	RAK	- 3 75	36	4

WHITE, TONY JOE

Groupy Girl	Monument	- 6 70	22	10

WHITFIELD, DAVID

Cara Mia	Decca	- 10 54	3	10
Santo Natale	Decca	- 11 54	2	10
Beyond The Stars	Decca	11 2 55	8	9
Mama	Decca	27 5 55	12	11
Everywhere	Decca	8 7 55	3	20
When You Lose The One You Love	Decca	25 11 55	7	11
My September Love	Decca	2 3 56	5	21
The Rudder And The Rock	Decca	17 3 56	19	1
My Son John	Decca	25 8 56	13	2
Adoration Waltz	Decca	25 1 57	11	8
On The Street Where You Live	Decca	20 6 58	18	8
I Believe	Decca	- 11 60	49	1

WHITMAN, SLIM

Rosemarie	London	15 7 55	1	19
Indian Love Call	London	29 7 55	8	12
China Doll	London	23 9 55	15	2
Tumbling Tumbleweeds	London	9 3 56	15	4
I'm A Fool	London	13 4 56	11	5
Serenade	London	3 8 56	9	9
I'll Take You Home Again Kathleen	London	19 4 57	5	11
Happy Anniversary	Un.Artists	26 10 74	14	10

WHITTAKER, ROGER

Leavin' (Durham Town)	Columbia	6 12 69	12	18

I Don't Believe In If					
Anymore (re-issue)	Columbia	9 5 70	8	18
New World In The Morning	Columbia	31 10 70	17	14
Why	Columbia	- 3 71	44	3
Mammy Blue	Columbia	- 10 71	31	10
The Last Farewell	EMI	9 8 75	2	14

WHO

I Can't Explain	Brunswick	27 3 65	8	13
Anyway, Anyhow, Anywhere	Brunswick	19 6 65	10	12
My Generation	Brunswick	13 11 65	2	13
Substitute	Reaction	19 3 66	5	13
A Legal Matter	Brunswick	- 3 66	32	6
I'm A Boy	Reaction	10 9 66	2	12
The Kids Are Alright	Brunswick	- 9 66	41	3
Happy Jack	Reaction	24 12 66	3	11
Pictures Of Lily	Track	6 5 67	4	10
The Last Time/Under My				
Thumb	Track	- 7 67	44	3
I Can See For Miles	Track	11 11 67	10	12
Dogs	Track	- 6 68	25	5
Magic Bus	Track	- 10 68	26	6
Pinball Wizard	Track	5 4 69	4	13
The Seeker	Track	16 5 70	19	11
Summertime Blues	Track	- 8 70	38	4
Won't Get Fooled Again	Track	31 7 71	9	12
Let's See Action	Track	27 11 71	16	12
Join Together	Track	8 7 72	9	9
Relay	Track	- 1 73	21	5
5.15/Water	Track	20 10 73	20	6
Squeeze Box	Polydor	14 2 76	10	9

WIGAN'S CHOSEN FEW

Footsee	Pye	8 2 75	9	12

WIGAN'S OVATION

Skiing In The Snow	Spark	12 4 75	12	10
Per-Son-Ally	Spark	- 6 75	38	6
Super Love	Spark	- 11 75	41	3

WILD, JACK

Something Beautiful	Capitol	- 5 70	46	2

WILDE, MARTY

Endless Sleep	Philips	18 7 58	4	12
Donna	Philips	21 3 59	4	13
A Teenager In Love	Philips	6 6 59	2	13
Sea Of Love	Philips	26 9 59	4	12
Bad Boy	Philips	5 12 59	6	8
Johnny Rocco	Philips	- 3 60	30	5
The Fight	Philips	- 5 60	47	1
Little Girl	Philips	25 12 60	17	9
Rubber Ball	Philips	15 1 61	10	9
Hide And Seek	Philips	- 7 61	47	2
Tomorrow's Clown	Philips	- 11 61	33	5
Jezebel	Philips	16 6 62	19	11
Ever Since You Said Goodbye	Philips	- 10 62	31	7

WILLIAMS, ANDY

Butterfly	London	26 4 57	1	12
I Like Your Kind Of Love	London	12 7 57	18	4
Stranger On The Shore	CBS	- 6 62	30	10
Can't Get Used To Losing You	CBS	20 4 63	2	17
A Fool Never Learns	CBS	- 2 64	40	4

Almost There	CBS	23	9 65	2	17
May Each Day	CBS	19	3 66	19	8
In The Arms Of Love	CBS	–	9 66	33	7
Music To Watch Girls By	CBS	–	5 67	33	6
More And More	CBS	–	8 67	45	1
Can't Keep My Eyes Off You	CBS	6	4 68	5	18
Happy Heart	CBS	28	6 69	19	9
Can't Help Falling In Love	CBS	14	3 70	3	17
It's So Easy	CBS	5	9 70	13	14
Home Lovin' Man	CBS	28	11 70	7	13
Where Do I Begin (Love Story)	CBS	3	4 71	4	18
Love Theme From 'The Godfather'	CBS	–	8 72	42	9
Solitaire	CBS	19	1 74	4	17
Getting Over You	CBS	–	5 74	35	5
You Lay So Easy On My Mind	CBS	–	5 75	32	7
Other Side Of Me	CBS	–	3 76	42	3

WILLIAMS, ANDY AND DAVID

I Don't Know Why	MCA	–	3 73	37	5

WILLIAMS, BILLY

I'm Gonna Sit Right Down And Write Myself A Letter	Vogue-Coral	24	8 57	20	1

WILLIAMS, DANNY

We Will Never Be As Young As This Again	HMV	–	5 61	44	3
The Miracle Of You	HMV	–	7 61	41	8
Moon River	HMV	4	11 61	2	20
Jeannie	HMV	10	2 62	14	14
Wonderful World Of The Young	HMV	28	4 62	8	12
Tears	HMV	–	7 62	22	7
My Own True Love	HMV	–	2 63	45	3

WILLIAMS, LARRY

Short Fat Fannie	London	21	9 57	15	3
Bony Maronie	London	24	1 58	12	7

WILLIAMS, MASON

Classical Gas	Warner Bros.	21	9 68	9	13

WILLIAMS, MAURICE AND THE ZODIACS

Stay	Top Rank	25	12 60	11	9

WILSON, AL

The Snake (re-issue)	Bell	–	8 75	41	5

WILSON, JACKIE

Reet Petite	Coral	29	11 57	3	12
To Be Loved	Coral	15	3 58	17	6
All My Love	Coral	–	9 60	33	7
Alone At Last	Coral	–	12 60	50	1
(Your Love Keeps Lifting Me) Higher And Higher (re-issue)	MCA	31	5 69	11	11
I Get The Sweetest Feeling (re-issue)	MCA	26	8 72	9	13

WING AND A PRAYER, FIFE AND DRUM CORPS

Baby Face	Atlantic	14	2 76	12	7

WINGS

Give Ireland Back To The Irish	Apple	18	3 72	16	8
Mary Had A Little Lamb	Apple	3	6 72	9	11
Hi Hi Hi/C Moon	Apple	6	1 73	5	13
Junior's Farm	Apple	14	12 74	16	10
Listen To What The Man Said	EMI	7	6 75	6	8
Letting Go	EMI	-	10 75	41	3

(see also: PAUL McCARTNEY, McCARTNEY'S WINGS)

EDGAR WINTER GROUP

Frankenstein	Epic	23	6 73	18	9

WISDOM, NORMAN

Wisdom Of A Fool	Columbia	15	3 57	20	2

WITHERS, BILL

Lean On Me	Sussex	9	9 72	18	9

WIZZARD

Ball Park Incident	Harvest	6	1 73	6	12
See My Baby Jive	Harvest	28	4 73	1	17
Angel Fingers	Harvest	1	9 73	1	10
I Wish It Could Be Christmas Everyday	Harvest	8	12 73	4	9
Rock And Roll Winter	Warner Bros.	4	5 74	6	7
This Is The Story Of My Love	Warner Bros.	-	8 74	34	4
Are You Ready To Rock?	Warner Bros.	11	1 75	8	10

WOLF, HOWLIN'

Smokestack Lightnin'	Pye	-	6 64	42	5

WOMBLES

The Wombling Song	CBS	9	2 74	4	23
Remember You're A Womble	CBS	13	4 74	3	16
Banana Rock	CBS	6	7 74	9	13
Minuetto Allegretto	CBS	2	11 74	16	9
Wombling Merry Christmas	CBS	21	12 74	2	8
Wombling White Tie And Tails	CBS	-	5 75	22	7
Super Womble	CBS	23	8 75	20	6
Let's Womble To The Party Tonight	CBS	-	12 75	34	5

WONDER, STEVIE

Uptight (Everything's Alright)	T.Motown	26	2 66	14	10
Blowin' In The Wind	T.Motown	-	8 66	36	5
A Place In The Sun	T.Motown	21	1 67	20	5
I Was Made To Love Her	T.Motown	5	8 67	5	15
I'm Wondering	T.Motown	-	10 67	22	8
Shoo-Be-Doo-Da-Day	T.Motown	-	5 68	46	4
For Once In My Life	T.Motown	4	1 69	3	13
I Don't Know Why	T.Motown	19	4 69	14	11
My Cherie Amour (re-issue)	T.Motown	2	8 69	4	16
Yester-Me, Yester-You, Yesterday	T.Motown	22	11 69	2	13

Never Had A Dream Come True	T.Motown	11	4 70	6	12
Signed, sealed, delivered, I'm Yours	T.Motown	1	8 70	15	10
Heaven Help Us All	T.Motown	-	11 70	30	11
We Can Work It Out	T.Motown	-	5 71	27	7
If You Really Love Me	T.Motown	19	2 72	20	8
Superstition	T.Motown	10	2 73	11	9
You Are The Sunshine Of My Life	T.Motown	26	5 73	7	11
Higher Ground	T.Motown	-	10 73	29	5
Living For The City	T.Motown	2	2 74	15	9
He's Misstra Know It All	T.Motown	27	4 74	10	9
You Havn't Done Nothin'	T.Motown	-	10 74	30	5
Boogie On Reggae Woman	T.Motown	1	2 75	12	7

WOOLEY, SHEB

Purple People Eater	MGM	27	6 58	11	9

WOOD, BRENTON

Gimme Little Sign	Liberty	3	2 68	8	13

WOOD, ROY

Dear Elaine	Harvest	8	9 73	18	8
Forever	Harvest	22	11 73	8	13
Going Down The Road	Harvest	29	6 74	14	7
Oh What A Shame	Jet	14	6 75	13	7

(see also: ELECTRIC LIGHT ORCHESTRA, MOVE, WIZZARD)

WOODWARD, EDWARD

The Way You Look Tonight	DJM	-	1 71	42	3

WRIGHT, BETTY

Shoorah Shoorah	RCA	-	1 75	27	7
Where Is The Love	RCA	-	4 75	25	7

WRIGHT, RUBY

Three Stars	Parlophone	23	5 59	8	6

WURZELS

see ADGE CUTLER

WYATT, ROBERT

I'm A Believer	Virgin	-	9 74	29	6

WYNETTE, TAMMY

Stand By Your Man	Epic	10	5 75	1	12
D.I.V.O.R.C.E.	Epic	12	7 75	12	7

WYNTER, MARK

Image Of A Girl	Decca	21	8 60	11	10
Kicking Up The Leaves	Decca	27	11 60	19	10
Dream Girl	Decca	19	2 61	14	8
Exclusively Yours	Decca	-	6 61	32	7
Venus In Blue Jeans	Pye	20	10 62	4	15
Go Away Little Girl	Pye	6	1 63	6	12
Shy Girl	Pye	-	6 63	28	6
It's Almost Tomorrow	Pye	30	11 63	12	12
Only You	Pye	-	4 64	38	4

YARDBIRDS

Good Morning Little Schoolgirl	Columbia	– 11 64	44	4
For Your Love	Columbia	27 3 65	2	12
Heart Full Of Soul	Columbia	26 6 65	2	13
Evil Hearted You/Still I'm Sad	Columbia	21 10 65	3	10
Shapes Of Things	Columbia	12 3 66	3	9
Over Under Sideways Down	Columbia	11 6 66	10	9
Happenings Ten Years Time Ago	Columbia	– 10 66	43	5

YIN AND YAN

If/Butch Soap	EMI	– 3 75	25	5

YOUNG, FARON

Four In The Morning	Mercury	/12 8 72	3	23

YOUNG IDEA

With A Little Help From My Friends	Columbia	15 7 67	10	6

YOUNG, JIMMY

Unchained Melody	Decca	6 5 55	1	18
Man From Laramie	Decca	16 9 55	1	12
Someone On Your Mind	Decca	23 12 55	13	5
The Chain Gang	Decca	16 3 56	9	5
More	Decca	12 10 56	4	14
Miss You	Columbia	2 11 63	15	13
Unchained Melody (re-issue)	Columbia	– 3 64	43	3

YOUNG, KAREN

Nobody's Child	Major Minor	27 9 69	6	20

YOUNG, NEIL

Heart Of Gold	Reprise	1 4 72	10	11

YOUNG RASCALS

Groovin'	Atlantic	17 6 67	8	13
A Girl Like You	Atlantic	– 8 67	37	4

YOUNG, RETTA

Sending Out An S.O.S.	All Platinum	– 5 75	28	7

ZACHARIAS, HELMUT AND HIS ORCHESTRA

Tokyo Melody	Polydor	14 11 64	9	10

ZAGER AND EVANS

In The Year 2525	RCA	16 8 69	1	13

ZANG, TOMMY

Hey Good Looking	Polydor	– 2 61	45	1

ZAVARONI, LENA

Ma, He's Making Eyes At Me	Philips	16 2 74	10	11
Personality	Philips	– 6 74	33	3

ZOMBIES

She's Not There	Decca	4 9 64	12	11
Tell Her No	Decca	– 2 65	42	5

Index.

RECORD TITLE	ARTIST
ABC	JACKSON FIVE
ABRAHAM, MARTIN AND JOHN	MARVIN GAYE
ACCIDENTS	THUNDERCLAP NEWMAN
ACTION	SWEET
ADIOS AMIGO	JIM REEVES
ADORATION WALTZ	DAVID WHITFIELD
AFRICAN WALTZ	JOHNNY DANKWORTH
AFTER THE GOLDRUSH	PRELUDE
AFTERGLOW	SMALL FACES
AFTERNOON OF THE RHINO	MIKE POST COALITION
AIN'T GONNA BE THAT WAY	MARV JOHNSON
AIN'T GONNA WASH FOR A WEEK	BROOK BROTHERS
AIN'T GOT NO - I GOT LIFE	NINA SIMONE
AIN'T MISBEHAVIN'	JOHNNY RAY
AIN'T MISBEHAVIN'	TOMMY BRUCE
AIN'T NO MOUNTAIN HIGH ENOUGH	DIANA ROSS
AIN'T NO SUNSHINE	MICHAEL JACKSON
AIN'T NOTHING BUT A HOUSE PARTY	SHOWSTOPPERS
AIN'T NOTHING LIKE THE REAL THING	MARVIN GAYE AND TAMMI TERRELL
AIN'T SHE SWEET	BEATLES WITH TONY SHERIDAN
AIN'T THAT A SHAME	FATS DOMINO
AIN'T THAT A SHAME	PAT BOONE
AIN'T THAT A SHAME	FOUR SEASONS
AIN'T THAT FUNNY	JIMMY JUSTICE
AIN'T THAT LOVING YOU, BABY	ELVIS PRESLEY
AIN'T TOO PROUD TO BEG	TEMPTATIONS
AIR THAT I BREATHE	HOLLIES
ALABAMA JUBILEE	FERKO STRING BAND
ALBATROSS	FLEETWOOD MAC
AL CAPONE	PRINCE BUSTER
AL DI DA	PERICOLI EMILIO
ALEXANDER GRAHAM BELL	SWEET
ALFIE	CILLA BLACK
ALL ALONE AM I	BRENDA LEE
ALL ALONG THE WATCHTOWER	JIMI HENDRIX
ALL AROUND MY HAT	STEELEYE SPAN
ALL BECAUSE OF YOU	GEORDIE
ALL BY MYSELF	ERIC CARMEN
ALL DAY AND ALL OF THE NIGHT	KINKS
ALL FALL DOWN	LINDISFARNE
ALL I EVER NEED IS YOU	SONNY AND CHER
ALL I EVER NEED IS YOUR SWEET LOVIN'	GLORIA GAYNOR
ALL I HAVE TO DO IS DREAM	EVERLY BROTHERS
ALL I HAVE TO DO IS DREAM	GLEN CAMPBELL WITH BOBBY GENTRY
ALL I REALLY WANT TO DO	BYRDS
ALL I REALLY WANT TO DO	CHER
ALL I SEE IS YOU	DUSTY SPRINGFIELD
ALL I WANT FOR CHRISTMAS IS A BEATLE	DORA BRYAN
ALL I WANT IS YOU	ROXY MUSIC
ALL KINDS OF EVERYTHING	DANA
ALL MY LOVE	JACKIE WILSON
ALL MY LOVE	CLIFF RICHARD
ALL MY LOVING	DOWLANDS
ALL OF A SUDDEN MY HEART SINGS	PAUL ANKA
ALL OF ME LOVES ALL OF YOU	BAY CITY ROLLERS
ALL OF MY LIFE	DIANA ROSS
ALL OR NOTHING	SMALL FACES

ALL OVER THE WORLD	FRANCOISE HARDY
ALL RIGHT NOW	FREE
ALL SHOOK UP	ELVIS PRESLEY
ALL STAR HIT PARADE	'DECCA' ARTISTS
ALL THAT I AM	ELVIS PRESLEY
ALL THE LOVE IN THE WORLD	CONSORTIUM
ALL THE WAY	FRANK SINATRA
ALL THE WAY FROM MEMPHIS	MOTT THE HOOPLE
ALL THE YOUNG DUDES	MOTT THE HOOPLE
ALL YOU NEED IS LOVE	BEATLES
ALLEY CAT SONG	DAVID THORNE
ALLEY-OOP	HOLLYWOOD ARGYLES
ALMOST THERE	ANDY WILLIAMS
ALONE	PETULA CLARK
ALONE	SOUTHLANDERS
ALONE AGAIN (NATURALLY)	GILBERT O'SULLIVAN
ALONE AT LAST	JACKIE WILSON
ALONG CAME CAROLINE	MICHAEL COX
ALRIGHT, ALRIGHT, ALRIGHT	MUNGO JERRY
ALRIGHT BABY	STEVENSON'S ROCKET
ALSO SPRACH ZARATHUSTRA-2001	DEODATO
ALSO SPRACH ZARATHUSTRA-2001	MAAZEL AND THE NEW PHILHARMONIC ORCHESTRA
ALTERNATE TITLE	MONKEES
ALWAYS	SAMMY TURNER
ALWAYS AND EVER	JOHNNY KIDD AND THE PIRATES
ALWAYS ON MY MIND	ELVIS PRESLEY
ALWAYS THE LONELY ONE	ALAN DREW
ALWAYS YOU AND ME	RUSS CONWAY
ALWAYS YOURS	GARY GLITTER
AM I A TOY OR A TREASURE	KAY STARR
AM I THAT EASY TO FORGET	ENGELBERT HUMPERDINCK
AM I THE SAME GIRL	DUSTY SPRINGFIELD
AMANDA	STUART GILLIES
AMATEUR HOUR	SPARKS
AMAZING GRACE	JUDY COLLINS
AMAZING GRACE	ROYAL SCOTS DRAGOON GUARDS
AMBUSH	OUTLAWS
AMERICA	SIMON AND GARFUNKEL
AMERICA	NICE
AMERICA	DAVID ESSEX
AMERICAN PIE	DON McLEAN
AMERICAN TRILOGY	ELVIS PRESLEY
AMERICAN WOMAN	GUESS WHO
AMONG MY SOUVENIRS	CONNIE FRANCIS
AMOR	BEN E. KING
AMOUREUSE	KIKI DEE
AN OLYMPIC RECORD	BARRON KNIGHTS
AND I LOVE YOU SO	PERRY COMO
AND THE HEAVENS CRIED	ANTHONY NEWLEY
AND THE SUN WILL SHINE	JOSE FELICIANO
AND THE WIND CRIES MARY	JIMI HENDRIX EXPERIENCE
AND YOU SMILED	MATT MONRO
ANGEL	ROD STEWART
ANGEL	ARETHA FRANKLIN
ANGEL FACE	GLITTER BAND
ANGEL FINGERS	WIZZARD
ANGEL OF THE MORNING	P.P. ARNOLD
ANGELA JONES	MICHAEL COX
ANGELS DON'T LIE	JIM REEVES
ANGIE	ROLLING STONES
ANGIE BABY	HELEN REDDY
ANGRY AT THE BIG OAK TREE	FRANK IFIELD
ANNABELLA	JOHN WALKER
ANNIE'S SONG	JOHN DENVER
ANNIVERSARY LOVE	ANITA HARRIS
ANOTHER DAY	PAUL McCARTNEY

ANOTHER SATURDAY NIGHT	SAM COOKE
ANOTHER SATURDAY NIGHT	CAT STEVENS
ANOTHER SLEEPLESS NIGHT	JIMMY CLANTON
ANOTHER TEAR FALLS	WALKER BROTHERS
ANOTHER TIME, ANOTHER PLACE	ENGELBERT HUMPERDINCK
ANSWER ME	RAY PETERSON
ANSWER ME	BARBARA DICKSON
ANY OLD IRON	PETER SELLARS
ANY OLD TIME (YOU'RE LONELY AND SAD)	FOUNDATIONS
ANYONE FOR TENNIS	CREAM
ANYONE WHO HAD A HEART	CILLA BLACK
ANYONE WHO HAD A HEART	DIONNE WARWICK
ANYONE WHO HAD A HEART	MARY MAY
ANYTHING GOES	HARPERS BIZARRE
ANYWAY, ANYHOW, ANYWHERE	WHO
ANYWAY THAT YOU WANT ME	TROGGS
ANYWAY YOU WANT IT	DAVE CLARK FIVE
APACHE	SHADOWS
APACHE	BERT WEEDON
APACHE DROPOUT	EDGAR BROUGHTON BAND
'APARTMENT' THEME	FERRANTE AND TEICHER
APEMAN	KINKS
APPLEJACK	JET HARRIS AND TONY MEEHAN
APRIL LOVE	PAT BOONE
AQUARIUS	PAUL JONES
AQUARIUS	FIFTH DIMENSION
ARE YOU BEING SERVED SIR	JOHN INMAN
ARE YOU GROWING TIRED OF MY LOVE	STATUS QUO
ARE YOU LONESOME TONIGHT	ELVIS PRESLEY
ARE YOU READY TO ROCK	WIZZARD
ARE YOU SURE	ALLISONS
ARMED AND EXTREMELY DANGEROUS	FIRST CHOICE
ARMY GAME	ARMY GAME T.V. CAST
ARNOLD LAYNE	PINK FLOYD
AROUND THE WORLD	BING CROSBY
AROUND THE WORLD	RONNIE HILTON
AROUND THE WORLD	GRACIE FIELDS
AROUND THE WORLD	MANTOVANI
ARRIVERDERCI DARLING	ANNE SHELTON
ARRIVERDERCI DARLING	EDNA SAVAGE
ART FOR ART'S SAKE	10 C.C.
AS I LOVE YOU	SHIRLEY BASSEY
AS LONG AS HE NEEDS ME	SHIRLEY BASSEY
AS LONG AS HE NEEDS ME	PACKABEATS
AS LONG AS I CAN SEE THE LIGHT	CREEDENCE CLEARWATER REVIVAL
AS TEARS GO BY	MARIANNE FAITHFUL
AS TIME GOES BY	RICHARD ALLAN
AS USUAL	BRENDA LEE
AS YOU LIKE IT	ADAM FAITH
ASHES TO ASHES	MINDBENDERS
ASIA MINOR	KOKOMO
AT THE CLUB	DRIFTERS
AT THE HOP	DANNY AND THE JUNIORS
AT THE PALACE	WILFRED BRAMBLE WITH HARRY H. CORBETT
AT THE TOP OF THE STAIRS	FORMATIONS
ATLANTIS	SHADOWS
ATLANTIS	DONOVAN
ATTACK	TOYS
AUGUST OCTOBER	ROBIN GIBB
AUTOBAHN	KRAFTWERK
AUTOMATICALLY SUNSHINE	SUPREMES
AUTUMN ALMANAC	KINKS
AUTUMN CONCERTO	GEORGE MELACHRINO
AVE MARIA	SHIRLEY BASSEY
AVENUES AND ALLEYWAYS	TONY CHRISTIE

BABETTE	TOMMY BRUCE
BABY	HOLLIES
BABY BABY	FRANKIE LYMON AND THE TEENAGERS
BABY BYE BYE	JERRY LEE LEWIS
BABY COME BACK	EQUALS
BABY DON'T GET HOOKED ON ME	MAC DAVIS
BABY DON'T GO	SONNY AND CHER
BABY FACE	LITTLE RICHARD
BABY FACE	BOBBY DARIN
BABY FACE	WING AND A PRAYER FIFE AND DRUM CORPS
BABY I DON'T CARE	BUDDY HOLLY
BABY I LOVE YOU	RONETTES
BABY I LOVE YOU	DAVE EDMUNDS
BABY I LOVE YOU	ARETHA FRANKLIN
BABY I LOVE YOU O.K.	KENNY
BABY I NEED YOUR LOVIN'	FOURMOST
BABY I'M A WANT YOU	BREAD
BABY I'M YOURS	PETER AND GORDON
BABY I'M YOURS	LINDA LEWIS
BABY IT'S YOU	DAVE BERRY AND THE CRUISERS
BABY JUMP	MUNGO JERRY
BABY LET ME TAKE YOU HOME	ANIMALS
BABY LOVE	SUPREMES
BABY LOVER	PETULA CLARK
BABY MAKE IT SOON	MARMALADE
BABY MY HEART	BUDDY HOLLY AND THE CRICKETS
BABY NEVER SAY GOODBYE	UNIT 4 + 2
BABY NOW THAT I'VE FOUND YOU	FOUNDATIONS
BABY PLEASE DON'T GO	THEM
BABY ROO	CONNIE FRANCIS
BABY SITTIN'	BOBBY ANGELO
BABY SITTIN' BOOGIE	BUZZ CLIFFORD
BABY TAKE A BOW	ADAM FAITH
BABY WE CAN'T GO WRONG	CILLA BLACK
BABY WHAT I MEAN	DRIFTERS
(BABY) YOU DON'T HAVE TO TELL ME	WALKER BROTHERS
BABY'S FIRST CHRISTMAS	CONNIE FRANCIS
BACHELOR BOY	CLIFF RICHARD
BACK HOME	ENGLAND WORLD CUP SQUAD
BACK IN MY ARMS AGAIN	SUPREMES
BACK OFF BOOGALOO	RINGO STARR
BACK ON MY FEET AGAIN	FOUNDATIONS
BACK SEAT OF MY CAR	PAUL McCARTNEY
BACK STREET LUV	CURVED AIR
BACKSTABBERS	O'JAYS
BACKSTAGE (I'M LONELY)	GENE PITNEY
BAD BAD BOY	NAZARETH
BAD BOY	MARTY WILDE
BAD MOON RISING	CREEDENCE CLEARWATER REVIVAL
BAD NIGHT	CAT STEVENS
BAD PENNY BLUES	HUMPHREY LYTTLETON
BAD TO ME	BILLY J. KRAMER AND THE DAKOTAS
BAD WEATHER	SUPREMES
BADGE	CREAM
BALL OF CONFUSION	TEMPTATIONS
BALL PARK INCIDENT	WIZZARD
BALLAD OF BONNIE AND CLYDE	GEORGIE FAME
BALLAD OF DAVY CROCKETT	BILL HAYES
BALLAD OF DAVY CROCKETT	MAX BYGRAVES
BALLAD OF DAVY CROCKETT	GARY MILLER
BALLAD OF JOHN AND YOKO	BEATLES
BALLAD OF PALADIN	DUANE EDDY
BALLAD OF SPOTTY MULDOON	PETER COOK AND DUDLEY MOORE
BALLAD OF THE GREEN BERETS	STAFF SERGEANT BARRY SADLER
BALLROOM BLITZ	SWEET
BAMA LAMA (BAMA) LOO	LITTLE RICHARD

BAMBINO	SPRINGFIELDS
BANANA BOAT SONG	HARRY BELAFONTE
BANANA ROCK	WOMBLES
BAND OF GOLD	DON CHERRY
BAND OF GOLD	FREDA PAYNE
BAND ON THE RUN	PAUL McCARTNEY AND WINGS
BAND PLAYED THE BOOGIE	C.C.S.
BANG A GONG (U.S. TITLE)	SEE 'GET IT ON'
BANG BANG	CHER
BANGERS AND MASH	PETER SELLARS AND SOPHIA LOREN
BANGIN' MAN	SLADE
BANGLA DESH	GEORGE HARRISON
BANJO BOY	JAN AND KJELD
BANJO BOY	GEORGE FORMBY
BANJO'S BACK IN TOWN	ALMA COGAN
BANKS OF THE OHIO	OLIVIA NEWTON-JOHN
BANNER MAN	BLUE MINK
BARBADOS	TYPICALLY TROPICAL
BARBARA ANN	BEACH BOYS
BAREFOOTIN'	ROBERT PARKER
BASS GUITAR	DUANE EDDY
BATTLE OF NEW ORLEANS	JOHNNY HORTON
BATTLE OF NEW ORLEANS	LONNIE DONEGAN
BATTLE'S O'ER	ANDY STEWART
BAUBLES, BANGLES AND BEADS	GEORGE SHEARING
BE-BOP-A-LULA	GENE VINCENT
BE MINE	LANCE FORTUNE
BE MINE	TREMELOES
BE MY BABY	RONETTES
BE MY GIRL	JIM DALE
BE MY GIRL	DENNISONS
BE MY GUEST	FATS DOMINO
BE THANKFUL FOR WHAT YOU'VE GOT	WILLIAM DE VAUGHN
BE YOUNG, BE FOOLISH, BE HAPPY	TAMS
BEACH BABY	FIRST CLASS
BEAT FOR BEATNIKS	JOHN BARRY
BEAT GOES ON	SONNY AND CHER
BEATNIK FLY	JOHNNY AND THE HURRICANES
BEAUTIFUL SUNDAY	DANIEL BOONE
BEAUTIFUL YOU	NEIL SEDAKA
BEAUTY IS ONLY SKIN DEEP	TEMPTATIONS
BECAUSE I LOVE YOU	GEORGIE FAME
BECAUSE OF LOVE	BILLY FURY
BECAUSE THEY'RE YOUNG	DUANE EDDY
BECAUSE THEY'RE YOUNG	JAMES DARREN
BEE-BUM	ANTHONY NEWLEY
BEG, STEAL OR BORROW	NEW SEEKERS
BEGGIN'	TIMEBOX
BEHIND A PAINTED SMILE	ISLEY BROTHERS
BEHIND CLOSED DOORS	CHARLIE RICH
BELFAST BOY	DON FARDON
BELLS OF AVIGNON	MAX BYGRAVES
BEN	MICHAEL JACKSON
BEND IT	DAVE DEE, DOZY, BEAKY, MICK AND TICH
BEND ME, SHAPE ME	AMERICAN BREED
BEND ME, SHAPE ME	AMEN CORNER
BERNADETTE	FOUR TOPS
BESAME MUCHO	JET HARRIS
BEST OF EVERYTHING	JOHNNY MATHIS
BEST OF MY LOVE	EAGLES
BEST PART OF BREAKING UP	SYMBOLS
BEST PART OF BREAKING UP	RONETTES
BEST THING THAT EVER HAPPENED	GLADYS KNIGHT AND THE PIPS
BET YER LIFE I DO	HERMAN'S HERMITS
BETCHA BY GOLLY WOW	STYLISTICS
BETTY BETTY BETTY	LONNIE DONEGAN

BEYOND THE SEA	BOBBY DARIN
BEYOND THE STARS	DAVID WHITFIELD
BIG BAD JOHN	JIMMY DEAN
BIG BEAT	FATS DOMINO
BIG BEAT BOOGIE	BERT WEEDON
BIG CITY	DANDY LIVINGSTONE
BIG EIGHT	JUDGE DREAD
BIG GIRLS DON'T CRY	FOUR SEASONS
BIG HUNK OF LOVE	ELVIS PRESLEY
BIG IRON	MARTY ROBBINS
BIG MAN	FOUR PREPS
BIG MAN IN A BIG HOUSE	LEROY VAN DYKE
BIG SEVEN	JUDGE DREAD
BIG SHIP	CLIFF RICHARD
BIG SIX	JUDGE DREAD
BIG SPENDER	SHIRLEY BASSEY
BIG TEN	JUDGE DREAD
BIG-TIME OPERATOR	ZOOT MONEY AND THE BIG ROLL BAND
BIG YELLOW TAXI	JONI MITCHELL
BILJO	CLODAGH ROGERS
BILL BAILEY	BOBBY DARIN
BILLY BOY	DICK CHARLESWORTH ORCHESTRA
BILLY, DON'T BE A HERO	PAPER LACE
BIRD DOG	EVERLY BROTHERS
BIRDS AND BEES	JEWEL AKENS
BIRDS AND BEES	WARM SOUNDS
BIRTH	PEDDLERS
BITCH	ROLLING STONES
BITCH IS BACK	ELTON JOHN
BITS AND PIECES	DAVE CLARK FIVE
BLACK AND WHITE	GREYHOUND
BLACK BEAR	FRANK CORDELL
'BLACK BEAUTY' T.V. THEME (GALLOPING HOME)	LONDON STRING CHORALE
BLACK-EYED BOYS	PAPER LACE
BLACK GIRL	FOUR PENNIES
BLACK HILLS OF DAKOTA	DORIS DAY
BLACK IS BLACK	LOS BRAVOS
BLACK MAGIC WOMAN	FLEETWOOD MAC
BLACK NIGHT	DEEP PURPLE
BLACK PEARL	HORACE FAITH
BLACK PUDDING BERTHA	GOODIES
BLACK STOCKINGS	JOHN BARRY
BLACK SUPERMAN	JOHNNY WAKELIN AND THE KINSHASA BAND
BLACK VELVET BAND	DUBLINERS
BLACKBERRY WAY	MOVE
BLACKSKIN BLUE-EYED BOYS	EQUALS
BLAME IT ON THE BOSSA NOVA	EYDIE GORME
BLAME IT ON THE PONY EXPRESS	JOHNNY JOHNSON AND THE BANDWAGON
BLANKET ON THE GROUND	BILLIE JO SPEARS
BLESS YOU	TONY ORLANDO
BLESS YOU	MARTHA REEVES AND THE VANDELLAS
BLOCKBUSTER	SWEET
BLOODNOCK'S ROCK AND ROLL	GOONS
BLOODSHOT EYES	MILLIE
BLOSSOM FELL	NAT 'KING' COLE
BLOSSOM FELL	DICKIE VALENTINE
BLOSSOM FELL	RONNIE HILTON
BLOWIN' IN THE WIND	PETER, PAUL AND MARY
BLOWIN' IN THE WIND	STEVIE WONDER
BLUE ANGEL	ROY ORBISON
BLUE ANGEL	GENE PITNEY
BLUE BAYOU	ROY ORBISON
BLUE CHRISTMAS	ELVIS PRESLEY
BLUE-EYED BOY	AL SAXON

BLUE EYES	DON PARTRIDGE
BLUE GIRL	BRUISERS
BLUE GUITAR	JUSTIN HAYWARD AND JOHN LODGE
BLUE IS THE COLOUR	CHELSEA FOOTBALL CLUB
BLUE JEAN BOP	GENE VINCENT
BLUE MOON	ELVIS PRESLEY
BLUE MOON	MARCELS
BLUE RIVER	ELVIS PRESLEY
BLUE STAR	CHARLIE APPLEWHITE
BLUE STAR	CYRIL STAPLETON
BLUE STAR	RON GOODWIN
BLUE SUEDE SHOES	CARL PERKINS
BLUE SUEDE SHOES	ELVIS PRESLEY
BLUE TURNS TO GREY	CLIFF RICHARD
BLUER THAN BLUE	ROLF HARRIS
BLUE WEEKEND	KARL DENVER
BLUEBELL POLKA	JIMMY SHAND
BLUEBERRY HILL	FATS DOMINO
BLUEBERRY HILL	JOHN BARRY
BO DIDDLEY	BUDDY HOLLY
BOAT THAT I ROW	LULU
BOBBY TOMORROW	BOBBY VEE
BOBBY'S GIRL	SUSAN MAUGHAN
BOHEMIAN RHAPSODY	QUEEN
BOLL WEEVIL SONG	BROOK BENTON
BONNY CAME BACK	DUANE EDDY
BONY MARONIE	LARRY WILLIAMS
BOO GA LOO PARTY	FLAMINGOS
BOOGIE DOWN	EDDIE KENDRICKS
BOOGIE ON REGGAE WOMAN	STEVIE WONDER
BOOK OF LOVE	MUDLARKS
BOOM BANG-A-BANG	LULU
BORN A WOMAN	SANDY POSEY
BORN TO BE WILD	STEPPENWOLF
BORN TO BE WITH YOU	CHORDETTES
BORN TO BE WITH YOU	DAVE EDMUNDS
BORN TO LIVE, BORN TO DIE	FOUNDATIONS
BORN TOO LATE	PONI-TAILS
BORN WITH A SMILE ON MY FACE	STEPHANIE DE SYKES
BORNE ON THE WIND	ROY ORBISON
BORSALINO	BOBBY CRUSH
BOSSA NOVA BABY	ELVIS PRESLEY
BOTH ENDS BURNING	ROXY MUSIC
BOTH SIDES NOW	JUDY COLLINS
BOXER	SIMON AND GARFUNKEL
BOY	LULU
BOY NAMED SUE	JOHNNY CASH
BOYS CRY	EDEN KANE
BRAND NEW KEY	MELANIE
BRANDY	SCOTT ENGLISH
BRAZIL	RITCHIE FAMILY
BRAZIL	CRISPY AND COMPANY
BRAZILIAN LOVE SONG	NAT 'KING' COLE
BREAD AND BUTTER	NEWBEATS
BREAK AWAY	BEACH BOYS
BREAK IT TO ME GENTLY	BRENDA LEE
BREAK THE RULES	STATUS QUO
BREAK UP TO MAKE UP	STYLISTICS
BREAKAWAY	SPRINGFIELDS
BREAKFAST ON PLUTO	DON PARTRIDGE
BREAKIN' IN A BRAND NEW BROKEN HEART	CONNIE FRANCIS
BREAKIN' UP IS BREAKIN' MY HEART	ROY ORBISON
BREAKING DOWN THE WALLS OF HEARTACHE	BAND WAGON
BREAKING UP IS HARD TO DO	NEIL SEDAKA

BREAKING UP IS HARD TO DO	PARTRIDGE FAMILY
BREATHLESS	JERRY LEE LEWIS
BREEZE AND I	CATERINA VALENTE
BREEZE AND I	FENTONES
BRIDGE OVER TROUBLED WATER	SIMON AND GARFUNKEL
BRIDGET THE MIDGET	RAY STEVENS
BRING A LITTLE WATER, SYLVIE	LONNIE DONEGAN
BRING IT ON HOME TO ME	ANIMALS
BRING IT ON HOME TO ME	ROD STEWART
BRINGING ON BACK THE GOOD TIMES	LOVE AFFAIR
BROKEN DOLL	TOMMY BRUCE
BROKEN DOWN ANGEL	NAZARETH
BROKEN HEARTED	KEN DODD
BROKEN HEARTED MELODY	SARAH VAUGHAN
BRONTOSAURUS	MOVE
BROTHER	C.C.S.
BROTHER LOUIE	HOT CHOCOLATE
BROWN EYED HANDSOME MAN	BUDDY HOLLY
BROWN SUGAR	ROLLING STONES
BUILD ME UP BUTTERCUP	FOUNDATIONS
BUILD YOUR LOVE	JOHNNY RAY
BUMP	KENNY
BUONA SERA	ACKER BILK
BURLESQUE	FAMILY
BURN BABY BURN	HUDSON-FORD
BURNING BRIDGES	JACK SCOTT
BURNING LOVE	ELVIS PRESLEY
BURNING OF THE MIDNIGHT LAMP	JIMI HENDRIX
BURUNDI BLACK	BURUNDI STEIPHENSON BLACK
BUS STOP	HOLLIES
BUSTED	RAY CHARLES
BUT I DO	CLARENCE 'FROGMAN' HENRY
BUT NOT FOR ME	KETTY LESTER
BUT YOU LOVE ME DADDY	JIM REEVES
BUT YOU'RE MINE	SONNY AND CHER
BUTCH SOAP	YIN AND YAN
BUTTERFINGERS	TOMMY STEELE
BUTTERFLY	CHARLIE GRACIE
BUTTERFLY	ANDY WILLIAMS
BUTTERFLY	DANYEL GERARD
BY THE DEVIL	BLUE MINK
BY THE LIGHT OF THE SILVERY MOON	LITTLE RICHARD
BY THE WAY	BIG THREE
BY THE WAY	TREMELOES
BY YOUR SIDE	PETERS AND LEE
BYE BYE BABY	JOHNNY OTIS SHOW WITH MARIE ADAMS
BYE BYE BABY	SYMBOLS
BYE BYE BABY	BAY CITY ROLLERS
BYE BYE BABY	TONY JACKSON
BYE BYE BLUES	BERT KAEMPFERT
BYE BY LOVE	EVERLY BROTHERS
'CADE'S COUNTRY' (THEME FROM)	HENRY MANCINI ORCHESTRA
CALCUTTA	LAWRENCE WELK
CALENDAR GIRL	NEIL SEDAKA
CALIFORNIA DREAMIN'	MAMAS AND PAPAS
CALIFORNIA GIRLS	BEACH BOYS
CALIFORNIA HERE I COME	FREDDIE CANNON
CALIFORNIA MAN	MOVE
CALIFORNIA SAGA	BEACH BOYS
CALL HER YOUR SWEETHEART	FRANK IFIELD
(CALL ME) NUMBER ONE	TREMELOES
CALL ME 'ROUND	PILOT
CALL ROSIE ON THE PHONE	GUY MITCHELL
CAN CAN '62	PETER JAY AND THE JAYWALKERS

CAN I TAKE YOU HOME, LITTLE GIRL	DRIFTERS
CAN I TRUST YOU	BACHELORS
CAN THE CAN	SUZI QUATRO
CAN THIS BE LOVE	MATT MONRO
CAN YOU DO IT	GEORDIE
CAN YOU FORGIVE ME	KARL DENVER
CAN YOU PLEASE CRAWL OUT YOUR WINDOW	BOB DYLAN
CAN'T BUY ME LOVE	ELLA FITZGERALD/BEATLES
CAN'T GET ALONG WITHOUT YOU	FRANKIE VAUGHAN
CAN'T GET ENOUGH	BAD COMPANY
CAN'T GET ENOUGH OF YOUR LOVE BABY	BARRY WHITE
CAN'T GET USE TO LOSING YOU	ANDY WILLIAMS
CAN'T HELP FALLING IN LOVE	ELVIS PRESLEY
CAN'T HELP FALLING IN LOVE	ANDY WILLIAMS
CAN'T KEEP IT IN	CAT STEVENS
CAN'T LIVE WITH YOU, CAN'T LIVE WITHOUT YOU	MINDBENDERS
CAN'T SAY HOW MUCH I LOVE YOU	DEMIS ROUSSOS
CAN'T TAKE MY EYES OFF YOU	ANDY WILLIAMS
CAN'T YOU HEAR MY HEART	DANNY RIVERS
CAN'T YOU HEAR MY HEARTBEAT	GOLDIE AND THE GINGERBREADS
CAN'T YOU HEAR THE BEAT OF A BROKEN HEART	IAN GREGORY
CAN'T YOU SEE THAT SHE'S MINE	DAVE CLARK FIVE
CANDIDA	DAWN
CANDLE IN THE WIND	ELTON JOHN
CANDY MAN	BRIAN POOLE AND THE TREMELOES
CANNONBALL	DUANE EDDY
CAPTAIN OF YOUR SHIP	REPARATA AND THE DELRONS
CARA MIA	DAVID WHITFIELD
CARAVAN	DUANE EDDY
CARELESS HANDS	DES O'CONNOR
CARIBBEAN HONEYMOON	FRANK WEIR
CARNIVAL IS OVER	SEEKERS
CAROLINA MOON	CONNIE FRANCIS
CAROLINE	STATUS QUO
CARRIE ANNE	HOLLIES
CARRY THAT WEIGHT	TRASH
CASANOVA	PETULA CLARK
CASINO ROYALE	HERB ALPERT AND THE TIJUANA BRASS
CAST YOUR FATE TO THE WIND	SOUNDS ORCHESTRAL
CAT CREPT IN	MUD
CATCH A FALLING STAR	PERRY COMO
CATCH THE WIND	DONOVAN
CATCH US IF YOU CAN	DAVE CLARK FIVE
CATERINA	PERRY COMO
CATHY'S CLOWN	EVERLY BROTHERS
CENTRAL PARK ARREST	THUNDERTHIGHS
CERTAIN SMILE	JOHNNY MATHIS
C'EST SI BON	CONWAY TWITTY
CHA CHA MOMMA BROWN	MARTINAS AND HIS ORCHESTRA
CHAIN GANG	JIMMY YOUNG
CHAIN GANG	SAM COOKE
CHAIN OF FOOLS	ARETHA FRANKLIN
CHAINS	COOKIES
CHAIRMAN OF THE BOARD	CHAIRMEN OF THE BOARD
CHANGE WITH THE TIMES	VAN McCOY
CHANGES	CRISPIAN ST. PETERS
CHANTILLY LACE	BIG BOPPER
CHANTILLY LACE	JERRY LEE LEWIS
CHAPEL OF LOVE	DIXIE CUPS
CHAPEL OF THE ROSES	MALCOLM VAUGHAN
CHARIOT	RHET STOLLER

CHARLESTON	TEMPERANCE SEVEN
CHARLIE BROWN	COASTERS
CHARMAINE	BACHELORS
CHARMING BILLY	JOHNNY PRESTON
CHELSEA	STAMFORD BRIDGE
CHERI BABE	HOT CHOCOLATE
CHERISH WHAT IS DEAR TO YOU	FREDA PAYNE
CHERRY PIE	JESS CONRAD
CHERRY PINK (AND APPLE BLOSSOM WHITE)	PEREZ PRADO
CHERRY PINK (AND APPLE BLOSSOM WHITE)	EDDIE CALVERT
CHERYL'S GOING HOME	ADAM FAITH
CHESTNUT MARE	BYRDS
CHICAGO	FRANK SINATRA
CHICK-A-BOOM	53RD AND 3RD
CHILDREN OF THE REVOLUTION	T. REX
CHILD'S PRAYER	HOT CHOCOLATE
CHILLI BOM BOM	TEMPERANCE SEVEN
CHINA DOLL	SLIM WHITMAN
CHINA TEA	RUSS CONWAY
CHINA TOWN	MOVE
CHIRPY CHIRPY CHEEP CHEEP	MIDDLE OF THE ROAD
CHIRPY CHIRPY CHEEP CHEEP	MAC AND KATIE KISSOON
CHOC ICE	LONG AND THE SHORT
CHRISTINE	MISS X
CHRISTMAS ALPHABET	DICKIE VALENTINE
CHRISTMAS IN DREADLAND	JUDGE DREAD
CHRISTMAS ISLAND	DICKIE VALENTINE
CHRISTMAS SONG	GILBERT O'SULLIVAN
CHRISTMAS WILL BE JUST ANOTHER LONELY DAY	BRENDA LEE
CINDERELLA ROCKAFELLA	ESTHER AND ABI OFARIM
CINDY INCIDENTALLY	FACES
CINDY, OH CINDY	EDDIE FISHER
CINDY, OH CINDY	TONY BRENT
CINDY'S BIRTHDAY	SHANE FENTON AND THE FENTONES
CIRCLES	NEW SEEKERS
CITY LIGHTS	DAVID ESSEX
CLAIR	GILBERT O'SULLIVAN
CLAPPING SONG	SHIRLEY ELLIS
CLARE	PAUL AND BARRY RYAN
CLASSICAL GAS	MASON WILLIAMS
CLAUDETTE	EVERLY BROTHERS
CLEAN UP YOUR OWN BACK YARD	ELVIS PRESLEY
CLEMENTINE	BOBBY DARIN
CLIMB EVERY MOUNTAIN	SHIRLEY BASSEY
CLOSE THE DOOR	STARGAZERS
CLOSE TO YOU	CARPENTERS
CLOSE YOUR EYES	TONY BENNETT
CLOUD NINE	TEMPTATIONS
CLOUD 99	ST. ANDREW'S CHORALE
CLOUDBURST	DON LANG
CLOUDS WILL SOON ROLL BY	TONY BRENT
CLOWN SHOES	JOHNNY BURNETTE
C'MON EVERYBODY	EDDIE COCHRAN
C'MON MARIANNE	GRAPEFRUIT
C MOON	WINGS
CO-CO	SWEET
COCONUT	NILSSON
COCONUT WOMAN	HARRY BELAFONTE
CODE OF LOVE	MIKE SARNE
COFFEE SONG	FRANK SINATRA
COLD LIGHT OF DAY	GENE PITNEY
COLD TURKEY	PLASTIC ONO BAND

COLETTE	BILLY FURY
COLOUR OF MY LIFE	JEFFERSON
COLOURS	DONOVAN
COMANCHEROS	LONNIE DONEGAN
COME ALONG PLEASE	BOB WALLIS
COME AND GET IT	BADFINGER
COME AND STAY WITH ME	MARIANNE FAITHFUL
COME AWAY MELINDA	BARRY ST. JOHN
COME BACK AND SHAKE ME	CLODAGH ROGERS
COME HOME	DAVE CLARK FIVE
COME ON	ROLLING STONES
COME ON HOME	WAYNE FONTANA
COME ON HOME	SPRINGFIELDS
COME ON LET'S GO	TOMMY STEELE
COME OUTSIDE	MIKE SARNE
COME OUTSIDE	JUDGE DREAD
COME ON OVER TO MY PLACE	DRIFTERS
COME PRIMA (MORE THAN EVER)	MARINO MARINI
COME PRIMA (MORE THAN EVER)	MALCOLM VAUGHAN
(COME ROUND HERE) I'M THE ONE YOU NEED	SMOKEY ROBINSON AND THE MIRACLES
COME SEE ABOUT ME	SUPREMES
COME SEE ME	PRETTY THINGS
COME SEPTEMBER	BOBBY DARIN
COME SOFTLY TO ME	FLEETWOODS
COME SOFTLY TO ME	FRANKIE VAUGHAN
COME SOFTLY TO ME	NEW SEEKERS
COME TO THE DANCE	BARRON KNIGHTS
COME TOGETHER	BEATLES
COME TOMORROW	MANFRED MANN
COME WHAT MAY	VICKY LEANDROS
COMIN' HOME	DELANEY AND BONNIE
COMIN' HOME BABY	MEL TORME
COMMUNICATION	DAVID McCALLUM
CONCRETE AND CLAY	UNIT 4 + 2
CONCRETE AND CLAY	RANDY EDELMAN
CONFUSION	LEE DORSEY
CONGRATULATIONS	CLIFF RICHARD
CONQUISTADOR	PROCOL HARUM
CONSCIENCE	JAMES DARREN
CONSIDER YOURSELF	MAX BYGRAVES
CONSTANTLY	CLIFF RICHARD
CONVERSATIONS	CILLA BLACK
CONVOY	C.W. McCALL
COOL WATER	FRANKIE LANE
CORINNE, CORINNA	RAY PETERSON
COSTAFINE TOWN	SPLINTER
COTTONFIELDS	HIGHWAYMEN
COTTONFIELDS	BEACH BOYS
COULD IT BE FOREVER	DAVID CASSIDY
COULD IT BE I'M FALLING IN LOVE?	STYLISTICS
COUNT ON ME	JULIE GRANT
COUNT TO ME	JULIE GRANT
COUNT YOUR BLESSINGS	BING CROSBY
COUNTING TEARDROPS	EMILE FORD AND THE CHECKMATES
COUNTRY BOY	FATS DOMINO
COUNTRY BOY	HEINZ
COUSIN NORMAN	MARMALADE
COWBOY JIMMY JOE	ALMA COGAN
COZ I LUV YOU	SLADE
CRACKIN' UP	TOMMY HUNT
CRACKLIN' ROSIE	NEIL DIAMOND
CRADLE OF LOVE	JOHNNY PRESTON
CRAWLING BACK	ROY ORBISON
CRAZY	MUD

CRAZY HORSES	OSMONDS
CRAZY OTTO RAG	STARGAZERS
CRAZY WORDS, CRAZY TUNE	DOROTHY PROVINE
CREEQUE ALLEY	MAMAS AND PAPAS
CREOLE JAZZ	ACKER BILK
CROCODILE ROCK	ELTON JOHN
CROSS TOWN TRAFFIC	JIMI HENDRIX EXPERIENCE
CROWD	ROY ORBISON
CRUEL SEA	DAKOTAS
CRY	GERRY MONROE
CRY LIKE A BABY	BOX TOPS
CRY MYSELF TO SLEEP	DEL SHANNON
CRY TO ME	PRETTY THINGS
CRYIN'	ROY ORBISON
CRYIN' TIME	RAY CHARLES
CRYING GAME	DAVE BERRY
CRYING IN THE CHAPEL	ELVIS PRESLEY
CRYING IN THE RAIN	EVERLY BROTHERS
CRYING, LAUGHING, LOVING, LYING	LABI SIFFRE
CRYING OVER YOU	KEN BOOTHE
CUM ON FEEL THE NOIZE	SLADE
CUMBERLAND GAP	LONNIE DONEGAN
CUMBERLAND GAP	VIPERS
CUPBOARD LOVE	JOHN LEYTON
CUPID	SAM COOKE
CUPID	JOHNNY NASH
CURLY	MOVE
CUT THE CAKE	AVERAGE WHITE BAND
CUTTY SARK	JOHN BARRY
D-DARLING	ANTHONY NEWLEY
DA DOO RON RON	CRYSTALS
DADDY DON'T YOU WALK SO FAST	DANIEL BOONE
DAMBUSTERS MARCH	R.A.F. BAND
DANCE DANCE DANCE	BEACH BOYS
DANCE OF THE CUCKOOS	BAND OF THE BLACK WATCH
DANCE ON	SHADOWS
DANCE ON	KATHY KIRBY
DANCE TO THE MUSIC	SLY AND THE FAMILY STONE
DANCE THE KUNG FU	CARL DOUGLAS
DANCE WITH ME	DRIFTERS
DANCE WITH THE DEVIL	COZY POWELL
DANCE WITH THE GUITAR MAN	DUANE EDDY
DANCIN' PARTY	CHUBBY CHECKER
DANCING IN THE STREET	MARTHA AND THE VANDELLAS
DANCING ON A SATURDAY NIGHT	BARRY BLUE
DANDELION	ROLLING STONES
DANIEL	ELTON JOHN
DARK LADY	CHER
DARK MOON	TONY BRENT
DARK TOWN STRUTTERS BALL	JOE BROWN AND THE BRUVVERS
DARLIN'	BEACH BOYS
DARLIN'	DAVID CASSIDY
DARLING BE HOME SOON	LOVIN' SPOONFUL
DAT	PLUTO
DAUGHTERS OF DARKNESS	TOM JONES
DAY AFTER DAY	BADFINGER
DAY BY DAY	HOLLY SHERWOOD
DAY DREAMER	DAVID CASSIDY
DAY I MET MARIE	CLIFF RICHARD
DAY IS OVER	ROYAL SCOTS DRAGOON GUARDS BAND
DAY THAT CURLY BILLY SHOT CRAZY SAM McGEE	HOLLIES
DAY THE RAINS CAME DOWN	JANE MORGAN
DAY TRIPPER	BEATLES
DAY TRIPPER	OTIS REDDING
DAY WITHOUT LOVE	LOVE AFFAIR

DAYDREAM	LOVIN' SPOONFUL
DAYDREAM BELIEVER	MONKEES
DAYS	KINKS
DAYTONA DEMON	SUZI QUATRO
DEAD END STREET	KINKS
DEAD OR ALIVE	LONNIE DONEGAN
DEADLIER THAN THE MALE	WALKER BROTHERS
DEAL	PAT CAMPBELL
DEAN AND I	10 C.C.
DEAR DELILAH	GRAPEFRUIT
DEAR ELAINE	ROY WOOD
DEAR LONELY HEARTS	NAT 'KING' COLE
DEAR MRS. APPLEBEE	DAVID GARRICK
DEATH OF A CLOWN	DAVE DAVIES
DEBORAH	T. REX
DECEMBER '63 (OH WHAT A NIGHT)	FOUR SEASONS
DECK OF CARDS	WINK MARTINDALE
DECK OF CARDS	MAX BYGRAVES
DEDICATED FOLLOWER OF FASHION	KINKS
DEDICATED TO THE ONE I LOVE	MAMAS AND PAPAS
DEEP FEELING	MIKE SAGAR
DEEP IN THE HEART OF TEXAS	DUANE EDDY
DEEP PURPLE	NINO TEMPO AND APRIL STEVENS
DEEP PURPLE	DONNY AND MARIE OSMOND
DEEPER AND DEEPER	FREDA PAYNE
DELAWARE	PERRY COMO
DELILAH	TOM JONES
DELILAH	SENSATIONAL ALEX HARVEY BAND
DELTA LADY	JOE COCKER
DESAFINADO	ELLA FITZGERALD
DESAFINADO	STAN GETZ AND CHARLIE BYRD
DESIDERATA	LES CRANE
DESPERATE DAN	LIEUTENANT PIGEON
DESTINY	ANNE MURRAY
DETROIT CITY	TOM JONES
DEVIL GATE DRIVE	SUZI QUATRO
DEVIL IN DISGUISE	ELVIS PRESLEY
DEVIL WOMAN	MARTY ROBBINS
DEVIL'S ANSWER	ATOMIC ROOSTER
DIAMOND DOGS	DAVID BOWIE
DIAMONDS	JET HARRIS AND TONY MEEHAN
DIAMONDS ARE FOREVER	SHIRLEY BASSEY
DIANA	PAUL ANKA
DIANE	BACHELORS
DICK-A-DUM-DUM	DES O'CONNOR
DID YOU EVER	NANCY SINATRA AND LEE HAZLEWOOD
DIDN'T I BLOW YOUR MIND THIS TIME	DELFONICS
DIGGIN' MY POTATOES	HEINZ
DING-A-DONG	TEACH-IN
DING DONG	GEORGE HARRISON
DISCO QUEEN	HOT CHOCOLATE
DISCO STOMP	HAMILTON BOHANNON
DISTANT DRUMS	JIM REEVES
D.I.V.O.R.C.E.	TAMMY WYNETTE
D.I.V.O.R.C.E.	BILLY CONNOLLY
DIZZY	TOMMY ROE
DO I LOVE YOU	RONETTES
DO IT AGAIN	BEACH BOYS
DO IT AGAIN	STEELY DAN
DO IT ANYWAY YOU WANNA	PEOPLE'S CHOICE
DO THE BIRD	VERNON GIRLS FEATURING MAUREEN
DO THE BUS STOP	FATBACK BAND
DO THE CLAM	ELVIS PRESLEY
DO THE FUNKY CHICKEN	RUFUS THOMAS

DO WHAT YOU DO WELL	NED MILLER
DO WHAT YOU GOTTA DO	FOUR TOPS
DO YOU KNOW THE WAY TO SAN JOSE	DIONNE WARWICK
DO YOU KNOW WHERE YOU'RE GOING TO	DIANA ROSS
DO YOU LOVE ME	BRIAN POOLE AND THE TREMELOES
DO YOU LOVE ME	DAVE CLARK FIVE
DO YOU LOVE ME	DEEP FEELING
DO YOU MIND	ANTHONY NEWLEY
DO YOU REALLY LOVE ME TOO (FOOL'S ERRAND)	BILLY FURY
DO YOU REMEMBER	SCAFFOLD
DO YOU WANNA DANCE	CLIFF RICHARD
DO YOU WANNA DANCE	BARRY BLUE
DO YOU WANNA TOUCH ME	GARY GLITTER
DO YOU WANT ME TO	FOUR PENNIES
DO YOU WANT TO KNOW A SECRET	BILLY J. KRAMER AND THE DAKOTAS
DOCK OF THE BAY	OTIS REDDING
DOCTOR FINLAY	ANDY STEWART
DOCTOR KILDARE	JOHNNY SPENCE
DOCTOR KILDARE	RICHARD CHAMBERLAIN
DOCTOR MY EYES	JACKSON FIVE
DOCTOR NO (JAMES BOND THEME)	JOHN BARRY
DOCTOR'S ORDERS	SUNNY
DOES YOUR CHEWING GUM LOSE IT'S FLAVOUR ON THE BEDPOST OVERNIGHT	LONNIE DONEGAN
DOESN'T ANYBODY KNOW MY NAME	VINCE HILL
DOGS	WHO
DOING ALRIGHT WITH THE BOYS	GARY GLITTER
DOLL HOUSE	KING BROTHERS
DOLLY MY LOVE	MOMENTS
DOMINIQUE	SINGING NUN
DON JUAN	DAVE DEE, DOZY, BEAKY, MICK AND TICH
DONALD, WHERE'S YOUR TROUSERS	ANDY STEWART
DONNA	RITCHIE VALENS
DONNA	MARTY WILDE
DONNA	10 C.C.
DON'T	ELVIS PRESLEY
DON'T ANSWER ME	CILLA BLACK
DON'T BE CRUEL	ELVIS PRESLEY
DON'T BE CRUEL	BILL BLACK COMBO
DON'T BE CRUEL	BILLY SWAN
DON'T BLAME ME	EVERLY BROTHERS
DON'T BLAME ME	FRANK IFIELD
DON'T BREAK THE HEART THAT LOVES YOU	CONNIE FRANCIS
DON'T BRING LULU	DOROTHY PROVINE
DON'T BRING ME DOWN	PRETTY THINGS
DON'T BRING ME DOWN	ANIMALS
DON'T BRING ME YOUR HEARTACHES	PAUL AND BARRY RYAN
DON'T CRY DADDY	ELVIS PRESLEY
DON'T DO IT BABY	MAC AND KATIE KISSOON
DON'T DO THAT	GEORDIE
DON'T EVER CHANGE	CRICKETS
DON'T FIGHT IT	WILSON PICKETT
DON'T FORBID ME	PAT BOONE
DON'T FORGET TO **CATCH** ME	CLIFF RICHARD
DON'T FORGET TO REMEMBER	BEE GEES
DON'T HANG ON	ORLONS
DON'T JUMP OFF THE ROOF, DAD	TOMMY COOPER
DON'T KNOCK THE ROCK	BILL HALEY AND THE COMETS
DON'T LET HIM TOUCH YOU	ANGELETTES
DON'T LET IT DIE	HURRICANE SMITH
DON'T LET ME BE MISUNDERSTOOD	ANIMALS
DON'T LET THE RAIN COME DOWN	RONNIE HILTON

DON'T LET THE SUN CATCH YOU CRYING	GERRY AND THE PACEMAKERS
DON'T LET THE SUN GO DOWN ON ME	ELTON JOHN
DON'T MAKE ME BLUE	BABBITY BLUE
DON'T MAKE ME OVER	SWINGING BLUE JEANS
DON'T MAKE MY BABY BLUE	SHADOWS
DON'T PLAY THAT SONG	BEN E. KING
DON'T PLAY YOUR ROCK AND ROLL TO ME	SMOKEY
DON'T SET ME FREE	RAY CHARLES
DON'T SLEEP IN THE SUBWAY	PETULA CLARK
DON'T STAY AWAY TOO LONG	PETERS AND LEE
DON'T STOP IT NOW	HOT CHOCOLATE
DON'T STOP LOVIN' ME BABY	PINKERTON'S ASSORTED COLOURS
DON'T STOP THE CARNIVAL	ALAN PRICE
DON'T STOP - TWIST	FRANKIE VAUGHAN
DON'T TALK TO HIM	CLIFF RICHARD
DON'T THAT BEAT ALL	ADAM FAITH
DON'T THROW AWAY ALL THOSE TEARDROPS	FRANKIE AVALON
DON'T THROW IT ALL AWAY	GARY BENSON
DON'T THROW YOUR LOVE AWAY	SEARCHERS
DON'T TREAT ME LIKE A CHILD	HELEN SHAPIRO
DON'T TRY TO CHANGE ME	CRICKETS
DON'T TURN AROUND	MERSEYBEATS
DON'T WORRY	JOHNNY BRANDON
DON'T WORRY	BILLY FURY
DON'T YOU KNOW	BUTTERSCOTCH
DON'T YOU KNOW IT	ADAM FAITH
DON'T YOU ROCK ME DADDY-O	VIPERS
DON'T YOU ROCK ME DADDY-O	LONNIE DONEGAN
DON'T YOU THINK ITS TIME	MIKE BERRY
DOO WAH DIDDY DIDDY	MANFRED MANN
DOOBEDOOD'N DOOBE	DIANA ROSS
DOOMSDAY	EVELYN THOMAS
DOOR IS STILL OPEN	DEAN MARTIN
DOUBLE BARREL	DAVE AND ANSEL COLLINS
007	DESMOND DEKKER AND THE ACES
DOWN BY THE LAZY RIVER	OSMONDS
DOWN DOWN	STATUS QUO
DOWN IN THE BOONDOCKS	BILLY JOE ROYAL
DOWN ON THE BEACH TONIGHT	DRIFTERS
DOWN ON THE CORNER	CREEDENCE CLEARWATER REVIVAL
DOWN THE DUSTPIPE	STATUS QUO
DOWN THE RIVER NILE	JOHN LEYTON
DOWN YONDER	JOHNNY AND THE HURRICANES
DOWNTOWN	PETULA CLARK
DRAGONFLY	TORNADOS
DREAM A LITTLE DREAM OF ME	MAMA CASS
DREAM BABY	ROY ORBISON
DREAM BABY	GLEN CAMPBELL
DREAM GIRL	MARK WYNTER
DREAM LOVER	BOBBY DARIN
DREAM OF OLIVER	SECOND CITY SOUND
DREAMBOAT	ALMA COGAN
DREAMBOAT	LIMMIE AND FAMILY COOKING
DREAMER	SUPERTRAMP
DREAMIN'	JOHNNY BURNETTE
DREAMS CAN TELL A LIE	NAT 'KING' COLE
DREAMS I DREAM	SHADOWS
DREAMS OF YOU	RALPH McTELL
DREAMY LADY	T. REX
DRINK UP THY ZIDER	ADGE CUTLER AND THE WURZELS
DRINKING SONG	MARIO LANZA
DRIVE-IN SATURDAY	DAVID BOWIE
DRIVIN' HOME	DUANE EDDY
DRUMMIN' UP A STORM	SANDY NELSON

DRUMS ARE MY BEAT	SANDY NELSON
DUELLING BANJOS	ERIC WEISSBERG AND STEVE MANDEL
DUM DUM	BRENDA LEE
D. W. WASHBURN	MONKEES
DYNA-MITE	MUD
DYNOMITE	TONY CAMILLO'S BAZUKA
EARLY IN THE MORNING	BUDDY HOLLY
EARLY IN THE MORNING	VANITY FAIR
EARTH ANGEL	CREWCUTS
EASIER SAID THAN DONE	ESCORTS
EAST WEST	HERMAN'S HERMITS
EASY GOING ME	ADAM FAITH
EASY EASY	SCOTLAND WORLD CUP SQUAD
EBB TIDE	RIGHTEOUS BROTHERS
EBONY EYES	EVERLY BROTHERS
EDELWEISS	VINCE HILL
EENY MEENY	SHOWSTOPPERS
EIGHT BY TEN	KEN DODD
EIGHT MILES HIGH	BYRDS
EIGHTEEN YELLOW ROSES	BOBBY DARIN
EL BIMBO	BIMBO JET
EL CONDOR PASA (IF I COULD)	JULIE FELIX
EL CONDOR PASA (IF I COULD)	SIMON AND GARFUNKEL
EL PASO	MARTY ROBBINS
ELEANOR RIGBY	BEATLES
ELEANOR RIGBY	RAY CHARLES
ELEANORE	TURTLES
ELECTED	ALICE COOPER
ELECTRIC LADY	GEORDIE
ELEPHANT TANGO	CYRIL STAPLETON
ELIZABETHAN REGGAE	BYRON LEE AND THE DRAGONAIRES
ELIZABETHAN SERENADE	GUNTHER KALLMAN CHOIR
ELMO JAMES	CHAIRMEN OF THE BOARD
ELOISE	BARRY RYAN
ELUSIVE BUTTERFLY	BOB LIND
ELUSIVE BUTTERFLY	VAL DOONICAN
EMERALD CITY	SEEKERS
EMMA	HOT CHOCOLATE
EMOTIONS	BRENDA LEE
END OF THE WORLD	SKEETER DAVIS
ENDLESS	DICKIE VALENTINE
ENDLESS SLEEP	MARTY WILDE
ENGINE ENGINE NO	ROGER MILLER
ENGLAND SWINGS	ROGER MILLER
ENGLISH COUNTRY GARDEN	JIMMIE RODGERS
ENTERTAINER (THEME FROM 'THE STING')	MARVIN HAMLISCH
ENTERTAINER (THEME FROM 'THE STING')	RAGTIMERS
ENTRY OF THE GLADIATORS	NERO AND THE GLADIATORS
ERNIE	BENNY HILL
ET MEME	FRANCOISE HARDY
EVE OF DESTRUCTION	BARRY McGUIRE
EVEN MORE PARTY POPS	RUSS CONWAY
EVEN THE BAD TIMES ARE GOOD	TREMELOES
EVER SINCE YOU SAID GOODBYE	MARTY WILDE
EVERLASTING LOVE	ROBERT KNIGHT
EVERLASTING LOVE	LOVE AFFAIR
EVERLOVIN'	RICKY NELSON
EVERMORE	RUBY MURRAY
EVERY DAY OF MY LIFE	MALCOLM VAUGHAN
EVERY LITTLE BIT HURTS	SPENCER DAVIS GROUP
EVERYBODY	TOMMY ROE
EVERYBODY GET TOGETHER	YOUNGBLOODS
EVERYBODY GET TOGETHER	DAVE CLARK FIVE

EVERYBODY GO HOME	CLODAGH ROGERS
EVERYBODY KNOWS	DAVE CLARK FIVE
EVERYBODY LOVES SOMEBODY	DEAN MARTIN
EVERYBODY'S GONNA BE HAPPY	KINKS
EVERYBODY'S SOMEBODY'S FOOL	CONNIE FRANCIS
EVERYBODY'S TALKIN'	NILSSON
EVERYBODY'S TWISTIN'	FRANK SINATRA
EVERYDAY	SLADE
EVERYDAY	MOODY BLUES
EVERYDAY	DON MACLEAN
EVERYDAY PEOPLE	SLY AND THE FAMILY STONE
EVERYONE'S GONE TO THE MOON	JONATHAN KING
EVERYTHING A MAN COULD EVER WANT	GLEN CAMPBELL
EVERYTHING I AM	PLASTIC PENNY
EVERYTHING I OWN	KEN BOOTHE
EVERYTHING IS BEAUTIFUL	RAY STEVENS
EVERYTHING WILL TURN OUT FINE	STEALERS WHEEL
EVERYTHING'S ALL RIGHT	MOJOS
EVERYTHING'S TUESDAY	CHAIRMEN OF THE BOARD
EVERYWHERE	DAVID WHITFIELD
EVIL HEARTED YOU	YARDBIRDS
EVIL WOMAN	ELECTRIC LIGHT ORCHESTRA
EXCERPT FROM A TEENAGE OPERA	KEITH WEST
EXCUSE ME BABY	MARK WYNTER
EXCLUSIVELY YOURS	MARK WYNTER
'EXCORCIST' THEME	SEE MIKE OLDFIELD'S SINGLE (THEME FROM 'TUBULAR BELLS')*
EXODUS	FERRANTE AND TEICHER
EXODUS	SEMPRINI
EXODUS	MANTOVANI
EXPERIMENTS WITH MICE	JOHNNY DANKWORTH
EXPRESS	B.T. EXPRESS
EXPRESSO BONGO (E.P.)	CLIFF RICHARD
EYE LEVEL	SIMON PARK ORCHESTRA
FA-FA-FA-FA (SAD SONG)	OTIS REDDING
FABULOUS	CHARLIE GRACIE
FAITHFUL HUSSAR	TED HEATH
FALL IN LOVE WITH YOU	CLIFF RICHARD
FALLIN'	CONNIE FRANCIS
FALLIN'	ROY ORBISON
FALLIN' IN LOVE	HAMILTON JOE FRANK AND REYNOLD
FALLING APART AT THE SEAMS	MARMALADE
FAME	DAVID BOWIE
FANCY PANTS	KENNY
FANLIGHT FANNY	CLINTON FORD
FAR AWAY	SHIRLEY BASSEY
FAR FAR AWAY	SLADE
FARAWAY PLACES	BACHELORS
FAREWELL	ROD STEWART
FAREWELL ANGELINA	JOAN BAEZ
FAREWELL IS A LONELY SOUND	JIMMY RUFFIN
FATHER CHRISTMAS DO NOT TOUCH ME	GOODIES
FATTIE BUM BUM	DIVERSIONS
FATTIE BUM BUM	CARL MALCOLM
F.B.I.	SHADOWS
FEEL LIKE MAKIN' LOVE	ROBERTA FLACK
FEEL LIKE MAKIN' LOVE	BAD COMPANY
FEEL SO FINE	JOHNNY PRESTON
FEEL THE NEED IN ME	DETROIT EMERALDS
FEELIN' GROOVY (FIFTY-NINTH STREET BRIDGE SONG)	HARPERS BIZARRE
FEELINGS	MORRIS ALBERT
FERRIS WHEEL	EVERLY BROTHERS

*MIKE OLDFIELD released in the U.S.A. only, as a single, a condensed
extract from 'Tubular Bells', as THEME FROM 'THE EXCORCIST' not to be
confused with MIKE OLDFIELD'S SINGLE, a different, British only release.

FERRY CROSS THE MERSEY	GERRY AND THE PACEMAKERS
FESTIVAL TIME	SAN REMO STRINGS
FEVER	PEGGY LEE
FEVER	HELEN SHAPIRO
FEVER	McCOYS
59TH STREET BRIDGE SONG (FEELIN' GROOVY)	HARPERS BIZARRE
FIFTY WAYS TO LEAVE YOUR LOVER	PAUL SIMON
FIGHT	MARTY WILDE
FINCHLEY CENTRAL	NEW VAUDEVILLE BAND
FIND MY WAY BACK HOME	NASHVILLE TEENS
FINDERS KEEPERS	CHAIRMEN OF THE BOARD
FINGER OF SUSPICION	DICKIE VALENTINE
FINGS AIN'T WHAT THEY USED TO BE	MAX BYGRAVES
FINGS AIN'T WHAT THEY USED TO BE	RUSS CONWAY
FIRE	ARTHUR BROWN
FIRE AND RAIN	JAMES TAYLOR
FIREBALL	DEEP PURPLE
FIREBALL XL5	DON SPENCER
FIRE BRIGADE	MOVE
FIRST CUT IS THE DEEPEST	P.P. ARNOLD
FIRST IMPRESSIONS	IMPRESSIONS
FIRST OF MAY	BEE GEES
FIRST TASTE OF LOVE	BEN E. KING
FIRST TIME	ADAM FAITH
FIRST TIME EVER I SAW YOUR FACE	ROBERTA FLACK
FISH MAN	IAN MENZIES
5.15	WHO
5-4-3-2-1	MANFRED MANN
FIVE LITTLE FINGERS	FRANKIE McBRIDE
FLIRT	JONATHAN KING
FLOATING IN THE WIND	HUDSON FORD
FLOWERS IN THE RAIN	MOVE
FLOWERS ON THE WALL	STATLER BROTHERS
FLOY JOY	SUPREMES
FLY ROBIN FLY	SILVER CONVENTION
FLYING MACHINE	CLIFF RICHARD
FOE-DEE-O-DEE	RUBETTES
FOGGY MOUNTAIN BREAKDOWN	LESTER FLATT AND EARL SCRUGGS
FOLK SINGER	TOMMY ROE
FOOL	ELVIS PRESLEY
FOOL	AL MATTHEWS
FOOL AM I	CILLA BLACK
FOOL NEVER LEARNS	ANDY WILLIAMS
FOOL NUMBER ONE	BRENDA LEE
FOOL ON THE HILL	SHIRLEY BASSEY
FOOL SUCH AS I	ELVIS PRESLEY
FOOLISH LITTLE GIRL	SHIRELLES
FOOLS RUSH IN	RICKY NELSON
FOOLS RUSH IN	BROOK BENTON
FOOT TAPPER	SHADOWS
FOOTSEE	WIGAN'S CHOSEN FEW
FOOTSTEPS	STEVE LAWRENCE
FOOTSTEPS	RONNIE CARROL
FOOTSTOMPIN' MUSIC	HAMILTON BOHANNON
FOR A PENNY	PAT BOONE
FOR ALL WE KNOW	CARPENTERS
FOR ALL WE KNOW	SHIRLEY BASSEY
(FOR GOD'S SAKE) GIVE MORE POWER TO THE PEOPLE	CHI-LITES
FOR LOVE	DAVID CASSIDY
FOR MAMA	MATT MONRO
FOR OLD TIME'S SAKE	MILLICAN AND NESBITT
FOR ONCE IN MY LIFE	TONY BENNET
FOR ONCE IN MY LIFE	STEVIE WONDER

FOR ONCE IN MY LIFE	DOROTHY SQUIRES
FOR THE GOOD TIMES	PERRY COMO
FOR WHOM THE BELL TOLLS	SIMON DUPREE
FOREVER	ROY WOOD
FOREVER AND EVER	SLIK
FOREVER CAME TODAY	DIANA ROSS AND THE SUPREMES
FOREVER KIND OF LOVE	BOBBY VEE
FORGET HIM	BOBBY RYDELL
FORGET ME NOT	EDEN KANE
FORGET ME NOT	MARTHA AND THE VANDELLAS
FORT WORTH JAIL	LONNIE DONEGAN
48 CRASH	SUZI QUATRO
FORTY MILES OF BAD ROAD	DUANE EDDY
FOR YOU	RICKY NELSON
FOR YOUR LOVE	JOE BROWN
FOUNTAINS OF ROME	EDMUND HOCKRIDGE
FOUR IN THE MORNING	FARON YOUNG
FOUR LITTLE HEELS	AVONS
FOUR LITTLE HEELS	BRIAN HYLAND
FOX ON THE RUN	SWEET
FOX ON THE RUN	MANFRED MANN
FOXY FOXY	MOTT THE HOOPLE
FRANKENSTEIN	EDGAR WINTER
FRANKIE AND JOHNNY	ACKER BILK
FRANKIE AND JOHNNY	SAM COOKE
FRANKIE AND JOHNNY	ELVIS PRESLEY
FREE ELECTRIC BAND	ALBERT HAMMOND
FREEDOM COME, FREEDOM GO	FORTUNES
FREIGHT TRAIN	CHAS McDEVITT AND NANCY WHISKY
FRIDAY ON MY MIND	EASYBEATS
FRIENDLY PERSUASION	PAT BOONE
FRIENDS	ARRIVAL
FRIENDS	BEACH BOYS
FRIGHTENED CITY	SHADOWS
FROM A JACK TO A KING	NED MILLER
FROM A WINDOW	BILLY J. KRAMER AND THE DAKOTAS
FROM HERE, TO THERE, TO YOU	HANK LOCKLIN
FROM ME TO YOU	BEATLES
FROM RUSSIA WITH LOVE	MATT MONRO
FROM RUSSIA WITH LOVE	JOHN BARRY
FROM THE BOTTOM OF MY HEART	MOODY BLUES
FROM THE UNDERWORLD	HERD
FROZEN ORANGE JOICE	PETER SARSTEDT
FUNKY BROADWAY	WILSON PICKETT
FUNKY GIBBON	GOODIES
FUNKY MOPED	JASPER CARROT
FUNKY NASSAU	BEGINNING OF THE END
FUNKY WEEKEND	STYLISTICS
FUNKY STREET	ARTHUR CONLEY
FUNNY ALL OVER	VERNON GIRLS FEATURING MAUREEN
FUNNY FAMILIAR FORGOTTEN FEELINGS	TOM JONES
FUNNY FUNNY	SWEET
FUNNY HOW LOVE CAN BE	IVY LEAGUE
FUNNY WAY OF LAUGHIN'	BURL IVES
GAL WITH YALLER SHOES	MICHAEL HOLLIDAY
GALLOPING HOME	LONDON STRING CHORALE
('BLACK BEAUTY' THEME)	
GALVESTON	GLEN CAMPBELL
GAMBLING BAR ROOM BLUES	SENSATIONAL ALEX HARVEY BAND
GAMBLING MAN	LONNIE DONEGAN
GAMES OF LOVE	WAYNE FONTANA
GAMES PEOPLE PLAY	JOE SOUTH
GAMES THAT LOVERS PLAY	DONALD PEERS
GARDEN OF EDEN	JOE VALINO

GARDEN OF EDEN	FRANKIE VAUGHAN
GARDEN OF EDEN	GARY MILLER
GARDEN OF EDEN	DICK JAMES
GARDEN PARTY	RICK NELSON
GASOLINE ALLEY BRED	HOLLIES
GATHER IN THE MUSHROOMS	BENNY HILL
GAUDETE	STEELEYE SPAN
GAYE	CLIFFORD T. WARD
GEE BABY	PETER SHELLEY
GEE WHIZ, IT'S YOU	CLIFF RICHARD
GENIE WITH THE LIGHT BROWN LAMP	SHADOWS
GENTLE ON MY MIND	GLEN CAMPBELL
GENTLE ON MY MIND	DEAN MARTIN
GEORGIA ON MY MIND	RAY CHARLES
GEORGY GIRL	SEEKERS
GERONIMO	SHADOWS
GET AWAY	GEORGIE FAME
GET BACK	BEATLES
GET DANCING	DISCO TEX AND THE SEX-O-LETTES
GET DOWN	GILBERT O'SULLIVAN
GET DOWN AND GET WITH IT	SLADE
GET DOWN TONIGHT	K.C. AND THE SUNSHINE BAND
GET IN THE SWING	SPARKS
GET IT ON ('BANG A GONG' U.S. TITLE)	T. REX
GET IT TOGETHER	CRISPY AND COMPANY
GET LOST	EDEN KANE
GET ME TO THE WORLD ON TIME	ELECTRIC PRUNES
GET OFF OF MY CLOUD	ROLLING STONES
GET OUT	HAROLD MELVIN AND THE BLUENOTES
GET OUT OF MY LIFE, WOMAN	LEE DORSEY
GET READY	TEMPTATIONS
GET UP I FEEL LIKE BEING A SEX MACHINE	JAMES BROWN
GET YOUR LOVE BACK	THREE DEGREES
GETTING A DRAG	LYNSEY DE PAUL
GETTING MIGHTY CROWDED	BETTY EVERETT
GETTING OVER YOU	ANDY WILLIAMS
GHETTO CHILD	DETROIT SPINNERS
GHOST RIDERS IN THE SKY	RAMRODS
GIDDY UP A DING DONG	FREDDIE BELL AND THE BELL BOYS
GIGI	VIC DAMONE
GIGI	BILLY ECKSTINE
GILLY GILLY OSSENFEFFER KATZENELLEN BOGEN BY THE SEA	MAX BYGRAVES
GIMME DAT DING	PIPKINS
GIMME GIMME GOOD LOVIN'	CRAZY ELEPHANT
GIMME LITTLE SIGN	BRENTON WOOD
GIMME SOME LOVING	SPENCER DAVIS GROUP
GIN GAN GOOLIE	SCAFFOLD
GIN HOUSE	AMEN CORNER
GINCHY	BERT WEEDON
GINNY COME LATELY	BRIAN HYLAND
GIRL	ST. LOUIS UNION
GIRL	TRUTH
GIRL CAN'T HELP IT	LITTLE RICHARD
GIRL DON'T COME	SANDIE SHAW
GIRL FROM IPANEMA	STAN GETZ AND CHARLIE BIRD WITH JOAO GILBERTO
GIRL LIKE YOU	CLIFF RICHARD
GIRL LIKE YOU	YOUNG RASCALS
GIRL OF MY BEST FRIEND	ELVIS PRESLEY
GIRL OF MY DREAMS	TONY BRENT
GIRL OF MY DREAMS	GERRY MONROE
GIRL SANG THE BLUES	EVERLY BROTHERS
GIRLIE	PEDDLERS

GIRLS	JOHNNY BURNETTE
GIRLS	MOMENTS AND WHATNAUTS
GIRLS, GIRLS, GIRLS	FOURMOST
GIRLS, GIRLS, GIRLS	STEVE LAWRENCE
GIRLS, GIRLS, GIRLS	SAILOR
GIVE A LITTLE LOVE	BAY CITY ROLLERS
GIVE AND TAKE	PIONEERS
GIVE, GIVE, GIVE	TOMMY STEELE
GIVE IRELAND BACK TO THE IRISH	WINGS
GIVE IT TO ME	TROGGS
GIVE IT TO ME NOW	KENNY
GIVE ME JUST A LITTLE MORE TIME	CHAIRMEN OF THE BOARD
GIVE ME LOVE (GIVE ME PEACE ON EARTH)	GEORGE HARRISON
GIVE ME ONE MORE CHANCE	DONALD PEERS
GIVE ME TIME	DUSTY SPRINGFIELD
GIVE ME YOUR WORD	TENNESSEE ERNIE FORD
GIVE ME YOUR WORD	BILLY FURY
GIVE MORE POWER TO THE PEOPLE	CHI-LITES
GIVE PEACE A CHANCE	PLASTIC ONO BAND
GIVING IT ALL AWAY	ROGER DALTREY
GLAD ALL OVER	DAVE CLARK FIVE
GLASS OF CHAMPAGNE	SAILOR
GLENDORA	PERRY COMO
GLOBETROTTER	TORNADOS
GLORIA	THEM
GO	GIGLIOLA CINQUETTI
GO AWAY LITTLE GIRL	MARK WYNTER
GO GO GO	CHUCK BERRY
GO NORTH	RICHARD BARNES
GO NOW	MOODY BLUES
GO ON BY	ALMA COGAN
GO TELL IT ON THE MOUNTAIN	PETER, PAUL AND MARY
GOD GAVE ROCK AND ROLL TO YOU	ARGENT
GOD ONLY KNOWS	BEACH BOYS
GODFATHER (LOVE THEME)	ANDY WILLIAMS
GOD'S GONNA PUNISH YOU	TYMES
GOIN' BACK	DUSTY SPRINGFIELD
GOIN' OUT OF MY HEAD	DODIE WEST
GOIN' UP COUNTRY	CANNED HEAT
GOING BACK TO MY HOME TOWN	HAL PAGE AND THE WHALERS
GOING DOWN THE ROAD	ROY WOOD
GOING HOME	OSMONDS
GOING TO A GO-GO	SMOKEY ROBINSON AND THE MIRACLES
GOING TO A GO-GO	SHARONETTES
GOLDEN AGE OF ROCK'N'ROLL	MOTT THE HOOPLE
GOLDEN LIGHTS	TWINKLE
GOLDEN SLUMBERS	TRASH
GOLDEN YEARS	DAVID BOWIE
GOLDFINGER	SHIRLEY BASSEY
GONE	SHIRLEY BASSEY
GONE, GONE, GONE	EVERLY BROTHERS
GONNA BUILD A MOUNTAIN	MATT MONRO
GONNA BUILD A MOUNTAIN	SAMMY DAVIS JR.
GONNA GET ALONG WITHOUT YOU NOW	TRINI LOPEZ
GONNA GIVE HER ALL THE LOVE I GOT	JIMMY RUFFIN
GONNA MAKE YOU A STAR	DAVID ESSEX
GONNA MAKE YOU AN OFFER YOU CAN'T REFUSE	JIMMY HELMS
GOO GOO BARABAJAGAL	DONOVAN (WITH JEFF BECK)
GOOD GOLLY MISS MOLLY	LITTLE RICHARD
GOOD GOLLY MISS MOLLY	SWINGING BLUE JEANS
GOOD GOLLY MISS MOLLY	JERRY LEE LEWIS
GOOD GRIEF CHRISTINA	CHICORY TIP
GOOD LIFE	TONY BENNETT

GOOD LOVE CAN NEVER DIE	ALVIN STARDUST
GOOD LOVIN' AIN'T THAT EASY TO COME BY	MARVIN GAYE AND TAMMI TERRELL
GOOD LOVIN' GONE BAD	BAD COMPANY
GOOD LUCK CHARM	ELVIS PRESLEY
GOOD MORNING	LEAPY LEE
GOOD MORNING FREEDOM	BLUE MINK
GOOD MORNING LITTLE SCHOOLGIRL	YARDBIRDS
GOOD MORNING STARSHINE	OLIVER
GOOD OLD ARSENAL	ARSENAL FOOTBALL CLUB
GOOD OLD ROCK'N'ROLL	DAVE CLARK FIVE
GOOD, THE BAD, AND THE UGLY	HUGO MONTENEGRO
GOOD TIME BABY	BOBBY RYDELL
GOOD TIMES	ERIC BURDON AND THE ANIMALS
GOOD TIMES	CLIFF RICHARD
GOOD TIMIN'	JIMMY JONES
GOOD VIBRATIONS	BEACH BOYS
GOODBYE	MARY HOPKIN
GOODBYE BLUEBIRD	WAYNE FONTANA
GOODBYE CRUEL WORLD	JAMES DARREN
GOODBYE IS JUST ANOTHER WORD	NEW SEEKERS
GOODBYE JIMMY GOODBYE	RUBY MURRAY
GOODBYE MY LOVE	SEARCHERS
GOODBYE MY LOVE	GLITTER BAND
GOODBYE, NOTHING TO SAY	JAVELLS FEATURING NOSMO KING
GOODBYE SAM, HELLO SAMANTHA	CLIFF RICHARD
GOODBYE TO LOVE	CARPENTERS
GOODBYE YELLOW BRICK ROAD	ELTON JOHN
GOODBYEE	PETER COOK AND DUDLEY MOORE
GOODBYEE	14 - 18
GOODNESS GRACIOUS ME	PETER SELLARS AND SOPHIA LOREN
GOODNIGHT	ROY ORBISON
GOODNIGHT MIDNIGHT	CLODAGH ROGERS
GOODNIGHT MRS. FLINTSTONE	PILTDOWN MEN
GOODNIGHT SWEET PRINCE	ACKER BILK
GOSSIP CALYPSO	BERNARD CRIBBINS
GOT A GIRL	FOUR PREPS
GOT A LOT O' LIVING TO DO	ELVIS PRESLEY
GOT MY MOJO WORKING	JIMMY SMITH
GOT TO BE THERE	MICHAEL JACKSON
GOT TO GET YOU INTO MY LIFE	CLIFF BENNET AND THE REBEL ROUSERS
GOTTA GET A DATE	FRANK IFIELD
GOTTA HAVE SOMETHIN' IN THE BANK, FRANK	FRANKIE VAUGHAN AND THE KAYE SISTERS
GOTTA SEE BABY TONIGHT	ACKER BILK
GOTTA SEE JANE	R. DEAN TAYLOR
GOVINDA	HARE KRISHNA TEMPLE
GRANADA	FRANK SINATRA
GRAND COULEE DAM	LONNIE DONEGAN
GRANDAD	CLIVE DUNN
GREAT BALLS OF FIRE	JERRY LEE LEWIS
GREAT BALLS OF FIRE	TINY TIM
GREAT PRETENDER	PLATTERS
GREAT SNOWMAN	BOB LUMAN
GREEN DOOR	JIM LOWE
GREEN DOOR	FRANKIE VAUGHAN
GREEN FIELDS	UNIT 4 + 2
GREEN GREEN GRASS OF HOME	TOM JONES
GREEN GREEN GRASS OF HOME	ELVIS PRESLEY
GREEN JEANS	FLEE RAKKERS
GREEN LEAVES OF SUMMER	BROTHERS FOUR
GREEN LEAVES OF SUMMER	KENNY BALL
GREEN MANALISHI	FLEETWOOD MAC
GREEN RIVER	CREEDENCE CLEARWATER REVIVAL
GREEN STREET GREEN	NEW VAUDEVILLE BAND

GREEN TAMBOURINE	LEMON PIPERS
GREEN TAMBOURINE	SUNDRAGON
GREENFIELDS	BROTHERS FOUR
GREENFIELDS	BEVERLY SISTERS
GROCI DI ORO	JOAN REGAN
GROOVE ME	KING FLOYD
GROOVER	T. REX
GROOVIN'	YOUNG RASCALS
GROOVIN' WITH MR. BLOE	MR. BLOE
GROOVEY KIND OF LOVE	MINDBENDERS
GROOVY	P.P. ARNOLD
GROOVY BABY	MICROBE
GROUPY GIRL	TONY JOE WHITE
GUANTANAMERA	SANDPIPERS
GUDBUY T'JANE	SLADE
GUILTY	PEARLS
GUITAR BOOGIE SHUFFLE	BERT WEEDON
GUITAR BOOGIE SHUFFLE	VIRTUES
GUITAR MAN	ELVIS PRESLEY
GUITAR MAN	BREAD
GUITAR TANGO	SHADOWS
GUNS OF NAVARONE	SKATALITES
GUNSLINGER	FRANKIE LANE
GURNEY SLADE	MAX HARRIS
GYPSIES, TRAMPS AND THIEVES	CHER
GYPSY EYES	JIMI HENDRIX EXPERIENCE
GYPSY ROVER	HIGHWAYMEN
GYPSY WOMAN	BRIAN HYLAND
HA HA SAID THE CROWN	MANFRED MANN
HALF AS NICE	AMEN CORNER
HALFWAY TO PARADISE	BILLY FURY
HALLELUJAH DAY	JACKSON FIVE
HALLELUJAH FREEDOM	JUNIOR CAMPBELL
HALLELUJAH, I LOVE HER SO	DICK JORDAN
HAND A HANDKERCHIEF TO HELEN	SUSAN MAUGHAN
HANDBAGS AND GLADRAGS	CHRIS FARLOWE
HANDFUL OF SONGS	TOMMY STEELE
HANDY MAN	JIMMY JONES
HANDY MAN	DEL SHANNON
HANG 'EM HIGH	HUGO MONTENEGRO
HANG ON IN THERE BABY	JOHNNY BRISTOL
HANG ON SLOOPY	McCOYS
HANG ON TO A DREAM	TIM HARDIN
HANGING ON	CLIFF RICHARD
HANKY PANKY	TOMMY JAMES AND THE SHONDELLS
HAPPENING	SUPREMES
HAPPENINGS TEN YEARS TIME AGO	YARDBIRDS
HAPPINESS	KEN DODD
HAPPINESS IS ME AND YOU	GILBERT O'SULLIVAN
HAPPY ANNIVERSARY	JANE MORGAN
HAPPY ANNIVERSARY	JOAN REGAN
HAPPY ANNIVERSARY	SLIM WHITMAN
HAPPY BIRTHDAY SWEET SIXTEEN	NEIL SEDAKA
HAPPY CHRISTMAS (WAR IS OVER)	JOHN LENNON AND THE PLASTIC
HAPPY CHRISTMAS (WAR IS OVER)	ONO BAND WITH THE HARLEM
HAPPY CHRISTMAS (WAR IS OVER)	COMMUNITY CHOIR
HAPPY DAYS AND LONELY NIGHTS	SUZI MILLER
HAPPY DAYS AND LONELY NIGHTS	FRANKIE VAUGHAN
HAPPY DAYS AND LONELY NIGHTS	RUBY MURRAY
HAPPY FEELING	HAMILTON BOHANNON
HAPPY GO LUCKY ME	GEORGE FORMBY
HAPPY GUITAR	TOMMY STEELE
HAPPY HEART	ANDY WILLIAMS
HAPPY JACK	WHO

HAPPY SONG	OTIS REDDING
HAPPY TO BE ON AN ISLAND IN THE SUN	DEMIS ROUSSOS
HAPPY TO MAKE YOUR ACQUAINTANCE	SAMMY DAVIS JR.
HAPPY TOGETHER	TURTLES
HAPPY WHISTLER	DON ROBERTSON
HARBOUR LIGHTS	PLATTERS
HARD DAY'S NIGHT	BEATLES
HARD DAY'S NIGHT	PETER SELLARS
HARD HEADED WOMAN	ELVIS PRESLEY
HARD RAIN'S A-GONNA FALL	BRIAN FERRY
HARD TO HANDLE	OTIS REDDING
HARD WAY	NASHVILLE TEENS
HARDHEARTED HANNAH	RAY CHARLES
HARDHEARTED HANNAH	TEMPERANCE SEVEN
HARE KRISHNA MANTRA	RADHA KRISHNA TEMPLE
HARLEM SHUFFLE	BOB AND EARL
HARMOUR LOVE	SYREETA
HARPER VALLEY P.T.A.	JEANNIE C. RILEY
HARVEST OF LOVE	BENNY HILL
HASTA LA VISTA	SYLVIA (SWEDISH)
HATS OFF TO LARRY	DEL SHANNON
HAVA NAGILA	SPOTNIKS
HAVE A DRINK ON ME	LONNIE DONEGAN
HAVE I STAYED TOO LONG	SONNY AND CHER
HAVE I THE RIGHT	HONEYCOMBS
HAVE PITY ON THE BOY	PAUL AND BARRY RYAN
HAVE YOU EVER LOVED SOMEBODY	PAUL AND BARRY RYAN
HAVE YOU EVER LOVED SOMEBODY	SEARCHERS
HAVE YOU EVER SEEN THE RAIN	CREEDANCE CLEARWATER REVIVAL
HAVE YOU SEEN HER	CHI-LITES
HAVE YOU SEEN YOUR MOTHER, BABY	ROLLING STONES
HAVING A PARTY	OSMONDS
HAVING MY BABY	PAUL ANKA
HAWAII TATTOO	WAIKIKIS
HAWAIIAN WEDDING SONG	JULIE RODGERS
HAWKEYE	FRANKIE LAINE
HE AIN'T HEAVY, HE'S MY BROTHER	HOLLIES
HE GOT WHAT HE WANTED	LITTLE RICHARD
HE'LL HAVE TO GO	JIM REEVES
HE'LL HAVE TO STAY	JEANNE BLACK
HE'S A REBEL	CRYSTALS
HE'S GONNA STEP ON YOU AGAIN	JOHN KONGOS
HE'S GOT NO LOVE	SEARCHERS
HE'S GOT THE WHOLE WORLD IN HIS HANDS	LAURIE LONDON
HE'S IN TOWN	ROCKIN' BERRIES
HE'S MISSTRA KNOW IT ALL	STEVIE WONDER
HE'S OLD ENOUGH TO KNOW BETTER	BROOK BROTHERS
HE'S SO FINE	CHIFFONS
HE'S THE ONE	BILLIE DAVIS
HEADLINE NEWS	EDWIN STARR
HEART	MAX BYGRAVES
HEART	RITA PAVONE
HEART AND SOUL	JAN AND DEAN
HEART OF A MAN	FRANKIE VAUGHAN
HEART OF A TEENAGE GIRL	CRAIG DOUGLAS
HEART OF A TEENAGE GIRL	GEORGE CHAKARIS
HEART OF GOLD	NEIL YOUNG
HEART OF STONE	KENNY
HEARTACHE	ROY ORBISON
HEARTACHES	PATSY CLINE
HEARTACHES	VINCE HILL
HEARTACHES BY THE NUMBER	GUY MITCHELL
HEARTBEAT	RUBY MURRAY
HEARTBEAT	ENGLAND SISTERS
HEARTBEAT	BUDDY HOLLY
HEARTBREAK HOTEL	ELVIS PRESLEY

HEARTFUL OF SOUL	YARDBIRDS
HEATHER HONEY	TOMMY ROE
HEAVEN HELP US ALL	STEVIE WONDER
HEAVEN IS MY WOMAN	VAL DOONICAN
HEAVEN IS THERE	JULIE FELIX
HEAVEN MUST HAVE SENT YOU	ELGINS
HEAVY MAKES YOU HAPPY	BOBBY BLOOM
HELEN WHEELS	PAUL McCARTNEY'S WINGS
HELL RAISER	SWEET
HELLO BUDDY	TREMELOES
HELLO DOLLY	LOUIS ARMSTRONG
HELLO DOLLY	FRANKIE VAUGHAN
HELLO DOLLY	FRANK SINATRA
HELLO DOLLY	BACHELORS
HELLO GOODBYE	BEATLES
HELLO HAPPINESS	DRIFTERS
HELLO, HELLO, I'M BACK AGAIN	GARY GLITTER
HELLO HOW ARE YOU	EASYBEATS
HELLO HURRAY	ALICE COOPER
HELLO I LOVE YOU	DOORS
HELLO JOSEPHINE	WAYNE FONTANA
HELLO LITTLE GIRL	FOURMOST
HELLO MARY LOU	RICKY NELSON
HELLO MUDDAH, HELLO FADDAH	ALAN SHERMAN
HELLO SUMMERTIME	BOBBY GOLDSBORO
HELLO SUSIE	AMEN CORNER
HELLO WORLD	TREMELOES
HELP	BEATLES
HELP IT ALONG	CLIFF RICHARD
HELP ME GIRL	ERIC BURDON AND THE ANIMALS
HELP ME MAKE IT THROUGH THE NIGHT	GLADYS KNIGHT AND THE PIPS
HELP ME MAKE IT THROUGH THE NIGHT	JOHN HOLT
HELP ME RHONDA	BEACH BOYS
HELP YOURSELF	TOM JONES
HELULE HELULE	TREMELOES
HER ROYAL MAJESTY	JAMES DARREN
HERCULES	FRANKIE VAUGHAN
HERE COME THE NICE	SMALL FACES
HERE COMES MY BABY	TREMELOES
HERE COMES SUMMER	JERRY KELLER
HERE COMES SUMMER	DAVE CLARK FIVE
HERE COMES THAT FEELING	BRENDA LEE
HERE COMES THE JUDGE	PIGMEAT MARKHAM
HERE COMES THE JUDGE	SHORTY LONG
HERE COMES THE NIGHT	THEM
HERE COMES THE NIGHT	LULU AND THE LUVVERS
HERE COMES THE STAR	HERMAN'S HERMITS
HERE I GO AGAIN	HOLLIES
HERE I GO AGAIN	ARCHIE BELL AND THE DRELLS
HERE I GO AGAIN	GUYS AND DOLLS
HERE IT COMES AGAIN	FORTUNES
HERE, THERE AND EVERYWHERE	EMMYLOU HARRIS
HERE WE GO AGAIN	RAY CHARLES
HERE WE GO ROUND THE MULBERRY BUSH	TRAFFIC
HERNANDO'S HIDEAWAY	JOHNNY RAY
HERNANDO'S HIDEAWAY	JOHNSTON BROTHERS
HEROES AND VILLAINS	BEACH BOYS
HEY AMERICA	JAMES BROWN
HEY BABY	BRUCE CHANNEL
HEY GIRL	SMALL FACES
HEY GIRL DON'T BOTHER ME	TAMS
HEY GOOD-LOOKING	TOMMY ZANG
HEY GOOD-LOOKING	BO DIDDLEY
HEY JOE	JIMI HENDRIX

HEY JUDE	BEATLES
HEY JUDE	WILSON PICKETT
HEY LITTLE GIRL	DEL SHANNON
HEY LITTLE LUCY	CONWAY TWITTY
HEY MAMA	JOE BROWN
HEY MISS PAYNE	CHEQUERS
HEY MISTER CHRISTMAS	SHOWADDYWADDY
HEY MR. MUSIC MAN	PETERS AND LEE
HEY PAULA	PAUL AND PAULA
HEY ROCK'N'ROLL	SHOWADDYWADDY
HEY THERE	ROSEMARY CLOONEY
HEY THERE	SAMMY DAVIS JR.
HEY THERE	JOHNNIE RAY
HEY THERE	LITA ROZA
HEY WILLY	HOLLIES
HEYKENS SERENADE	ROYAL SCOTS DRAGOON GUARDS BAND
HI HI HAZEL	TROGGS
HI HI HAZEL	GENO WASHINGTON AND THE RAM JAM BAND
HI HI HI	WINGS
HI-HEEL SNEAKERS	TOMMY TUCKER
HI HO SILVER LINING	JEFF BECK
HI-LILI, HI-LO	RICHARD CHAMBERLAIN
HI-LILI, HI-LO	ALAN PRICE
HIDE AND SEEK	MARTY WILDE
HIDEAWAY	DAVE DEE, DOZY, BEAKY, MICK AND TICH
HIGH CLASS BABY	CLIFF RICHARD AND THE SHADOWS
HIGH HOPES	FRANK SINATRA
HIGH IN THE SKY	AMEN CORNER
HIGH SCHOOL CONFIDENTIAL	JERRY LEE LEWIS
HIGH TIME	PAUL JONES
HIGH VOLTAGE	JOHNNY AND THE HURRICANES
HIGHER AND HIGHER	JACKIE WILSON
HIGHER GROUND	STEVIE WONDER
HIGHFLY	JOHN MILES
HIGHWAY CODE	MASTERSINGERS
HIGHWAY SONG	NANCY SINATRA
HIGHWAYS OF MY LIFE	ISLEY BROTHERS
HIGHWIRE	LINDA CARR AND THE LOVE SQUAD
HIPPY HIPPY SHAKE	SWINGING BLUE JEANS
HIS GIRL	GUESS WHO
HIS LATEST FLAME	ELVIS PRESLEY
HIT AND MISS	JOHN BARRY
HIT THE ROAD JACK	RAY CHARLES
HITCHIN' A RIDE	VANITY FARE
HOCUS POCUS	FOCUS
HOLD BACK THE NIGHT	TRAMMPS
HOLD BACK TOMORROW	MIKI AND GRIFF
HOLD ME	P.J. PROBY
HOLD ME CLOSE	DAVID ESSEX
HOLD ME TIGHT	JOHNNY NASH
HOLD MY HAND	DON CORNELL
HOLD ON TO LOVE	PETER SKELLERN
HOLD TIGHT	DAVE DEE, DOZY, BEAKY, MICK AND TICH
HOLD YOUR HEAD UP	ARGENT
HOLE IN MY SHOE	TRAFFIC
HOLE IN THE BUCKET	HARRY BELAFONTE
HOLE IN THE GROUND	BERNARD CRIBBINS
HOLY COW	LEE DORSEY
HOLY CITY	MOIRA ANDERSON
HOLY ROLLER	NAZARETH
HOMBURG	PROCOL HARUM
HOME OF THE BRAVE	JODY MILLER
HOMELOVIN' MAN	ANDY WILLIAMS
HOMELY GIRL	CHI-LITES
HOMEWARD BOUND	SIMON AND GARFUNKEL

HOMEWARD BOUND	QUIET FIVE
HONALOOCHIE BOOGIE	MOTT THE HOOPLE
HONEST I DO	DANNY STORM
HONEY	BOBBY GOLDSBORO
HONEY	GEORGE McCRAE
HONEY CHILE	MARTHA REEVES AND THE VANDELLAS
HONEY COME BACK	GLEN CAMPBELL
HONEY HONEY	SWEET DREAMS
HONEY I NEED	PRETTY THINGS
HONEYCOMB	JIMMIE RODGERS
HONKY CAT	ELTON JOHN
HONKY TONK TRAIN BLUES	KEITH EMERSON
HONKY TONK WOMEN	ROLLING STONES
HOOKED ON A FEELING	JONATHAN KING
HOOTS MON	LORD ROCKINGHAM'S XI
HORSE WITH NO NAME	AMERICA
HOT DIGGITY	PERRY COMO
HOT DIGGITY	MICHAEL HOLLIDAY
HOT DIGGITY	STARGAZERS
HOT LOVE	T. REX
HOT PEPPER	FLOYD CRAMER
HOT SHOT	BARRY BLUE
HOUND DOG	ELVIS PRESLEY
HOUSE IN THE COUNTRY	PRETTY THINGS
HOUSE OF THE RISING SUN	ANIMALS
HOUSE OF THE RISING SUN	FRIJID PINK
HOUSE THAT JACK BUILT	ALAN PRICE
HOUSE WITH LOVE IN IT	FOUR LADS
HOUSE WITH LOVE IN IT	VERA LYNN
HOW ABOUT THAT	ADAM FAITH
HOW CAN I BE SURE	RASCALS
HOW CAN I BE SURE	DAVID CASSIDY
HOW CAN I BE SURE	DUSTY SPRINGFIELD
HOW CAN I MEET HER	EVERLY BROTHERS
HOW CAN I TELL HER	FOURMOST
HOW COME	RONNIE LANE
HOW COULD WE DARE TO BE WRONG	COLIN BLUNSTONE
HOW DO YOU DO IT	GERRY AND THE PACEMAKERS
HOW DO YOU KNOW IT'S LOVE	TERESA BREWER
HOW DO YOU SPEAK TO AN ANGEL	DEAN MARTIN
HOW DOES IT FEEL	SLADE
HOW DOES THAT GRAB YOU, DARLIN'	NANCY SINATRA
HOW GLAD I AM	KIKI DEE
HOW HIGH THE MOON	ELLA FITZGERALD
HOW HIGH THE MOON	GLORIA GAYNOR
HOW LONG	ACE
HOW LONG HAS IT BEEN	JIM REEVES
HOW MANY TEARS	BOBBY VEE
HOW SOON	HENRY MANCINI
HOW SWEET IT IS (TO BE LOVED BY YOU)	MARVIN GAYE
HOW SWEET IT IS (TO BE LOVED BY YOU)	JUNIOR WALKER AND THE ALL STARS
HOW WONDERFUL TO KNOW	PEARL CARR AND TEDDY JOHNSON
HUBBLE BUBBLE TOIL AND TROUBLE	MANFRED MANN
HULLO MY DARLINGS	CHARLIE DRAKE
HULLO YOUNG LOVERS	PAUL ANKA
HUMMINGBIRD	FRANKIE LANE
HUNDRED POUNDS OF CLAY	GENE McDANIELS
HUNDRED POUNDS OF CLAY	CRAIG DOUGLAS
HUNGRY FOR LOVE	JOHNNY KIDD AND THE PIRATES
HUNT	BARRY RYAN
HURDY GURDY MAN	DONOVAN
HURRICANE	BOB DYLAN
HURT BY LOVE	INEZ FOXX

HURT SO GOOD	SUSAN CADOGAN
HUSH ... NOT A WORD TO MARY	JOHN ROWLES
HUSTLE	VAN McCOY
HYPNOSIS	MUD
I AIN'T GOT TIME ANYMORE	CLIFF RICHARD
I AIN'T LYING	GEORGE McCRAE
I ALMOST LOST MY MIND	PAT BOONE
I AM A ROCK	SIMON AND GARFUNKEL
I AM ... I SAID	NEIL DIAMOND
I AM WHAT I AM	GREYHOUND
I APOLOGISE	P.J. PROBY
I BEG OF YOU	ELVIS PRESLEY
I BELIEVE	DAVID WHITFIELD
I BELIEVE	BACHELORS
I BELIEVE I'M GONNA LOVE YOU	FRANK SINATRA
I BELIEVE IN FATHER CHRISTMAS	GREG LAKE
I BELIEVE IN LOVE	HOT CHOCOLATE
I BELONG	KATHY KIRBY
I CAN DANCE	BRIAN POOLE AND THE TREMELOES
I CAN DO IT	RUBETTES
I CAN HEAR MUSIC	BEACH BOYS
I CAN HEAR THE GRASS GROW	MOVE
I CAN HELP	BILLY SWAN
I CAN SEE CLEARLY NOW	JOHNNY NASH
I CAN SEE FOR MILES	WHO
I CAN SING A RAINBOW	DELLS
I CAN TAKE OR LEAVE YOUR LOVING	HERMAN'S HERMITS
I CAN'T CONTROL MYSELF	TROGGS
I CAN'T EXPLAIN	WHO
I CAN'T GET NEXT TO YOU	TEMPTATIONS
I CAN'T GIVE YOU ANYTHING BUT	
MY LOVE	STYLISTICS
I CAN'T HELP	ELVIS PRESLEY
I CAN'T HELP IT	JOHNNY TILLOTSON
I CAN'T HELP MYSELF	DONNIE ELBERT
I CAN'T HELP MYSELF	FOUR TOPS
I CAN'T LEAVE YOU ALONE	GEORGE McCRAE
I CAN'T LET GO	HOLLIES
I CAN'T LET MAGGIE GO	HONEYBUS
I CAN'T MAKE IT	SMALL FACES
I CAN'T MAKE IT ALONE	P.J. PROBY
I CAN'T STAND IT	SPENCER DAVIS GROUP
I CAN'T STAND THE RAIN	ANNE PEEBLES
I CAN'T STOP	OSMONDS
I CAN'T STOP LOVING YOU	RAY CHARLES
I CAN'T TELL A WALTZ FROM A TANGO	ALMA COGAN
I CAN'T TELL THE BOTTOM FROM THE	
TOP	HOLLIES
I CAN'T TURN YOU LOOSE	OTIS REDDING
I CLOSE MY EYES	DUSTY SPRINGFIELD
I COULD EASILY FALL	CLIFF RICHARD
I COULD NEVER LOVE ANOTHER	TEMPTATIONS
I COULDN'T LIVE WITHOUT YOUR LOVE	PETULA CLARK
I COUNT THE TEARS	DRIFTERS
I CRIED FOR YOU	RICKY STEVENS
I DID WHAT I DID FOR MARIA	TONY CHRISTIE
I DIDN'T KNOW I LOVED YOU	GARY GLITTER
(TILL I SAW YOU ROCK'N'ROLL)	
I DIDN'T MEAN TO HURT YOU	ROCKIN' BERRIES
I DIG YOU BABY	MARVIN RAINWATER
I DO, I DO, I DO	ABBA
I DON'T BELIEVE IN IF ANYMORE	ROGER WHITTAKER
I DON'T BELIEVE IN MIRACLES	COLIN BLUNSTONE
I DON'T BLAME YOU AT ALL	SMOKEY ROBINSON AND THE MIRACLES
I DON'T CARE	LOS BRAVOS

I DON'T NEED ANYTHING	SANDIE SHAW
I DON'T KNOW HOW TO LOVE HIM	PETULA CLARK
I DON'T KNOW HOW TO LOVE HIM	MURRAY HEAD WITH YVONNE ELLIMAN
I DON'T KNOW WHY	EDEN KANE
I DON'T KNOW WHY	ANDY AND DAVID WILLIAMS
I DON'T KNOW WHY	STEVIE WONDER
I DON'T LOVE YOU (BUT I THINK I LIKE YOU)	GILBERT O'SULLIVAN
I DON'T WANT OUR LOVING TO DIE	HERD
I DON'T WANT TO GO ON WITHOUT YOU	MOODY BLUES
I ENJOY BEING A GIRL	PAT SUZUKI
I FEEL A CRY COMING ON	HANK LOCKLIN
I FEEL FINE	BEATLES
I FEEL FREE	CREAM
I FEEL LOVE COMING ON	FELICE TAYLOR
I FEEL SO BAD	ELVIS PRESLEY
I FEEL SOMETHING	CHER
I FOUGHT THE LAW (AND THE LAW WON)	BOBBY FULLER FOUR
I FOUND OUT THE HARD WAY	FOUR PENNIES
I FOUND SUNSHINE	CHI-LITES
I GET A KICK OUT OF YOU	GARY SHEARSTON
I GET A LITTLE SENTIMENTAL OVER YOU	NEW SEEKERS
I GET AROUND	BEACH BOYS
I GET SO EXCITED	EQUALS
I GET THE MUSIC IN ME	KIKI DEE
I GET THE SWEETEST FEELING	JACKIE WILSON
I GO APE	NEIL SEDAKA
I GOT RHYTHM	HAPPENINGS
I GOT STUNG	ELVIS PRESLEY
I GOT YOU	JAMES BROWN
I GOT YOU BABE	SONNY AND CHER
I GUESS I'LL ALWAYS LOVE YOU	ISLEY BROTHERS
I HAD TOO MUCH TO DREAM LAST NIGHT	ELECTRIC PRUNES
I HEAR A SYMPHONY	SUPREMES
I HEAR YOU KNOCKING	GALE STORM
I HEAR YOU KNOCKING	DAVE EDMUNDS
I HEARD A HEART BREAK LAST NIGHT	JIM REEVES
I HEARD IT THROUGH THE GRAPEVINE	GLADYS KNIGHT AND THE PIPS
I HEARD IT THROUGH THE GRAPEVINE	MARVIN GAYE
I HONESTLY LOVE YOU	OLIVIA NEWTON-JOHN
I JUST CAN'T HELP BELIEVING	ELVIS PRESLEY
I JUST DON'T KNOW WHAT TO DO WITH MYSELF	DUSTY SPRINGFIELD
I JUST GO FOR YOU	JIMMY JONES
I KEEP RINGING MY BABY	SOUL BROTHERS
I KNOW	PERRY COMO
I KNOW A PLACE	PETULA CLARK
I KNOW I'M LOSING YOU	TEMPTATIONS
I KNOW WHAT I LIKE	GENESIS
I KNOW WHERE I'M GOING	COUNTRYMEN
I LEFT MY HEART IN SAN FRANCISCO	TONY BENNET
I LIKE IT	GERRY AND THE PACEMAKERS
I LIKE YOUR KIND OF LOVE	ANDY WILLIAMS
I LIVE FOR THE SUN	VANITY FAIR
I LOVE BEING IN LOVE WITH YOU	ADAM FAITH
I LOVE HER	PAUL AND BARRY RYAN
I LOVE HOW YOU LOVE ME	PARIS SISTERS
I LOVE HOW YOU LOVE ME	JIMMY CRAWFORD
I LOVE HOW YOU LOVE ME	MAUREEN EVANS
I LOVE HOW YOU LOVE ME	PAUL AND BARRY RYAN
I LOVE MUSIC	O'JAYS
I LOVE MY DOG	CAT STEVENS

I LOVE THE WAY YOU LOVE	MARV JOHNSON
I LOVE TO LOVE	TINA CHARLES
I LOVE YOU	CLIFF RICHARD
I LOVE YOU BABY	PAUL ANKA
I LOVE YOU BABY	FREDDIE AND THE DREAMERS
I LOVE YOU BECAUSE	AL MARTINO
I LOVE YOU BECAUSE	JIM REEVES
I LOVE YOU LOVE ME LOVE	GARY GLITTER
I LOVE YOU SO MUCH IT HURTS	CHARLIE GRACIE
I LOVE YOU YES I DO	MERSEYBEATS
I MAY NEVER PASS THIS WAY AGAIN	ROBERT EARL
I MAY NEVER PASS THIS WAY AGAIN	PERRY COMO
I MET A GIRL	SHADOWS
I MISS YOU BABY	MARV JOHNSON
I MUST BE SEEING THINGS	GENE PITNEY
I NEED YOUR LOVE SO BAD	FLEETWOOD MAC
I NEED YOU NOW	EDDIE FISHER
I NEED YOUR LOVE TONIGHT	ELVIS PRESLEY
I ONLY HAVE EYES FOR YOU	ART GARFUNKEL
I ONLY LIVE TO LOVE YOU	CILLA BLACK
I ONLY WANT TO BE WITH YOU	DUSTY SPRINGFIELD
I PRETEND	DES O'CONNOR
I PUT A SPELL ON YOU	ALAN PRICE
I PUT A SPELL ON YOU	NINA SIMONE
I REMEMBER YOU	FRANK IFIELD
I SAW HER AGAIN LAST NIGHT	MAMAS AND PAPAS
I SAW LINDA YESTERDAY	DOUG SHELDON
I SAW THE LIGHT	TODD RUNDGREN
I SAY A LITTLE PRAYER	ARETHA FRANKLIN
I SECOND THAT EMOTION	SMOKEY ROBINSON AND THE MIRACLES
I SECOND THAT EMOTION	DIANA ROSS AND THE SUPREMES
I SEE A STAR	MOUTH AND MACNEAL
I SHALL BE RELEASED	TREMELOES
I SHOT THE SHERIFF	ERIC CLAPTON
I SHOULD CARE	FRANK IFIELD
I SHOULD HAVE KNOWN BETTER	NATURALS
I SPY FOR THE F.B.I.	JAMO THOMAS
I STAND ACCUSED	MERSEYBEATS
I STILL BELIEVE	RONNIE HILTON
I STILL LOVE YOU ALL	KENNY BALL
I TALKED TO THE TREES	LEE MARVIN AND CLINT EASTWOOD
I THANK YOU	SAM AND DAVE
I THINK I LOVE YOU	PARTRIDGE FAMILY
I THINK OF YOU	MERSEYBEATS
I THINK OF YOU	PERRY COMO
I THINK OF YOU	DETROIT EMERALDS
I THREW IT ALL AWAY	BOB DYLAN
I TOLD YOU SO	JIMMY JONES
I UNDERSTAND	G-CLEFS
I UNDERSTAND	FREDDIE AND THE DREAMERS
I WANNA BE YOUR MAN	ROLLING STONES
I WANNA DANCE WIT CHOO	DISCO TEX AND THE SEX-O-LETTES
I WANNA GO HOME	LONNIE DONEGAN
I WANNA LOVE MY LIFE AWAY	GENE PITNEY
I WANNA STAY HERE	MIKI AND GRIFF
I WANNA STAY WITH YOU	GALLAGHER AND LYLE
I WANT CANDY	BRIAN POOLE AND THE TREMELOES
I WANT TO BE WANTED	BRENDA LEE
I WANT TO GIVE	PERRY COMO
I WANT TO GO WITH YOU	EDDY ARNOLD
I WANT TO HOLD YOUR HAND	BEATLES
I WANT TO STAY HERE	STEVE LAWRENCE AND EYDIE GORME
I WANT TO WALK YOU HOME	FATS DOMINO
I WANT YOU	BOB DYLAN
I WANT YOU BACK	JACKSON FIVE

I WANT YOU, I NEED YOU, I LOVE YOU	ELVIS PRESLEY
I WANT YOU TO BE MY BABY	BILLIE DAVIS
I WAS KAISER BILL'S BATMAN	WHISTLING JACK SMITH
I WAS MADE TO LOVE HER	STEVIE WONDER
I WHO HAVE NOTHING	SHIRLEY BASSEY
I WHO HAVE NOTHING	TOM JONES
I WILL	BILLY FURY
I WILL DRINK THE WINE	FRANK SINATRA
I WILL RETURN	SPRINGWATER
I WILL SEE YOU THERE	LINDA KENDRICK
I WILL SURVIVE	ARRIVAL
I WISH I COULD SHIMMY LIKE MY SISTER KATE	OLYMPICS
I WISH IT COULD BE CHRISTMAS EVERY DAY	WIZZARD
I WISH IT WOULD RAIN	TEMPTATIONS
I WISH IT WOULD RAIN	FACES
I WONDER	BRENDA LEE
I WONDER	JANE FROMAN
I WONDER	DICKIE VALENTINE
I WONDER	CRYSTALS
I WON'T COME IN WHILE HE'S THERE	JIM REEVES
I WON'T FORGET YOU	JIM REEVES
I WON'T LAST ANOTHER DAY WITHOUT YOU	CARPENTERS
I WOULDN'T TRADE YOU FOR THE WORLD	BACHELORS
I WRITE THE SONGS	DAVID CASSIDY
ICE CREAM MAN	TORNADOS
ICE IN THE SUN	STATUS QUO
I'D DO ANYTHING	MIKE PRESTON
I'D LIKE TO TEACH THE WORLD TO SING	NEW SEEKERS
I'D LOVE YOU TO WANT ME	LOBO
I'D NEVER FIND ANOTHER YOU	BILLY FURY
I'D RATHER GO BLIND	CHICKEN SHACK
IDLE ON PARADE (E.P.)	ANTHONY NEWLEY
IF	TELLY SAVALAS
IF	YIN AND YAN
IF A MAN ANSWERS	BOBBY DARIN
IF EVERY DAY WAS LIKE CHRISTMAS	ELVIS PRESLEY
IF HE TELLS YOU	ADAM FAITH
IF I CAN DREAM	ELVIS PRESLEY
IF I COULD (EL CONDOR PASA)	SIMON AND GARFUNKEL
IF I COULD (EL CONDOR PASA)	JULIE FELIX
IF I COULD	DAVID ESSEX
IF I COULD BUILD MY WORLD AROUND YOU	MARVIN GAYE AND TAMMI TERRELL
IF I DIDN'T CARE	DAVID CASSIDY
IF I GIVE MY HEART TO YOU	JOAN REGAN
IF I GIVE MY HEART TO YOU	DORIS DAY
IF I HAD A HAMMER	PETER, PAUL AND MARY
IF I HAD A HAMMER	TRINI LOPEZ
IF I KNEW THEN WHAT I KNOW NOW	VAL DOONICAN
IF I LOVED YOU	PERRY COMO
IF I LOVED YOU	RICHARD ANTHONY
IF I NEEDED SOMEONE	HOLLIES
IF I ONLY HAD TIME	JOHN ROWLES
IF I RULED THE WORLD	HARRY SECOMBE
IF I RULED THE WORLD	TONY BENNETT
IF I THOUGHT YOU'D EVER CHANGE YOUR MIND	CILLA BLACK
IF I WERE A CARPENTER	BOBBY DARIN
IF I WERE A CARPENTER	FOUR TOPS
IF I WERE A RICH MAN	TOPOL
IF IT WASN'T FOR THE REASON THAT I LOVE YOU	MIKI ANTHONY

IF NOT FOR YOU	OLIVIA NEWTON-JOHN
IF ONLY TOMORROW	RONNIE CARROL
IF SHE SHOULD COME TO YOU	ANTHONY NEWLEY
IF THE WHOLE WORLD STOPPED LOVING	VAL DOONICAN
IF YOU BELIEVE	JOHNNY RAY
IF YOU CAN WANT	SMOKEY ROBINSON AND THE MIRACLES
IF YOU COULD READ MY MIND	GORDON LIGHTFOOT
IF YOU DON'T KNOW ME BY NOW	HAROLD MELVIN AND THE BLUENOTES
IF YOU DON'T WANT MY LOVE	ROBERT JOHN
IF YOU GO AWAY	TERRY JACKS
IF YOU GOTTA GO, GO NOW	MANFRED MANN
IF YOU GOTTA MAKE A FOOL OF SOMEBODY	FREDDIE AND THE DREAMERS
IF YOU LOVE HER	DICK EMERY
IF YOU LOVE ME	MARY HOPKIN
IF YOU REALLY LOVE ME	STEVIE WONDER
IF YOU TALK IN YOUR SLEEP	ELVIS PRESLEY
IF YOU THINK YOU KNOW HOW TO LOVE ME	SMOKEY
IF YOU WANNA BE HAPPY	JIMMY SOUL
IF YOU WERE MINE, MARY	EDDY ARNOLD
IF YOU'RE READY	STAPLE SINGERS
IKO IKO	DIXIE-CUPS
IL NOSTRO CONCERTO	UMBERTO BINDI
IL SILENZIO	NINI ROSSO
I'LL ALWAYS LOVE MY MAMA	INTRUDERS
I'LL BE HOME	PAT BOONE
I'LL BE THERE	BOBBY DARIN
I'LL BE THERE	GERRY AND THE PACEMAKERS
I'LL BE THERE	JACKIE TRENT
I'LL BE THERE	JACKSON FIVE
I'LL BE TRUE TO YOU	HOLLIES
I'LL BE WITH YOU IN APPLEBLOSSOM TIME	ROSEMARY JUNE
I'LL BE YOUR HERO	VINCE TAYLOR
I'LL COME RUNNING	CLIFF RICHARD
I'LL COME WHEN YOU CALL	RUBY MURRAY
I'LL CUT YOUR TAIL OFF	JOHN LEYTON
I'LL DO FOR YOU ANYTHING YOU WANT ME TO	BARRY WHITE
I'LL GET BY	CONNIE FRANCIS
I'LL GET BY	SHIRLEY BASSEY
I'LL GIVE YOU THE EARTH	KEITH MITCHELL
I'LL GO ON HOPING	DES O'CONNOR
I'LL KEEP YOU SATISFIED	BILLY J. KRAMER AND THE DAKOTAS
I'LL LOVE YOU FOREVER TODAY	CLIFF RICHARD
I'LL NEVER FALL IN LOVE AGAIN	DIONNE WARWICK
I'LL NEVER FALL IN LOVE AGAIN	BOBBY GENTRY
I'LL NEVER FALL IN LOVE AGAIN	TOM JONES
I'LL NEVER FIND ANOTHER YOU	SEEKERS
I'LL NEVER GET OVER YOU	JOHNNY KIDD AND THE PIRATES
I'LL NEVER GET OVER YOU	EVERLY BROTHERS
I'LL NEVER QUITE GET OVER YOU	BILLY FURY
I'LL NEVER STOP LOVING YOU	DORIS DAY
I'LL PICK A ROSE FOR MY ROSE	MARV JOHNSON
I'LL REMEMBER TONIGHT	PAT BOONE
I'LL SAY FOREVER MY LOVE	JIMMY RUFFIN
I'LL SEE YOU IN MY DREAMS	PAT BOONE
I'LL STOP AT NOTHING	SANDIE SHAW
I'LL STAY BY YOU	KENNY LYNCH
I'LL STEP DOWN	GARY MILLS
I'LL TAKE YOU HOME	CLIFF BENNET AND THE REBEL ROUSERS
I'LL TAKE YOU HOME	DRIFTERS
I'LL TAKE YOU HOME AGAIN KATHLEEN	SLIM WHITMAN

I'LL TAKE YOU THERE	STAPLE SINGERS
I'LL TRY ANYTHING	DUSTY SPRINGFIELD
I'LL WALK WITH GOD	MARIO LANZA
I'M A BELIEVER	MONKEES
I'M A BELIEVER	ROBERT WYATT
I'M A BETTER MAN	ENGELBERT HUMPERDINCK
I'M A BOY	WHO
I'M A CLOWN	DAVID CASSIDY
I'M A FOOL	SLIM WHITMAN
I'M A FOOL TO CARE	JOE BARRY
I'M A MAN	SPENCER DAVIS GROUP
I'M A MAN	CHICAGO
I'M A MIDNIGHT MOVER	WILSON PICKETT
I'M A MOODY GUY	SHANE FENTON AND THE FENTONES
I'M A TIGER	LULU
I'M ALIVE	HOLLIES
I'M COMING HOME	TOM JONES
I'M COMING HOME, CINDY	TRINI LOPEZ
I'M CONFESSIN'	FRANK IFIELD
I'M COUNTING ON YOU	PETULA CLARK
I'M CRYING	ANIMALS
I'M DOIN' FINE NOW	NEW YORK CITY
I'M FOREVER BLOWING BUBBLES	WEST HAM UNITED
I'M FREE	WHO
I'M FREE	ROGER DALTREY
I'M GOING HOME	GENE VINCENT
I'M GONNA BE STRONG	GENE PITNEY
I'M GONNA BE A COUNTRY GIRL AGAIN	BUFFY SAINTE-MARIE
I'M GONNA BE WARM THIS WINTER	CONNIE FRANCIS
I'M GONNA CHANGE EVERYTHING	JIM REEVES
I'M GONNA GET MARRIED	LLOYD PRICE
I'M GONNA GET ME A GUN	CAT STEVENS
I'M GONNA GET THERE SOMEHOW	VAL DOONICAN
I'M GONNA KNOCK ON YOUR DOOR	EDDIE HODGES
I'M GONNA KNOCK ON YOUR DOOR	JIMMY OSMOND
I'M GONNA LOVE YOU JUST A LITTLE BIT MORE BABY	BARRY WHITE
I'M GONNA MAKE YOU LOVE ME	DIANA ROSS AND THE SUPREMES
I'M GONNA MAKE YOU MINE	LOU CHRISTIE
I'M GONNA RUN AWAY FROM YOU	TAMMI LYNN
I'M GONNA SIT RIGHT DOWN	BILLY WILLIAMS
I'M IN A DIFFERENT WORLD	FOUR TOPS
I'M IN FAVOUR OF FRIENDSHIP	SMITH BROTHERS
I'M IN LOVE	FOURMOST
I'M IN LOVE AGAIN	FATS DOMINO
I'M INTO SOMETHING GOOD	HERMAN'S HERMITS
I'M JUST A BABY	LOUISE CORDET
I'M JUST A SINGER	MOODY BLUES
I'M LEAVING	ELVIS PRESLEY
I'M LEAVING IT UP TO YOU	DALE AND GRACE
I'M LEAVING IT UP TO YOU	DONNY AND MARIE OSMOND
I'M LEFT, YOU'RE RIGHT, SHE'S GONE	ELVIS PRESLEY
I'M LIVING IN SHAME	DIANA ROSS AND THE SUPREMES
I'M LOOKING OUT THE WINDOW	CLIFF RICHARD
I'M LOST WITHOUT YOU	BILLY FURY
I'M MANDY, FLY ME	10 C.C.
I'M NOT A JUVENILE DELINQUENT	FRANKIE LYMON AND THE TEENAGERS
I'M NOT IN LOVE	10 C.C.
I'M ON FIRE	5,000 VOLTS
I'M ON MY WAY	DEAN PARRISH
I'M ON MY WAY TO A BETTER PLACE	CHAIRMEN OF THE BOARD
I'M READY FOR LOVE	MARTHA REEVES AND THE VANDELLAS
I'M SHY MARY ELLEN, I'M SHY	BOB WALLIS
I'M SO CRAZY	K.C. AND THE SUNSHINE BAND

I'M SORRY	PLATTERS
I'M SORRY	BRENDA LEE
I'M SORRY I MADE YOU CRY	CONNIE FRANCIS
I'M STARTING TO GO STEADY (WITH THE BLUES)	JOHNNY PRESTON
I'M STILL GONNA NEED YOU	OSMONDS
I'M STILL IN LOVE WITH YOU	AL GREEN
I'M STILL WAITING	DIANA ROSS
I'M STONE IN LOVE WITH YOU	STYLISTICS
I'M STONE IN LOVE WITH YOU	JOHNNY MATHIS
I'M TELLING YOU NOW	FREDDIE AND THE DREAMERS
I'M THE LEADER OF THE GANG	GARY GLITTER
I'M THE LONELY ONE	CLIFF RICHARD
I'M THE ONE	GERRY AND THE PACEMAKERS
I'M THE ONE YOU NEED	SMOKEY ROBINSON AND THE MIRACLES
I'M THE URBAN SPACEMAN	BONZO DOG DOO DAH BAND
I'M WALKIN'	FATS DOMINO
I'M WALKING BACKWARDS FOR CHRISTMAS	GOONS
I'M WONDERING	STEVIE WONDER
IMAGE	HANK LEVINE
IMAGE OF A GIRL	SAFARIS
IMAGE OF A GIRL	MARK WYNTER
IMAGE OF A GIRL	NELSON KEENE
IMAGINE	JOHN LENNON
IMAGINE ME, IMAGINE YOU	FOX
IMPORTANCE OF YOUR LOVE	VINCE HILL
IN A BROKEN DREAM	PYTHON LEE JACKSON
IN A LITTLE SPANISH TOWN	BING CROSBY
IN AND OUT OF LOVE	DIANA ROSS AND THE SUPREMES
IN-CROWD	DOBIE GRAY
IN-CROWD	BRYAN FERRY
IN DREAMS	ROY ORBISON
IN DULCE JUBILO	MIKE OLDFIELD
IN FOR A PENNY	SLADE
IN MY CHAIR	STATUS QUO
IN MY OWN TIME	FAMILY
IN OLD LISBON	FRANK CHACKSFIELD
IN SUMMER	BILLY FURY
IN THE ARMS OF LOVE	ANDY WILLIAMS
IN THE BAD BAD OLD DAYS	FOUNDATIONS
IN THE BEGINNING	FRANKIE LAINE
IN THE CHAPEL IN THE MOONLIGHT	BACHELORS
IN THE COUNTRY	CLIFF RICHARD
IN THE GHETTO	ELVIS PRESLEY
IN THE HALL OF THE MOUNTAIN KING	NERO AND THE GLADIATORS
IN THE MEANTIME	GEORGIE FAME
IN THE MIDDLE OF AN ISLAND	TONY BENNET
IN THE MIDDLE OF AN ISLAND	KING BROTHERS
IN THE MIDDLE OF NOWHERE	DUSTY SPRINGFIELD
IN THE MIDDLE OF THE HOUSE	ALMA COGAN
IN THE MIDDLE OF THE HOUSE	JIMMY PARKINSON
IN THE MIDNIGHT HOUR	WILSON PICKETT
IN THE MOOD	ERNIE FIELDS
IN THE MOOD	SOUND 9418
IN THE SUMMERTIME	MUNGO JERRY
IN THE YEAR 2525	ZAGER AND EVANS
IN THOUGHTS OF YOU	BILLY FURY
INBETWEENIES	GOODIES
INDESCRIBABLY BLUE	ELVIS PRESLEY
INDIAN LOVE CALL	SLIM WHITMAN
INDIAN LOVE CALL	KARL DENVER
INDIAN LOVE CALL	RAY STEVENS
INDIAN RESERVATION	DON FARDON
INDIANA WANTS ME	R. DEAN TAYLOR
INSIDE AMERICA	JUGGY JONES

INSIDE LOOKING OUT	ANIMALS
INSIDE LOOKING OUT	GRAND FUNK RaILROAD
INSTANT KARMA	JOHN LENNON AND THE PLASTIC ONO BAND
IRE FEELINGS	RUPIE EDWARDS
IRON HORSE	CHRISTIE
IS A BLUEBIRD BLUE	CONWAY TWITTY
IS IT BECAUSE	HONEYCOMBS
IS IT REALLY OVER	JIM REEVES
IS IT TRUE	BRENDA LEE
IS THIS THE WAY TO AMARILLO	TONY CHRISTIE
IS THIS WHAT I GET FOR LOVING YOU BABY	MARIANNE FAITHFUL
ISLAND GIRL	ELTON JOHN
ISLAND IN THE SUN	HARRY BELAFONTE
ISLAND IN THE SUN	RIGHTEOUS BROTHERS
ISLAND OF DREAMS	SPRINGFIELDS
ISN'T LIFE STRANGE	MOODY BLUES
ISRAELITES	DESMOND DEKKER AND THE ACES
IT AIN'T ME BABE	JOHNNY CASH
IT DOESN'T MATTER ANY MORE	BUDDY HOLLY
IT DON'T COME EASY	RINGO STARR
IT HAPPENED TODAY	CURVED AIR
IT HURTS SO MUCH	JIM REEVES
IT HURTS TO BE IN LOVE	GENE PITNEY
IT KEEPS RAINING	FATS DOMINO
IT KEEPS RIGHT ON A HURTIN'	JOHNNY TILLOTSON
IT MAY BE WINTER OUTSIDE	LOVE UNLIMITED
IT MEK	DESMOND DEKKER AND THE ACES
IT MIGHT AS WELL RAIN UNTIL SEPTEMBER	CAROLE KING
IT MUST BE HIM	VIKKI CARR
IT MUST BE LOVE	LABI SIFFRE
IT ONLY TOOK A MINUTE	JOE BROWN
IT OUGHT TO SELL A MILLION	LYN PAUL
IT SHOULD HAVE BEEN ME	YVONNE FAIR
IT STARTED ALL OVER AGAIN	BRENDA LEE
IT TAKES TWO	MARVIN GAYE AND KIM WESTON
IT WAS EASIER TO HURT HER	WAYNE FONTANA
ITALIAN THEME	CYRIL STAPLETON
ITCHYCOO PARK	SMALL FACES
IT'LL BE ME	CLIFF RICHARD
IT'S A MAN'S MAN'S MAN'S WORLD	JAMES BROWN
IT'S A RAGGY WALTZ	DAVE BRUBECK
IT'S A SHAME	MOTOWN SPINNERS
IT'S A SIN TO TELL A LIE	GERRY MONROE
IT'S ALL IN THE GAME	TOMMY EDWARDS
IT'S ALL IN THE GAME	CLIFF RICHARD
IT'S ALL IN THE GAME	FOUR TOPS
IT'S ALL OVER	CLIFF RICHARD
IT'S ALL OVER NOW	ROLLING STONES
IT'S ALL OVER NOW	SHANE FENTON AND THE FENTONES
IT'S ALL OVER NOW, BABY BLUE	JOAN BAEZ
IT'S ALL UP TO YOU	JIM CAPALDI
IT'S ALMOST TOMORROW	DREAMWEAVERS
IT'S ALMOST TOMORROW	MARK WYNTER
IT'S AN OPEN SECRET	JOYSTRINGS
IT'S BEEN NICE	EVERLY BROTHERS
IT'S BEEN SO LONG	GEORGE McRAE
IT'S BETTER TO HAVE	DON COVAY
IT'S FOR YOU	CILLA BLACK
IT'S GETTING BETTER	MAMA CASS
IT'S GONNA BE A COLD COLD CHRISTMAS	DANA
IT'S GONNA BE ALRIGHT	GERRY AND THE PACEMAKERS
IT'S GOOD NEWS WEEK	HEDGEHOPPERS ANONYMOUS

IT'S GROWING	TEMPTATIONS
IT'S IMPOSSIBLE	PERRY COMO
IT'S IN HIS KISS	BETTY EVERETT
IT'S IN HIS KISS	LINDA LEWIS
IT'S JUST A LITTLE BIT TOO LATE	WAYNE FONTANA
IT'S LATE	RICKY NELSON
IT'S LIKE A SAD OLD MOVIE	PICKETTYWITCH
IT'S LOVE	KEN DODD
IT'S LOVE THAT REALLY COUNTS	MERSEYBEATS
IT'S MY LIFE	ANIMALS
IT'S MY PARTY	LESLEY GORE
IT'S MY TIME	EVERLY BROTHERS
IT'S NICE TO BE TRAVELLIN'	FRANK SINATRA
IT'S NOT UNUSUAL	TOM JONES
IT'S NOW OR NEVER	ELVIS PRESLEY
IT'S ONE OF THOSE NIGHTS	PARTRIDGE FAMILY
IT'S ONLY LOVE	TONY BLACKBURN
IT'S ONLY MAKE BELIEVE	CONWAY TWITTY
IT'S ONLY MAKE BELIEVE	BILLY FURY
IT'S ONLY ROCK'N'ROLL	ROLLING STONES
IT'S OVER	ROY ORBISON
IT'S SO EASY	ANDY WILLIAMS
IT'S SO EASY	CRICKETS
IT'S THE SAME OLD SONG	FOUR TOPS
IT'S THE SAME OLD SONG	WEATHERMEN
IT'S TIME FOR LOVE	CHI-LITES
IT'S TIME TO CRY	PAUL ANKA
IT'S TOO LATE	CAROLE KING
IT'S TOO LATE NOW	SWINGING BLUE JEANS
IT'S TOO LATE NOW	LONG JOHN BALDRY
IT'S TOO SOON TO KNOW	PAT BOONE
IT'S UP TO YOU	RICKY NELSON
IT'S UP TO YOU PETULA	EDISON LIGHTHOUSE
IT'S WONDERFUL TO BE LOVED BY YOU	JIMMY RUFFIN
IT'S YOU	FREDDIE STAR
IT'S YOU THAT I LOVE	MARION RYAN
IT'S YOUR DAY TODAY	P.J. PROBY
IT'S YOUR THING	ISLEY BROTHERS
ITSY BITSY TEENY WEENY YELLOW POLKA DOT BIKINI	BRIAN HYLAND
I'VE BEEN A BAD BAD BOY	PAUL JONES
I'VE BEEN DRINKING	JEFF BECK GROUP WITH ROD STEWART
I'VE BEEN HURT	GUY DARRELL
I'VE BEEN LONELY FOR SO LONG	FREDERICK KNIGHT
I'VE BEEN WRONG BEFORE	CILLA BLACK
I'VE GOT A THING ABOUT YOU BABY	ELVIS PRESLEY
I'VE GOT YOU ON MY MIND	DORIAN GREY
I'VE GOT YOU ON MY MIND	WHITE PLAINS
I'VE GOT YOU UNDER MY SKIN	FOUR SEASONS
I'VE GOTTA GET A MESSAGE TO YOU	BEE GEES
I'VE LOST YOU	ELVIS PRESLEY
I'VE PASSED THIS WAY BEFORE	JIMMY RUFFIN
I'VE TOLD EVERY LITTLE STAR	LINDA SCOTT
I'VE WAITED SO LONG	ANTHONY NEWLEY
IVORY TOWER	THREE KAYES
IVY WILL CLING	ARNOLD STANG
JA-DA	JOHNNY AND THE HURRICANES
JACK IN THE BOX	CLODAGH ROGERS
JACK O'DIAMONDS	LONNIE DONEGAN
JACKIE	SCOTT WALKER
JACQUELINE	BOBBY HELMS
JAILHOUSE ROCK	ELVIS PRESLEY
JAILHOUSE ROCK EP	ELVIS PRESLEY
JAMBALAYA	FATS DOMINO

JAMBALAYA	CARPENTERS
JAMES BOND (DR. NO)	JOHN BARRY
JANUARY	PILOT
JARROW SONG	ALAN PRICE
JE T'AIME-MOI NON PLUS (LOVE AT FIRST SIGHT)	JANE BIRKIN AND SERGE GAINSBOURG
JE T'AIME-MOI NON PLUS (LOVE AT FIRST SIGHT)	JUDGE DREAD
JE T'AIME-MOI NON PLUS (LOVE AT FIRST SIGHT)	SOUNDS NICE
JEALOUS HEART	CADETS
JEALOUS HEART	CONNIE FRANCIS
JEALOUS MIND	ALVIN STARDUST
JEALOUSY	BILLY FURY
JEAN GENIE	DAVID BOWIE
JEANNIE	DANNY WILLIAMS
JEANNIE, JEANNIE, JEANNIE	EDDIE COCHRAN
JEEPSTER	T. REX
JENNIFER ECCLES	HOLLIES
JENNIFER JUNIPER	DONOVAN
JENNY JENNY	LITTLE RICHARD
JENNY TAKES A RIDE	MITCH RYDER AND THE DETROIT WHEELS
JERUSALEM	HERB ALPERT AND THE TIJUANA BRASS
JESAMINE	CASUALS
JESUS	CLIFF RICHARD
JESUS CHRIST SUPERSTAR	MURRAY HEAD AND YVONNE ELLIMAN
JET	McCARTNEY'S WINGS
JET BLACK MACHINE	VINCE TAYLOR
JEZEBEL	MARTY WILDE
JIG-A-JIG	EAST OF EDEN
JIMMY MACK	MARTHA REEVES AND THE VANDELLAS
JIMMY UNKNOWN	LITA ROZA
JIMMY'S GIRL	JOHNNY TILLOTSON
JINGLE BELL ROCK	MAX BYGRAVES
JINGLE BELL ROCK	CHUBBY CHECKER WITH BOBBY RYDELL
JIVE TALKIN'	BEE GEES
JOANNA	SCOTT WALKER
JOHN AND JULIE	EDDIE CALVERT
JOHN, I'M ONLY DANCING	DAVID BOWIE
JOHNNY ANGEL	SHELLEY FABARES
JOHNNY ANGEL	PATTI LYNN
JOHNNY B. GOODE	CHUCK BERRY
JOHNNY B. GOODE	JIMI HENDRIX
JOHNNY DAY	ROLF HARRIS
JOHNNY GET ANGRY	CAROLE DEENE
JOHNNY REGGAE	PIGLETS
JOHNNY REMEMBER ME	JOHN LEYTON
JOHNNY ROCCO	MARTY WILDE
'JOHNNY STACCATO' THEME	ELMER BERNSTEIN
JOHNNY WILL	PAT BOONE
JOIN TOGETHER	WHO
JOURNEY	DUNCAN BROWNE
JOY OF LIVING	CLIFF RICHARD AND HANK MARVIN
JOY TO THE WORLD	THREE DOG NIGHT
JOYBRINGER	MANFRED MANN
JUDY IN DISGUISE (WITH GLASSES)	JOHN FRED AND HIS PLAYBOY BAND
JUDY TEEN	COCKNEY REBEL
JUKE BOX JIVE	RUBETTES
JULIE-ANN	KENNY
JULIE DO YA LOVE ME	BOBBY SHERMAN
JULIE DO YA LOVE ME	WHITE PLAINS
JULIET	FOUR PENNIES
JUMBO	BEE GEES
JUMPING JACK FLASH	ROLLING STONES
JUNGLE FEVER	CHAKACHAS

JUNIOR'S FARM	WINGS
JUST A LITTLE BIT	UNDERTAKERS
JUST A LITTLE BIT BETTER	HERMAN'S HERMITS
JUST A LITTLE BIT TOO LATE	WAYNE FONTANA
JUST A LITTLE MISUNDERSTANDING	CONTOURS
JUST A LITTLE TOO MUCH	RICKY NELSON
JUST A SMILE	PILOT
JUST AS MUCH AS EVER	NAT 'KING' COLE
JUST DON'T WANT TO BE LONELY	MAIN INGREDIENT
JUST FOR KICKS	MIKE SARNE
JUST FOR YOU	FREDDIE AND THE DREAMERS
JUST FOR YOU	GLITTER BAND
JUST KEEP IT UP	DEE CLARK
JUST LIKE A WOMAN	MANFRED MANN
JUST LIKE EDDIE	HEINZ
JUST LIKE ME	HOLLIES
JUST LISTEN TO MY HEART	SPOTNIKS
JUST LOVING YOU	ANITA HARRIS
JUST MY IMAGINATION	TEMPTATIONS
JUST MY SOUL RESPONDING	SMOKEY ROBINSON
JUST ONE LOOK	DORIS TROY
JUST ONE LOOK	HOLLIES
JUST ONE LOOK	FAITH, HOPE AND CHARITY
JUST ONE SMILE	GENE PITNEY
JUST OUT OF REACH	KEN DODD
JUST SEVEN NUMBERS	FOUR TOPS
JUST WALK IN MY SHOES	GLADYS KNIGHT AND THE PIPS
JUST WALKING IN THE RAIN	JOHNNY RAY
KANSAS CITY	TRINI LOPEZ
KANSAS CITY STAR	ROGER MILLER
KARA KARA	NEW WORLD
KEEP A-KNOCKING	LITTLE RICHARD
KEEP AWAY FROM OTHER GIRLS	HELEN SHAPIRO
KEEP IT OUT OF SIGHT	PAUL AND BARRY RYAN
KEEP ON	BRUCE CHANNEL
KEEP ON DANCING	BAY CITY ROLLERS
KEEP ON RUNNING	SPENCER DAVIS GROUP
KEEP ON TRUCKIN'	EDDIE KENDRICKS
KEEP SEARCHIN'	DEL SHANNON
KEEP THE CUSTOMER SATISFIED	MARSHA HUNT
KEEP YOUR HANDS OFF MY BABY	LITTLE EVA
KEEPER OF THE CASTLE	FOUR TOPS
KELLY	WAYNE GIBSON
KENTUCKY RAIN	ELVIS PRESLEY
KEWPIE DOLL	PERRY COMO
KEWPIE DOLL	FRANKIE VAUGHAN
KICKING UP THE LEAVES	MARK WYNTER
KIDDIO	BROOK BENTON
KIDS ARE ALRIGHT	WHO
KILLER QUEEN	QUEEN
KILLING ME SOFTLY WITH HIS SONG	ROBERTA FLACK
KING CREOLE	ELVIS PRESLEY
KING KONG	TERRY LIGHTFOOT
KING MIDAS IN REVERSE	HOLLIES
KING OF KINGS	EZZ RECO AND THE LAUNCHERS WITH BOYSIE GRANT
KING OF CLOWNS	NEIL SEDAKA
KING OF THE COPS	BILLY HOWARD
KING OF THE ROAD	ROGER MILLER
KING OF THE RUMBLING SPIRES	T. REX
KISS ME GOODBYE	PETULA CLARK
KISS ME HONEY HONEY KISS ME	SHIRLEY BASSEY
KISS ME QUICK	ELVIS PRESLEY
KISSES SWEETER THAN MINE	JIMMIE RODGERS

KISSES SWEETER THAN MINE	FRANKIE VAUGHAN
KISSIN' COUSINS	ELVIS PRESLEY
KISSING IN THE BACK ROW OF THE MOVIES	DRIFTERS
KITES	SIMON DUPREE
KITTY	CAT STEVENS
KNEE DEEP IN THE BLUES	GUY MITCHELL
KNEE DEEP IN THE BLUES	TOMMY STEELE
KNOCKIN' ON HEAVEN'S DOOR	BOB DYLAN
KNOCKIN' ON HEAVEN'S DOOR	ERIC CLAPTON
KNOCK KNOCK WHO'S THERE	MARY HOPKIN
KNOCK ON WOOD	EDDIE FLOYD
KNOCK ON WOOD	DAVID BOWIE
KNOCK ON WOOD	OTIS REDDING WITH CARLA THOMAS
KNOCK THREE TIMES	DAWN
KOMMOTION	DUANE EDDY
KON-TIKI	SHADOWS
KOOKIE, KOOKIE, LEND ME YOUR COMB	ED BYRNES AND CONNIE STEVENS
KOOKIE LITTLE PARADISE	FRANKIE VAUGHAN
KUM BAYA	SANDPIPERS
KUNG FU FIGHTING	CARL DOUGLAS
LA BAMBA	CRICKETS
LA BOOGA ROOGA	SURPRISE SISTERS
LA DE DAH	JACKIE DENNIS
LA DERNIERE VALSE	MIRIELLE MATTHIEU
LA LA LA	MASSIEL
LA LA MEANS I LOVE YOU	DELFONICS
LA YENKA	JOHNNY AND CHARLEY
LADY BARBARA	PETER NOONE AND HERMAN'S HERMITS
LADY D'ARBANVILLE	CAT STEVENS
LADY ELEANOR	LINDISFARNE
LADY GODIVA	PETER AND GORDON
LADY IS A TRAMP	BUDDY GRECO
LADY JANE	DAVID GARRICK
LADY LOVE BUG	CLODAGH RODGERS
LADY LUCKY	LLOYD PRICE
LADY MADONNA	BEATLES
LADY MARMALADE	LABELLE
LADY ROSE	MUNGO JERRY
LADY WILLPOWER	GARY PUCKETT AND THE UNION GAP
LADYBIRD	NANCY SINATRA AND LEE HAZLEWOOD
LAMPLIGHT	DAVID ESSEX
LANA	ROY ORBISON
LAND OF 1000 DANCES	WILSON PICKETT
LANGUAGE OF LOVE	JOHN D. LOUDERMILK
LAS VEGAS	TONY CHRISTIE
LAST FAREWELL	ROGER WHITTAKER
LAST NIGHT	MERSEYBEATS
LAST NIGHT IN SOHO	DAVE DEE, DOZY, BEAKY, MICK AND TICH
LAST NIGHT WAS MADE FOR LOVE	BILLY FURY
LAST TIME	ROLLING STONES
LAST TIME	WHO
LAST TIME I SAW HIM	DIANA ROSS
LAST TRAIN TO SAN FERNANDO	JOHNNY DUNCAN
LAST WALTZ	ENGELBERT HUMPERDINCK
LAUGH AT ME	SONNY BONO
LAUGHING GNOME	DAVID BOWIE
LAUGHTER IN THE RAIN	NEIL SEDAKA
LAUREL AND HARDY	EQUALS
LAW OF THE LAND	TEMPTATIONS
LAWDY MISS CLAWDY	ELVIS PRESLEY
LAY DOWN	STRAWBS
LAY DOWN YOUR ARMS	ANNE SHELTON
LAY LADY LAY	BOB DYLAN

LAYLA	DEREK AND THE DOMINOES
LAZY RIVER	BOBBY DARIN
LAZY SUNDAY	SMALL FACES
LAZYBONES	JONATHAN KING
LEADER OF THE PACK	SHANGRI-LAS
LEAN ON ME	BILL WITHERS
LEAP UP AND DOWN	ST. CECILIA
LEARNIN' THE BLUES	FRANK SINATRA
LEARNING THE GAME	BUDDY HOLLY
LEAVE A LITTLE LOVE	LULU
LEAVE IT	SCAFFOLD (MIKE McGEAR ONLY)
LEAVIN' DURHAM TOWN	ROGER WHITTAKER
LEAVING HERE	BIRDS
LEAVING ON A JET PLANE	PETER, PAUL AND MARY
LEEDS UNITED	LEEDS UNITED F.C.
LEFT BANK	WINIFRED ATWELL
LEGAL MATTER	WHO
LEGEND OF XANADU	DAVE DEE, DOZY, BEAKY, MICK AND TICH
'LEGION'S LAST PATROL'	KEN THORNE ORCHESTRA
LEGO SKANGA	RUPIE EDWARDS
LES BICYCLETTES DE BELSIZE	ENGELBERT HUMPERDINCK
LESSON NO. 1	RUSS CONWAY
LESSONS IN LOVE	ALLISONS
LET IT ALL HANG OUT	JONATHAN KING
LET IT BE	BEATLES
LET IT ROCK	CHUCK BERRY
LET IT ROCK	ROLLING STONES
LET ME BE THE NUMBER ONE	DOOLEY SILVERSPOON
LET ME BE THE ONE	SHADOWS
LET ME CRY ON YOUR SHOULDER	KEN DODD
LET ME GO LOVER	JOAN WEBER
LET ME GO LOVER	TERESA BREWER
LET ME GO LOVER	DEAN MARTIN
LET ME GO LOVER	RUBY MURRAY
LET ME GO LOVER	KATHY KIRBY
LET ME COME ON HOME	OTIS REDDING
LET ME IN	OSMONDS
LET ME TRY AGAIN	TAMMY JONES
LET MY NAME BE SORROW	MARY HOPKIN
LET THE HEARTACHES BEGIN	LONG JOHN BALDRY
LET THE LITTLE GIRL DANCE	BILLY BLAND
LET THE MUSIC PLAY	BARRY WHITE
LET THE SUNSHINE IN	FIFTH DIMENSION
LET THE SUNSHINE IN	PEDDLERS
LET THE WATER RUN DOWN	P.J. PROBY
LET THERE BE DRUMS	SANDY NELSON
LET THERE BE LOVE	NAT 'KING' COLE WITH GEORGE SHEARING
LET THERE BE PEACE ON EARTH	MICHAEL WARD
LET TRUE LOVE BEGIN	NAT 'KING' COLE
LET YOUR YEAH BE YEAH	PIONEERS
LET'S	SARAH VAUGHAN
LET'S BE FRIENDS	JOHNNY NASH
LET'S CALL IT QUITS	SLADE
LET'S DANCE	CHRIS MONTEZ
LET'S DO THE HUSTLE	M AND O BAND
LET'S DO THE LATIN HUSTLE	EDDIE DRENNON AND BBS UNLIMITED
LET'S GET IT ON	MARVIN GAYE
LET'S GET TOGETHER	HAYLEY MILLS
LET'S GET TOGETHER	BIG BEN BANJO BAND
LET'S GET TOGETHER AGAIN	GLITTER BAND
LET'S GO	ROUTERS
LET'S GO STEADY AGAIN	NEIL SEDAKA
LET'S GO TO SAN FRANCISCO	FLOWERPOT MEN
LET'S HANG ON	FOUR SEASONS
LET'S HANG ON	JOHNNY JOHNSON AND THE BANDWAGON

LET'S HAVE A BALL	WINIFRED ATWELL
LET'S HAVE A DING DONG	WINIFRED ATWELL
LET'S HAVE A PARTY	WINIFRED ATWELL
LET'S HAVE A PARTY	ELVIS PRESLEY
LET'S HAVE A PARTY	WANDA JACKSON
LET'S HAVE ANOTHER PARTY	WINIFRED ATWELL
LET'S JUMP THE BROOMSTICK	BRENDA LEE
LET'S PRETEND	LULU
LET'S PUT IT ALL TOGETHER	STYLISTICS
LET'S SEE ACTION	WHO
LET'S SLIP AWAY	CLEO LAINE
LET'S SPEND THE NIGHT TOGETHER	ROLLING STONES
LET'S STAY TOGETHER	AL GREEN
LET'S TALK ABOUT LOVE	HELEN SHAPIRO
LET'S THINK ABOUT LIVING	BOB LUMAN
LET'S TURKEY TROT	LITTLE EVA
LET'S TWIST AGAIN	CHUBBY CHEKKER
LET'S TWIST AGAIN	JOHN ASHER
LET'S WOMBLE TO THE PARTY TONIGHT	WOMBLES
LET'S WORK TOGETHER	CANNED HEAT
LETTER	LONG AND THE SHORT
LETTER	MINDBENDERS
LETTER	BOX TOPS
LETTER	JOE COCKER
LETTER FULL OF TEARS	BILLY FURY
LETTER TO LUCILLE	TOM JONES
LETTING GO	WINGS
LIES IN YOUR EYES	SWEET
LIFE IS A LONG SONG	JETHRO TULL
LIFE IS A MINESTRONE	10 C.C.
LIFE IS A ROCK (BUT THE RADIO ROLLED ME)	REUNION
LIFE ON MARS	DAVID BOWIE
LIGHT FLIGHT	PENTANGLE
LIGHT MY FIRE	DOORS
LIGHT MY FIRE	JOSE FELICIANO
LIGHT OF LOVE	T. REX
LIGHT UP THE FIRE	PARCHMENT
LIGHTNIN' STRIKES	LOU CHRISTIE
LIGHTNING TREE	SETTLERS
LIGHTS OF CINCINATTI	SCOTT WALKER
LIKE A BABY	LEN BARRY
LIKE A BUTTERFLY	MAC AND KATIE KISSOON
LIKE A CHILD	JULIE ROGERS
LIKE A ROLLING STONE	BOB DYLAN
LIKE AN OLD TIME MOVIE	SCOTT MACKENZIE
LIKE DREAMERS DO	APPLEJACKS
LIKE I DO	MAUREEN EVANS
LIKE I'VE NEVER BEEN GONE	BILLY FURY
LIKE SISTER AND BROTHER	DRIFTERS
LIKE STRANGERS	EVERLY BROTHERS
LIKE WE USED TO BE	GEORGIE FAME
'LIKELY LADS' THEME (WHATEVER HAPPENED TO YOU)	HIGHLY LIKELY
LI'L RED RIDING HOOD	SAM THE SHAM AND THE PHARAOHS
LILY THE PINK	SCAFFOLD
LIMBO ROCK	CHUBBY CHECKER
LINDA LU	JOHNNY KIDD AND THE PIRATES
LION SLEEPS TONIGHT	SEE 'WIMOWEH'
LIPSTICK ON YOUR COLLAR	CONNIE FRANCIS
LIQUIDATOR	HARRY J AND THE ALL STARS
LISTEN LITTLE GIRL	KEITH KELLY
LISTEN TO ME	BUDDY HOLLY
LISTEN TO ME	HOLLIES
LISTEN TO THE MUSIC	DOOBIE BROTHERS

LISTEN TO THE OCEAN	NINA AND FREDERICK
LISTEN TO WHAT THE MAN SAID	WINGS
LITTLE ARROWS	LEAPY LEE
LITTLE BANK OF GOLD	JAMES GILREATH
LITTLE BERNADETTE	HARRY BELAFONTE
LITTLE BIT ME, A LITTLE BIT YOU	MONKEES
LITTLE BIT OF LOVE	FREE
LITTLE BITTY TEAR	BURL IVES
LITTLE BITTY TEAR	MIKI AND GRIFF
LITTLE BLACK BOOK	JIMMY DEAN
LITTLE BLUE BIRD	VINCE HILL
LITTLE BOY LOST	MICHAEL HOLLIDAY
LITTLE BOY SAD	JOHNNY BURNETTE
LITTLE BROWN JUG	GLENN MILLER ORCHESTRA
LITTLE BY LITTLE	DUSTY SPRINGFIELDS
LITTLE CHILDREN	BILLY J. KRAMER AND THE DAKOTAS
LITTLE CHRISTINE	DICK JORDAN
LITTLE DARLIN'	DIAMONDS
LITTLE DARLIN'	RUBETTES
LITTLE DARLING I NEED YOU	MARVIN GAYE
LITTLE DEVIL	NEIL SEDAKA
LITTLE DONKEY	BEVERLEY SISTERS
LITTLE DONKEY	NINA AND FREDERICK
LITTLE DROPS OF SILVER	GERRY MONROE
LITTLE DRUMMER BOY	BEVERLEY SISTERS
LITTLE DRUMMER BOY	ROYAL SCOTS DRAGOON GUARDS BAND
LITTLE GIRL	MARTY WILDE
LITTLE GIRL	TROGGS
LITTLE GREEN APPLES	ROGER MILLER
LITTLE LOVE,A LITTLE KISS	KARL DENVER
LITTLE LOVE AND UNDERSTANDING	GILBERT BECAUD
LITTLE LOVIN'	NEIL SEDAKA
LITTLE LOVING	FOURMOST
LITTLE MAN	SONNY AND CHER
LITTLE MISS LONELY	HELEN SHAPIRO
LITTLE PIECE OF LEATHER	DONNIE ELBERT
LITTLE RED RIDING HOOD	(SEE "LI'L RED RIDING HOOD")
LITTLE RED ROOSTER	ROLLING STONES
LITTLE SISTER	ELVIS PRESLEY
LITTLE STAR	ELEGANTS
LITTLE THINGS	BOBBY GOLDSBORO
LITTLE THINGS	DAVE BERRY
LITTLE THINGS MEAN A LOT	ALMA COGAN
LITTLE THINGS MEAN A LOT	KITTY KALLEN
LITTLE TOWN FLIRT	DEL SHANNON
LITTLE WHITE BERRY	ROY CASTLE
LITTLE WHITE BULL	TOMMY STEELE
LITTLE WILLIE	SWEET
LITTLE YOU	FREDDIE AND THE DREAMERS
LIVE AND LET DIE	PAUL McCARTNEY'S WINGS
LIVELY	LONNIE DONEGAN
LIVING DOLL	CLIFF RICHARD
LIVING FOR THE CITY	STEVIE WONDER
LIVING FOR YOU	SONNY AND CHER
LIVING IN HARMONY	CLIFF RICHARD
LIVING IN THE PAST	JETHRO TULL
L-L-LUCY	MUD
LOCOMOTION	LITTLE EVA
LOCOMOTION	VERNON GIRLS FEATURING MAUREEN
LOLA	KINKS
LOLLIPOP	CHORDETTES
LOLLIPOP	MUDLARKS
L.O.L.O.	BEE GEES
LONDON BOYS	T. REX

LONELY	ACKER BILK
LONELY	EDDIE COCHRAN
LONELY BALLERINA	MANTOVANI
LONELY BOY	PAUL ANKA
LONELY BOY, LONELY GUITAR	DUANE EDDY
LONELY BULL	HERB ALPERT AND THE TIJUANA BRASS
LONELY CITY	JOHN LEYTON
LONELY DAYS	BEE GEES
LONELY DAYS, LONELY NIGHTS	DON DOWNING
'LONELY MAN' THEME	CLIFF ADAMS ORCHESTRA
LONELY ONE	DUANE EDDY
LONELY PUP	ADAM FAITH
LONELY RIDER	JOHN LEYTON
LONELY STREET	CLARENCE 'FROGMAN' HENRY
LONELY TEENAGER	DION
LONELY THIS CHRISTMAS	MUD
LONESOME	ADAM FAITH
LONESOME NO. 1	DON GIBSON
LONG AND WINDING ROAD	RAY MORGAN
LONG AS I CAN SEE THE LIGHT	CREEDENCE CLEARWATER REVIVAL
LONG COOL WOMAN IN A BLACK DRESS	HOLLIES
LONG-HAIRED LOVER FROM LIVERPOOL	LITTLE JIMMY OSMOND
LONG-LEGGED GIRL (WITH THE SHORT DRESS ON)	ELVIS PRESLEY
LONG-LEGGED WOMAN DRESSED IN BLACK	MUNGO JERRY
LONG LIVE LOVE	SANDIE SHAW
LONG LIVE LOVE	OLIVIA NEWTON-JOHN
LONG LOST LOVER	THREE DEGREES
LONG SHOT KICK THE BUCKET	PIONEERS
LONG TALL GLASSES	LEO SAYER
LONG TALL SALLY	LITTLE RICHARD
LONGTIME BOY	NINA AND FREDERICK
LONLINESS	DES O'CONNOR
LOO-BE-LOO	CHUCKS
LOOK AROUND	VINCE HILL
LOOK AT ME	MOMENTS
LOOK BEFORE YOU LEAP	DAVE CLARK FIVE
LOOK FOR A STAR	GARY MILLS
LOOK HOMEWARD ANGEL	JOHNNY RAY
LOOK OF LOVE	GLADYS KNIGHT AND THE PIPS
LOOK THROUGH ANY WINDOW	HOLLIES
LOOK WHAT YOU DONE FOR ME	AL GREEN
LOOK WHO IT IS	HELEN SHAPIRO
LOOK WOT YOU DUN	SLADE
LOOKIN' THROUGH THE WINDOWS	JACKSON FIVE
LOOKING HIGH HIGH HIGH	BRYAN JOHNSON
LOOKING THROUGH THE EYES OF LOVE	GENE PITNEY
LOOKING THROUGH THE EYES OF LOVE	PARTRIDGE FAMILY
LOOKS, LOOKS, LOOKS	SPARKS
LOOP DE LOOP	FRANKIE VAUGHAN
LOOP DI LOVE	JONATHAN KING
LORELEI	LONNIE DONEGAN
LOSING YOU	BRENDA LEE
LOSING YOU	DUSTY SPRINGFIELD
LOST JOHN	LONNIE DONEGAN
LOUIE LOUIE	KINGSMEN
L.O.V.E.	AL GREEN
LOVE AND MARRIAGE	FRANK SINATRA
LOVE AT FIRST SIGHT	SEE 'JE T'AIME-MOI NON PLUS'
LOVE CHILD	DIANA ROSS AND THE SUPREMES
LOVE GAMES	DRIFTERS
LOVE GROWS (WHERE MY ROSEMARY GOES)	EDISON LIGHTHOUSE

LOVE HER	WALKER BROTHERS
LOVE HURTS	JIM CAPALDI
LOVE I HAVE FOR YOU	LANCE FORTUNE
LOVE I LOST	HAROLD MELVIN AND THE BLUENOTES
LOVE IN THE SUN	GLITTER BAND
LOVE IN YOUR EYES	VICKY LEANDROS
LOVE IS A GOLDEN RING	FRANKIE LAINE
LOVE IS A MANY-SPLENDOURED THING	FOUR ACES
LOVE IS ALL	MALCOLM ROBERTS
LOVE IS ALL	ENGELBERT HUMPERDINCK
LOVE IS ALL AROUND	TROGGS
LOVE IS BLUE	PAUL MAURIAT
LOVE IS BLUE	DELLS
LOVE IS BLUE	JEFF BECK GROUP
LOVE IS HERE AND NOW YOU'RE GONE	SUPREMES
LOVE IS LIFE	HOT CHOCOLATE
LOVE IS LIKE A VIOLIN	KEN DODD
LOVE IS LOVE	BARRY RYAN
LOVE IS STRANGE	EVERLY BROTHERS
LOVE IS THE DRUG	ROXY MUSIC
LOVE IS THE TENDER TRAP	FRANK SINATRA
LOVE, KISSES AND HEARTACHES	MAUREEN EVANS
LOVE LETTERS	KETTY LESTER
LOVE LETTERS	ELVIS PRESLEY
LOVE LETTERS IN THE SAND	PAT BOONE
LOVE LETTERS IN THE SAND	VINCE HILL
LOVE LIKE A MAN	TEN YEARS AFTER
LOVE LIKE YOU AND ME	GARY GLITTER
LOVE LIKE YOURS	IKE AND TINA TURNER
LOVE, LOVE, LOVE	BOBBY HEBB
LOVE, LOVES TO LOVE, LOVE	LULU
LOVE MACHINE	MIRACLES
LOVE MACHINE	ELVIS PRESLEY
LOVE MAKES THE WORLD GO ROUND	PERRY COMO
LOVE MAN	OTIS REDDING
LOVE ME	DIANA ROSS
LOVE ME AS THOUGH THERE WERE NO TOMORROW	NAT 'KING' COLE
LOVE ME BABY	SUSAN CADOGAN
LOVE ME FOREVER	EYDIE GORME
LOVE ME DO	BEATLES
LOVE ME FOR A REASON	OSMONDS
LOVE ME FOREVER	MARION RYAN
LOVE ME LIKE I LOVE YOU	BAY CITY ROLLERS
LOVE ME LOVE MY DOG	PETER SHELLEY
LOVE ME OR LEAVE ME	SAMMY DAVIS JR.
LOVE ME OR LEAVE ME	DORIS DAY
LOVE ME TENDER	ELVIS PRESLEY
LOVE ME TENDER	RICHARD CHAMBERLAIN
LOVE ME TONIGHT	TOM JONES
LOVE ME WARM AND TENDER	PAUL ANKA
LOVE ME WITH ALL YOUR HEART	KARL DENVER
LOVE OF THE COMMON PEOPLE	NICKY THOMAS
LOVE OF THE LOVED	CILLA BLACK
LOVE ON A MOUNTAIN TOP	ROBERT KNIGHT
LOVE OR MONEY	BLACKWELLS
LOVE REALLY HURTS WITHOUT YOU	BILLY OCEAN
LOVE STORY (WHERE DO I BEGIN)	SHIRLEY BASSEY
LOVE STORY (WHERE DO I BEGIN)	ANDY WILLIAMS
LOVE STORY	JETHRO TULL
LOVE THE ONE YOU'RE WITH	STEPHEN STILLS
LOVE THEME FROM 'THE GODFATHER'	ANDY WILLIAMS
LOVE TRAIN	O'JAYS
LOVE WILL KEEP US TOGETHER	CAPTAIN AND TENILLE
LOVE YOU SAVE	JACKSON FIVE
LOVE'S BEEN GOOD TO ME	FRANK SINATRA

LOVE'S JUST A BROKEN HEART	CILLA BLACK
LOVE'S MADE A FOOL OF YOU	BUDDY HOLLY
LOVE'S THEME	LOVE UNLIMITED ORCHESTRA
LOVER PLEASE	VERNON GIRLS
LOVER'S CONCERTO	TOYS
LOVERS OF THE WORLD UNITE	DAVID AND JONATHAN
LOVES ME LIKE A ROCK	PAUL SIMON
LOVESICK BLUES	FRANK IFIELD
LOVIN' THINGS	MARMALADE
LOVIN' UP A STORM	JERRY LEE LEWIS
LOVING YOU	MINNIE RIPPERTON
LOVING YOU AIN'T EASY	PAGLIARO
LOVING YOU IS SWEETER THAN EVER	FOUR TOPS
LOW RIDER	WAR
LUCILLE	LITTLE RICHARD
LUCILLE	EVERLY BROTHERS
LUCKY DEVIL	CARL DOBKINS
LUCKY DEVIL	FRANK IFIELD
LUCKY FIVE	RUSS CONWAY
LUCKY LIPS	CLIFF RICHARD
LUCKY OLD SUN	VELVETS
LUCY IN THE SKY WITH DIAMONDS	ELTON JOHN
LULLABY OF THE LEAVES	VENTURES
LUMBERED	LONNIE DONEGAN
LYIN' EYES	EAGLES
MA,HE'S MAKING EYES AT ME	JOHNNY OTIS SHOW WITH MARIE ADAMS AND THE THREE TONS OF JOY
MA,HE'S MAKING EYES AT ME	LENA ZAVARONI
MA-MA-MA-BELLE	ELECTRIC LIGHT ORCHESTRA
MACARTHUR PARK	RICHARD HARRIS
MACARTHUR PARK	BILLY VAUGHAN
MACHINE GUN	COMMODORES
MACK THE KNIFE (SEE ALSO THREEPENNY OPERA)	LOUIS ARMSTRONG
MACK THE KNIFE (SEE ALSO THREEPENNY OPERA)	BOBBY DARIN
MACK THE KNIFE (SEE ALSO THREEPENNY OPERA)	ELLA FITZGERALD
MAD ABOUT YOU	BRUCE RUFFIN
MAD PASSIONATE LOVE	BERNARD BRESSLAW
MADE YOU	ADAM FAITH
MADISON	RAY ELLINGTON
MAGGIE MAY	VIPERS
MAGGIE MAY	ROD STEWART
MAGGIE'S FARM	BOB DYLAN
MAGIC	PILOT
MAGIC BUS	WHO
MAGIC MOMENTS	PERRY COMO
MAGIC ROUNDABOUT	JASPER CARROT
MAGICAL MYSTERY TOUR (E.P.)	BEATLES
MAGNIFICENT SEVEN	JOHN BARRY
MAGNIFICENT SEVEN	AL CAIDA
MAIGRET THEME	JOE LOSS
MAIN ATTRACTION	PAT BOONE
MAIS OUI	KING BROTHERS
MAJORCA	PETULA CLARK
MAKE A DAFT NOISE FOR CHRISTMAS	GOODIES
MAKE IT A PARTY	WINIFRED ATWELL
MAKE IT EASY ON YOURSELF	WALKER BROTHERS
MAKE IT WITH YOU	BREAD
MAKE LOVE TO ME	JOHN LEYTON
MAKE ME AN ISLAND	JOE DOLAN
MAKE ME SMILE	COCKNEY REBEL
MAKE THE WORLD GO AWAY	EDDY ARNOLD

MAKE THE WORLD GO AWAY	DONNY AND MARIE OSMOND
MAKIN' LOVE	FLOYD ROBINSON
MAKIN' WHOOPEE	RAY CHARLES
MAKING TIME	CREATION
MALT AND BARLEY BLUES	McGUINESS FLINT
MAMA	DAVID WHITFIELD
MAMA	CONNIE FRANCIS
MAMA	B.J. THOMAS
MAMA	DAVE BERRY
MAMA MIA	ABBA
MAMA NEVER TOLD ME	SISTER SLEDGE
MAMA TOLD ME NOT TO COME	THREE DOG NIGHT
MAMA WEER ALL CRAZEE NOW	SLADE
MAMA'S PEARL	JACKSON FIVE
MAMBO ITALIANO	ROSEMARY CLOONEY
MAMBO ITALIANO	DEAN MARTIN
MAMBO ROCK	BILL HALEY AND HIS COMETS
MAMMY BLUE	ROGER WHITTAKER
MAN FROM LARAMIE	AL MARTINO
MAN FROM LARAMIE	JIMMY YOUNG
MAN FROM MADRID	TONY OSBOURNE
MAN FROM NAZARETH	JOHN PAUL JOANS
MAN IN BLACK	COZY POWELL
MAN OF MYSTERY	SHADOWS
MAN OF THE WORLD	FLEETWOOD MAC
MAN ON FIRE	FRANKIE VAUGHAN
MAN THAT GOT AWAY	JUDY GARLAND
MAN WHO SOLD THE WORLD	LULU
MAN WITHOUT LOVE	ENGELBERT HUMPERDINCK
MAN WITHOUT LOVE	KENNETH McKELLAR
MAN WITH THE GOLDEN ARM	ELMER BERNSTEIN
MAN WITH THE GOLDEN ARM	JET HARRIS
MANCHESTER UNITED	MANCHESTER UNITED F.C.
MANDOLINS IN THE MOONLIGHT	PERRY COMO
MANDY	EDDIE CALVERT
MANDY	BARRY MANILOW
MANY TEARS AGO	CONNIE FRANCIS
MARBLE BREAKS, IRON BENDS	PETER FENTON
MARCH OF THE MODS	JOE LOSS
MARCH OF THE SIAMESE CHILDREN	KENNY BALL
MARCHETA	KARL DENVER
MARGIE	FATS DOMINO
MARIA	P.J. PROBY
MARIA ELENA	LOS INDIOS TABAJAROS
MARIA ELENA	GENE PITNEY
MARIANNE	HILLTOPPERS
MARIANNE	CLIFF RICHARD
MARIE	BACHELORS
MARJORINE	JOE COCKER
MAROC SEVEN	SHADOWS
MARRAKESH EXPRESS	CROSBY, STILLS AND NASH
MARRIED	BROOK BROTHERS
MARRY ME	MIKE PRESTON
MARTA	BACHELORS
MARY ANNE	SHADOWS
MARY HAD A LITTLE LAMB	WINGS
MARY JANE	DEL SHANNON
MARY'S BOY CHILD	HARRY BELAFONTE
MASSACHUSSETS	BEE GEES
MATTHEW AND SON	CAT STEVENS
MAY EACH DAY	ANDY WILLIAMS
MAY I HAVE THE NEXT DREAM WITH YOU	MALCOLM ROBERTS
MAY YOU ALWAYS	McGUIRE SISTERS
MAY YOU ALWAYS	JOAN REGAN

MAYBE BABY	CRICKETS
MAYBE I KNOW	LESLEY GORE
MAYBE TOMORROW	BILLY FURY
McDONALD'S CAVE	PILTDOWN MEN
ME AND JULIO DOWN BY THE SCHOOLYARD	PAUL SIMON
ME AND MRS. JONES	BILLY PAUL
ME AND MY LIFE	TREMELOES
ME AND MY SHADOW	SAMMY DAVIS JR. WITH FRANK SINATRA
ME AND YOU AND A DOG NAMED BOO	LOBO
ME, THE PEACEFUL HEART	LULU
MEAN GIRL	STATUS QUO
MEAN, MEAN, MEAN	WANDA JACKSON
MEAN STREAK	CLIFF RICHARD
MEAN TO ME	SHAYE COGAN
MEAN WOMAN BLUES	ROY ORBISON
MECCA	CHEETAHS
MEET ME ON THE CORNER	MAX BYGRAVES
MEET ME ON THE CORNER	LINDISFARNE
MELLOW YELLOW	DONOVAN
MELODY OF LOVE	INK SPOTS
MELTING POT	BLUE MINK
MEMORIES ARE MADE OF THIS	DEAN MARTIN
MEMORIES ARE MADE OF THIS	DAVE KING
MEMORIES ARE MADE OF THIS	VAL DOONICAN
MEMPHIS TENNESSEE	CHUCK BERRY
MEMPHIS TENNESSEE	DAVE BERRY AND THE CRUISERS
MERCI, CHERIE	VINCE HILL
MERRY CHRISTMAS, DARLING	CARPENTERS
MERRY CHRISTMAS, EVERYBODY	SLADE
MERRY PLOUGHBOY	DERMOT O'BRIEN
MESS OF BLUES	ELVIS PRESLEY
MESSAGE TO MARTHA	ADAM FAITH
MESSAGE TO MARTHA	LOU JOHNSON
MESSAGE UNDERSTOOD	SANDIE SHAW
MESSING ABOUT ON THE RIVER	JOSH MACRAE
METAL GURU	T. REX
MEXICALI ROSE	KARL DENVER
MEXICAN	FENTONES
MEXICO	LONG JOHN BALDRY
MICHAEL	HIGHWAYMEN
MICHAEL	LONNIE DONEGAN
MICHAEL	GENO WASHINGTON AND THE RAM JAM BAND
MICHAEL AND THE SLIPPER TREE	EQUALS
MICHELLE	DAVID AND JONATHAN
MICHELLE	OVERLANDERS
MIDDLE OF THE HOUSE	JIMMY PARKINSON
MIDNIGHT AT THE OASIS	MARIA MULDAUR
MIDNIGHT IN MOSCOW	KENNY BALL
MIDNIGHT RIDER	PAUL DAVIDSON
MIDNIGHT SPECIAL	PAUL EVANS AND THE CURLS
MIDNIGHT TO SIX MAN	PRETTY THINGS
MIGHTY JOE	SHOCKING BLUE
MIGHTY QUINN	MANFRED MANN
MIKE OLDFIELD'S SINGLE (THEME FROM 'TUBULAR BELLS')	MIKE OLDFIELD
MILKY WAY	SHEER ELEGANCE
MILLION DRUMS	TONY SHEVETON
MILLY MOLLY MANDY	GLYN POOLE
MILORD	EDITH PIAF
MILORD	FRANKIE VAUGHAN
MIND GAMES	JOHN LENNON
MINUETTO ALLEGRETTO	WOMBLES
MINUTE OF YOUR TIME	TOM JONES

MINUTE YOUR GONE	CLIFF RICHARD
MIRACLE OF YOU	DANNY WILLIAMS
MIRROR MIRROR	PINKERTON'S ASSORTED COLOURS
MISS, HIT AND RUN	BARRY BLUE
MISS YOU	JIMMY YOUNG
MISS YOU NIGHTS	CLIFF RICHARD
MISSY MISSY	PAUL AND BARRY RYAN
MISTY	JOHNNY MATHIS
MISTY	RAY STEVENS
M'LADY	SLY AND THE FAMILY STONE
MOBILE	RAY BURNS
MOCKING BIRD HILL	MIGIL FIVE
MOCKINGBIRD	INEZ AND CHARLIE FOXX
MOCKINGBIRD	CARLY SIMON AND JAMES TAYLOR
MONA LISA	CONWAY TWITTY
MONDAY, MONDAY	MAMAS AND PAPAS
MONEY HONEY	BAY CITY ROLLERS
MONEY (THAT'S WHAT I WANT)	BERN ELLIOTT AND THE FENMEN
MONKEY MAN	MAYTALS
MONKEY SPANNER	DAVE AND ANSEL COLLINS
MONSIEUR DUPONT	SANDIE SHAW
MONSTER MASH	BOBBY 'BORIS' PICKETT AND THE CRYPT KICKERS
MONTEGO BAY	BOBBY BLOOM
MONTEGO BAY	FREDDIE NOTES AND THE RUDIES
MONY MONY	TOMMY JAMES AND THE SHONDELLS
MOODY RIVER	PAT BOONE
MOON HOP	DERRICK MORGAN
MOON RIVER	DANNY WILLIAMS
MOON RIVER	GREYHOUND
MOON SHADOW	CAT STEVENS
MOON TALK	PERRY COMO
MOONGLOW (THEME FROM 'PICNIC')	MORRIS STOLOFF
MOONGLOW (THEME FROM 'PICNIC')	SOUNDS ORCHESTRAL
MOONIN'	CHRIS FARLOWE
MOONLIGHT GAMBLER	FRANKIE LAINE
MOONLIGHT SERENADE	GLENN MILLER ORCHESTRA
MOONLIGHTING	LEO SAYER
MOONSHINE SALLY	MUD
MORE	PERRY COMO
MORE	JIMMY YOUNG
MORE AND MORE PARTY POPS	RUSS CONWAY
MORE I SEE YOU	CHRIS MONTEZ
MORE I SEE YOU	JOY MARSHALL
MORE GOOD OLD ROCK'N'ROLL	DAVE CLARK FIVE
MORE MONEY FOR YOU AND ME	FOUR PREPS
MORE MORE	ANDY WILLIAMS
MORE PARTY POPS	RUSS CONWAY
MORE THAN EVER	SEE 'COME PRIMA'
MORE THAN I CAN SAY	BOBBY VEE
MORE THAN LOVE	KEN DODD
MORNING	VAL DOONICAN
MORNING HAS BROKEN	CAT STEVENS
MORNING SIDE OF THE MOUNTAIN	DONNY AND MARIE OSMOND
MORNING TOWN RIDE	SEEKERS
MOST BEAUTIFUL GIRL	CHARLIE RICH
MOTHER AND CHILD REUNION	PAUL SIMON
MOTHER-IN-LAW	ERNIE K-DOE
MOTHER OF MINE	NEIL REID
MOTOR BIKING	CHRIS SPEDDING
MOTORCYCLE MICHAEL	JO ANNE CAMPBELL
MOULDY OLD DOUGH	LIEUTENANT PIGEON
MOUNTAIN GREENERY	MEL TORME
MOUNTAIN OF LOVE	KENNY LYNCH
MOUNTAINS HIGH	DICK AND DEEDEE

MOVE IN A LITTLE CLOSER	HARMONY GRASS
MOVE IT	CLIFF RICHARD
MOVE IT BABY	SCOTT SIMON
MOVE ON UP	CURTIS MAYFIELD
MOVE OVER DARLING	DORIS DAY
MOVIE STAR	HARPO
MOVIN'	BRASS CONSTRUCTION
MOZART (SYMPHONY NO.) 40	WALDO DE LOS RIOS
MOZART (SYMPHONY NO.) 40	SOVEREIGN COLLECTION
MR. BASS MAN	JOHNNY CYMBAL
MR. BLUE	MIKE PRESTON
MR. CUSTER	CHARLIE DRAKE
MR. GUITAR	BERT WEEDON
MR. PORTER	MICKIE MOST
MR. PRESIDENT	DAVE DEE, DOZY, BEAKY, MICK AND TICH
MR. RAFFLES	COCKNEY REBEL
MR. SANDMAN	CHORDETTES
MR. SANDMAN	FOUR ACES
MR. SANDMAN	DICKIE VALENTINE
MR. SANDMAN	MAX BYGRAVES
MR. SECOND CLASS	SPENCER DAVIS GROUP
MR. SOFT	COCKNEY REBEL
MR. SUCCESS	FRANK SINATRA
MR. TAMBOURINE MAN	BYRDS
MR. WONDERFUL	PEGGY LEE
MRS. MILLS MEDLEY	MRS. MILLS
MRS. ROBINSON	SIMON AND GARFUNKEL
MRS. ROBINSON (E.P.)	SIMON AND GARFUNKEL
MS. GRACE	TYMES
MULE SKINNER BLUES (MULE TRAIN)	RUSTY DRAPER
MULE SKINNER BLUES (MULE TRAIN)	FENDERMEN
MULE TRAIN	FRANK IFIELD
MULTIPLICATION	BOBBY DARIN
MUSIC	JOHN MILES
MUSIC TO WATCH GIRLS BY	ANDY WILLIAMS
MUSIC FROM 'SIX WIVES OF HENRY VIII'	B.B.C. ORCHESTRA
MUSKRAT	EVERLY BROTHERS
MUSKRAT RAMBLE	FREDDIE CANNON
MUST BE MADISON	JOE LOSS
MUST BE SANTA	TOMMY STEELE
MUST TO AVOID	HERMAN'S HERMITS
MUSTANG SALLY	WILSON PICKETT
MUSTAPHA	BOB AZZAM AND HIS ORCHESTRA
MUSTAPHA	STAIFFI AND HIS MUSTAPHAS
MY BABY LEFT ME	DAVE BERRY AND THE CRUISERS
MY BABY LOVES LOVIN'	WHITE PLAINS
MY BLUE HEAVEN	FRANK SINATRA
MY BONNIE	BEATLES WITH TONY SHERIDAN
MY BOOMERANG WON'T COME BACK	CHARLIE DRAKE
MY BOY	ELVIS PRESLEY
MY BOY FLAT TOP	FRANKIE VAUGHAN
MY BOY LOLLIPOP	MILLIE (SMALL)
MY BOYFRIEND'S BACK	ANGELS
MY BROTHER JAKE	FREE
MY CHERIE AMOUR	STEVIE WONDER
MY CHILD	CONNIE FRANCIS
MY COO CA CHOO	ALVIN STARDUST
MY DING-A-LING	CHUCK BERRY
MY DIXIE DARLING	LONNIE DONEGAN
MY EYES ADORED YOU	FRANKIE VALLI
MY FRIEND	ROY ORBISON
MY FRIEND JACK	SMOKE
MY FRIEND STAN	SLADE
MY FRIEND THE SEA	PETULA CLARK
MY GENERATION	WHO

MY GIRL	TEMPTATIONS
MY GIRL	OTIS REDDING
MY GIRL JOSEPHINE	FATS DOMINO
MY GUY	MARY WELLS
MY HAPPINESS	CONNIE FRANCIS
MY HEART	GENE VINCENT
MY HEART HAS A MIND OF ITS OWN	CONNIE FRANCIS
MY HEART'S SYMPHONY	GARY LEWIS AND THE PLAYBOYS
MY KIND OF GIRL	MATT MONRO
MY KIND OF GIRL	FRANK SINATRA WITH COUNT BASIE
MY LAST NIGHT WITH YOU	ARROWS
MY LITTLE BABY	MIKE BERRY AND THE OUTLAWS
MY LITTLE CORNER OF THE WORLD	ANITA BRYANT
MY LITTLE GIRL	CRICKETS
MY LITTLE GIRL	AUTUMN
MY LITTLE LADY	TREMELOES
MY LITTLE ONE	MARMALADE
MY LOVE	PETULA CLARK
MY LOVE	PAUL McCARTNEY'S WINGS
MY LOVE AND DEVOTION	MATT MONRO
MY LOVE FOR YOU	JOHNNY MATHIS
MY LOVER'S PRAYER	OTIS REDDING
MY MAMMY	HAPPENINGS
MY MAN AND ME	LYNSEY DE PAUL
MY MAN IS A SWEET MAN	MILLIE JACKSON
MY MARIE	ENGELBERT HUMPERDINCK
MY MIND'S EYE	SMALL FACES
MY NAME IS JACK	MANFRED MANN
MY OLD MAN'S A DUSTMAN	LONNIE DONEGAN
MY ONE SIN	NAT 'KING' COLE
MY OWN TRUE LOVE	DANNY WILLIAMS
MY PRAYER	PLATTERS
MY PRAYER	GERRY MONROE
MY SENTIMENTAL FRIEND	HERMAN'S HERMITS
MY SEPTEMBER LOVE	DAVID WHITFIELD
MY SHIP IS COMING IN	WALKER BROTHERS
MY SON, MY SON	VERA LYNN
MY SPECIAL ANGEL	MALCOLM VAUGHAN
MY SPECIAL DREAM	SHIRLEY BASSEY
MY SUNDAY BABY	DALE SISTERS
MY SWEET LORD	GEORGE HARRISON
MY TRUE LOVE	JACK SCOTT
MY UKELELE	MAX BYGRAVES
MY WAY	FRANK SINATRA
MY WAY	DOROTHY SQUIRES
MY WAY	EDDIE COCHRAN
MY WAY OF GIVING	CHRIS FARLOWE
MY WHITE BICYCLE	NAZARETH
MY WOMAN'S MAN	DAVE DEE (SOLO)
MY WORLD OF BLUE	KARL DENVER
MYSTERY GIRL	JESS CONRAD
NA NA HEY HEY KISS HIM GOODBYE	STEAM
NA NA IS THE SADDEST WORD	STYLISTICS
NA NA NA	COZY POWELL
NADINE	CHUCK BERRY
NAIROBI	TOMMY STEELE
NAPPY LOVE	GOODIES
NASHVILLE CATS	LOVIN' SPOONFUL
NATHAN JONES	SUPREMES
NATURAL BORN BOOGIE	HUMBLE PIE
NATURAL HIGH	BLOODSTONE
NATURAL SINNER	FAIRWEATHER
NATURE BOY	BOBBY DARIN
NATURE'S TIME FOR LOVE	JOE BROWN

NAUGHTY LADY OF SHADY LANE	AMES BROTHERS
NAUGHTY LADY OF SHADY LANE	DEAN MARTIN
NEANDERTHAL MAN	HOTLEGS
NEAR YOU	MIGIL FIVE
NEED A SHOT OF RHYTHM AND BLUES	JOHNNY KIDD AND THE PIRATES
NEEDLES AND PINS	SEARCHERS
NEITHER ONE OF US	GLADYS KNIGHT AND THE PIPS
NEVER BE ANYONE ELSE BUT YOU	RICKY NELSON
NEVER BEFORE	DEEP PURPLE
NEVER CAN SAY GOODBYE	JACKSON FIVE
NEVER CAN SAY GOODBYE	GLORIA GAYNOR
NEVER DO A TANGO WITH AN ESKIMO	ALMA COGAN
NEVER ENDING SONG OF LOVE	NEW SEEKERS
NEVER FONNA FALL IN LOVE AGAIN	DANA
NEVER GOODBYE	KARL DENVER
NEVER HAD A DREAM COME TRUE	STEVIE WONDER
NEVER LET GO	JOHN BARRY
NEVER MIND	CLIFF RICHARD AND THE SHADOWS
NEVER NEVER GONNA GIVE YA UP	BARRY WHITE
NEVER, NEVER, NEVER	SHIRLEY BASSEY
NEVER ON SUNDAY	MANUEL AND HIS MUSIC OF THE MOUNTAINS
NEVER ON SUNDAY	CHAQUITE
NEVER ON SUNDAY	LYNN CORNELL
NEVER ON SUNDAY	DON COSTA
NEVER ON SUNDAY	MAKADOPOLOUS
NEVER TURN YOUR BACK ON MOTHER EARTH	SPARKS
NEVER WED AN OLD MAN	DUBLINERS
NEVERTHELESS	FRANKIE VAUGHAN
NEVERTHELESS	NEW SEEKERS
NEW ORLEANS	GARY 'U.S.' BONDS
NEW ORLEANS	HARLEY QUINNE
NEW ORLEANS	BERN ELLIOT AND THE FENMEN
NEW PIANO MEDLEY	CHARLIE KUNZ
NEW WORLD IN THE MORNING	ROGER WHITTAKER
NEW YORK CITY	T. REX
NEW YORK GROOVE	HELLO
NEW YORK MINING DISASTER 1941	BEE GEES
NEXT DOOR TO AN ANGEL	NEIL SEDAKA
NEXT TIME	CLIFF RICHARD
NICE 'N' EASY	FRANK SINATRA
NICE ONE CYRIL	COCKEREL CHORUS
NIGHT	FOUR SEASONS
NIGHT CHICAGO DIED	PAPER LACE
NIGHT HAS A THOUSAND EYES	BOBBY VEE
NIGHT IS YOUNG	GARY MILLER
NIGHT OF FEAR	MOVE
NIGHT OF THE LONG GRASS	TROGGS
NIGHT OF THE VAMPIRE	MOON TREKKERS
NIGHT THEY DROVE OLD DIXIE DOWN	JOAN BAEZ
NIGHTS IN WHITE SATIN	MOODY BLUES
NINE TIMES OUT OF TEN	CLIFF RICHARD
NINETEENTH NERVOUS BREAKDOWN	ROLLING STONES
98.6	BYSTANDERS
98.6	KEITH
99 WAYS	TAB HUNTER
96 TEARS	? AND THE MYSTERIANS
NO ARMS COULD EVER HOLD YOU	BACHELORS
NO FACE, NO NAME, NO NUMBER	TRAFFIC
NO HONESTLY	LYNSEY DE PAUL
NO MATTER HOW I TRY	GILBERT O'SULLIVAN
NO MATTER WHAT	BADFINGER
NO MATTER WHAT SIGN YOU ARE	DIANA ROSS AND THE SUPREMES
NO MILK TODAY	HERMAN'S HERMITS

NO MORE	McGUIRE SISTERS
NO MORE MR. NICE GUY	ALICE COOPER
NO MULE'S FOOL	FAMILY
NO ONE BUT YOU	BILLY ECKSTINE
NO ONE CAN BREAK A HEART LIKE YOU	DAVE CLARK FIVE
NO ONE CAN MAKE MY SUNSHINE SMILE	EVERLY BROTHERS
NO ONE TO CRY TO	RAY CHARLES
NO ONE WILL EVER KNOW	FRANK IFIELD
NO OTHER LOVE	RONNIE HILTON
NO PARTICULAR PLACE TO GO	CHUCK BERRY
NO REGRETS	SHIRLEY BASSEY
NO WOMAN, NO CRY	BOB MARLEY AND THE WAILERS
NOBODY I KNOW	PETER AND GORDON
NOBODY LOVES LIKE AN IRISHMAN	LONNIE DONEGAN
NOBODY NEEDS YOUR LOVE	GENE PITNEY
NOBODY'S CHILD	KAREN YOUNG
NOBODY'S DARLING BUT MINE	FRANK IFIELD
NOBODY'S FOOL	JIM REEVES
NON HO L'ETA	GIGLIOLA CINQUETTI
NORMAN	CAROL DEENE
NORTH TO ALASKA	JOHNNY HORTON
NOT AS A STRANGER	FRANK SINATRA
NOT FADE AWAY	ROLLING STONES
NOT RESPONSIBLE	TOM JONES
NOT TOO LITTLE, NOT TOO MUCH	CHRIS SANFORD
NOTHIN' TO DO	MICHAEL HOLLIDAY
NOTHING CAN STOP ME NOW	GENE CHANDLER
NOTHING COMES EASY	SANDIE SHAW
NOTHING RHYMED	GILBERT O'SULLIVAN
NOW	VAL DOONICAN
NOW I'M HERE	QUEEN
NOW WE'RE THROUGH	POETS
NOWHERE MAN	THREE GOOD REASONS
NOWHERE TO RUN	MARTHA REEVES AND THE VANDELLAS
NUMBER NINE DREAM	JOHN LENNON
NUMBER ONE	TREMELOES
NUTBUSH CITY LIMITS	IKE AND TINA TURNER
NUT ROCKER	B. BUMBLE AND THE STINGERS
OB-LA-DI, OB-LA-DA	MARMALADE
OB-LA-DI, OB-LA-DA	BEDROCKS
OBSESSION	REG OWEN
ODE TO BILLY JOE	BOBBY GENTRY
OH BABE, WHAT WOULD YOU SAY	HURRICANE SMITH
OH BOY	CRICKETS
OH BOY	MUD
OH CAROL	NEIL SEDAKA
OH GIRL	CHI-LITES
OH HAPPY DAY	EDWIN HAWKINS SINGERS
OH HOW I MISS YOU	BACHELORS
OH LONESOME ME	CRAIG DOUGLAS
OH ME, OH MY	LULU
OH NO NOT MY BABY	MANFRED MANN
OH NO NOT MY BABY	ROD STEWART
OH OH I'M FALLING IN LOVE AGAIN	JIMMIE RODGERS
OH PRETTY WOMAN	ROY ORBISON
OH SUZANNA	SINGING DOGS
OH WELL	FLEETWOOD MAC
OH WHAT A DAY	CRAIG DOUGLAS
OH WHAT A NIGHT	FOUR SEASONS
OH WHAT A SHAME	ROY WOOD
OH YES, YOU'RE BEAUTIFUL	GARY GLITTER
OL' MACDONALD	FRANK SINATRA
OLD FASHIONED WAY	CHARLES AZNAVOUR
OLD OAKEN BUCKET	TOMMY SANDS

OLD PIANNA RAG	DICKIE VALENTINE
OLD RIVERS	WALTER BRENNAN
OLD RUGGED CROSS	ETHNA CAMPBELL
OLD SMOKEY	JOHNNY AND THE HURRICANES
OLIVE TREE	SEEKERS (JUDITH DURHAM SOLO)
OLYMPIC RECORD	BARRON KNIGHTS
ON A CAROUSEL	HOLLIES
ON A SATURDAY NIGHT	TERRY DACTYL AND THE DINOSAURS
ON A SLOW BOAT TO CHINA	EMILE FORD AND THE CHECKMATES
ON HORSEBACK	MIKE OLDFIELD
ON MOTHER KELLY'S DOORSTEP	DANNY LA RUE
ON MY WORD	CLIFF RICHARD
ON THE BEACH	CLIFF RICHARD
ON THE REBOUND	FLOYD KRAMER
ON THE ROAD AGAIN	CANNED HEAT
ON THE STREET WHERE YOU LIVE	VIC DAMONE
ON THE STREET WHERE YOU LIVE	DAVID WHITFIELD
ON WITH THE MOTLEY	HARRY SECOMBE
ONCE	GENEVIEVE
ONCE BITTEN, TWICE SHY	IAN HUNTER
ONCE I HAD A SWEETHEART	PENTANGLE
ONCE IN EVERY LIFETIME	KEN DODD
ONCE THERE WAS A TIME	TOM JONES
ONCE UPON A DREAM	BILLY FURY
ONCE UPON A TIME	TOM JONES
ONCE UPON A TIME	MARVIN GAYE WITH MARY WELLS
ONE AND ONE IS ONE	MEDICINE HEAD
ONE BAD APPLE	OSMONDS
ONE BROKEN HEART FOR SALE	ELVIS PRESLEY
ONE FINE DAY	CHIFFONS
ONE HEART BETWEEN TWO	DAVE BERRY AND THE CRUISERS
ONE INCH ROCK	T. REX
ONE MAN BAND	LEO SAYER
ONE MORE DANCE	ESTHER AND ABI OFARIM
ONE MORE SUNRISE	DICKIE VALENTINE
ONE NIGHT	ELVIS PRESLEY
ONE NIGHT	MUD
10538 OVERTURE	ELECTRIC LIGHT ORCHESTRA
ONE OF THOSE NIGHTS	EAGLES
ONE OF US MUST KNOW	BOB DYLAN
ONE ROAD	LOVE AFFAIR
ONE TO CRY	ESCORTS
1-2-3	LEN BARRY
1-2-3 O'LEARY	DES O'CONNOR
ONE WAY LOVE	CLIFF BENNET AND THE REBEL ROUSERS
ONEDIN LINE	VIENNA PHILHARMONIC ORCHESTRA
ONION SONG	MARVIN GAYE WITH TAMMI TERRELL
ONLY MAN ON THE ISLAND	TOMMY STEELE
ONLY ONE WOMAN	MARBLES
ONLY SIXTEEN	CRAIG DOUGLAS
ONLY SIXTEEN	SAM COOKE
ONLY THE HEARTACHES	HOUSTON WELLS
ONLY THE ONLY	ROY ORBISON
ONLY YESTERDAY	CARPENTERS
ONLY YOU	PLATTERS
ONLY YOU	HILLTOPPERS
ONLY YOU	MARK WYNTER
ONLY YOU	RINGO STARR
ONLY YOU	JEFF COLLINS
ONLY YOU CAN	FOX
ONWARD CHRISTIAN SOLDIERS	HARRY SIMEONE CHORALE
OOH BABY	GILBERT O'SULLIVAN
OOH I DO	LYNSEY DE PAUL
OOH LA LA	KEITH KELLY
OOH LA LA	JOE HENDERSON

OOH-WAKKA-DOO-WAKKA-DAY	GILBERT O'SULLIVAN
OPEN UP	MUNGO JERRY
OPERATOR	MANHATTAN TRANSFER
OPUS 17	FOUR SEASONS
ORANGE BLOSSOM SPECIAL	SPOTNIKS
OTHER MAN'S GRASS	PETULA CLARK
OTHER SIDE OF ME	ANDY WILLIAMS
OUR DAY WILL COME	RUBY AND THE ROMANTICS
OUR FAVOURITE MELODIES	CRAIG DOUGLAS
OUR LAST SONG TOGETHER	NEIL SEDAKA
OUR WORLD	BLUE MINK
OUT DEMONS OUT	EDGAR WINTER GROUP
OUT OF MY MIND	JOHNNY TILLOTSON
OUT OF THIS WORLD	TONY HATCH
OUT OF TIME	CHRIS FARLOWE
OUT OF TIME	ROLLING STONES
OUT OF TIME	DAN McCAFFERTY
OUT OF TOWN	MAX BYGRAVES
OUT ON THE FLOOR	DOBIE GREY
OUTA SPACE	BILLY PRESTON
OVER AND OVER	DAVE CLARK FIVE
OVER AND OVER	JAMES BOYS
OVER, UNDER, SIDEWAYS, DOWN	YARDBIRDS
OVER YOU	FREDDIE AND THE DREAMERS
'OWEN M.D.' THEME (SLEEPY SHORES)	JOHNNY PEARSON ORCHESTRA
PABLO	RUSS CONWAY
PACK UP YOUR SORROWS	JOAN BAEZ
PAINT IT BLACK	ROLLING STONES
PAINTER MAN	CREATION
PALISADES PARK	FREDDIE CANNON
PAMELA PAMELA	WAYNE FONTANA
PANDORA'S BOX	PROCUL HARUM
PAPA LOVES MAMA	JOAN REGAN
PAPA LOVES MAMBO	PERRY COMO
PAPA WAS A ROLLING STONE	TEMPTATIONS
PAPA OOM MOW MOW	SHARONETTES
PAPA OOM MOW MOW	GARY GLITTER
PAPA'S GOT A BRAND NEW BAG	JAMES BROWN
PAPER DOLL	WINDSOR DAVIES AND DON ESTELLE
PAPER PLANE	STATUS QUO
PAPER ROSES	ANITA BRYANT
PAPER ROSES	KAYE SISTERS
PAPER ROSES	MAUREEN EVANS
PAPER ROSES	MARIE OSMOND
PAPER SUN	TRAFFIC
PAPER TIGER	SUE THOMPSON
PAPERBACK WRITER	BEATLES
PARADISE	FRANK IFIELD
PARADISE LOST	HERD
PARALYSED	ELVIS PRESLEY
PARANOID	BLACK SABBATH
PART OF THE UNION	STRAWBS
PART TIME LOVE	GLADYS KNIGHT AND THE PIPS
PARTY DOLL	BUDDY KNOX
PARTY'S OVER	LONNIE DONEGAN
PASADENA	TEMPERANCE SEVEN
PASSING BREEZE	RUSS CONWAY
PASSING STRANGERS	SARAH VAUGHAN AND BILLY ECKSTINE
PATCHES	CLARENCE CARTER
PATHS OF PARADISE	JOHNNY RAY
PATRICIA	PEREZ PRADO
PAY TO THE PIPER	CHAIRMAN OF THE BOARD
PEACEFUL	GEORGIE FAME
PEEK-A-BOO	NEW VAUDEVILLE BAND

PEEK-A-BOO	STYLISTICS
PEGGY SUE	BUDDY HOLLY
PEGGY SUE GOT MARRIED	BUDDY HOLLY
PENNY ARCADE	ROY ORBISON
PENNY LANE	BEATLES
PEOPLE	TYMES
PEOPLE LIKE YOU, PEOPLE LIKE ME	GLITTER BAND
PEPE	DUANE EDDY
PEPE	RUSS CONWAY
PEPITO	LOS MACHUCAMBOS
PEPPER BOX	PEPPERS
PEPPERMINT TWIST	JOEY DEE AND THE STARLITERS
PEPPERMINT TWIST	DANNY PEPPERMINT AND THE JUMPING JACKS
PEPYS' DIARY	BENNY HILL
PERFIDIA	VENTURES
PERSONALITY	LLOYD PRICE
PERSONALITY	LENA ZAVARONI
PER-SON-AL-LY	WIGAN'S OVATION
'PERSUADERS' THEME	JOHN BARRY
PETER AND THE WOLF	CLYDE VALLEY STOMPERS
PETER GUNN	DUANE EDDY
PETITE FLEUR	CHRIS BARBER
PHILADELPHIA FREEDOM	ELTON JOHN
PHOTOGRAPH	RINGO STARR
PIANISSIMO	KEN DODD
PIANO PARTY	WINIFRED ATWELL
PICK A BALE OF COTTON	LONNIE DONEGAN
PICKIN' A CHICKEN	EVE BOSWELL
PICK UP THE PIECES	HUDSON-FORD
PICK UP THE PIECES	AVERAGE WHITE BAND
PICKNEY GAL	DESMOND DEKKER AND THE ACES
PICNIC	SEE 'MOONGLOW'
PICTURE OF YOU	JOE BROWN
PICTURES IN THE SKY	MEDICINE HEAD
PICTURES OF LILY	WHO
PICTURES OF MATCHSTICK MEN	STATUS QUO
PIED PIPER	STEVE RACE
PIED PIPER	CRISPIAN ST. PETERS
PIED PIPER	BOB ANDY AND MARCIA GRIFFITHS
PILLOW TALK	SYLVIA
PILTDOWN RIDES AGAIN	PILTDOWN MEN
PINBALL	BRIAN PROTHEROE
PINBALL WIZARD	WHO
PINBALL WIZARD	NEW SEEKERS
PINBALL WIZARD	ELTON JOHN
PIPELINE	CHANTAYS
PISTOL PACKING MAMA	GENE VINCENT
PLACE IN THE SUN	SHADOWS
PLACE IN THE SUN	STEVIE WONDER
PLASTIC MEN	KINKS
PLAY ME LIKE YOU PLAY YOUR OLD GUITAR	DUANE EDDY
PLAYGROUND	ANITA HARRIS
PLEASANT VALLEY SUNDAY	MONKEES
PLEASE DON'T ASK ABOUT BARBARA	BOBBY VEE
PLEASE DON'T GO	DONALD PEERS
PLEASE DON'T TEASE	CLIFF RICHARD
PLEASE HELP ME I'M FALLING	HANK LOCKLIN
PLEASE HELP ME I'M FALLING	BROOK BROTHERS
PLEASE MR. POSTMAN	CARPENTERS
PLEASE PLEASE ME	BEATLES
PLEASE STAY	CRYIN' SHAMES
PLEASE TELL HIM THAT I SAID HELLO	DANA
PLENTY GOOD LOVIN'	CONNIE FRANCIS

POACHER	RONNIE LANE
POETRY IN MOTION	JOHNNY TILLOTSON
POISON IVY	PARAMOUNTS
POISON IVY	COASTERS
POLK SALAD ANNIE	ELVIS PRESLEY
PONY TIME	CHUBBY CHECKER
POOLHALL RICHARD	FACES
POOR JENNY	EVERLY BROTHERS
POOR LITTLE FOOL	RICKY NELSON
POOR MAN'S SON	ROCKIN' BERRIES
POOR ME	ADAM FAITH
POOR PEOPLE OF PARIS	WINIFRED ATWELL
POPCORN	HOT BUTTER
POP GOES THE WEASEL	ANTHONY NEWLEY
POPPA JOE	SWEET
PORT AU PRINCE	WINIFRED ATWELL
PORTRAIT OF MY LOVE	MATT MONRO
PORTUGUESE WASHER WOMEN	JOE 'FINGERS' CARR
POSITIVELY 4TH STREET	BOB DYLAN
POWER TO ALL OUR FRIENDS	CLIFF RICHARD
POWER TO THE PEOPLE	JOHN LENNON AND THE PLASTIC ONO BAND
PRETTY BLUE EYES	CRAIG DOUGLAS
PRETTY FLAMINGO	MANFRED MANN
PRETTY JENNY	JESS CONRAD
PRETTY LITTLE ANGEL EYES	CURTIS LEE
PRETTY PAPER	ROY ORBISON
PRETTY THINGS	BO DIDDLEY
PRETTY WOMAN	ROY ORBISON
PRETTY WOMAN	JUICY LUCY
PRICE OF LOVE	EVERLY BROTHERS
PRINCESS	TOMMY STEELE
PRINCESS IN RAGS	GENE PITNEY
PRIVATE NUMBER	JUDY CLAY AND WILLIAM BELL
PRIZE OF GOLD	JOAN REGAN
PROBLEMS	EVERLY BROTHERS
PROMISED LAND	CHUCK BERRY
PROMISED LAND	ELVIS PRESLEY
PROMISES	KEN DODD
PROUD MARY	CREEDANCE CLEARWATER REVIVAL
PROUD MARY	CHECKMATES LIMITED WITH SONNY CHARLES
PROUD ONE	OSMONDS
PSYCHEDELIC SHOCK	TEMPTATIONS
PUB WITH NO BEER	SLIM DUSTY
PUCKWUDGIE	CHARLIE DRAKE
PUFF	KENNY LYNCH
PUPPET MAN	TOM JONES
PUPPET ON A STRING	SANDIE SHAW
PUPPY LOVE	PAUL ANKA
PUPPY LOVE	DONNY OSMOND
PUPPY SONG	DAVID CASSIDY
PURELY BY COINCIDENCE	SWEET SENSATION
PURPLE HAZE	JIMI HENDRIX
PURPLE PEOPLE EATER	SHEB WOOLEY
PUSHBIKE SONG	MIXTURES
PUT A LIGHT IN THE WINDOW	SOUTHLANDERS
PUT A LITTLE LOVE IN YOUR HEART	DAVE CLARK FIVE
PUT YOUR HEAD ON MY SHOULDER	PAUL ANKA
PUT YOURSELF IN MY PLACE	ISLEY BROTHERS
PUTTIN' ON THE STYLE	LONNIE DONEGAN
PYJAMARAMA	ROXY MUSIC
QUANDO LN'INNAMORO	SANDPIPERS
QUE SERA SERA (WHATEVER WILL BE, WILL BE)	DORIS DAY

QUE SERA SERA (WHATEVER WILL BE, WILL BE)	GENO WASHINGTON AND HIS RAM JAM BAND
QUEEN FOR TONIGHT	HELEN SHAPIRO
QUEEN OF CLUBS	K.C. AND THE SUNSHINE BAND
QUEEN OF 1964	NEIL SEDAKA
QUESTION	MOODY BLUES
QUESTIONS I CAN'T ANSWER	HEINZ
QUICK JOEY SMALL	KASENETZ-KATZ SWINGING ORCHESTRAL CIRCUS
QUITE A PARTY	FIREBALLS
QUITE RIGHTLY SO	PROCOL HARUM
RACE WITH THE DEVIL	GUN
RADANCER	MARMALADE
RAG DOLL	FOUR SEASONS
RAG MAMA RAG	BAND
RAGAMUFFIN MAN	MANFRED MANN
RAGS TO RICHES	ELVIS PRESLEY
RAGTIME COWBOY JOE	CHIPMUNKS
RAIN	JOSE FELICIANO
RAIN	BRUCE RUFFIN
RAIN	STATUS QUO
RAIN AND TEARS	APHRODITE'S CHILD
RAIN FOREST	BIDDU ORCHESTRA
RAIN RAIN RAIN	FRANKIE LAINE
RAINBOW	MARMALADE
RAINBOW	PETERS AND LEE
RAINBOW CHASER	NIRVANA
RAINBOW VALLEY	LOVE AFFAIR
RAINDROPS KEEP FALLING ON MY HEAD	B.J. THOMAS
RAINDROPS KEEP FALLING ON MY HEAD	SACHA DISTEL
RAINDROPS KEEP FALLING ON MY HEAD	BOBBY GENTRY
RAINY DAY WOMEN NOS. 12 AND 35	BOB DYLAN
RAISE YOUR HAND	EDDIE FLOYD
RAISED ON ROCK	ELVIS PRESLEY
RAM BUNK SHUSH	VENTURES
RAM GOAT LIVER	PLUTO
RAMBLIN' ROSE	NAT 'KING' COLE
RAMONA	BACHELORS
RANDY	BLUE MINK
RAUNCHY	BILL JUSTIS
RAUNCHY	KEN MACKINTOSH
RAVE ON	BUDDY HOLLY
RAWHIDE	FRANKIE LAINE
RAZZLE DAZZLE	BILL HALEY AND HIS COMETS
REACH FOR THE STARS	SHIRLEY BASSEY
REACH OUT AND TOUCH	DIANA ROSS
REACH OUT FOR ME	DIONNE WARWICK
REACH OUT I'LL BE THERE	FOUR TOPS
REACH OUT I'LL BE THERE	GLORIA GAYNOR
REACHING FOR THE BEST	EXCITERS
READY FOR LOVE	JIMMY JONES
READY OR NOT, HERE I COME	DELFONICS
READY, WILLING AND ABLE	DORIS DAY
REAL LOVE	RUBY MURRAY
REASON TO BELIEVE	ROD STEWART
REBEL, REBEL	DAVID BOWIE
REBEL ROUSER	DUANE EDDY
RED BALLOON	DAVE CLARK FIVE
RED DRESS	ALVIN STARDUST
RED RED WINE	JIMMY JAMES AND THE VAGABONDS
RED RED WINE	TONY TRIBE
RED RIVER ROCK	JOHNNY AND THE HURRICANES
RED SAILS IN THE SUNSET	FATS DOMINO
REELIN' AND ROCKIN'	DAVE CLARK FIVE

REELIN' AND ROCKIN'	CHUCK BERRY
REET PETITE	JACKIE WILSON
REFLECTIONS	DIANA ROSS AND THE SUPREMES
REFLECTIONS OF MY LIFE	MARMALADE
REGGAE TUNE	ANDY FAIRWEATHER-LOWE
RELAY	WHO
RELEASE ME	ENGELBERT HUMPERDINCK
REMEMBER	BAY CITY ROLLERS
REMEMBER	ROCK CANDY
REMEMBER	JIMI HENDRIX EXPERIENCE
REMEMBER (WALKING IN THE SAND)	SHANGRI-LAS
REMEMBER ME	DIANA ROSS
REMEMBER ME THIS WAY	GARY GLITTER
REMEMBER YOU'RE A WOMBLE	WOMBLES
REMEMBER YOU'RE MINE	PAT BOONE
REMINISCING	BUDDY HOLLY
RENTA SANTA	CHRIS HILL
RESCUE ME	FONTELLA BASS
RESPECT	ARETHA FRANKLIN
RESPONSIBLE	TOM JONES
RESTLESS	JOHNNY KIDD AND THE PIRATES
RESURRECTION SHUFFLE	ASHTON, GARDNER AND DYKE
RETURN OF DJANGO	UPSETTERS
RETURN OF THE RED BARON	ROYAL GUARDSMEN
RETURN TO ME	DEAN MARTIN
RETURN TO SENDER	ELVIS PRESLEY
REVEILLE ROCK	JOHNNY AND THE HURRICANES
REVIVAL	CHRIS BARBER
RHAPSODY IN THE RAIN	LOU CHRISTIE
RHINESTONE COWBOY	GLEN CAMPBELL
RHYTHM AND GREENS	SHADOWS
RICE IS NICE	LEMON PIPERS
RIDE A WHITE SWAN	T. REX
RIDE A WILD HORSE	DEE CLARK
RIDE AWAY	ROY ORBISON
RIDE MY SEE-SAW	MOODY BLUES
RIDE ON BABY	CHRIS FARLOWE
RIDERS IN THE SKY	RAMRODS
RIDERS ON THE STORM	DOORS
RIGHT BACK WHERE WE STARTED FROM	MAXINE NIGHTINGALE
'RIGHT', SAID FRED	BERNARD CRIBBINS
RIGHT THING TO DO	CARLY SIMON
RIGHT THING TO SAY	NAT 'KING' COLE
RIGHT WHEEL LEFT HAMMER SHAM	TREMELOES
RING-A-DING-GIRL	RONNIE CARROL
RING OF BRIGHT WATER	VAL DOONICAN
RING OF FIRE	DUANE EDDY
RING OF FIRE	ERIC BURDON AND THE ANIMALS
RING RING	ABBA
RINGO	LORNE GREEN
RIP IT UP	BILL HALEY AND HIS COMETS
RIP IT UP	ELVIS PRESLEY
RISE AND FALL OF FLINGEL BUNT	SHADOWS
RISING SUN	MEDICINE HEAD
RIVER	KEN DODD
RIVER DEEP, MOUNTAIN HIGH	IKE AND TINA TURNER
RIVER DEEP, MOUNTAIN HIGH	SUPREMES AND FOUR TOPS
RIVER, STAY 'WAY FROM MY DOOR	FRANK SINATRA
RIVERS RUN DRY	VINCE HILL
ROAD RUNNER	JUNIOR WALKER
ROBIN HOOD	GARY MILLER
ROBIN HOOD	DICK JAMES
ROBIN'S RETURN	NEVILLE DICKIE
ROBOT	TORNADOS
ROBOT MAN	CONNIE FRANCIS

ROCHDALE COWBOY	MIKE HARDING
ROCK-A-BEATIN' BOOGIE	BILL HALEY AND HIS COMETS
ROCK-A-BILLY	GUY MITCHELL
ROCK-A-BYE YOUR BABY	JERRY LEWIS
ROCK-A-DOOBLE DOO	LINDA LEWIS
ROCK-A-HULA BABY	ELVIS PRESLEY
ROCK AND ROLL (I GAVE YOU THE BEST YEARS OF MY LIFE)	KEVIN JOHNSON
ROCK AND ROLL PART 2	GARY GLITTER
ROCK AND ROLL SUICIDE	DAVID BOWIE
ROCK AND ROLL WALTZ	KAY STARR
ROCK AND ROLL WINTER	WIZZARD
ROCK AROUND THE CLOCK	BILL HALEY AND HIS COMETS
ROCK ISLAND LINE	LONNIE DONEGAN
ROCK ME GENTLY	ANDY KIM
ROCK'N'ROLL BABY	STYLISTICS
ROCK'N'ROLL LADY	SHOWADDYWADDY
ROCK'N'SOUL	HUES CORPORATION
ROCK ON	DAVID ESSEX
ROCK ON BROTHER	CHEQUERS
ROCK THE BOAT	HUES CORPORATION
ROCK THE JOINT	BILL HALEY AND HIS COMETS
ROCK WITH THE CAVEMAN	TOMMY STEELE
ROCK YOUR BABY	GEORGE McCRAE
ROCKET	MUD
ROCKET MAN	SPOTNIKS
ROCKET MAN	ELTON JOHN
ROCKIN' ALONE	MIKI AND GRIFF
ROCKIN' ROUND THE CHRISTMAS TREE	BRENDA LEE
ROCKIN' ROBIN	MICHAEL JACKSON
ROCKIN' THROUGH THE RYE	BILL HALEY AND HIS COMETS
ROCKING GOOSE	JOHNNY AND THE HURRICANES
ROCKING RED WING	SAMMY MASTERS
ROCKY	AUSTIN ROBERTS
ROLL AWAY THE STONE	MOTT THE HOOPLE
ROLL ON DOWN THE HIGHWAY	BACHMAN-TURNER OVERDRIVE
ROLL OVER BEETHOVEN	ELECTRIC LIGHT ORCHESTRA
ROLL OVER LAY DOWN	STATUS QUO
ROLLIN' STONE	DAVID ESSEX
ROMANTICA	JANE MORGAN
ROMEO	PETULA CLARK
ROOF TOP SINGING	NEW WORLD
ROSALYN	PRETTY THINGS
ROSE GARDEN	LYNN ANDERSON
ROSE GARDEN	NEW WORLD
ROSE GARDEN	SANDIE SHAW
ROSEMARIE	SLIM WHITMAN
ROSES ARE RED	BOBBY VINTON
ROSES ARE RED	RONNIE CARROLL
ROSES OF PICARDY	VINCE HILL
ROSETTA	GEORGIE FAME AND ALAN PRICE
ROSIE	DON PARTRIDGE
ROULETTE	RUSS CONWAY
ROUND EVERY CORNER	PETULA CLARK
ROYAL EVENT	RUSS CONWAY
RUB-A-DUB-DUB	EQUALS
RUBBER BALL	MARTY WILDE
RUBBER BALL	BOBBY VEE
RUBBER BALL	AVONS
RUBBER BULLETS	10 C.C.
RUBY ANN	MARTY ROBBINS
RUBY (DON'T TAKE YOUR LOVE TO TOWN)	KENNY ROGERS AND THE FIRST EDITION
RUBY TUESDAY	ROLLING STONES
RUBY TUESDAY	MELANIE

RUDDER AND THE ROCK	DAVID WHITFIELD
RUDY'S IN LOVE	LOCOMOTIVE
RUMOURS	HOT CHOCOLATE
RUN	SANDIE SHAW
RUN BABY RUN	NEWBEATS
RUN RUDOLPH RUN	CHUCK BERRY
RUN RUN RUN	JO JO GUNNE
RUN TO HIM	BOBBY VEE
RUN TO ME	BEE GEES
RUN TO MY LOVIN' ARMS	BILLY FURY
RUN TO THE DOOR	CLINTON FORD
RUN TO THE DOOR	JACKIE LEE
RUNAROUND SUE	DION
RUNAROUND SUE	DOUG SHELDON
RUNAWAY	DEL SHANNON
RUNNIN' AWAY	SLY AND THE FAMILY STONE
RUNNIN' SCARED	ROY ORBISON
RUNNING BEAR	JOHNNY PRESTON
RUPERT	JACKIE LEE
SABRE DANCE	LOVE SCULPTURE
SACREMENTO	MIDDLE OF THE ROAD
SAD MOVIES	CAROLE DEENE
SAD MOVIES MAKE ME CRY	SUE THOMPSON
SAD SWEET DREAMER	SWEET SENSATION
SAILING	ROD STEWART
SAILOR	PETULA CLARK
SAILOR	ANNE SHELTON
ST. THERESA OF THE ROSES	MALCOLM VAUGHAN
SAINTS ROCK AND ROLL	BILL HALEY AND HIS COMETS
SALLY	GERRY MONROE
SALLY ANN	JOE BROWN AND THE BRUVVERS
SALLY G	WINGS
SALLY DON'T YOU GRIEVE	LONNIE DONEGAN
SAL'S GOT A SUGAR LIP	LONNIE DONEGAN
SALTY DOG	PROCUL HARUM
SAM	KEITH WEST
SAMBA PA TI	SANTANA
SAMSON AND DELILAH	MIDDLE OF THE ROAD
SAN ANTONIA ROSE	FLOYD CRAMER
SAN BERNARDINO	CHRISTIE
SAN FRANCISCAN NIGHTS	ERIC BURDON AND THE ANIMALS
SAN FRANCISCO	SCOTT McKENZIE
SANCTUS	TROUBADOURS DU ROI BAUDOIN
SANTA BRING MY BABY BACK TO ME	ELVIS PRESLEY
SANTA CLAUS IS COMING TO TOWN	JACKSON FIVE
SANTA CLAUS IS COMING TO TOWN	CARPENTERS
SANTA LIJA	ENGELBERT HUMPERDINCK
SANTO NATALE	DAVID WHITFIELD
SATISFACTION	ROLLING STONES
SATISFACTION	OTIS REDDING
SATISFACTION	ARETHA FRANKLIN
SATISFACTION	BUBBLEROCK
SATISFACTION GUARANTEED	HAROLD MELVIN AND THE BLUENOTES
SATISFIED	LULU AND THE LUVVERS
SATURDAY GIG	MOTT THE HOOPLE
SATURDAY NIGHT AT THE DUCKPOND	CONGARS
SATURDAY NIGHT AT THE MOVIES	DRIFTERS
SATURDAY NIGHT'S ALRIGHT FOR FIGHTING	ELTON JOHN
SAVAGE	SHADOWS
SAVE ME	DAVE DEE, DOZY, BEAKY, MICK AND TICH
SAVE ME	SILVER CONVENTION
SAVE THE LAST DANCE FOR ME	DRIFTERS

SAVED BY THE BELL	ROBIN GIBB
SAY, HAS ANYBODY SEEN MY SWEET GYPSY ROSE	DAWN
SAY I WON'T BE THERE	SPRINGFIELDS
SAY IT WITH FLOWERS	RUSS CONWAY WITH DOROTHY SQUIRES
SAY WONDERFUL THING	RONNIE CARROLL
SAY YOU DON'T MIND	COLIN BLUNSTONE
SAY YOU'RE MY GIRL	ROY ORBISON
SCARLET RIBBONS	HARRY BELAFONTE
SCARLETT O'HARA	JET HARRIS AND TONY MEEHAN
SCHOOL DAYS	CHUCK BERRY
SCHOOL LOVE	BARRY BLUE
SCHOOL'S OUT	ALICE COOPER
SCOTCH ON THE ROCKS	BAND OF THE BLACK WATCH
SCOTTISH SOLDIER	ANDY STEWART
SCULLERY	CLIFFORD T. WARD
SEA OF HEARTBREAK	DON GIBSON
SEA OF LOVE	MARTY WILDE
SEAGULL	RAINBOW COTTAGE
SEAGULL'S NAME WAS NELSON	PETER E. BENNETT
SEALED WITH A KISS	BRIAN HYLAND
SEARCHIN'	HOLLIES
SEASIDE SHUFFLE	TERRY DACTYL AND THE DINOSAURS
SECOND HAND ROSE	BARBRA STREISAND
SECRET LOVE	KATHY KIRBY
SECRETS THAT YOU KEEP	MUD
SEE EMILY PLAY	PINK FLOYD
SEE ME, FEEL ME	SEEKERS
SEE MY BABY JIVE	WIZZARD
SEE MY FRIENDS	KINKS
SEE YOU LATER, ALLIGATOR	BILL HALEY AND HIS COMETS
SEEKER	WHO
SEMI-DETACHED SUBURBAN MR. JONES	MANFRED MANN
SEND IN THE CLOWNS	JUDY COLLINS
SEND ME THE PILLOW	JOHNNY TILLOTSON
SENDING OUT AN S.O.S.	RETTA YOUNG
SEPTEMBER IN THE RAIN	DINAH WASHINGTON
SERANATA	TONY BENNETT
SERANATA	SARAH VAUGHAN
SERENADE	MARIO LANZA
SERENADE	SLIM WHITMAN
SET ME FREE	KINKS
SEVEN DAFFODILS	MOJOS
SEVEN DAFFODILS	CHEROKEES
SEVEN DAYS	ANNE SHELTON
SEVEN DRUNKEN NIGHTS	DUBLINERS
SEVEN LITTLE GIRLS	PAUL EVANS AND THE CURLS
SEVEN LITTLE GIRLS	AVONS
SEVEN ROOMS OF GLOOM	FOUR TOPS
SEVEN SEAS OF RHYE	QUEEN
7-6-5-4-3-2-1 BLOW YOUR WHISTLE	RIMSHOTS
SEVENTEEN	BOYD BENNET
SEVENTEEN	FRANKIE VAUGHAN
SEVENTH SON	GEORGIE FAME
76 TROMBONES	KING BROTHERS
SEXY	M.F.S.B.
SH-BOOM	CREWCUTS
SH-BOOM	STAN FREBURG
SHA LA LA	SHIRELLES
SHA LA LA	MANFRED MANN
SHA LA LA	AL GREEN
SHA LA LA LA LEE	SMALL FACES
SHADY LADY	GENE PITNEY
SHAFT THEME	ISAAC HAYES

SHAKE	OTIS REDDING
SHAKE RATTLE AND ROLL	BILL HALEY AND HIS COMETS
SHAKIN' ALL OVER	JOHNNY KIDD AND THE PIRATES
SHAME	ALAN PRICE
SHAME AND SCANDAL IN THE FAMILY	LANCE PERCIVAL
SHAME, SHAME, SHAME	JIMMY REED
SHAME, SHAME, SHAME	SHIRLEY AND CO.
SHANG-A-LANG	BAY CITY ROLLERS
SHANTY TOWN (007)	DESMOND DEKKER AND THE ACES
SHAPES OF THINGS	YARDBIRDS
SHARING YOU	BOBBY VEE
SHAZAM	DUANE EDDY
SHE	CHARLES AZNAVOUR
SHE LOVES YOU	BEATLES
SHE NEEDS LOVE	WAYNE FONTANA
SHE SHE LITTLE SHEILA	GENE VINCENT
SHE SOLD MAGIC	LOU CHRISTIE
SHE WEARS MY RING	SOLOMON KING
SHE'D RATHER BE WITH ME	TURTLES
SHEILA	TOMMY ROE
SHEPHERD'S SONG	TONY OSBOURNE
SHERRY	FOUR SEASONS
SHERRY	ADRIAN BAKER
SHE'S A LADY	TOM JONES
SHE'S A WINNER	INTRUDERS
SHE'S ABOUT A MOVER	SIR DOUGLAS QUINTET
SHE'S GONE	BUDDY KNOX
SHE'S GOT IT	LITTLE RICHARD
SHE'S GOT YOU	PATSY CLINE
SHE'S NEW TO YOU	SUSAN MAUGHAN
SHE'S NOT THERE	ZOMBIES
SHE'S NOT THERE	COLIN BLUNSTONE
SHE'S NOT YOU	ELVIS PRESLEY
SHIFTING, WHISPERING SANDS	EAMMON ANDREWS
SHIFTING, WHISPERING SANDS	BILLY VAUGHN
SHINDIG	SHADOWS
SHINE	JOE BROWN AND THE BRUVVERS
SHINE ON SILVER SUN	STRAWBS
SHIPS IN THE NIGHT	BE-BOP DELUXE
SHIRALEE	TOMMY STEELE
SHOES	REPARATA (SOLO)
SHOO-BE-DOO-DAH-DAY	STEVIE WONDER
SHOORAH SHOORAH	BETTY WRIGHT
SHORTNIN' BREAD	VISCOUNTS
SHOT OF RHYTHM AND BLUES	JOHNNY KIDD AND THE PIRATES
SHOTGUN	JUNIOR WALKER AND THE ALL-STARS
SHOTGUN WEDDING	ROY C
SHOUT	LULU AND THE LUVVERS
SHOW ME GIRL	HERMAN'S HERMITS
SHOW ME YOU'RE A WOMAN	MUD
SHOW MUST GO ON	LEO SAYER
SHOWDOWN	ELECTRIC LIGHT ORCHESTRA
SHY GIRL	MARK WYNTER
SI TU DOIS PARTIR	FAIRPORT CONVENTION
SICKMAN BLUES	GOODIES
SIDE-SADDLE	RUSS CONWAY
SIGN OF THE TIMES	PETULA CLARK
SIGNED, SEALED, DELIVERED	STEVIE WONDER
SILENCE IS GOLDEN	TREMELOES
SILHOUETTES	HERMAN'S HERMITS
SILLY LOVE	10 C.C.
SILVER MACHINE	HAWKWIND
SILVERY RAIN	CLIFF RICHARD
SIMON SAYS	1910 FRUITGUM CO.

SIMON SMITH AND HIS AMAZING DANCING BEAR	ALAN PRICE
SIMPLE GAME	FOUR TOPS
SINCE YOU'VE BEEN GONE	ARETHA FRANKLIN
SINCERELY	McGUIRE SISTERS
SING A HAPPY SONG	GEORGE McCRAE
SING A LITTLE SONG	DESMOND DEKKER AND THE ACES
SING A SONG OF FREEDOM	CLIFF RICHARD
SING BABY SING	STYLISTICS
SING DON'T SPEAK	BLACKFOOT SUE
SING IT WITH JOE	JOE HENDERSON
SINK LIKE AN ANGEL	JERRY LORDAN
SING LITTLE BIRDY	PEARL CARR AND TEDDY JOHNSON
SING WITH SHAND	JIMMY SHAND
SINGER SANG HIS SONG	BEE GEES
SINGING DOGS	SINGING DOGS
SINGING THE BLUES	GUY MITCHELL
SINGING THE BLUES	TOMMY STEELE
SINGLE GIRL	SANDY POSIE
SINS OF A FAMILY	P.F. SLOANE
SISTER JANE	NEW WORLD
SITTIN' IN THE PARK	GEORGIE FAME
SITTIN' ON A FENCE	TWICE AS MUCH
SIX TEENS	SWEET
634-5789	WILSON PICKETT
SIX WIVES OF HENRY VIII	B.B.C. ORCHESTRA
SIXTEEN REASONS	CONNIE STEVENS
SIXTEEN TONS	TENNESSEE ERNIE FORD
SIXTY MINUTE MAN	TRAMMPS
SKIING IN THE SNOW	WIGAN'S OVATION
SKIFFLE PARTY (E.P.)	LONNIE DONEGAN
SKIFFLE SESSION (E.P.)	LONNIE DONEGAN
SKWEEZE ME, PLEAZE ME	SLADE
SKY BLUE SHIRT	NORMAN BROOK
SKY HIGH	JIGSAW
SKY PILOT	ERIC BURDON AND THE ANIMALS
SKY WRITER	JACKSON FIVE
SKYLARK	MICHAEL HOLLIDAY
SLEEPWALK	SANTO AND JOHNNY
SLEEPY JOE	HERMAN'S HERMITS
SLEEPY SHORES ('OWEN M.D.' THEME)	JOHNNY PEARSON
SLIP AND SLIDE	MEDICINE HEAD
SLOOP 'JOHN B'	BEACH BOYS
SLOW TWISTIN'	CHUBBY CHECKER
SMALL SAD SAM	PAUL McLEAN
SMARTY PANTS	FIRST CHOICE
SMOKE GETS IN YOUR EYES	PLATTERS
SMOKE GETS IN YOUR EYES	BLUE HAZE
SMOKE GETS IN YOUR EYES	BRYAN FERRY
SMOKESTACK LIGHTNIN'	HOWLIN' WOLF
SMOKEY BLUES AWAY	NEW GENERATION
SMOKIN' IN THE BOYS' ROOM	BROWNSVILLE STATION
SNAKE	AL WILSON
SNAKE IN THE GRASS	DAVE DEE, DOZY, BEAKY, MICK AND TICH
SNOOPY VS. THE RED BARON	ROYAL GUARDSMEN
SNOOPY VS. THE RED BARON	HOTSHOTS
SNOW COACH	RUSS CONWAY
SNOWBIRD	ANNE MURRAY
SO DEEP IS THE NIGHT	KEN DODD
SO DO I	KENNY BALL
SO GOOD	ROY ORBISON
SO IN LOVE WITH YOU	FREDDIE BRECK
SO IT WILL ALWAYS BE	EVERLY BROTHERS
SO LONG, BABY	DEL SHANNON

SO MUCH IN LOVE	TYMES
SO MUCH IN LOVE	MIGHTY AVENGERS
SO MUCH LOVE	TONY BLACKBURN
SO SAD	EVERLY BROTHERS
SO TIRED	FRANKIE VAUGHAN
SOFTLY AS I LEAVE YOU	MATT MONRO
SOFTLY SOFTLY	RUBY MURRAY
SOFTLY SOFTLY	EQUALS
SOFTLY WHISPERING I LOVE YOU	CONGREGATION
SOLDIER BLUE	BUFFY SAINTE-MARIE
SOLDIER BOY	CHEETAHS
SOLDIER BOY	SHIRELLES
SOLEY SOLEY	MIDDLE OF THE ROAD
SOLID GOLD EASY ACTION	T. REX
SOLITAIRE	ANDY WILLIAMS
SOLITAIRE	CARPENTERS
SOME KIND OF A SUMMER	DAVID CASSIDY
SOME KINDA EARTHQUAKE	DUANE EDDY
SOME KINDA FUN	CHRIS MONTEZ
SOME OF YOUR LOVIN'	DUSTY SPRINGFIELD
SOME OTHER GUY	BIG THREE
SOME PEOPLE	CAROLE DEENE
SOME THINGS YOU NEVER GET USED TO	DIANA ROSS AND THE SUPREMES
SOMEBODY	STARGAZERS
SOMEBODY ELSE'S GIRL	BILLY FURY
SOMEBODY HELP ME	SPENCER DAVIS GROUP
SOMEBODY TO LOVE	BRAD NEWMAN
SOMEDAY (YOU'LL WANT ME)	JODIE SANDS
SOMEDAY (YOU'LL WANT ME)	RICKY NELSON
SOMEDAY MAN	MONKEES
SOMEDAY ONE DAY	SEEKERS
SOMEDAY WE'LL BE TOGETHER	DIANA ROSS AND THE SUPREMES
SOMEDAY WE'RE GONNA LOVE AGAIN	SEARCHERS
SOMEONE	JOHNNY MATHIS
SOMEONE ELSE'S BABY	ADAM FAITH
SOMEONE MUST HAVE HURT YOU A LOT	FRANKIE VAUGHAN
SOMEONE ON YOUR MIND	JIMMY YOUNG
SOMEONE SAVED MY LIFE TONIGHT	ELTON JOHN
SOMEONE SOMEONE	BRIAN POOLE AND THE TREMELOES
SOMEONE'S TAKEN MARIA AWAY	ADAM FAITH
SOMETHIN' STUPID	FRANK AND NANCY SINATRA
SOMETHING	GEORGIE FAME
SOMETHING	BEATLES
SOMETHING	SHIRLEY BASSEY
SOMETHING BETTER BEGINNING	HONEYCOMBS
SOMETHING BEAUTIFUL	JACK WILD
SOMETHING 'BOUT YOU BABY I LIKE	TOM JONES
SOMETHING FOR THE GIRL WITH EVERYTHING	SPARKS
SOMETHING HERE IN MY HEART	PAPER DOLLS
SOMETHING IN THE AIR	THUNDERCLAP NEWMAN
SOMETHING MISSING	PETULA CLARK
SOMETHING OLD, SOMETHING NEW	FANTASTICS
SOMETHING ON MY MIND	CHRIS ANDREWS
SOMETHING TELLS ME	CILLA BLACK
SOMETHING'S BEEN MAKING ME BLUE	SMOKEY
SOMETHING'S BURNING	KENNY ROGERS AND THE FIRST EDITION
SOMETHING'S GONNA HAPPEN TONIGHT	SEE 'SOMETHING TELLS ME'
SOMETHING'S GOTTA GIVE	SAMMY DAVIS JR.
SOMETHING'S GOTTEN HOLD OF MY HEART	GENE PITNEY
SOMETHING'S HAPPENING	HERMAN'S HERMITS
SOMEWHERE	P.J. PROBY
SOMEWHERE IN THE COUNTRY	GENE PITNEY

SOMEWHERE MY LOVE	RAY CONNIFF SINGERS
SOMEWHERE MY LOVE	MIKE SAMMES SINGERS
SOMEWHERE MY LOVE	MANUEL AND HIS MUSIC OF THE MOUNTAINS
SON OF A PREACHER MAN	DUSTY SPRINGFIELD
SON OF HICKORY HOLLER'S TRAMP	O.C. SMITH
SON OF MARY	HARRY BELAFONTE
SON OF MY FATHER	CHICORY TIP
SON, THIS IS SHE	JOHN LEYTON
SONG OF JOY	MIGUEL DE LOS RIOS
SONG OF MEXICO	TONY MEEHAN
SONG OF MY LIFE	PETULA CLARK
SONG OF THE DREAMER	JOHNNIE RAY
SONG SUNG BLUE	NEIL DIAMOND
SOOTHE ME	SAM AND DAVE
SORROW	MERSEYS
SORRY DOESN'T ALWAYS MAKE IT RIGHT	DIANA ROSS
SORRY ROBBIE	BERT WEEDON
SORRY SUZANNE	HOLLIES
S.O.S.	ABBA
S.O.S.	EDWIN STARR
SOUL CLAP	BOOKER T. AND THE MGs
SOUL COAXING	RAYMOND LEFEVRE ORCHESTRA
SOUL DEEP	BOX TOPS
SOUL FINGER	BAR KAYS
SOUL LIMBO	BOOKER T. AND THE MGs
SOUL MAN	SAM AND DAVE
SOUL SERENADE	WILLIE MITCHELL
SOUL SISTER, BROWN SUGAR	SAME AND DAVE
SOUND OF SILENCE	BACHELORS
SOUND YOUR FUNKY HORN	K.C. AND THE SUNSHINE BAND
SOUTH AFRICAN MAN	HAMILTON BOHANNON
SPACE ODDITY	DAVID BOWIE
SPANISH EYES	AL MARTINO
SPANISH FLEA	HERB ALPERT AND THE TIJUANA BRASS
SPANISH HARLEM	JIMMY JUSTICE
SPANISH HARLEM	SOUNDS INCORPORATED
SPANISH HARLEM	ARETHA FRANKLIN
SPANISH WINE	CHRIS WHITE
SPARTANS	SOUNDS INCORPORATED
SPEAK TO ME PRETTY	BRENDA LEE
SPECIAL YEARS	VAL DOONICAN
SPEEDY GONZALES	PAT BOONE
SPIDERS AND SNAKES	JIM STAFFORD
SPINNIN' AND SPINNIN'	SYREETA
SPIRIT IN THE SKY	NORMAN GREENBAUM
SPIRIT IS WILLING	PETER STRAKER WITH DR. TELENY
SPLISH SPLASH	BOBBY DARIN
SPLISH SPLASH	CHARLIE DRAKE
SPOOKY	CLASSICS IV
SQUEEZE BOX	WHO
STAGGER LEE	LLOYD PRICE
STAIRWAY OF LOVE	MICHAEL HOLLIDAY
STAIRWAY OF LOVE	TERRY DENE
STAIRWAY TO HEAVEN	NEIL SEDAKA
STAND BY ME	JOHN LENNON
STAND BY ME	KENNY LYNCH
STAND BY YOUR MAN	TAMMY WYNETTE
STANDING IN THE ROAD	BLACKFOOT SUE
STANDING IN THE SHADOW OF LOVE	FOUR TOPS
STANDING ON THE CORNER	FOUR LADS
STANDING ON THE CORNER	KING BROTHERS
STANDING ON THE INSIDE	NEIL SEDAKA
STAR	STEALERS WHEEL

STAR DUST	BILLY WARD AND HIS DOMINOES
STAR ON A T.V. SHOW	STYLISTICS
STARBRIGHT	JOHNNY MATHIS
STARDUST	DAVID ESSEX
STARMAN	DAVID BOWIE
STARRY EYED	MICHAEL HOLLIDAY
STARRY NIGHT	JOYSTRINGS
STARS AND STRIPES	ACKER BILK
STARS SHINE IN YOUR EYES	RONNIE HILTON
START MOVIN'	SAL MINEO
START MOVIN'	TERRY DENE
STAY	MAURICE WILLIAMS
STAY	HOLLIES
STAY AWHILE	DUSTY SPRINGFIELD
STAY WITH ME	BLUE MINK
STAY WITH ME	FACES
STAY WITH ME BABY	WALKER BROTHERS
STAYING IN	BOBBY VEE
STEEL GUITAR AND A GLASS OF WINE	PAUL ANKA
STEP BY STEP	STEVE PERRY
STEP BY STEP	JOE SIMON
STEP INSIDE LOVE	CILLA BLACK
STEP INTO A DREAM	WHITE PLAINS
STEP INTO CHRISTMAS	ELTON JOHN
STILL	KARL DENVER
STILL	KEN DODD
STILL I'M SAD	YARDBIRDS
STILL WATER (LOVE)	FOUR TOPS
STING (ENTERTAINER)	RAGTIMERS
STING (ENTERTAINER)	MARVIN HAMLISCH
STINGRAY	SHADOWS
STIR IT UP	JOHNNY NASH
STONED LOVE	SUPREMES
STONEY END	BARBRA STREISAND
STOOD UP	RICKY NELSON
STOP FEELING SORRY FOR YOURSELF	ADAM FAITH
STOP HER ON SIGHT	EDWIN STARR
STOP IN THE NAME OF LOVE	SUPREMES
STOP, LOOK AND LISTEN	DIANA ROSS AND MARVIN GAYE
STOP, LOOK AND LISTEN	WAYNE FONTANA
STOP, STOP, STOP	HOLLIES
STOP THAT GIRLS	CHRIS ANDREWS
STOP THE WAR NOW	EDWIN STARR
STORM IN A TEACUP	FORTUNES
STORY OF MY LIFE	MICHAEL HOLLIDAY
STORY OF MY LIFE	GARY MILLER
STORY OF MY LIFE	DAVE KING
STORY OF THREE LOVES	WINIFRED ATWELL
STORY OF TINA	RONNIE HARRIS
STORY OF TINA	AL MARTINO
STOW AWAY	BARBARA LYON
STRANGE BAND	FAMILY
STRANGE BREW	CREAM
STRANGE KIND OF WOMAN	DEEP PURPLE
STRANGE LADY IN TOWN	FRANKIE LAINE
STRANGER	SHADOWS
STRANGER IN PARADISE	TONY BENNETT
STRANGER IN PARADISE	DON CORNELL
STRANGER IN PARADISE	TONY MARTIN
STRANGER IN PARADISE	BING CROSBY
STRANGER IN PARADISE	FOUR ACES
STRANGER IN PARADISE	EDDIE CALVERT
STRANGER IN TOWN	DEL SHANNON
STRANGER ON THE SHORE	ACKER BILK

STRANGER ON THE SHORE	ANDY WILLIAMS
STRANGERS IN THE NIGHT	FRANK SINATRA
STRAWBERRY BLONDE	FRANK D'RONE
STRAWBERRY FAIR	ANTHONY NEWLEY
STRAWBERRY FIELDS FOREVER	BEATLES
STREAK	RAY STEVENS
STREET CALLED HOPE	GENE PITNEY
STREET LIFE	ROXY MUSIC
STREETS OF LONDON	RALPH McTELL
STRONG LOVE	SPENCER DAVIS GROUP
STUCK IN THE MIDDLE WITH YOU	STEALERS WHEEL
STUCK ON YOU	ELVIS PRESLEY
STUPID CUPID	CONNIE FRANCIS
SUBSTITUTE	WHO
SUBTERRANEAN HOMESICK BLUES	BOB DYLAN
SUCH A NIGHT	ELVIS PRESLEY
SUCU SUCU	JOE LOSS
SUCU SUCU	TED HEATH
SUCU SUCU	LAURIE JOHNSON
SUCU SUCU	NINA AND FREDERICK
SUCU SUCU	PING PIN AND AL VERLAINE
SUDDENLY THERE'S A VALLEY	JO STAFFORD
SUDDENLY THERE'S A VALLEY	PETULA CLARK
SUDDENLY THERE'S A VALLEY	LEE LAWRENCE
SUDDENLY YOU LOVE ME	TREMELOES
SUE'S GONNA BE MINE	DEL SHANNON
SUGAR AND SPICE	SEARCHERS
SUGAR BABY LOVE	RUBETTES
SUGAR BEE	CANNED HEAT
SUGAR CANDY KISSES	MAC AND KATIE KISSOON
SUGAR ME	LYNSEY DE PAUL
SUGAR MOON	PAT BOONE
SUGAR SHACK	JIMMY GILMER AND THE FIREBALLS
SUGAR SUGAR	ARCHIES
SUGAR SUGAR	SAKHARIN
SUGARTIME	McGUIRE SISTERS
SUGARTIME	ALMA COGAN
SUGARTIME	JIM DALE
SUGAR TOWN	NANCY SINATRA
SUKI YAKI	KYU SAKAMOTO
SUKI YAKI	KENNY BALL
SULTANA	TITANIC
SUMMER (THE FIRST TIME)	BOBBY GOLDSBORO
SUMMER BREEZE	ISLEY BROTHERS
SUMMER HOLIDAY	CLIFF RICHARD
SUMMER IN THE CITY	LOVIN' SPOONFUL
SUMMER IS OVER	FRANK IFIELD
SUMMER NIGHTS	MARIANNE FAITHFUL
SUMMER OF '42	BIDDU ORCHESTRA
SUMMER PLACE (THEME)	PERCY FAITH
SUMMER PLACE (THEME)	NORRIE PARAMOUR
SUMMER SET	ACKER BILK
SUMMER WIND	FRANK SINATRA
SUMMERLOVE SENSATION	BAY CITY ROLLERS
SUMMERTIME	BILLY STEWART
SUMMERTIME	MARCELS
SUMMERTIME	AL MARTINO
SUMMERTIME BLUES	EDDIE COCHRAN
SUMMERTIME BLUES	WHO
SUN AIN'T GONNA SHINE ANYMORE	WALKER BROTHERS
SUN ARISE	ROLF HARRIS
SUNDOWN	GORDON LIGHTFOOT
SUNNY	BOBBY HEBB
SUNNY	GEORGIE FAME

SUNNY AFTERNOON	KINKS
SUNNY HONEY GIRL	CLIFF RICHARD
SUNSHINE DAY	OSIBISA
SUNSHINE GIRL	HERMAN'S HERMITS
SUNSHINE OF YOUR LOVE	LOUIS ARMSTRONG
SUNSHINE OF YOUR LOVE	CREAM
SUNSHINE SUPERMAN	DONOVAN
SUPER LOVE	WIGAN'S OVATION
SUPERGIRL	GRAHAM BONNEY
SUPERSHIP	GEORGE BENSON
SUPERSTAR	CARPENTERS
SUPERSTAR	TEMPTATIONS
SUPERSONIC ROCKET SHIP	KINKS
SUPERSTITION	STEVIE WONDER
SUPERWOMBLE	WOMBLES
SURF CITY	JAN AND DEAN
SURFIN' U.S.A.	BEACH BOYS
SURRENDER	DIANA ROSS
SURROUND YOURSELF WITH SORROW	CILLA BLACK
SUSANNAH'S STILL ALIVE	DAVE DAVIES
SUSIE DARLIN'	TOMMY ROE
SUSPICION	TERRY STAFFORD
SUSPICIOUS MINDS	ELVIS PRESLEY
SUZANNE BEWARE OF THE DEVIL	DANDY LIVINGSTONE
SWAN LAKE	CATS
SWAY	BOBBY RYDELL
SWEARIN' TO GOD	FRANKIE VALLI
SWEET CAROLINE	NEIL DIAMOND
SWEET CHEATIN' RITA	ALVIN STARDUST
SWEET DREAM	JETHRO TULL
SWEET DREAMS	DAVE SAMPSON
SWEET DREAMS	TOMMY McLAIN
SWEET DREAMS	ROY BUCHANAN
SWEET HITCH-HIKER	CREEDANCE CLEARWATER REVIVAL
SWEET ILLUSION	JUNIOR CAMPBELL
SWEET IMPOSSIBLE YOU	BRENDA LEE
SWEET INSPIRATION	JOHNNY JOHNSON AND THE BANDWAGON
SWEET LITTLE SIXTEEN	CHUCK BERRY
SWEET LITTLE SIXTEEN	JERRY LEE LEWIS
SWEET NUTHINS	BRENDA LEE
SWEET NUTHINS	SEARCHERS
SWEET OLD-FASHIONED GIRL	TERESA BREWER
SWEET PEA	MANFRED MANN
SWEET SENSATION	MELODIANS
SWEET SOUL MUSIC	ARTHUR CONLEY
SWEET TALKING GUY	CHIFFONS
SWEET UNDERSTANDING LOVE	FOUR TOPS
SWEET WILLIAM	MILLIE (SMALL)
SWEETER THAN YOU	RICKY NELSON
SWEETHEART	ENGELBERT HUMPERDINCK
SWEETIE PIE	EDDIE COCHRAN
SWEETS FOR MY SWEET	SEARCHERS
SWING LOW SWEET CHARIOT	ERIC CLAPTON
SWING THAT HAMMER	MIKE COTTON
SWING YOUR DADDY	JIM GILSTRAP
SWINGIN' IN THE RAIN	NORMAN VAUGHAN
SWINGIN' LOW	OUTLAWS
SWINGING ON A STAR	BIG DEE IRWIN AND LITTLE EVA
SWINGING SCHOOL	BOBBY RYDELL
SWINGING SHEPHERD BLUES	TED HEATH
SWINGING SHEPHERD BLUES	ELLA FITZGERALD
SWISS MAID	DEL SHANNON
SYLVIA	FOCUS
SYLVIA'S MOTHER	DR. HOOK AND THE MEDICINE SHOW

SYMPATHY	RARE BIRD
TAKE A HEART	SORROW
TAKE A LOOK AROUND	TEMPTATIONS
TAKE A MESSAGE TO MARY	EVERLY BROTHERS
TAKE FIVE	DAVE BRUBECK
TAKE GOOD CARE OF HER	ADAM WADE
TAKE GOOD CARE OF MY BABY	BOBBY VEE
TAKE GOOD CARE OF YOURSELF	THREE DEGREES
TAKE IT OR LEAVE IT	SEARCHERS
TAKE IT TO THE LIMIT	EAGLES
TAKE ME BACK 'OME	SLADE
TAKE ME FOR WHAT I'M WORTH	SEARCHERS
TAKE ME GIRL I'M READY	JUNIOR WALKER AND THE ALL-STARS
TAKE ME HIGH	CLIFF RICHARD
TAKE ME HOME COUNTRY ROADS	OLIVIA NEWTON-JOHN
TAKE ME IN YOUR ARMS AND LOVE ME	GLADYS KNIGHT AND THE PIPS
TAKE ME IN YOUR ARMS AND LOVE ME	DOOBIE BROTHERS
TAKE ME TO THE MARDI GRAS	PAUL SIMON
TAKE ME TO YOUR HEART AGAIN	VINCE HILL
TAKE THESE CHAINS FROM MY HEART	RAY CHARLES
TAKE TO THE MOUNTAINS	RICHARD BARNES
TAKE YOUR MAMA FOR A RIDE	LULU
TALKIN' ARMY BLUES	JOSH MACRAE
TALL DARK STRANGER	ROSE BRENNAN
TALLAHASSEE LASSIE	FREDDY CANNON
TALLAHASSEE LASSIE	TOMMY STEELE
TALLY MEN	JEFF BECK GROUP
TAMMY	DEBBIE REYNOLDS
TANSY	ALEX TANSY
TAP TURNS ON THE WATER	C.C.S.
TASTE OF HONEY	ACKER BILK
TAVERN IN THE TOWN	TERRY LIGHTFOOT
TCHAIKOVSKY ONE	SECOND CITY SOUND
TEA FOR TWO CHA CHA	TOMMY DORSEY
TEACH ME TO TWIST	CHUBBY CHECKER AND BOBBY RYDELL
TEACH ME TONIGHT	DECASTRO SISTERS
TEACHER	JETHRO TULL
TEAR FELL	TERESA BREWER
TEARDROP CITY	MONKEES
TEARDROPS	SANTO AND JOHNNY
TEARS	KEN DODD
TEARS	DANNY WILLIAMS
TEARS I CRIED FOR YOU	GLITTER BAND
TEARS IN THE WIND	CHICKEN SHACK
TEARS OF A CLOWN	SMOKEY ROBINSON AND THE MIRACLES
TEARS ON MY PILLOW	JOHNNY NASH
TEARS ON THE TELEPHONE	CLAUDE FRANCOIS
TEARS WON'T WASH AWAY THE HEARTACHES	KEN DODD
TEASE ME	KEITH KELLY
TEDDY BEAR	ELVIS PRESLEY
TEEN ANGEL	MARK DINNING
TEEN BEAT	SANDY NELSON
TEENAGE DREAM	T. REX
TEENAGE IDOL	RICKY NELSON
TEENAGER IN LOVE	MARTY WILDE
TEENAGER IN LOVE	CRAIG DOUGLAS
TEENAGE LAMENT	ALICE COOPER
TEENAGE RAMPAGE	SWEET
TEENSVILLE	CHET ATKINS
TELEGRAM SAM	T. REX
TELL HER I'M NOT AT HOME	IKE AND TINA TURNER
TELL HER NO	ZOMBIES

TELL HIM	HELLO
TELL HIM	EXCITERS
TELL HIM	BILLIE DAVIS
TELL IT TO MY FACE	KEITH
TELL IT TO THE RAIN	FOUR SEASONS
TELL LAURA I LOVE HER	RICKY VALANCE
TELL ME WHAT HE SAID	HELEN SHAPIRO
TELL ME WHAT YOU WANT	JIMMY RUFFIN
TELL ME WHEN	APPLEJACKS
TELL ME WHY	ELVIS PRESLEY
TELL ME WHY	ALVIN STARDUST
TELSTAR	TORNADOS
TEMMA HARBOUR	MARY HOPKIN
TEMPTATION	EVERLY BROTHERS
TEN SWINGING BOTTLES	PETE CHESTER AND THE CHESTERNUTS
TEQUILA	CHAMPS
TERESA	JOE DOLAN
TERRY	TWINKLE
THANK U VERY MUCH	SCAFFOLD
THANKS A LOT	BRENDA LEE
THANKS FOR SAVING MY LIFE	BILLY PAUL
THANKS FOR THE MEMORY	SLADE
THAT GIRL BELONGS TO YESTERDAY	GENE PITNEY
THAT LADY	ISLEY BROTHERS
THAT MEANS A LOT	P.J. PROBY
THAT NOISE	ANTHONY NEWLEY
THAT OLD BLACK MAGIC	SAMMY DAVIS JR.
THAT SAME OLD FEELING	PICKETTYWITCH
THAT'LL BE THE DAY	CRICKETS
THAT'S HOW A LOVE SONG WAS BORN	RAY BURNS
THAT'S HOW STRONG MY LOVE IS	IN-CROWD
THAT'S LIFE	FRANK SINATRA
THAT'S LOVE	BILLY FURY
THAT'S MY HOME	ACKER BILK
THAT'S NICE	NEIL CHRISTIAN
THAT'S THE WAY	HONEYCOMBS
THAT'S THE WAY	CHARLES DICKENS
THAT'S THE WAY GOD PLANNED IT	BILLY PRESTON
THAT'S THE WAY I LIKE IT	K.C. AND THE SUNSHINE BAND
THAT'S WHAT I WANT	MARAUDERS
THAT'S WHAT I WANT TO BE	NEIL REID
THAT'S WHAT LIFE IS ALL ABOUT	BING CROSBY
THAT'S WHAT LOVE WILL DO	JOE BROWN
THAT'S WHEN I SEE THE BLUE	JIM REEVES
THAT'S WHEN THE MUSIC TAKES ME	NEIL SEDAKA
THAT'S WHY I'M CRYING	IVY LEAGUE
THAT'S YOU	NAT 'KING' COLE
THEM THERE EYES	EMILE FORD AND THE CHECKMATES
THEME FOR A DREAM	CLIFF RICHARD
THEME FOR YOUNG LOVERS	SHADOWS
THEME FROM DIXIE	DUANE EDDY
THEN CAME YOU	DIONNE WARWICK
THEN HE KISSED ME	CRYSTALS
THEN I KISSED HER	BEACH BOYS
THEN YOU CAN TELL ME GOODBYE	CASINOS
THERE ARE MORE QUESTIONS THEN ANSWERS	JOHNNY NASH
THERE BUT FOR FORTUNE	JOAN BAEZ
THERE GOES MY EVERYTHING	ENGELBERT HUMPERDINCK
THERE GOES MY EVERYTHING	ELVIS PRESLEY
THERE GOES MY FIRST LOVE	DRIFTERS
THERE GOES THAT SONG AGAIN	GARY MILLER
THERE IT GO	VIKKI CARR
THERE IS A MOUNTAIN	DONOVAN

THERE, I'VE SAID IT AGAIN	BOBBY VINTON
THERE, I'VE SAID IT AGAIN	AL SAXON
THERE MUST BE A WAY	FRANKIE VAUGHAN
THERE WILL NEVER BE ANOTHER YOU	CHRIS MONTEZ
THERE WON'T BE MANY COMING HOME	ROY ORBISON
THERE'LL NEVER BE ANYONE ELSE BUT YOU	RICKY NELSON
THERE'S A KIND OF HUSH	HERMAN'S HERMITS
THERE'S A KIND OF HUSH	CARPENTERS
THERE'S A HEARTACHE FOLLOWING ME	JIM REEVES
THERE'S A WHOLE LOT OF LOVING GOING ON	GUY AND DOLLS
THERE'S ALWAYS SOMETHING THERE TO REMIND ME	SANDIE SHAW
THERE'S GONNA BE A SHOWDOWN	ARCHIE BELL AND THE DRELLS
THESE BOOTS ARE MADE FOR WALKING	NANCY SINATRA
THEY LONG TO BE CLOSE TO YOU	CARPENTERS
THEY'RE COMING TO TAKE ME AWAY, HA, HA	NAPOLEON XIV
THING CALLED LOVE	JOHNNY CASH
THINGS	BOBBY DARIN
THINGS GET BETTER	EDDIE FLOYD
THINK	ARETHA FRANKLIN
THINK	CHRIS FARLOWE
THINK	BRENDA LEE
THINK ABOUT THAT	DANDY LIVINGSTONE
THINK ABOUT YOUR CHILDREN	MARY HOPKIN
THINK IT ALL OVER	SANDIE SHAW
THINK IT OVER	CRICKETS
THINK OF ME (WHEREVER YOU ARE)	KEN DODD
THINK SOMETIMES ABOUT ME	SANDIE SHAW
THINKIN' AIN'T FOR ME	PAUL JONES
THINKING OF YOU BABY	DAVE CLARK FIVE
THIRD FINGER, LEFT HAND	PEARLS
THIS AND THAT	TOM JONES
THIS DOOR SWINGS BOTH WAYS	HERMAN'S HERMITS
THIS FLIGHT TONIGHT	NAZARETH
THIS GOLDEN RING	FORTUNES
THIS GUY'S IN LOVE WITH YOU	HERB ALPERT
THIS IS IT	ADAM FAITH
THIS IS MY SONG	PETULA CLARK
THIS IS MY SONG	HARRY SECOMBE
THIS IS THE STORY OF MY LOVE	WIZZARD
THIS LITTLE BIRD	MARIANNE FAITHFUL
THIS LITTLE BIRD	NASHVILLE TEENS
THIS MONDAY MORNING FEELING	TITO SIMON
THIS OLD HEART OF MINE	ISLEY BROTHERS
THIS OLD HEART OF MINE	ROD STEWART
THIS OLE HOUSE	ROSEMARY CLOONEY
THIS OLE HOUSE	BILLIE ANTHONY
THIS STRANGE EFFECT	DAVE BERRY AND THE CRUISERS
THIS TIME	TROY SHONDELL
THIS TOWN AIN'T BIG ENOUGH	SPARKS
THIS WHEEL'S ON FIRE	JULIE DRISCOLL WITH THE BRIAN AUGER TRINITY
THIS WILL BE	NATALIE COLE
THIS WORLD IS NOT MY HOME	JIM REEVES
TIGER FEET	MUD
THOSE WERE THE DAYS	MARY HOPKIN
THOU SHALT NOT STEAL	FREDDIE AND THE DREAMERS
THOUSAND STARS	BILLY FURY
THREE BELLS	BROWNS
THREE BELLS	BRIAN POOLE AND THE TREMELOES
THREE LITTLE WORDS	APPLEJACKS
THREE NIGHTS A WEEK	FATS DOMINO

THREE PENNY OPERA (MACK THE KNIFE)	RICHARD HAYMAN AND JAN AUGUST
THREE PENNY OPERA (MACK THE KNIFE)	DICK HYMAN TRIO
THREE PENNY OPERA (MACK THE KNIFE)	BILLY VAUGHN
THREE STARS	TOMMY DEE WITH CAROL KAY AND THE TEEN-AIRES
THREE STEPS TO HEAVEN	RUBY WRIGHT
THREE STEPS TO HEAVEN	EDDIE COCHRAN
THROW DOWN A LINE	CLIFF RICHARD AND HANK MARVIN
THUNDERBALL	TOM JONES
THUS SPAKE ZARATHUSTRA (ALSO SPRACH ZARATHUSTRA) ('2001')	DEODATO
THUS SPAKE ZARATHUSTRA (ALSO SPRACH ZARATHUSTRA) ('2001')	MAAZEL AND THE NEW PHILHARMONIC ORCHESTRA
TICKET TO RIDE	BEATLES
TICKLE ME	ALAN PRICE
TIE A YELLOW RIBBON ROUND THE OLD OAK TREE	DAWN
TIE ME KANGAROO DOWN, SPORT	ROLF HARRIS
TIJUANA TAXI	HERB ALPERT
'TIL I KISSED YOU	EVERLY BROTHERS
TILL	TOM JONES
TILL	TONY BENNETT
TILL	DOROTHY SQUIRES
TILL THE END OF THE DAY	KINKS
TILL THERE WAS YOU	PEGGY LEE
TIME	CRAIG DOUGLAS
TIME ALONE WILL TELL	MALCOLM ROBERTS
TIME AND THE RIVER	NAT 'KING' COLE
TIME DRAGS BY	CLIFF RICHARD
TIME FOR LIVING	ASSOCIATION
TIME HAS COME	ADAM FAITH
TIME HAS COME	P.P. ARNOLD
TIME INBETWEEN	CLIFF RICHARD
TIME IS TIGHT	BOOKER T. AND THE MGs
TIME SELLER	SPENCER DAVIS GROUP
TIME WILL TELL	IAN GREGORY
TIMES THEY ARE A-CHANGIN'	BOB DYLAN
TIMES THEY ARE A-CHANGIN'	PETER, PAUL AND MARY
TIMES THEY ARE A-CHANGIN'	IAN CAMPBELL FOLK GROUP
TIN SOLDIER	SMALL FACES
TIPS OF MY FINGERS	DES O'CONNOR
TIRED OF BEING ALONE	AL GREEN
TIRED OF WAITING FOR YOU	KINKS
TO BE LOVED	MALCOLM VAUGHAN
TO KNOW HIM IS TO LOVE HIM	TEDDY BEARS
TO KNOW HIM IS TO LOVE HIM	PETER AND GORDON
TO LOVE SOMEBODY	NINA SIMONE
TO MAKE A BIG MAN CRY	P.J. PROBY
TO WHOM IT MAY CONCERN	CHRIS ANDREWS
TOAST OF LOVE	THREE DEGREES
TOBACCO ROAD	NASHVILLE TEENS
TODAY	SANDIE SHAW
TODAY'S TEARDROPS	ROY ORBISON
TOGETHER	CONNIE FRANCIS
TOGETHER	RAY CHARLES
TOGETHER	P.J. PROBY
TOGETHERNESS	MIKE PRESTON
TOKOLOSHE MAN	JOHN KONGOS
TOKYO MELODY	HELMUT ZACHARIAS
TOM DOOLEY	KINGSTON TRIO
TOM HARK	ELIAS AND HIS ZIG ZAG JIVE FLUTES
TOM PILLIBI	JACQUELINE BOYER

TOM THE PEEPER	ACT ONE
TOM TOM TURNAROUND	NEW WORLD
TOMBOY	PERRY COMO
TOMORROW	SANDIE SHAW
TOMORROW	JOHNNY BRANDON
TOMORROW RISING	CLIFF RICHARD
TOMORROW TOMORROW	BEE GEES
TOMORROW'S CLOWN	MARTY WILDE
TONIGHT	RUBETTES
TONIGHT	MOVE
TONIGHT	SHIRLEY BASSEY
TONIGHT	VELVETS
TONIGHT IN TOKYO	SANDIE SHAW
TOO BEAUTIFUL TO LAST	ENGELBERT HUMPERDINCK
TOO BIG	SUZI QUATRO
TOO BUSY THINKIN' 'BOUT MY BABY	MARVIN GAYE
TOO BUSY THINKIN' 'BOUT MY BABY	MARDI GRAS
TOO GOOD	LITTLE TONY
TOO GOOD TO BE FORGOTTEN	CHI-LITES
TOO MANY BEAUTIFUL GIRLS	CLINTON FORD
TOO MANY RIVERS	BRENDA LEE
TOO MUCH	ELVIS PRESLEY
TOO MUCH TEQUILA	CHAMPS
TOO SOON TO KNOW	ROY ORBISON
TOO YOUNG	DONNY OSMOND
TOO YOUNG TO GO STEADY	NAT 'KING' COLE
TOP OF THE WORLD	CARPENTERS
TOP TEEN BABY	GARY MILLS
TORRERO	JULIUS LA ROSA
TOSSING AND TURNING	IVY LEAGUE
TOUCH ME IN THE MORNING	DIANA ROSS
TOUCH ME, TOUCH ME	DAVE DEE, DOZY, BEAKY, MICK AND TICH
TOUCH TOO MUCH	ARROWS
TOUS LES GARCONS ET LES FILLES	FRANCOISE HARDY
TOWER OF STRENGTH	GENE McDANIELS
TOWER OF STRENGTH	FRANKIE VAUGHAN
TOWN CRIER	CRAIG DOUGLAS
TOWN WITHOUT PITY	GENE PITNEY
TOY	CASUALS
TOY BALLOONS	RUSS CONWAY
TRACKS OF MY TEARS	LINDA RONSTADT
TRACKS OF MY TEARS	SMOKEY ROBINSON AND THE MIRACLES
TRACY	CUFFLINKS
TRAGEDY	ARGENT
TRAIL OF THE LONESOME PINE	LAUREL AND HARDY
TRAIN OF LOVE	ALMA COGAN
TRAIN TO SKAVILLE	ETHIOPIANS
TRAIN TOUR TO RAINBOW CITY	PYRAMIDS
TRAINS AND BOATS AND PLANES	BURT BACHARACH
TRAINS AND BOATS AND PLANES	BILLY J. KRAMER AND THE DAKOTAS
TRAMP	OTIS REDDING AND CARLA THOMAS
TRANSISTOR RADIO	BENNY HILL
TRAVELLIN' HOME	VERA LYNN
TRAVELLIN' MAN	RICKY NELSON
TRAVELLING BAND	CREEDENCE CLEARWATER REVIVAL
TRAVELLING LIGHT	CLIFF RICHARD AND THE SHADOWS
TREAT HER RIGHT	ROY HEAD
TRIBUTE TO A KING	WILLIAM BELL
TRIBUTE TO BUDDY HOLLY	MIKE BERRY AND THE OUTLAWS
TRIBUTE TO JIM REEVES	LARRY CUNNINGHAM AND THE MIGHTY AVONS
TROMBONE	KREWCUTS
T-R-O-U-B-L-E	ELVIS PRESLEY
TROUBLE IS MY MIDDLE NAME	BROOK BROTHERS
TROUBLE IS MY MIDDLE NAME	FOUR PENNIES
TROUBLE WITH HARRY	ALFIE AND HARRY

TRUCK ON (TYKE)	T. REX
TRUDIE	JOE HENDERSON
TRUE LOVE	BING CROSBY AND GRACE KELLY
TRUE LOVE	RICHARD CHAMBERLAIN
TRUE LOVE	TERRY LIGHTFOOT
TRUE LOVE FOR EVERMORE	BACHELORS
TRUE LOVE WAYS	BUDDY HOLLY
TRUE LOVE WAYS	PETER AND GORDON
TRY A LITTLE KINDNESS	GLEN CAMPBELL
TRY A LITTLE TENDERNESS	OTIS REDDING
TRY MY WORLD	GEORGIE FAME
TRY TO REMEMBER	GLADYS KNIGHT AND THE PIPS
TRY TO UNDERSTAND	LULU
TRYIN' TO GET TO YOU	ELVIS PRESLEY
TRYING TO FORGET	JIM REEVES
T.S.O.P.	M.F.S.B.
TUBULAR BELLS ('EXORCIST' THEME)	MIKE OLDFIELD
TULIPS FROM AMSTERDAM	MAX BYGRAVES
TUMBLING DICE	ROLLING STONES
TUMBLING TUMBLEWEEDS	SLIM WHITMAN
TURN IT DOWN	SWEET
TURN, TURN, TURN	BYRDS
TURN YOUR RADIO ON	RAY STEVENS
TURQUOISE	DONOVAN
TUTTI FRUTTI	LITTLE RICHARD
TUXEDO JUNCTION	MANHATTAN TRANSFER
TWEEDLEDEE	GEORGIA GIBBS
TWEEDLEDEE	FRANKIE VAUGHAN
TWEEDLEDEE	LITTLE JIMMY OSMOND
TWEEDLEDEE, TWEEDLEDUM	MIDDLE OF THE ROAD
TWELFTH OF NEVER	CLIFF RICHARD
TWELFTH OF NEVER	DONNY OSMOND
TWELFTH STREET RAG	BERT WEEDON
TWELVE STEPS TO LOVE	BRIAN POOLE AND THE TREMELOES
TWENTIETH CENTURY BOY	T. REX
25 MILES	EDWIN STARR
25 OR 6 TO 4	CHICAGO
24 HOURS FROM TULSA	GENE PITNEY
24 SYCAMORE	GENE PITNEY
20 TINY FINGERS	STARGAZERS
20 TINY FINGERS	ALMA COGAN
20 TINY FINGERS	CORONETS
TWILIGHT TIME	PLATTERS
TWINKIE LEE	GARY WALKER
TWINKLE TOES	ROY ORBISON
TWIST	CHUBBY CHECKER
TWIST AND SHOUT	BRIAN POOLE AND THE TREMELOES
TWIST, TWIST	LES CHAKADRAS
TWISTING THE NIGHT AWAY	SAM COOKE
'TWIXT TWELVE AND TWENTY	PAT BOONE
TWO DIFFERENT WORLDS	RONNIE HILTON
TWO KINDS OF TEARDROPS	DEL SHANNON
TWO LITTLE BOYS	ROLF HARRIS
TWO SILHOUETTES	DEL SHANNON
TWO STREETS	VAL DOONICAN

2001
  (ALSO SPRACH ZARATHUSTRA)
  (THUS SPAKE ZARATHUSTRA)
	DEODATA

2001
  (ALSO SPRACH ZARATHUSTRA)
  (THUS SPAKE ZARATHUSTRA)
	MAAZEL AND THE NEW PHILHARMONIC
	  ORCHESTRA

UGLY DUCKLING	MIKE REID
UH HUH	KEITH KELLY
UM UM UM UM UM UM	MAJOR LANCE

UM UM UM UM UM UM	WAYNE FONTANA
UN BANC, UNE ARBRE, UNE RUE	SEVERINE
UNA PALOMA BLANCA	GEORGE BAKER SELECTION
UNA PALOMA BLANCA	JONATHAN KING
UNCHAINED MELODY	AL HIBBLER
UNCHAINED MELODY	LES BAXTER
UNCHAINED MELODY	LIBERACE
UNCHAINED MELODY	JIMMY YOUNG
UNCHAINED MELODY	RIGHTEOUS BROTHERS
UNDER MY THUMB	WHO
UNDER MY THUMB	WAYNE GIBSON
UNDER THE BRIDGES OF PARIS	EARTHA KITT
UNDER THE BRIDGES OF PARIS	DEAN MARTIN
UNDERNEATH THE BLANKET GO	GILBERT O'SULLIVAN
UNITED WE STAND	BROTHERHOOD OF MAN
UNIVERSAL	SMALL FACES
UNSQUARE DANCE	DAVE BRUBECK
UNTIL IT'S TIME FOR YOU TO GO	FOUR PENNIES
UNTIL IT'S TIME FOR YOU TO GO	ELVIS PRESLEY
UNTIL YOU COME BACK TO ME	ARETHA FRANKLIN
UP AROUND THE BEND	CREEDENCE CLEARWATER REVIVAL
UP IN A PUFF OF SMOKE	POLLY BROWN
UP ON THE ROOF	KENNY LYNCH
UP ON THE ROOF	JULIE GRANT
UP THE LADDER TO THE ROOF	SUPREMES
UP THE POOL	JETHRO TULL
UP, UP AND AWAY	JOHNNY MANN SINGERS
UPTIGHT (EVERYTHING'S ALRIGHT)	STEVIE WONDER
URBAN GUERILLA	HAWKWIND
URGE	FREDDIE CANNON
U.S. MALE	ELVIS PRESLEY
VACATION	CONNIE FRANCIS
VADO VIA	DRUPI
VALENTINO	CONNIE FRANCIS
VALLERI	MONKEES
VALLEY OF TEARS	BUDDY HOLLY
VALLEY OF THE DOLLS	DIONNE WARWICK
VAYA CON DIOS	MILLICAN AND NESBITT
VEHICLE	IDES OF MARCH
VENI, VIDI, VICI	RONNIE HILTON
VENTURA HIGHWAY	AMERICA
VENUS	SHOCKING BLUE
VENUS IN BLUE JEANS	MARK WYNTER
VERY PRECIOUS LOVE	DORIS DAY
VERY THOUGHT OF YOU	TONY BENNETT
VICTORIA	KINKS
VIETNAM	JIMMY CLIFF
VINCENT	DON McLEAN
VIRGIN MARY	LONNIE DONEGAN
VIRGINIA PLAIN	ROXY MUSIC
VISIONS	CLIFF RICHARD
VIVA BOBBY JOE	EQUALS
VIVA EL FULHAM	COTTAGERS
VIVA LAS VEGAS	ELVIS PRESLEY
VOICE IN THE WILDERNESS	CLIFF RICHARD
VOICES IN THE SKY	MOODY BLUES
VOLARE	DOMENICO MODUGNO
VOLARE	MARINO MARINI
VOLARE	DEAN MARTIN
VOLARE	BOBBY RYDELL
VOODOO CHILE	JIMI HENDRIX
WADE IN THE WATER	RAMSEY LEWIS TRIO
WAIT FOR ME	MALCOLM VAUGHAN
WAIT FOR ME DARLING	JOAN REGAN

WAIT FOR ME MARIANNE	MARMALADE
WAKE UP LITTLE SUSIE	EVERLY BROTHERS
WAKE UP LITTLE SUSIE	KING BROTHERS
WALK AWAY	SHANE FENTON
WALK AWAY	MATT MONRO
WALK AWAY FROM LOVE	DAVID RUFFIN
WALK AWAY RENEE	FOUR TOPS
WALK, DON'T RUN	VENTURES
WALK, DON'T RUN	JOHN BARRY
WALK HAND IN HAND	TONY MARTIN
WALK HAND IN HAND	RONNIE CARROLL
WALK HAND IN HAND	JIMMY PARKINSON
WALK HAND IN HAND	GERRY AND THE PACEMAKERS
WALK IN THE BLACK FOREST	HORST JANOWSKI
WALK IN THE NIGHT	JUNIOR WALKER AND THE ALL-STARS
WALK LIKE A MAN	FOUR SEASONS
WALK ON	ROY ORBISON
WALK ON BY	LEROY VAN DYKE
WALK ON BY	DIONNE WARWICK
WALK ON GILDED SPLINTERS	MARSHA HUNT
WALK ON THE WILD SIDE	LOU REED
WALK RIGHT BACK	EVERLY BROTHERS
WALK RIGHT BACK	PERRY COMO
WALK RIGHT IN	ROOFTOP SINGERS
WALK TALL	VAL DOONICAN
WALK WITH FAITH IN YOUR HEART	BACHELORS
WALK WITH ME	SEEKERS
WALK WITH ME MY ANGEL	DON CHARLES
WALK WITH ME, TALK WITH ME, DARLING	FOUR TOPS
WALKIN' BACK TO HAPPINESS	HELEN SHAPIRO
WALKIN' IN THE RAIN WITH THE ONE I LOVE	LOVE UNLIMITED
WALKIN' TALL	ADAM FAITH
WALKIN' THE DOG	DENNISONS
WALKING	C.C.S.
WALKING ALONE	RICHARD ANTHONY
WALKING IN RHYTHM	BLACKBYRDS
WALKING IN THE RAIN	RONETTES
WALKING IN THE RAIN	WALKER BROTHERS
WALKING IN THE RAIN	PARTRIDGE FAMILY
WALKING MIRACLE	ESSEX
WALKING MIRACLE	LIMMIE AND FAMILY COOKING
WALKING MY CAT NAMED DOG	NORMA TANEGA
WALKING THE FLOOR OVER YOU	PAT BOONE
WALKING TO NEW ORLEANS	FATS DOMINO
WALL STREET SHUFFLE	10 C.C.
WALLS FELL DOWN	MARBLES
WAM BAM	HANDLEY FAMILY
WANDERER	DION
WANDERIN' EYES	CHARLIE GRACIE
WANDERIN' EYES	FRANKIE VAUGHAN
WANDERIN' STAR	LEE MARVIN
WANTED	PERRY COMO
WANTED	AL MARTINO
WAR	EDWIN STARR
WAR LORD	SHADOWS
WARM AND TENDER LOVE	PERCY SLEDGE
WARMED OVER KISSES	BRIAN HYLAND
WARPAINT	BROOK BROTHERS
WATCH ME	LABI SIFFRE
WATCHING THE RIVER FLOW	BOB DYLAN
WATER	GENO WASHINGTON AND THE RAM-JAM BAND
WATER IS OVER MY HEAD	ROCKIN' BERRIES
WATER WATER	TOMMY STEELE

WATERLOO	ABBA
WATERLOO SUNSET	SMALL FACES
WAY BACK HOME	JUNIOR WALKER AND THE ALL-STARS
WAY DOWN YONDER IN NEW ORLEANS	FREDDIE CANNON
WAY I WANT TO TOUCH YOU	CAPTAIN AND TENILLE
WAY IT USED TO BE	ENGELBERT HUMPERDINCK
WAY OF LIFE	FAMILY DOGG
WAY WE WERE	BARBRA STREISAND
WAY YOU LOOK TONIGHT	DENNY SEYTON
WAY YOU LOOK TONIGHT	LETTERMEN
WAY YOU LOOK TONIGHT	EDWARD WOODWARD
WAYWARD WIND	GOGI GRANT
WAYWARD WIND	TEX RITTER
WAYWARD WIND	FRANK IFIELD
WE ARE IN LOVE	ADAM FAITH
WE ARE NOT ALONE	FRANKIE VAUGHAN
WE CAN WORK IT OUT	BEATLES
WE CAN WORK IT OUT	STEVIE WONDER
WE DO IT	R. & J. STONE
WE LOVE EACH OTHER	CHARLIE RICH
WE LOVE YOU	ROLLING STONES
WE SHALL OVERCOME	JOAN BAEZ
WE WILL	GILBERT O'SULLIVAN
WE WILL MAKE LOVE	RUSS HAMILTON
WE WILL NEVER BE AS YOUNG AS THIS	DANNY WILLIAMS
WEAK SPOT	EVELYN THOMAS
WEAR MY RING AROUND YOUR NECK	ELVIS PRESLEY
WEATHER FORECAST	MASTERSINGERS
WEDDING	JULIE ROGERS
WEDDING BELL BLUES	FIFTH DIMENSION
WEDDING BELLS	EDDIE FISHER
WEDDING RING	RUSS HAMILTON
WEE TOM	LORD ROCKINGHAM'S XI
WEEKEND	EDDIE COCHRAN
WEIGHT	BAND
WELCOME HOME	PETERS AND LEE
WELCOME TO MY WORLD	JIM REEVES
WE'LL BE WITH YOU	POTTERS
WE'LL FIND OUR DAY	STEPHANIE DE SYKES
WE'LL SING IN THE SUNSHINE	LANCASTRIANS
WELL I ASK YOU	EDEN KANE
WE'RE GONNA GO FISHIN'	HANK LOCKLIN
WE'RE ONLY YOUNG ONCE	AVONS
WE'RE THROUGH	HOLLIES
WEST OF ZANZIBAR	ANTHONY STEELE AND THE RADIO REVELLER
WESTERN MOVIES	OLYMPICS
WET DREAM	MAX ROMEO
WE'VE GOTTA GET OUT OF THIS PLACE	ANIMALS
WE'VE ONLY JUST BEGUN	CARPENTERS
WHAT A CRAZY WORLD WE LIVE IN	JOE BROWN AND THE BRUVVERS
WHAT A DIFFERENCE A DAY MAKES	ESTHER PHILIPS
WHAT A MOUTH	TOMMY STEELE
WHAT A PARTY	FATS DOMINO
WHAT A WOMAN IN LOVE WON'T DO	SANDIE POSEY
WHAT A WONDERFUL WORLD	LOUIS ARMSTRONG
WHAT AM I GONNA DO WITH YOU	BARRY WHITE
WHAT AM I TO YOU	KENNY LYNCH
WHAT ARE YOU DOING SUNDAY	DAWN
WHAT BECOMES OF THE BROKEN-HEARTED	JIMMY RUFFIN
WHAT DO YOU SAY	CHUBBY CHECKER
WHAT DO YOU WANT	ADAM FAITH
WHAT DO YOU WANT TO MAKE THOSE EYES AT ME FOR	EMILE FORD AND THE CHECKMATES
WHAT DOES IT TAKE TO WIN YOUR LOVE	JUNIOR WALKER AND THE ALL-STARS

WHAT GOOD AM I	CILLA BLACK
WHAT HAVE THEY DONE TO MY SONG MA	NEW SEEKERS
WHAT HAVE THEY DONE TO THE RAIN	SEARCHERS
WHAT IN THE WORLD'S COME OVER YOU	JACK SCOTT
WHAT IN THE WORLD'S COME OVER YOU	ROCKIN' BERRIES
WHAT IN THE WORLD'S COME OVER YOU	TAM WHITE
WHAT IS A MAN	FOUR TOPS
WHAT IS LIFE	OLIVIA NEWTON-JOHN
WHAT IS TRUTH	JOHNNY CASH
WHAT KIND OF FOOL AM I	ANTHONY NEWLEY
WHAT KIND OF FOOL AM I	SHIRLEY BASSEY
WHAT KIND OF FOOL AM I	SAMMY DAVIS JR.
WHAT MADE MILWAUKEE FAMOUS (MADE A LOSER OUT OF ME)	ROD STEWART
WHAT NOW	ADAM FAITH
WHAT NOW MY LOVE	SONNY AND CHER
WHAT NOW MY LOVE	SHIRLEY BASSEY
WHAT TO DO	BUDDY HOLLY
WHAT WILL MARY SAY	JOHNNY MATHIS
WHAT WOULD I BE	VAL DOONICAN
WHATCHA GONNA DO ABOUT IT	DORIS TROY
WHATCHA GONNA DO ABOUT IT	SMALL FACES
WHATCHA GONNA DO NOW	CHRIS ANDREWS
WHAT'D I SAY	JERRY LEE LEWIS
WHATEVER GETS YOU THROUGH THE NIGHT	JOHN LENNON
WHATEVER HAPPENED TO YOU ('LIKELY LADS' THEME)	HIGHLY LIKELY
WHATEVER WILL BE WILL BE (QUE SERA SERA)	DORIS DAY
WHATEVER WILL BE WILL BE (QUE SERA SERA)	GENO WASHINGTON AND THE RAM JAM BAND
WHAT'S NEW PUSSYCAT	TOM JONES
WHAT'S YOUR NAME	CHICORY TIP
WHEELS	STRING-A-LONGS
WHEELS CHA-CHA	JOE LOSS
WHEN	KALIN TWINS
WHEN A MAN LOVES A WOMAN	PERCY SLEDGE
WHEN BOUZOUKIS PLAYED	VICKY LEANDROS
WHEN I COME HOME	SPENCER DAVIS GROUP
WHEN I FALL IN LOVE	NAT 'KING' COLE
WHEN I FALL IN LOVE	DONNY OSMOND
WHEN I GET HOME	SEARCHERS
WHEN I GROW UP TO BE A MAN	BEACH BOYS
WHEN I WAS YOUNG	ERIC BURDON AND THE ANIMALS
WHEN I'M DEAD AND GONE	McGUINNESS FLINT
WHEN JOHNNY COMES MARCHING HOME	ADAM FAITH
WHEN JULIE COMES AROUND	CUFFLINKS
WHEN LOVE COMES ALONG	MATT MONRO
WHEN MY LOVE COMES ROUND AGAIN	KEN DODD
WHEN MEXICO GAVE UP THE RHUMBA	MITCHELL TOROK
WHEN MY LITTLE GIRL IS SMILING	DRIFTERS
WHEN MY LITTLE GIRL IS SMILING	CRAIG DOUGLAS
WHEN MY LITTLE GIRL IS SMILING	JIMMY JUSTICE
WHEN THE GIRL IN YOUR ARMS IS THE GIRL IN YOUR HEART	CLIFF RICHARD
WHEN THE MORNING SUN DRIES THE DEW	QUIET FIVE
WHEN THE SUMMERTIME IS OVER	JACKIE TRENT
WHEN THE SUN COMES SHINING THROUGH	LONG JOHN BALDRY
WHEN TWO WORLDS COLLIDE	JIM REEVES
WHEN WE WERE YOUNG	SOLOMON KING
WHEN WILL I BE LOVED	EVERLY BROTHERS
WHEN WILL I SEE YOU AGAIN	THREE DEGREES

WHEN WILL THE GOOD APPLES FALL	SEEKERS
WHEN WILL YOU SAY I LOVE YOU	BILLY FURY
WHEN YOU ARE A KING	WHITE PLAINS
WHEN YOU GET RIGHT DOWN TO IT	RONNIE DYSON
WHEN YOU LOSE THE ONE YOU LOVE	DAVID WHITFIELD
WHEN YOU WALK IN THE ROOM	SEARCHERS
WHEN YOU'RE YOUNG AND IN LOVE	MARVELETTES
WHERE ARE YOU GOING TO MY LOVE	BROTHERHOOD OF MAN
WHERE ARE YOU NOW	JACKIE TRENT
WHERE DID ALL THE GOOD TIMES GO	DONNY OSMOND
WHERE DID OUR LOVE GO	SUPREMES
WHERE DID OUR LOVE GO	DONNIE ELBERT
WHERE DO I BEGIN ('LOVE STORY')	ANDY WILLIAMS
WHERE DO I BEGIN ('LOVE STORY')	SHIRLEY BASSEY
WHERE DO YOU GO TO MY LOVELY	PETER SARSTEDT
WHERE IS THE LOVE	BETTY WRIGHT
WHERE IS THE LOVE	ROBERTA FLACK AND DONNY HATHAWAY
WHERE IS TOMORROW	CILLA BLACK
WHERE THE BOYS ARE	CONNIE FRANCIS
WHERE THE HAPPY PEOPLE GO	TRAMMPS
WHERE WERE YOU ON OUR WEDDING DAY	LLOYD PRICE
WHERE WILL THE DIMPLE BE	ROSEMARY CLOONEY
WHERE WILL YOU BE	SUE NICHOLLS
WHEREVER YOU ARE	KEN DODD
WHICH WAY YOU GOIN' BILLY	POPPY FAMILY
WHILE I LIVE	KENNY DAMON
WHISKEY IN THE JAR	THIN LIZZY
WHISPERING	BACHELORS
WHISPERING	NINO TEMPO AND APRIL STEVENS
WHISPERING GRASS	WINDSOR DAVIES AND DON ESTELLE
WHISPERING HOPE	JIM REEVES
WHITE CHRISTMAS	FREDDIE STARR
WHITE CLIFFS OF DOVER	ACKER BILK
WHITE CLIFFS OF DOVER	RIGHTEOUS BROTHERS
WHITE HORSES	JACKY
WHITE ROOM	CREAM
WHITE SILVER SANDS	BILL BLACK COMBO
WHITE SPORTS COAT	KING BROTHERS
WHITE SPORTS COAT	TERRY DENE
WHITE XMAS	FREDDIE STARR
WHITER SHADE OF PALE	PROCOL HARUM
WHO AM I	ADAM FAITH
WHO ARE WE	RONNIE HILTON
WHO COULD BE BLUER	JERRY LORDAN
WHO DO YOU LOVE	JUICY LUCY
WHO DO YOU THINK YOU ARE	CANDLEWICK GREEN
WHO LOVES YOU	FOUR SEASONS
WHO PUT THE LIGHTS OUT	DANA
WHO PUT THE BOMP	VISCOUNTS
WHO WAS IT	HURRICANE SMITH
WHO'S IN THE STRAWBERRY PATCH WITH SALLY	DAWN
WHO'S SORRY NOW	JOHNNY RAY
WHO'S SORRY NOW	CONNIE FRANCIS
WHOLE LOTTA LOVE	C.C.S.
WHOLE LOTTA SHAKIN' GOIN' ON	JERRY LEE LEWIS
WHOLE LOTTA WOMAN	MARVIN RAINWATER
WHY	ROGER WHITTAKER
WHY	FRANKIE AVALON
WHY	ANTHONY NEWLEY
WHY	DONNY OSMOND
WHY BABY WHY	PAT BOONE
WHY CAN'T WE BE LOVERS	DOZIER-HOLLAND
WHY CAN'T WE LIVE TOGETHER	TIMMY THOMAS

WHY CAN'T YOU	CLARENCE 'FROGMAN' HENRY
WHY DID YOU DO IT	STRETCH
WHY DO FOOLS FALL IN LOVE	FRANKIE LYMON AND THE TEENAGERS
WHY DO FOOLS FALL IN LOVE	ALMA COGAN
WHY DON'T THEY UNDERSTAND	GEORGE HAMILTON
WHY MUST WE FALL IN LOVE	SUPREMES AND TEMPTATIONS
WHY NOT NOW	MATT MONRO
WHY NOT TONIGHT	MOJOS
WHY, OH, WHY, OH, WHY	GILBERT O'SULLIVAN
WHY, WHY, BYE, BYE	BOB LUMAN
WICHITA LINEMAN	GLEN CAMPBELL
WIDE-EYED AND LEGLESS	ANDY FAIRWEATHER-LOWE
WILD CAT	GENE VINCENT
WILD HONEY	BEACH BOYS
WILD IN THE COUNTRY	ELVIS PRESLEY
WILD LOVE	MUNGO JERRY
WILD ONE	BOBBY RYDELL
WILD ONE	SUZI QUATRO
WILD SIDE OF LIFE	JOSH MACRAE
WILD SIDE OF LIFE	TOMMY QUICKLY
WILD THING	TROGGS
WILD THING	GOODIES
WILD WIND	JOHN LEYTON
WILD WORLD	JIMMY CLIFF
WILL I WHAT	MIKE SARNE
WILL YOU LOVE ME TOMORROW	SHIRELLES
WILL YOU LOVE ME TOMORROW	MELANIE
WILLIE AND THE HAND-JIVE	CLIFF RICHARD
WILLIE CAN	ALMA COGAN
WILLOW TREE	IVY LEAGUE
WIMOWEH (LION SLEEPS TONIGHT)	TOKENS
WIMOWEH (LION SLEEPS TONIGHT)	KARL DENVER
WINCHESTER CATHEDRAL	NEW VAUDEVILLE BAND
WIND CRIES MARY	JIMI HENDRIX
WIND ME UP	CLIFF RICHARD
WINDMILL IN OLD AMSTERDAM	RONNIE HILTON
WINDMILLS OF YOUR MIND	NOEL HARRISON
WINDOW SHOPPING	R. DEAN TAYLOR
WINTER WONDERLAND	JOHNNY MATHIS
WINTER WORLD OF LOVE	ENGELBERT HUMPERDINCK
WIPE OUT	SURFARIS
WISDOM OF A FOOL	NORMAN WISDOM
WISDOM OF A FOOL	RONNIE CARROLL
WISHIN' AND HOPIN'	MERSEYBEATS
WISHING	BUDDY HOLLY
WISHING WELL	FREE
WITCH	RATTLES
WITCH DOCTOR	DAVID SEVILLE
WITCH DOCTOR	DON LANG
WITCH QUEEN OF NEW ORLEANS	REDBONE
WITCHCRAFT	FRANK SINATRA
WITCH'S BREW	JANIE JONES
WITCH'S PROMISE	JETHRO TULL
WITH A GIRL LIKE YOU	TROGGS
WITH A LITTLE HELP FROM MY FRIENDS	YOUNG IDEA
WITH A LITTLE HELP FROM MY FRIENDS	JOE COCKER
WITH A LITTLE HELP FROM MY FRIENDS	JOE BROWN
WITH ALL MY HEART	PETULA CLARK
WITH PEN IN HAND	VIKKI CARR
WITH THE EYES OF A CHILD	CLIFF RICHARD
WITH THESE HANDS	TOM JONES
WITH THESE HANDS	SHIRLEY BASSEY

WITH YOUR LOVE	MALCOLM VAUGHAN
WITHOUT HER	HERB ALPERT AND THE TIJUANA BRASS
WITHOUT LOVE THERE IS NOTHING	TOM JONES
WITHOUT YOU	MATT MONRO
WITHOUT YOU	NILSSON
WOE IS ME	HELEN SHAPIRO
W.O.L.D.	HARRY CHAPIN
WOMAN	PETER AND GORDON
WOMAN IN LOVE	FRANKIE LAINE
WOMAN IN LOVE	FOUR ACES
WOMAN IN LOVE	RONNIE HILTON
WOMAN WOMAN	GARY PUCKETT AND UNION GAP
WOMAN'S PLACE	GILBERT O'SULLIVAN
WOMBLING MERRY CHRISTMAS	WOMBLES
WOMBLING SONG	WOMBLES
WOMBLING WHITE TIE AND TAILS	WOMBLES
WONDER OF YOU	ELVIS PRESLEY
WONDERBOY	KINKS
WONDERFUL DREAM	ANNE-MARIE DAVID
WONDERFUL LAND	SHADOWS
WONDERFUL TIME UP THERE	PAT BOONE
WONDERFUL WORLD	SAM COOKE
WONDERFUL WORLD	HERMAN'S HERMITS
WONDERFUL WORLD, BEAUTIFUL PEOPLE	JIMMY CLIFF
WONDERFUL WORLD OF THE YOUNG	DANNY WILLIAMS
WONDROUS PLACE	BILLY FURY
WON'T GET FOOLED AGAIN	WHO
WON'T SOMEBODY DANCE WITH ME	LYNSEY DE PAUL
WOODEN HEART	ELVIS PRESLEY
WOODSTOCK	MATTHEW'S SOUTHERN COMFORT
WOOLY BULLY	SAM THE SHAM AND THE PHARAOHS
WORDS	ALLISONS
WORDS	BEE GEES
WORDS OF LOVE	MAMAS AND PAPAS
WORKIN' FOR THE MAN	ROY ORBISON
WORKIN' IN THE COALMINE	LEE DORSEY
WORKING MY WAY BACK TO YOU	FOUR SEASONS
WORKING ON A BUILDING OF LOVE	CHAIRMEN OF THE BOARD
WORLD	BEE GEES
WORLD OF BROKEN HEARTS	AMEN CORNER
WORLD OF OUR OWN	SEEKERS
WORLD IN MY ARMS	NAT 'KING' COLE
WORLD WE KNEW	FRANK SINATRA
WOULDN'T IT BE NICE	BEACH BOYS
WRAPPING PAPER	CREAM
WRECK OF THE ANTOINETTE	DAVE DEE, DOZY, BEAKY, MICK AND TICH
WRITING ON THE WALL	TOMMY STEELE
YA YA TWIST	PETULA CLARK
YAKETY YAK	COASTERS
YEARS MAY COME, YEARS MAY GO	HERMAN'S HERMITS
YEH YEH	GEORGIE FAME
YELLOW RIVER	CHRISTIE
YELLOW ROSE OF TEXAS	STAN FREBURG
YELLOW ROSE OF TEXAS	MITCH MILLER
YELLOW ROSE OF TEXAS	GARY MILLER
YELLOW ROSE OF TEXAS	RONNIE HILTON
YELLOW SUBMARINE	BEATLES
YEP	DUANE EDDY
YES MY DARLING DAUGHTER	EYDIE GORME
YES TONIGHT JOSEPHINE	JOHNNY RAY
YESTERDAY	MATT MONRO
YESTERDAY	BEATLES
YESTERDAY	RAY CHARLES
YESTERDAY HAS GONE	CUPID'S INSPIRATION

YESTERDAY MAN	CHRIS ANDREWS
YESTERDAY ONCE MORE	CARPENTERS
YESTERDAY'S DREAMS	FOUR TOPS
YESTERDAY'S GONE	CHAD AND JEREMY
YESTERME YESTERYOU YESTERDAY	STEVIE WONDER
YING TONG SONG	GOONS
YOU	JOHNNY JOHNSON AND THE BANDWAGON
YOU AIN'T GOING NOWHERE	BYRDS
YOU AIN'T LIVING UNTIL YOU'RE LOVING	MARVIN GAYE AND TAMMI TERRELL
YOU ALWAYS HURT THE ONE YOU LOVE	CONNIE FRANCIS
YOU ALWAYS HURT THE ONE YOU LOVE	CLARENCE 'FROGMAN' HENRY
YOU ARE AWFUL	DICK EMERY
YOU ARE BEAUTIFUL	JOHNNY MATHIS
YOU ARE EVERYTHING	PEARLS
YOU ARE EVERYTHING	MARVIN GAYE AND DIANA ROSS
YOU ARE MY DESTINY	PAUL ANKA
YOU ARE MY FIRST LOVE	RUBY MURRAY
YOU ARE THE SUNSHINE OF MY LIFE	STEVIE WONDER
YOU BELONG TO ME	GARY GLITTER
YOU BETTER COME HOME	PETULA CLARK
YOU CAME, YOU SAW, YOU CONQUERED	PEARLS
YOU CAN DO MAGIC	LIMMIE AND FAMILY COOKING
YOU CAN GET IT, IF YOU REALLY WANT IT	DESMOND DEKKER AND THE ACES
YOU CAN NEVER STOP ME LOVING YOU	KENNY LYNCH
YOU CAN'T BE TRUE TO TWO	DAVE KING
YOU CAN'T HURRY LOVE	SUPREMES
YOU COULD'VE BEEN A LADY	HOT CHOCOLATE
YOU DON'T HAVE TO BE A BABY TO CRY	CARAVELLES
YOU DON'T HAVE TO BE IN THE ARMY (TO FIGHT IN THE WAR)	MUNGO JERRY
YOU DON'T HAVE TO SAY YOU LOVE ME	DUSTY SPRINGFIELD
YOU DON'T HAVE TO SAY YOU LOVE ME	ELVIS PRESLEY
YOU DON'T HAVE TO SAY YOU LOVE ME	GUYS AND DOLLS
YOU DON'T KNOW	HELEN SHAPIRO
YOU DON'T KNOW ME	RAY CHARLES
YOU DON'T KNOW WHAT YOU'VE GOT	RAL DONNER
YOU DON'T OWE ME A THING	JOHNNIE RAY
YOU GAVE ME SOMEBODY TO LOVE	MANFRED MANN
YOU GOT SOUL	JOHNNY NASH
YOU GOT WHAT IT TAKES	MARV JOHNSON
YOU GOT WHAT IT TAKES	DAVE CLARK FIVE
YOU KEEP ME HANGIN' ON	SUPREMES
YOU KEEP ME HANGIN' ON	VANILLA FUDGE
(YOU KEEP ME) HANGING ON	CLIFF RICHARD
YOU KEEP RUNNING AWAY	FOUR TOPS
YOU MAKE IT MOVE	DAVE DEE, DOZY, BEAKY, MICK AND TICH
YOU MAKE ME FEEL BRAND NEW	STYLISTICS
YOU, ME AND US	ALMA COGAN
YOU MEAN EVERYTHING TO ME	NEIL SEDAKA
YOU MUST HAVE BEEN A BEAUTIFUL BABY	BOBBY DARIN
YOU MY LOVE	FRANK SINATRA
YOU NEED HANDS	MAX BYGRAVES
YOU NEVER CAN TELL	CHUCK BERRY
YOU ONLY LIVE TWICE	NANCY SINATRA
YOU ONLY YOU	RITA PAVONE
YOU SEE THE TROUBLE WITH ME	BARRY WHITE
YOU TALK TOO MUCH	JOE JONES
YOU WANT IT, YOU GOT IT	DETROIT EMERALDS
YOU WEAR IT WELL	ROD STEWART
YOU WERE MADE FOR ME	FREDDIE AND THE DREAMERS
YOU WERE ON MY MIND	CRISPIAN ST. PETERS
YOU WERE THERE	HEINZ

YOU WON'T BE LEAVING	HERMAN'S HERMITS
YOU WON'T FIND ANOTHER FOOL LIKE ME	NEW SEEKERS
YOU YOU YOU	ALVIN STARDUST
YOU'LL ALWAYS BE A FRIEND	HOT CHOCOLATE
YOU'LL ANSWER TO ME	CLEO LAINE
YOU'LL NEVER GET TO HEAVEN	DIONNE WARWICK
YOU'LL NEVER KNOW	SHIRLEY BASSEY
YOU'LL NEVER KNOW WHAT YOU'RE MISSING TILL YOU TRY	EMILE FORD AND THE CHECKMATES
YOU'LL NEVER WALK ALONE	GERRY AND THE PACEMAKERS
YOU'LL NEVER WALK ALONE	ELVIS PRESLEY
YOUNG AND FOOLISH	RONNIE HILTON
YOUNG AND FOOLISH	EDMUND HOCKRIDGE
YOUNG AND FOOLISH	DEAN MARTIN
YOUNG, GIFTED AND BLACK	BOB AND MARCIA
YOUNG GIRL	GARY PUCKETT AND UNION GAP
YOUNG LOVE	SONNY JAMES
YOUNG LOVE	TAB HUNTER
YOUNG LOVE	DONNY OSMOND
YOUNG LOVERS	PAUL AND PAULA
YOUNG NEW MEXICAN PUPPETEER	TOM JONES
YOUNG ONES	CLIFF RICHARD
YOUNG WORLD	RICKY NELSON
YOUNGER GIRL	CRITTERS
YOUR BABY AIN'T YOUR BABY ANYMORE	PAUL DA VINCI
YOUR BABY'S GONE SURFIN'	DUANE EDDY
YOUR CHEATING HEART	RAY CHARLES
YOU REALLY GOT ME	KINKS
YOUR HURTIN' KIND OF LOVE	DUSTY SPRINGFIELD
YOUR MA SAID YOU CRIED IN YOUR SLEEP LAST NIGHT	DOUG SHELDON
YOUR MAGIC PUT A SPELL ON ME	L.J. JOHNSON
YOUR SONG	ELTON JOHN
YOUR TENDER LOOK	JOE BROWN AND THE BRUVVERS
YOUR TIME HASN'T COME YET BABY	ELVIS PRESLEY
YOU'RE A LADY	PETER SKELLERN
YOU'RE ALL I NEED TO GET BY	MARVIN GAYE AND TAMMI TERRELL
YOU'RE ALL I NEED TO GET BY	ARETHA FRANKLIN
YOU'RE BREAKING MY HEART	KEELEY SMITH
YOU'RE DRIVING ME CRAZY	TEMPERANCE SEVEN
YOU'RE FREE TO GO	JIM REEVES
YOU'RE MY EVERYTHING	MAX BYGRAVES
YOU'RE MY GIRL	ROY ORBISON
YOU'RE MY GIRL	ROCKIN' BERRIES
YOU'RE MY SOUL AND INSPIRATION	RIGHTEOUS BROTHERS
YOU'RE MY WORLD	CILLA BLACK
YOU'RE NO GOOD	SWINGING BLUE JEANS
YOU'RE READY NOW	FRANKIE VALLI
YOU'RE SIXTEEN	JOHNNY BURNETTE
YOU'RE SIXTEEN	RINGO STARR
YOU'RE SO VAIN	CARLY SIMON
YOU'RE SUCH A GOOD-LOOKING WOMAN	JOE DOLAN
YOU'RE THE ONE	KATHY KIRBY
YOU'RE THE ONE	PETULA CLARK
YOU'RE THE ONLY GOOD THING THAT'S HAPPENED TO ME	JIM REEVES
YOU'RE THE ONLY ONE	VAL DOONICAN
YOU'RE THE REASON WHY	RUBETTES
YOU'VE COME BACK	P.J. PROBY
YOU'VE GONE	ALICE BABS
YOU'VE GOT A FRIEND	JAMES TAYLOR
YOU'VE GOT LOVE	BUDDY HOLLY
YOU'VE GOT ME DANGLING ON A STRING	CHAIRMEN OF THE BOARD
YOU'VE GOT TO HIDE YOUR LOVE AWAY	SILKIE

YOU'VE GOT YOUR TROUBLES	FORTUNES
YOU'VE GOTTA STOP	ELVIS PRESLEY
YOU'VE LOST THAT LOVIN' FEELING	RIGHTEOUS BROTHERS
YOU'VE LOST THAT LOVIN' FEELING	CILLA BLACK
YOU'VE LOST THAT LOVIN' FEELING	TELLY SAVALAS
YOU'VE MADE ME SO VERY HAPPY	BLOOD, SWEAT AND TEARS
YOU'VE NEVER BEEN IN LOVE LIKE THIS BEFORE	UNIT 4 + 2
YOU'VE NOT CHANGED	SANDIE SHAW
YUMMY, YUMMY, YUMMY	OHIO EXPRESS
Z - CARS THEME	JOHN KEATING
Z - CARS THEME	NORRIE PARAMOUR ORCHESTRA
ZABADAK	DAVE DEE, DOZY, BEAKY, MICK AND TICH
ZAMBEZI	LOU BUSCH
ZAMBEZI	EDDIE CALVERT
ZING WENT THE STRINGS OF MY HEART	TRAMMPS
ZIP-A-DEE DOO DAH	BOB B. SOXX AND THE BLUE JEANS
ZIP GUN BOOGIE	T. REX
ZOO	COMMODORES
ZORBA'S DANCE	MARCELLO MINGRABI

TOP ARTISTS

1. Based On Most Chart-Toppers

1.	Beatles	17
2.	Elvis Presley	16
3.	Cliff Richard	8
4.	Rolling Stones	8
5.	Slade	6
6.	Shadows	5
7.	Everly Brothers	4
8.	Frank Ifield	4
9.	T. Rex	4
10.	Lonnie Donegan	3
11.	Roy Orbison	3
12.	Gerry and Pacemakers	3
13.	Searchers	3
14.	Manfred Mann	3
15.	Kinks	3
16.	Sandie Shaw	3
17.	Georgie Fame	3
18.	Rod Stewart	3
19.	Donny Osmond	3
20.	Gary Glitter	3
21.	Mud	3

TOP ARTISTS

2. Based On Most Top 50 Entries

(a) International

1.	Elvis Presley	91
2.	Cliff Richard	62
3.	Frank Sinatra	32
4.	Beatles	31
5.	Supremes	30
6.	Lonnie Donegan	28
7.	Everly Brothers	28
8.	Roy Orbison	28
9.	Hollies	27
10.	Petula Clark	26
11.	Buddy Holly	26
12.	Jim Reeves	26
13.	Shadows	26
14.	Frankie Vaughan	25
15.	Shirley Bassey	25
16.	Billy Fury	25
17.	Tom Jones	25
18.	Four Tops	25
19.	Connie Francis	24
20.	Adam Faith	24
21.	Pat Boone	23
22.	Perry Como	22
23.	Duane Eddy	22
24.	Brenda Lee	22
25.	Rolling Stones	22
26.	Dave Clark Five	22
27.	Who	22
28.	Stevie Wonder	22

(b) American Artists

1.	Elvis Presley	91
2.	Frank Sinatra	32
3.	Supremes	30
4.	Everly Brothers	28
5.	Roy Orbison	28
6.	Buddy Holly	26
7.	Jim Reeves	26
8.	Shirley Bassey	25
9.	Four Tops	25
10.	Connie Francis	24
11.	Pat Boone	23
12.	Perry Como	22
13.	Duane Eddy	22
14.	Brenda Lee	22
15.	Stevie Wonder	22
16.	Andy Williams	21
17.	Gene Pitney	21
18.	Beach Boys	21
19.	Temptations	21
20.	Neil Sedaka	19
21.	Nat King Cole	18
22.	Drifters	18
23.	Bill Haley	17
24.	Fats Domino	17
25.	Marvin Gaye	17
26.	Ray Charles	16
27.	Otis Redding	16
28.	Bobby Darin	15

(c) British Artists

1.	Cliff Richard	62
2.	Beatles	31

3.	Lonnie Donegan	28
4.	Hollies	27
5.	Petula Clark	26
6.	Shadows	26
7.	Frankie Vaughan	25
8.	Billy Fury	25
9.	Tom Jones	25
10.	Adam Faith	24
11.	Rolling Stones	22
12.	Dave Clark Five	22
13.	Who	22
14.	T. Rex	21
15.	Herman's Hermits	20
16.	Cilla Black	19
17.	Kinks	19
18.	Ken Dodd	18
19.	Manfred Mann	18
20.	Sandie Shaw	18
21.	Russ Conway	17
22.	Bachelors	17
23.	Dusty Springfield	17
24.	Slade	17
25.	David Bowie	16
26.	Elton John	16
27.	Tommy Steele	15
28.	Lulu	15
29.	Dave Dee, Dozy, Beaky, Mick and Tich	15
30.	Engelbert Humperdinck	15
31.	Sweet	15

NUMBER 1 RECORDS 1955 - 1975

1955

					Weeks at No. 1
Jan	7	Dickie Valentine	Finger of Suspicion	Decca	1
Jan	14	Rosemary Clooney	Mambo Italiano	Philips	3
Feb	4	Eddie Fisher	I Need You Now	HMV	2
Feb	18	Ruby Murray	Softly Softly	Columbia	3
Mar	11	Tennessee Ernie Ford	Give Me Your Word	Capitol	7
Apr	29	Perez Prado	Cherry Pink And Apple Blossom White	HMV	2
May	13	Tony Bennett	Stranger In Paradise	Philips	2
May	27	Eddie Calvert	Cherry Pink And Apple Blossom White	Columbia	4
June	24	Jimmy Young	Unchained Melody	Decca	3
July	15	Alma Cogan	Dreamboat	HMV	2
July	29	Slim Whitman	Rosemarie	London	11
Oct	14	Jimmy Young	Man From Laramie	Decca	4
Nov	11	Johnston Brothers	Hernandos Hideaway	Decca	2
Nov	25	Bill Haley and the Comets	Rock Around The Clock	Brunswick	3
Dec	16	Dickie Valentine	Christmas Alphabet	Decca	3

1956

Jan	6	Bill Haley and the Comets	Rock Around The Clock	Brunswick	2
Jan	20	Tennessee Ernie Ford	Sixteen Tons	Capitol	4
Feb	17	Dean Martin	Memories Are Made Of This	Capitol	4
Mar	16	Dream Weavers	It's Almost Tomorrow	Brunswick	2
Mar	30	Kay Starr	Rock And Roll Waltz	HMV	1
Apr	6	Dream Weavers	It's Almost Tomorrow	Brunswick	1
Apr	13	Winifred Attwell	Poor People Of Paris	Decca	3
May	4	Ronnie Hilton	No Other Love	HMV	6
June	15	Pat Boone	I'll Be Home	London	5
July	20	Frankie Lymon and the Teenagers	Why Do Fools Fall In Love	Columbia	3
Aug	10	Doris Day	Whatever Will Be Will Be	Philips	6
Sept	21	Anne Shelton	Lay Down Your Arms	Philips	4
Oct	19	Frankie Laine	Woman In Love	Philips	4
Nov	16	Johnnie Ray	Just Walkin' In The Rain	Philips	7

1957

Jan	4	Guy Mitchell	Singing The Blues	Philips	1
Jan	11	Tommy Steele	Singing The Blues	Decca	1
Jan	18	Guy Mitchell	Singing The Blues	Philips	1
Jan	25	Frankie Vaughan	Garden Of Eden	Philips	4
Feb	22	Tab Hunter	Young Love	London	7

					Weeks at No. 1

1957-(cont.)

Apr 12	Lonnie Donegan	Cumberland Gap	Pye Nixa	5
May 17	Guy Mitchell	Rock-a-Billy	Philips	1
May 24	Andy Williams	Butterfly	London	2
June 7	Johnnie Ray	Yes Tonight Josephine	Philips	3
June 28	Lonnie Donegan	Gamblin' Man/ Putting On The Style	Nixa	2
July 12	Elvis Presley	All Shook Up	HMV	7
Aug 30	Paul Anka	Diana	Columbia	9
Nov 1	Crickets	That'll Be The Day	Vogue-Coral	3
Nov 22	Harry Belafonte	Mary's Boy Child	RCA	7

1958

Jan 10	Jerry Lee Lewis	Great Balls Of Fire	London	2
Jan 24	Elvis Presley	Jailhouse Rock	RCA	3
Feb 14	Michael Holliday	The Story Of My Life	Columbia	2
Feb 28	Perry Como	Magic Moments	RCA	8
Apr 25	Marvin Rainwater	Whole Lotta Woman	MGM	3
May 16	Connie Francis	Who's Sorry Now?	MGM	6
June 27	Vic Damone	On The Street Where You Live	Philips	2
July 4	Everly Brothers	All I Have To Do Is Dream/Claudette	London	7
Aug 22	Kalin Twins	When	Brunswick	5
Sept 26	Connie Francis	Carolina Moon/ Stupid Cupid	MGM	6
Nov 7	Tommy Edwards	It's All In The Game	MGM	3
Nov 28	Lord Rockingham's XI	Hoots Mon	Decca	3
Dec 19	Conway Twitty	It's Only Make Believe	MGM	5

1959

Jan 24	Elvis Presley	I Got Stung/One Night	RCA	5
Feb 22	Platters	Smoke Gets In Your Eyes	Mercury	5
Apr 4	Russ Conway	Side Saddle	Columbia	2
Apr 18	Buddy Holly	It Doesn't Matter Anymore	Coral	2
May 2	Elvis Presley	A Fool Such As I/I Need Your Love Tonight	RCA	7
June 20	Russ Conway	Roulette	Columbia	1
June 27	Bobby Darin	Dream Lover	London	5
Aug 1	Cliff Richard	Livin' Doll	Columbia	4
Aug 29	Craig Douglas	Only Sixteen	Rank	7
Oct 17	Cliff Richard	Travellin' Light	Columbia	7
Dec 5	Adam Faith	What Do You Want	Parlophone	6

1960

Jan 9	Emile Ford	What Do You Want To Make Those Eyes At Me For?	Pye	1
Jan 16	Anthony Newley	Why	Decca	6
Feb 27	Adam Faith	Poor Me	Parlophone	1

				Weeks at No. 1

1960-(cont.)

Mar	6	Johnny Preston	Running Bear	Mercury	2
Mar	20	Lonnie Donegan	My Old Man's A Dustman	Pye	5
Apr	24	Everly Brothers	Cathy's Clown	Warner	9
June	26	Jimmy Jones	Good Timin'	MGM	4
July	24	Cliff Richard	Please Don't Tease	Columbia	3
Aug	14	Shadows	Apache	Columbia	6
Sept	23	Ricky Valance	Tell Laura I Love Her	Columbia	2
Oct	7	Roy Orbison	Only The Lonely	London	3
Oct	30	Elvis Presley	It's Now Or Never	RCA	8
Dec	25	Johnny Tillotson	Poetry In Motion	London	3

1961

Jan	15	Elvis Presley	Are You Lonesome Tonight?/I Gotta Know	RCA	4
Feb	12	Everly Brothers	Walk Right Back/ Ebony Eyes	Warner	4
Mar	12	Elvis Presley	Wooden Heart	RCA	4
Apr	2	Allisons	Are You Sure?	Fontana	2
Apr	16	Temperance Seven	You're Driving Me Crazy	Parlophone	2
Apr	30	Marcels	Blue Moon	Pye Int.	2
May	14	Del Shannon	Runaway	London	1
May	14	Elvis Presley	Surrender	RCA	5
June	18	Del Shannon	Runaway	London	1
June	25	Everly Brothers	Temptation	Warner	4
July	29	Eden Kane	Well I Ask You	Decca	1
Aug	5	Helen Shapiro	You Don't Know	Columbia	2
Aug	19	John Leyton	Johnny Remember Me	Top Rank	5
Sept	23	Shadows	Kon-Tiki	Columbia	1
Sept	30	Highwaymen	Michael (Row The Boat Ashore)	HMV	1
Oct	7	Helen Shapiro	Walkin' Back To Happiness	Columbia	4
Nov	4	Elvis Presley	His Latest Flame	RCA	3
Nov	25	Bobby Vee	Take Good Care Of My Baby	London	1
Dec	2	Frankie Vaughan	Tower Of Strength	Philips	2
Dec	23	Acker Bilk	Stranger On The Shore	Columbia	2

1962

Jan	20	Cliff Richard	The Young Ones	Columbia	5
Feb	24	Elvis Presley	Rock A Hula Baby/ Can't Help Falling In Love With You	RCA	4
Mar	24	Shadows	Wonderful Land	Columbia	8
May	19	B. Bumble and the Stingers	Nut Rocker	Top Rank	1
May	26	Elvis Presley	Good Luck Charm	RCA	5
June	30	Mike Sarne	Come Outside	Parlophone	2
July	14	Ray Charles	I Can't Stop Loving You	HMV	2
July	28	Frank Ifield	I Remember You	Columbia	7
Sept	15	Elvis Presley	She's Not You	RCA	3
Oct	6	Tornadoes	Telstar	Decca	5
Nov	10	Frank Ifield	Lovesick Blues	Columbia	5
Dec	15	Elvis Presley	Return To Sender	RCA	3

					Weeks at No. 1

1963

Jan	6	Cliff Richard	The Next Time/ Bachelor Boy	Columbia	3
Jan	27	Shadows	Dance On	Columbia	1
Feb	3	Jet Harris/Tony Meehan	Diamonds	Decca	3
Feb	24	Frank Ifield	Wayward Wind	Columbia	3
Mar	16	Cliff Richard	Summer Holiday	Columbia	2
Mar	30	Shadows	Foottapper	Columbia	1
Apr	6	Gerry and the Pacemakers	How Do You Do It?	Columbia	4
May	4	Beatles	From Me To You	Parlophone	7
June	22	Gerry and the Pacemakers	I Like It	Columbia	4
July	20	Frank Ifield	Confessin'	Columbia	2
Aug	3	Elvis Presley	Devil In Disguise	RCA	1
Aug	10	Searchers	Sweets For My Sweet	Pye	2
Aug	24	Billy J Kramer and the Dakotas	Bad To Me	Parlophone	3
Sept	14	Beatles	She Loves You	Parlophone	4
Oct	12	Brian Poole and the Tremeloes	Do You Love Me?	Decca	3
Nov	2	Gerry and the Pacemakers	You'll Never Walk Alone	Columbia	4
Nov	30	Beatles	She Loves You	Parlophone	2
Dec	14	Beatles	I Want To Hold Your Hand	Parlophone	5

1964

Jan	18	Dave Clark Five	Glad All Over	Columbia	2
Feb	1	Searchers	Needles And Pins	Pye	3
Feb	22	Bachelors	Diane	Decca	1
Feb	29	Cilla Black	Anyone Who Had A Heart	Parlophone	3
Mar	21	Billy J. Kramer and the Dakotas	Little Children	Parlophone	2
Apr	4	Beatles	Can't Buy Me Love	Parlophone	3
Apr	25	Peter and Gordon	World Without Love	Columbia	2
May	9	Searchers	Don't Throw Your Love Away	Pye	2
May	23	Four Pennies	Juliet	Philips	1
May	30	Cilla Black	You're My World	Parlophone	4
June	27	Roy Orbison	It's Over	London	2
July	11	Animals	The House Of The Rising Sun	Columbia	1
July	18	Rolling Stones	It's All Over Now	Decca	1
July	25	Beatles	Hard Day's Night	Parlophone	3
Aug	15	Manfred Mann	Doo Wah Diddy Diddy	HMV	2
Aug	29	Honeycombs	Have I The Right?	Pye	2
Sept	11	Kinks	You Really Got Me	Pye	2
Sept	26	Herman's Hermits	I'm Into Something Good	Columbia	2
Oct	10	Roy Orbison	Oh, Pretty Woman	London	2
Oct	24	Sandie Shaw	(There's) Always Something There To Remind Me	Pye	3
Nov	14	Roy Orbison	Oh, Pretty Woman	London	1
Nov	21	Supremes	Baby Love	Stateside	2
Dec	5	Rolling Stones	Little Red Rooster	Decca	1
Dec	12	Beatles	I Feel Fine	Parlophone	5

1965

Date	Artist	Title	Label	Weeks at No. 1
Jan 16	Georgie Fame	Yeh Yeh	Columbia	2
Jan 30	Moody Blues	Go Now	Decca	1
Feb 6	Righteous Brothers	You've Lost That Lovin' Feeling	London	2
Feb 20	Kinks	Tired Of Waiting For You	Pye	1
Feb 27	Seekers	I'll Never Find Another You	Columbia	2
Mar 13	Tom Jones	It's Not Unusual	Decca	1
Mar 20	Rolling Stones	The Last Time	Decca	3
Apr 10	Unit 4+2	Concrete And Clay	Decca	1
Apr 17	Cliff Richard	The Minute You're Gone	Columbia	1
Apr 24	Beatles	Ticket To Ride	Parlophone	3
May 15	Roger Miller	King Of The Road	Philips	1
May 22	Jackie Trent	Where Are You Now My Love	Pye	1
May 29	Sandie Shaw	Long Live Love	Pye	3
June 19	Elvis Presley	Crying In The Chapel	RCA	2
June 26	Hollies	I'm Alive	Parlophone	3
July 24	Byrds	Mr. Tambourine Man	CBS	2
Aug 7	Beatles	Help	Parlophone	3
Aug 28	Sonny and Cher	I Got You Babe	Atlantic	2
Sept 11	Rolling Stones	Satisfaction	Decca	2
Sept 23	Walker Brothers	Make It Easy On Yourself	Philips	1
Sept 30	Ken Dodd	Tears	Columbia	5
Nov 6	Rolling Stones	Get Off Of My Cloud	Decca	3
Nov 27	Seekers	The Carnival Is Over	Columbia	3
Dec 18	Beatles	Day Tripper/We Can Work It Out	Parlophone	5

1966

Date	Artist	Title	Label	Weeks at No. 1
Jan 22	Spencer Davis Group	Keep On Runnin'	Fontana	1
Jan 29	Overlanders	Michelle	Pye	3
Feb 19	Nancy Sinatra	These Boots Are Made For Walking	Reprise	4
Mar 3	Walker Brothers	Sun Ain't Gonna Shine Anymore	Philips	4
Apr 16	Spencer Davis Group	Somebody Help Me	Fontana	2
Apr 30	Dusty Springfield	You Don't Have To Say You Love Me	Philips	1
May 7	Manfred Mann	Pretty Flamingo	HMV	3
May 28	Rolling Stones	Paint It Black	Decca	1
June 4	Frank Sinatra	Strangers In The Night	Reprise	3
June 25	Beatles	Paperback Writer	Parlophone	2
July 9	Kinks	Sunny Afternoon	Pye	2
July 23	Georgie Fame	Get Away	Columbia	1
July 30	Chris Farlowe	Out Of Time	Immediate	1
Aug 6	Troggs	With A Girl Like You	Fontana	2
Aug 20	Beatles	Eleanor Rigby/ Yellow Submarine	Parlophone	4
Sept 17	Small Faces	All Or Nothing	Decca	1
Sept 24	Jim Reeves	Distant Drums	RCA	5
Oct 29	Four Tops	Reach Out I'll Be There	Motown	3
Nov 19	Beach Boys	Good Vibrations	Capitol	2
Dec 3	Tom Jones	Green Green Grass Of Home	Decca	6

					Weeks at No. 1

1967

Jan	14	Monkees	I'm A Believer	RCA	4
Feb	18	Petula Clark	This Is My Song	Pye	2
Mar	4	Engelbert Humperdinck	Release Me	Decca	6
Apr	15	Frank and Nancy Sinatra	Somethin' Stupid	Reprise	2
Apr	29	Sandie Shaw	Puppet On A String	Pye	3
May	20	Tremeloes	Silence Is Golden	CBS	3
June	10	Procol Harum	A Whiter Shade Of Pale	Deram	6
July	22	Beatles	All You Need Is Love	Parlophone	3
Aug	12	Scott MacKenzie	San Francisco	CBS	4
Sept	9	Engelbert Humperdinck	The Last Waltz	Decca	5
Oct	14	Bee Gees	Massachussetts	Polydor	4
Nov	11	Foundations	Baby Now That I've Found You	Pye	2
Nov	25	Long John Baldry	Let The Heartaches Begin	Pye	2
Dec	9	Beatles	Hello Goodbye	Parlophone	7

1968

Jan	27	Georgie Fame	The Ballad Of Bonnie And Clyde	CBS	1
Feb	3	Love Affair	Everlasting Love	CBS	2
Feb	17	Manfred Mann	The Mighty Quinn	Fontana	2
Mar	2	Esther and Abi Ofarim	Cinderella Rockafella	Fontana	3
Mar	23	Dave Dee & Co.	Legend Of Xanadu	Fontana	1
Mar	30	Beatles	Lady Madonna	Parlophone	2
Apr	13	Cliff Richard	Congratulations	Columbia	2
Apr	27	Louis Armstrong	Wonderful World	Stateside	4
May	25	Union Gap	Young Girl	CBS	4
June	22	Rolling Stones	Jumping Jack Flash	Decca	2
July	6	Equals	Baby Come Back	President	3
July	27	Des O'Connor	I Pretend	Columbia	1
Aug	3	Tommy James and the Shondells	Mony Mony	Roulette	2
Aug	17	The Crazy World of Arthur Brown	Fire	Track	1
Aug	24	Tommy James and the Shondells	Mony Mony	Roulette	1
Aug	31	Beach Boys	Do It Again	Capitol	1
Sept	7	Bee Gees	I Gotta Get A Message To You	Polydor	1
Sept	14	Beatles	Hey Jude	Apple	2
Sept	28	Mary Hopkins	Those Were The Days	Apple	6
Nov	9	Joe Cocker	With A Little Help From My Friends	Regal Zonophone	1
Nov	16	Hugo Montenegro	The Good, The Bad And The Ugly	RCA	4
Dec	14	Scaffold	Lily The Pink	Columbia	3

1969

Jan	4	Marmalade	Ob-La-Di-Ob-La-Da	CBS	1
Jan	11	Scaffold	Lily The Pink	Columbia	1
Jan	18	Marmalade	Ob-La-Di-Ob-La-Da	CBS	2
Feb	1	Fleetwood Mac	Albatross	Blue Horizon	1
Feb	8	Move	Blackberry Way	Regal Zonophone	1
Feb	15	Amen Corner	(If Paradise Was) Half As Nice	Immediate	2

				Weeks at No. 1
		1969-(cont.)		
Mar 1	Peter Sarstedt	Where Do You Go To My Lovely	United Artists	4
Mar 29	Marvin Gaye	I Heard It Thru' The Grapevine	Tamla Motown	3
Apr 19	Desmond Dekker and the Aces	The Israelites	Pyramid	1
Apr 26	Beatles	Get Back	Apple	6
June 7	Tommy Roe	Dizzy	Stateside	1
June 14	Beatles	Ballad Of John And Yoko	Apple	3
July 5	Thunderclap Newman	Something In The Air	Track	3
July 26	Rolling Stones	Honky Tonk Women	Decca	5
Aug 30	Zager and Evans	In The Year 2525	RCA	3
Sept 20	Creedence Clearwater Revival	Bad Moon Rising	Liberty	3
Oct 11	Jane Birkin and Serge Gainsbourg	Je T'Aime Moi Non Plus	Major Minor	1
Oct 18	Bobbie Gentry	I'll Never Fall In Love Again	Capitol	1
Oct 25	Archies	Sugar Sugar	RCA	8
Dec 20	Rolf Harris	Two Little Boys	Columbia	6
		1970		
Jan 31	Edison Lighthouse	Love Grows	Bell	5
Mar 7	Lee Marvin	Wanderin' Star	Paramount	4
Apr 4	Simon and Garfunkel	Bridge Over Troubled Water	CBS	2
Apr 18	Dana	All Kinds Of Everything	Rex	2
May 2	Norman Greenbaum	Spirit In The Sky	Reprise	2
May 16	England World Cup Squad	Back Home	Pye	3
June 6	Christie	Yellow River	CBS	1
June 13	Mungo Jerry	In The Summertime	Dawn	8
Aug 1	Elvis Presley	The Wonder Of You	RCA	6
Sept 12	Smokey Robinson and the Miracles	The Tears Of A Clown	Motown	1
Sept 19	Freda Payne	Band Of Gold	Invictus	6
Oct 31	Matthews Southern Comfort	Woodstock	UNI	3
Nov 21	Jimi Hendrix	Voodoo Chile	Track	1
Nov 28	Dave Edmunds	I Hear You Knocking	MAM	7
		1971		
Jan 9	Clive Dunn	Grandad	Columbia	3
Jan 31	George Harrison	My Sweet Lord	Apple	5
Mar 6	Mungo Jerry	Baby Jump	Dawn	2
Mar 20	T. Rex	Hot Love	Fly	6
May 1	Dave and Ansell Collins	Double Barrel	Technique	2
May 15	Dawn	Knock Three Times	Bell	5
June 19	Middle of the Road	Chirpy Chirpy Cheep Cheep	RCA	5
July 24	T. Rex	Get It On	Fly	4
Aug 21	Diana Ross	I'm Still Waiting	Motown	3

				Weeks at No. 1
		1971-(cont.)		
Sept 18	Tams	Hey Girl Don't Bother Me	Probe	3
Oct 9	Rod Stewart	Maggie May/Reason To Believe	Mercury	5
Nov 13	Slade	Cos I Luv You	Polydor	4
Dec 11	Benny Hill	Ernie	Columbia	4
		1972		
Jan 8	New Seekers	I'd Like To Teach The World To Sing	Polydor	4
Feb 5	T. Rex	Telegram Sam	T. Rex	2
Feb 19	Chicory Tip	Son Of My Father	CBS	4
Mar 18	Nilsson	Without You	RCA	4
Apr 15	Royal Scots Dragoon Guards	Amazing Grace	RCA	5
May 20	T. Rex	Metal Guru	T. Rex	4
June 10	Don McLean	Vincent	UA	2
July 1	Slade	Take Me Back 'Ome	Polydor	1
July 8	Donny Osmond	Puppy Love	MGM	5
Aug 12	Alice Cooper	School's Out	Warner	3
Sept 2	Rod Stewart	You Wear It Well	Mercury	1
Sept 9	Slade	Mama Weer All Crazee Now	Polydor	3
Sept 30	David Cassidy	How Can I Be Sure	Bell	2
Oct 14	Lieutenant Pigeon	Mouldy Old Dough	Decca	4
Nov 11	Gilbert O'Sullivan	Clair	MAM	2
Nov 25	Chuck Berry	My Ding-A-Ling	Chess	4
Dec 23	Little Jimmy Osmond	Long Haired Lover From Liverpool	MGM	5
		1973		
Jan 27	Sweet	Blockbuster	RCA	5
Mar 3	Slade	Cum On Feel The Noize	Polydor	4
Mar 31	Donny Osmond	Twelfth Of Never	MGM	1
Apr 7	Gilbert O'Sullivan	Get Down	MAM	2
Apr 21	Dawn	Tie A Yellow Ribbon Round The Old Oak Tree	Bell	4
May 19	Wizzard	See My Baby Jive	Harvest	4
June 16	Suzie Quatro	Can The Can	RAK	1
June 23	10 C.C.	Rubber Bullets	UK	1
June 30	Slade	Skweeze Me, Pleeze Me	Polydor	3
July 21	Peters and Lee	Welcome Home	Philips	1
July 28	Gary Glitter	I'm The Leader Of The Gang	Bell	4
Aug 25	Donny Osmond	Young Love	MGM	4
Sept 22	Wizzard	Angel Fingers	Harvest	1
Sept 29	Simon Park Orchestra	Eye Level	Columbia	4
Oct 27	David Cassidy	Daydreamer	Bell	3
Nov 17	Gary Glitter	I Love You Love Me Love	Bell	4
Dec 15	Slade	Merry Christmas Everybody	Polydor	5

				Weeks at No. 1

1974

Jan 19	New Seekers	You Won't Find Another Fool Like Me	Polydor	1
Jan 26	Mud	Tiger Feet	RAK	4
Feb 23	Suzi Quatro	Devil Gate Drive	RAK	2
Mar 9	Alvin Stardust	Jealous Mind	Magnet	1
Mar 16	Paper Lace	Billy Don't Be A Hero	Bus Stop	3
Apr 6	Terry Jacks	Seasons In The Sun	Bell	4
May 4	Abba	Waterloo	Epic	2
May 18	Rubettes	Sugar Baby Love	Polydor	4
June 15	Ray Stevens	The Streak	Janus	1
June 22	Gary Glitter	Always Yours	Bell	1
June 29	Charles Azvanour	She	Barclay	4
July 27	George McCrae	Rock Your Baby	Jay Boy	3
Aug 17	Three Degrees	When Will I See You Again	Philadelphia International	2
Aug 31	Osmonds	Love Me For A Reason	MGM	3
Sept 21	Carl Douglas	Kung Fu Fighting	Pye	3
Oct 12	John Denver	Annie's Song	RCA	1
Oct 19	Sweet Sensation	Sad Sweet Dreamer	Pye	1
Oct 26	Ken Boothe	Everything I Own	Trojan	3
Nov 16	David Essex	I'm Gonna Make You A Star	CBS	3
Dec 7	Barry White	You're My First, My Last, My Everything	20th Century	2
Dec 21	Mud	Lonely This Christmas	RAK	3

1975

Jan 18	Status Quo	Down Down	Vertigo	1
Jan 25	Tymes	Ms. Grace	RCA	1
Feb 1	Pilot	January	EMI	3
Feb 22	Steve Harley and Cockney Rebel	Make Me Smile (Come Up And See Me)	EMI	2
Mar 8	Telly Savalas	If	MCA	2
Mar 22	Bay City Rollers	Bye Bye Baby	Bell	6
May 3	Mud	Oh Boy	RAK	2
May 17	Tammy Wynette	Stand By Your Man	Epic	3
June 7	Windsor Davies/ Don Estelle	Whispering Grass	EMI	3
June 28	10 C.C.	I'm Not In Love	Mercury	2
July 12	Johnny Nash	Tears On My Pillow	CBS	1
July 19	Bay City Rollers	Give A Little Love	Bell	3
Aug 9	Typically Tropical	Barbados	Gull	1
Aug 16	Stylistics	I Can't Give You Anything (But My Love)	Avco	3
Sept 6	Rod Stewart	Sailing	Warner Bros.	4
Oct 4	David Essex	Hold Me Close	CBS	3
Oct 25	Art Garfunkel	I Only Have Eyes For You	CBS	2
Nov 8	David Bowie	Space Oddity	RCA	2
Nov 22	Billy Connolly	D.I.V.O.R.C.E.	Polydor	1
Nov 29	Queen	Bohemian Rhapsody	EMI	9